Visions of Turmoil and Eternal Rest

Also by Warren A. Shipton:

The Pattern of Salvation

Clear Minds in Healthy Bodies (English and Chinese editions)

Health IQ

The Golden River That Flows through Time

Visions of Turmoil and Eternal Rest

Warren A. Shipton & Ebenezer A. Belete

authorHOUSE®

AuthorHouse™
1663 Liberty Drive
Bloomington, IN 47403
www.authorhouse.com
Phone: 1-800-839-8640

First published by AuthorHouse 09/12/2011

ISBN: 978-1-4567-8159-0 (sc)
ISBN: 978-1-4567-8160-6 (ebk)

Printed in the United States of America

Contents

"And we have the word of the prophets made more certain, and you will do well to pay attention to it, as to a light shining in a dark place, until the day dawns and the morning star rises in your hearts. Above all, you must understand that no prophecy of Scripture came about by the prophet's own interpretation."

2 Peter 1:19, 20, New International Version

List of Illustrations

List of Tables

Foreword

What you are holding in your hands is a long overdue resource produced by people of proven track record as scholars, educators, administrators, preachers and evangelists. The editors are individuals who understand the needs of both the seekers and the presenters and who always look for fresh ways of presenting the eternal truths from the Word of God.

I believe that "Visions of Turmoil and Eternal Rest" makes a unique contribution as it shares with the readers the insights of some of the best available Adventist scholarship and also contains some of the inspired comments from the writings of Ellen G. White.

The initial chapters of this resource, written by a number of eminent Adventist scholars, sets the tone for the rest of the resource as they provide good insights on the topics of inspiration, the great controversy theme, the methods of Bible study and various approaches to prophetic interpretation.

This resource clearly supports the historical method of prophetic interpretation that in turn affirms the very reason for being, for the Seventh-day Adventist Church is a prophetic movement foretold in the apocalyptic literature. If you are looking for a material that is both faithful to the teachings of the Bible and at the same time fully supportive and affirming of the unique prophetic identity of the Seventh-day Adventist Church, then this is it.

As a pastor/evangelist I will be delighted to use this resource. As a church administrator I would like to recommend this resource to both pastors and lay members who wish to use the material as a soul winning resource. I also recommend it to anyone who desires to better understand the prophecies of Daniel and Revelation as they are so relevant for the time in which we live.

Once again I wish to commend the editors for producing such a valuable resource. I believe it will be a blessing to all those who wish to better understand the time in which we live in the light of the Bible prophecy. Even though the world at times seems to be in turmoil, Bible prophecy tells us that the future is bright for all those who choose to put their trust in God. The very purpose of prophecy is to assure us that God is in control and that His purposes ultimately will be fulfilled.

Pr David Stojcic (DipTheo, BAA, MLM)
Chief Executive Officer and President
Seventh-day Adventist Church (Northern Australian Conference) Ltd

Foreword

Preface

The Bible is a book of God's dealings with humanity and of His plans to resolve the problem of sin in a manner consistent with His character. This means that we can establish principles for daily living from the pages of Holy Writ. As human beings we desire to know something about God's long term plan to resolve forever the issue of suffering in the world in which we live. Jesus' own disciples asked similar questions as recorded in Matthew chapter 24. The record is as follows: Now as He sat on the Mount of Olives, the disciples came to Him privately, saying, "Tell us, when will these things be? And what will be the sign of Your coming, and of the end of the age?" (vs. 3).

A more complete answer to the disciples' questions is given in the books of Daniel and Revelation. Daniel's book was already part of the Scriptures in Christ's day, and He indicated to His followers that they should study its messages. The apostle Mark (13:14) records Jesus' conversation as follows: "So when you see the 'abomination of desolation,' spoken of by Daniel the prophet, standing where it ought not" (let the reader understand), "then let those who are in Judea flee to the mountains." The beloved apostle John's work in Revelation found its way into the canon of Scripture with a little more difficulty, but we are glad that it is there. Both these books complement each other and help to fulfill the belief that "Surely the Lord GOD does nothing, Unless He reveals His secret to His servants the prophets" (Amos 3:7).

Both books talk about events that will happen near the end of world history. This is given in coded language that makes it challenging to interpret. However, the principles of interpretation are generally supplied elsewhere in the Bible so that the overall pattern of events can be understood. Indeed, we are given great confidence in the tools that the Bible has given us for interpretation when we compare Scripture with the historical record. This is particularly true for the book of Daniel. And with the confidence gained there, we can launch into the book of Revelation. In our study together we will go down this pathway of discovery.

We should treasure what God has chosen to reveal to mankind. He wishes all to accept His offer of salvation and to respond in obedience. Let us imagine that we are part of the audience the great prophet Moses addressed in the following words: "The secret *things belong* to the LORD our God, but those *things which are* revealed *belong* to us and to our children forever, that *we* may do all the words of this law" (Deuteronomy 29:29).

As we study the books of Daniel and Revelation together we need to understand that "prophecy is for believers" (1 Corinthians 14:22) and when unbelievers understand the compassion of God and His wisdom they will acknowledge that "the secrets of his heart are revealed; and so [the unbelieving listener], falling down on *his* face, he will worship God and report that God is truly among you [the believers]" (vs. 25). God is interested in saving you, the reader, and using you as an instrument to prepare others for Christ's second coming.

This series of studies was designed specifically to answer the needs of Seventh-day Adventist students at Asia-Pacific International University studying in the Faculty of Education and Psychology. It is our fervent hope that many more will be benefited through this work. We have endeavoured to make it as relevant as possible to people living and working in Asia. The texts quoted are from the New King James Version of the Bible in the main body of the studies and generally elsewhere, unless stated otherwise.

Preface

Acknowledgments

No work can be prepared effectively without the help of others. In completing this work we have relied heavily on the information collected by those who have gone before. The sources from which we acquired information are given solely in the basic references section in the interests of ease of reading the material. Where specific information is quoted, the source of this is noted in the text. We have indicated the source of relevant information in the writings of Ellen G. White, but this is not exhaustive.

Specific thanks are due to our respective families who have watched over us as we have completed this work. We are very appreciative for the time that Thitaree Sirikulpat spent in word processing and in the layout of diagrams and art work. She designed the book cover using an image purchased from Fotolia (http://www.fotolia.com/). Special thanks are due to Brian Wilson from the Translation and Cultural Research Centre, Asia-Pacific International University, and to Jan Shipton for commenting on the manuscript.

We thank all who enabled us to share this information with others. Our thanks extend to the Biblical Research Institute and Adventist Affirm. These organizations graciously allowed us to use previously published information, which we have acknowledged in the text.

Acknowledgments

Abbreviations Used

The books of the Bible have been abbreviated according to the Modern Language Associate (MLA) style (http://hbl.gcc.edu/abbreviationsMLA.htm). Versions of the Bible are referred to using standard abbreviations (http://bible-translation.110mb.com/english.htm).

Ellen White materials are quoted as follows: *The Acts of the Apostles*, page 10, would be referred to as follows: (AA 10). A table of abbreviations is given hereunder. The material quoted or highlighted in the studies may be accessed through the Ellen G. White Estate website (http://www.whiteestate.org/search/search.asp).

Seventh-day Adventists believe that the gift of prophecy did not cease with the apostles and that Ellen White is one individual in modern times that possessed keys to understanding Scripture well worth considering. She placed the Bible foremost and advised others to do likewise. As we study her writings, it is evident that she had a depth of understanding of the Bible and its relevance that is remarkable, and which has proved beneficial to believers and those not of the faith.

AA	The Acts of the Apostles
AG	God's Amazing Grace
BC	The Seventh-day Adventist Bible Commentary (vol. 1-1BC; 2BC, etc., for volumes 2-7)
CC	Conflict and Courage
COL	Christ's Object Lessons
DA	The Desire of Ages
Ed	Education
EW	Early Writings
FLB	The Faith I Live By
FW	Faith and Works
GC	The Great Controversy between Christ and Satan
Letter	Ellen G. White Letters
Mar	Maranatha (The Lord Is Coming)
MCP	Mind, Character, and Personality (vol. 1-1MCP; vol. 2-2MCP)
MR	Manuscript Releases
MS	Ellen G. White Manuscript
PK	The Story of Patriarchs and Prophets
PP	The Story of Prophets and Kings
RC	The Remnant Church
RH	The Advent Review and Sabbath Herald
SC	Steps to Christ
SG	Spiritual Gifts (vol. 1-1SG; 2SG, etc., for volumes 2-4)
SM	Selected Messages (book 1-1SM; 2SM, etc., for books 2 and 3)
SP	The Spirit of Prophecy (vol. 1-1SP; 2SP, etc., for volumes 2-4)
SR	The Story of Redemption
ST	Signs of the Times
T	Testimonies for the Church (vol. 1-1T; 2T, etc., for volumes 2-9)
TA	The Truth about Angels
YI	Youth's Instructor

Chapter 1

What Prophecy Means to This Church

Frank B. Holbrook

What is a Seventh-day Adventist? A common description is that a Seventh-day Adventist is a Christian who observes the seventh-day Sabbath and who is preparing for the Saviour's second coming. That is true, but the perspective is larger.

The real distinctive frame holding together the picture of truth as perceived by Seventh-day Adventists is their understanding of the prophecies of Daniel and Revelation. In these apocalyptic prophecies [prophecies predicting universal destruction] Adventists have found their times, their identity, and their task. Seventh-day Adventists arrive at their interpretations of Bible prophecy by employing the principles of the 'historicist school' of prophetic interpretation. This historicist view (also known as the 'continuous historical' view) sees the prophecies of Daniel and Revelation unfolding at various points in historical time, often encompassing the sweep of history from the times of Daniel and John (the human authors of these books) to the establishment of God's eternal kingdom.

A biblical illustration of this unrolling of the prophetic scroll along the continuum of human history is the prophetic dream given to the Neo-Babylonian king Nebuchadnezzar and its interpretation by the prophet Daniel (see Dan. 2:31-45). In his dream the king saw an image of a man composed of various metals of descending values: golden head, silver chest and arms, bronze belly and thighs, iron legs, feet and toes made of iron and clay. The dream concluded with a large stone, mysteriously quarried without human assistance from the side of a mountain that fell with devastating force upon the statue, smashing it to pieces. As the wind blew these metallic elements away 'like the chaff of the summer threshing floors,' the stone 'became a great mountain, and filled the whole earth' (Dan. 2:35).

Daniel clearly identified the golden head as symbolizing the empire of Babylon under Nebuchadnezzar (vss. 37, 38). It was to be followed by three successive world kingdoms corresponding to the three different metals. History records that these were Medo-Persia, Grecia, and the 'iron monarchy' of Rome. In the latter part of the fifth century A.D. the empire of Rome in the West was fully broken up. Its parts came to form the nations of Western Europe-symbolized by the strengths and weaknesses of the feet and toes composed of iron and clay. The 'stone,' which will ultimately destroy these and all other human, political entities, is the eternal kingdom that 'the God of heaven will set up' at the end of human history (see vss. 44, 45, RSV).

Thus the historicist system of interpretation sees in the apocalyptic prophecies of Daniel and Revelation the hand of Divine Providence moving across the ages, overruling events to bring about the fulfillment of God's purposes.

Jesus, our Lord, saw a similar unrolling of the prophetic scroll in Daniel 9:24-27, part of a much longer prophecy given to Daniel by the angel Gabriel in the early years of the Medo-Persian Empire. In this portion, several important predictions were made. A period of 'seventy weeks' was to be allotted to

Israel subsequent to their release from Babylonian captivity. On the principle that in apocalyptic prophecy a symbolic 'day' equals a literal year, this period translates into 490 years (70 weeks of seven days each equals 490 days, or 490 actual years). Near the close of this time the long-awaited Messiah would appear. This could and should have been Israel's finest hour when the Saviour of the world would 'make an end of sins,' would 'make reconciliation for iniquity,' and would 'bring in everlasting righteousness' (vs. 24).

But there was a shadow—a dark side to the prophetic picture. It implied a rejection of the Messiah, who would 'be cut off, but not for himself.' Tragic retribution would follow in the destruction of both Jerusalem and its Temple (vs. 26).

The Messianic aspects of this prophecy met their respective fulfillments in the life, ministry, and atoning death of Jesus Christ. But the destruction of the city and the Temple were still future events when the Saviour gave His important discourse on Olivet two days prior to His passion (see Matt. 24). On the basis of the prophecy recorded in Daniel 9, our Lord pointed to the impending national ruin (see Matt. 24:15; cf. chap. 24:1, 2; Luke 21:20-24), which met a fiery fulfillment by Roman arms about forty years later, in A.D.70.

Daniel 9:26, to which Jesus alluded, is a part of a much larger vision occupying chapters 8 and 9 of Daniel's book and symbolizing events that extend from Persian times to the onset of God's final judgment (see chapter 8:13, 14). Here again is another striking example of the historicist perspective of apocalyptic prophecy that serves to confirm and to strengthen faith in God's leading across the centuries through all the play and counter play of satanic opposition and human pride and ambition.

Historicism and the Reformation

The Millerites, the immediate spiritual forebears of Seventh-day Adventists, were historicists; that is, they interpreted Daniel and Revelation in harmony with the principles of the 'historical school' of prophetic interpretation. But the method was by no means original with the Millerites of mid-nineteenth-century America; they simply reflected and elaborated upon the labors of many earlier Bible students of the Reformation and post-Reformation eras.

Sixteenth-century-Reformation preaching of the apocalyptic prophecies of Daniel and Revelation tended to center on what the Reformers believed to be a Christian apostasy that had arisen within European Christendom and which they saw symbolized in the little horn (chapter 7), the leopard beast (Rev. 13), and the woman seated on the scarlet-colored beast (Rev. 17). This preaching had a telling effect upon Europe.

In the Counter-Reformation, which inevitably followed, Rome, rising to the challenge, sought to divert the damaging import of these applications. The result was the publishing of the initial argumentation for what would later become two distinctive, but diverse, methods of prophetic interpretation: the futurist and the preterist systems. Catholic and Protestant scholars alike agree on the origin of these two distinctively different systems, both of which are in conflict with the historicist method and the interpretations derived thereby.

Futurism

Toward the close of his life, the Spanish Jesuit Francisco Ribera (1537-1591) published a 500 page commentary on the book of Revelation. He assigned the first few chapters to ancient Rome but proposed that the bulk of the prophecies would be fulfilled in a brief three and one half year period at the *end* of the Christian era. In that short space antichrist (a *single* individual, according to Ribera) would rebuild the Jerusalem Temple, deny Christ, abolish Christianity, be received by the Jews, pretend to be god, and conquer the world. Thus the Protestant contention that the apocalyptic symbols of antichrist denoted an apostate religious *system* was countered, and the focus of the prophecies was diverted from the present to the far distant future.

Preterism

Another Spanish Jesuit, Luis de Alcazar (1554-1613), also published a scholarly work on Revelation, this one posthumously in 1614. The result of a forty-year endeavor to refute the Protestant challenge, Alcazar's publication developed a system of interpretation known as preterism (from the Latin *praeter,* meaning 'past'). His thesis, the opposite of Ribera's, was that all the prophecies of Revelation had been fulfilled in the past, that is, by the fifth and sixth centuries A.D., the early centuries of Christianity. He asserted that this prophetic book simply described a two-fold war by the church—its victory over the Jewish synagogue on the one hand (chapters 1-11) and Roman paganism on the other (chapters 12-19). Chapters 21 and 22 Alcazar applied to the Roman Catholic Church as the New Jerusalem, glorious and triumphant.

With the passage of time, these distinctive systems of counter interpretations began successfully to penetrate Protestant thought. Preterism was the first; it began to enter Protestantism in the late eighteenth century. Its present form is linked with the rise and spread of higher critical methodologies and approaches to Scripture study. Preterist interpretations of the prophecies have today become the standard view of liberal Protestantism.

The seeds of Catholic futurism, although refuted at first, eventually took root in the soil of Protestantism during the first quarter of the nineteenth century. Futurism, amplified with other elements (for example, many futurists teach a secret, pretribulation rapture), is currently followed in some form by most conservative Protestant bodies.

Thus in the centuries following the Reformation, Rome's countermoves to deflect the Reformers' application of the apocalyptic prophecies from herself have been largely successful. The futurist system of interpretation, as it functions today, wipes the Christian era clean of any prophetic significance by removing the bulk of the prophecies of Revelation (and certain aspects of Daniel) to the end of the age for their fulfillment. The preterist system accomplishes the same objective by relegating the prophecies of both books to the past. According to preterism, the significant prophetic portions of Daniel are assigned to second century B.C. events and the times of Antiochus IV Epiphanes; Revelation is restricted to Judaism and Rome in the first five hundred years of our era. Thus for most Protestants and Catholics the Christian era from the sixth century until the end of time stands totally devoid of prophetic significance as far as the books of Daniel and Revelation are concerned.

Seventh-day Adventists stand virtually alone today as exponents of the 'historicist school' or prophetic interpretation. If our interpretations of prophecy and our self-understanding differ from those of Christian friends outside our ranks (or from some critics who may arise from within our communion), it is largely because we as a people have been and are committed to a historicist system of prophetic interpretation, which we believe is soundly biblical.

Our Times and Task

In Daniel 7 the prophet records the first of several visions given to him personally. This vision parallels the prophetic dream given many years earlier to Nebuchadnezzar. However, instead of a metal image to symbolize the sequence of history, Daniel is shown the same world empires of Babylon, Medo-Persia, Grecia, and Rome as wild beasts—lion, bear, leopard, and a fourth creature, which bore no similarity to anything in nature. In Daniel 7 the division of Rome into the nations of Western Europe is symbolized by ten horns that rise from the head of the fourth beast. Two new elements, however, are introduced into this vision: (1) a little horn that rises among the nations of Western Europe with 'eyes like the eyes of man, and a mouth speaking great things' (vs. 8)—namely, the antichrist; (2) the opening phase of the final judgment.

Two things are immediately noteworthy about the prophetic description of the judgment. First, it takes place *in heaven.* 'I beheld,' Daniel says, 'till the thrones were cast down [placed], and the Ancient of days did sit, whose garment was white as snow, and the hair of His head like the pure wool: His throne was like the fiery flame, and His wheels as burning fire. A fiery stream issued and came forth from before Him: thousand thousands ministered unto Him, and ten thousand times ten thousand stood before Him: the judgment was set, and the books were opened' (vss. 9, 10, KJV).

Second, this heavenly court scene occurs *before* the advent of Jesus. It is a preadvent judgment that begins and functions in probationary time. At its close Daniel sees another scene in heaven that confirms this observation. 'I saw in the night visions, and behold, one like the son of man came with the clouds of heaven, and came to the Ancient of days, and they brought him near before him. And there was given him dominion, and glory, and a kingdom, that all people, nations, and languages, should serve him: his dominion is an everlasting dominion, which shall not pass away, and his kingdom that which shall not be destroyed' (vss. 13, 14). At His trial Jesus Christ identified Himself with this heavenly 'Son of man' described by Daniel (cf. Matt. 26:63, 64).

According to Daniel 7, it is at the close of this heavenly judgment scene that Christ will receive His kingdom and all those worthy to be His subjects under His eternal reign. *Then* He will descend the second time to this earth, not as a lowly babe, but as 'King of kings, and Lord of lords,' to bring the rule of Satan and sin to an end and to take His people to Himself.

But when will this preadvent judgment phase take place? Does prophecy specify a time for this awesome event other than in general terms—at the end of the age? Seventh-day Adventists believe that it does. In Daniel's second vision (Dan. 8 and 9), which again parallels and further elaborates on the dream and vision given earlier in chapters 2 and 7, the preadvent judgment is described as a 'cleansing' of the heavenly sanctuary or temple.

A time element of 2300 prophetic 'days' is given, or a period of 2300 years according to the year-day principle. Beginning with the 70-week prophecy (an integral part of the vision and interpretation of Dan. 8 and 9) in 457 B.C., at the time of Artaxerxes' decree that restored Jewish autonomy, these 2300 years span the centuries, extending to the fall of A.D. 1844. At that time, in heaven 'the judgment was set, and the books were opened' (Dan. 7:10), and the process of cleansing the heavenly sanctuary, or restoring it to its rightful state, was begun (Dan. 8:14).

It is these lines of prophecy found in Daniel chapters 2, 7, 8, and 9, interpreted along historicist principles that cause Seventh-day Adventists to sense the seriousness of the era in which the world now lives since 1844. The preadvent judgment is in progress, the first phase of the final judgment. In 1844 the world entered as it were the last inning in the game of life, the last lap of the race. Christ entered His final phase of priestly mediatorial ministry. Mercy began making her last plea to a doomed planet. The sands of probationary time have nearly run through time's hourglass, and Jesus Christ is about to lay aside His role as man's intercessor and to come as the rightful owner and ruler of this world.

It is in the awesome setting of this preadvent judgment that Seventh-day Adventists believe that Daniel's companion book, the book of Revelation, identifies their movement and end-time task. According to the prophet John the gospel invitation, along with certain specific emphases, is to be proclaimed worldwide just prior to our Lord's return (see Rev. 14:6-14). This special end-time work is symbolized by three angels who each have a message for the inhabitants of earth as they fly through the sky. Note some of the specifics: The first angel is described as preaching 'the everlasting gospel' to a global audience, crying in a loud voice, "Fear God, and give glory to Him; *for the hour of His judgment is come* [Greek, 'has come']: and worship Him that made heaven, and earth, and the sea, and the fountains of waters" (vs. 7, KJV). The second angel announces the fall of mystical Babylon, and the third warns against the worship of the beast, its image, and the receiving of its mark.

In these prophetic scenes, Seventh-day Adventists see delineated their task—a global outreach to announce to their fellow men that the hour of God's judgment has come, that the preadvent judgment in heaven, as described by Daniel, has begun and is now in progress. As probation inexorably moves towards its close, their appeal to every race and culture is to accept the salvation that is offered in Jesus Christ, to come back to the worship of God who created mankind and to respect and to give honor to Him by living in harmony with His law, including the observance of His Sabbath as stated in the fourth precept. This task involves warnings, as well, against apostasy and the substitution of false worship and institutions in the place of what God has commanded.

The world today is like that of Noah. There is a strange abandonment to every form of wickedness and pleasure with little thought for the future. It will not be long before the solemn pronouncement will be made: 'He that is unjust, let him be unjust still: and he which is filthy, let him be filthy still: and he that is righteous, let him be righteous still: and he that is holy, let him be holy still. And, behold, I come quickly; and my reward is with me, to give every man according as his work shall be' (Rev. 22:11-12). Consequently, while Adventists seek to present Christ as the center of every doctrine and to emphasize the centrality of His atoning death, yet it is the urgency and the seriousness of the present judgment hour that impels this people to reach out by every possible means 'to every nation, and kindred, and tongue, and people' (chapter 14:6) with Heaven's balm of healing grace.

Note

Used with permission from the Biblical Research Institute; published in Ministry, *July 1983. Online: http://www.adventistbiblicalresearch.org/documents/What%20Prophecy%20Means%20to%20Church.htm*

Chapter 2

The Authority of the Bible

George W. Reid

What about the manuscript sources of the various Bible translations? Is it true that the most faithful source is the Textus Receptus compiled by Erasmus and used as the basis for the Luther Bible, French Bible, and the King James English Bible?

While at one time this was probably correct, it is no longer the case. In creating the Textus Receptus, Erasmus, although a great scholar, had access to only eight manuscripts, all from the so-called Byzantine family of biblical manuscripts. And the oldest of Erasmus' documents dated only from the ninth century. This meant that his oldest manuscript represented at least eight centuries of copying and re-copying, which allowed substantial opportunity for errors to creep in through accidental miscopying or scribal additions and omissions. However, Erasmus' version was superior to anything else at that time.

This situation no longer applies today. Since the time of Erasmus, Luther, and the King James translators, we have discovered far older biblical manuscripts that date to the fifth, fourth, and in fragments even to the second century. Such sources have at least a 500 year copying advantage over the best manuscript Erasmus consulted. Therefore they offer much less chance of accidental mistakes. Two of these, Codex Sinaiticus and Codex Alexandrinus, are on display at the present time in the British Museum. Expert specialists have studied them carefully and have found no evidence that someone has tampered with the text.

Based on a huge number of manuscripts, including the most ancient available texts, in the late 1800s two famed British scholars, professors Wescott and Hort, prepared a new composite biblical text, one superior in quality to that of Erasmus. It became the basis of the English revision of the King James Version published in full in 1885. Immediately after its publication Ellen White began to consult it and often incorporated its readings into her books and articles. Clearly she had no reluctance to use it because of its manuscript base. In 1901 an American version of the 1885 English Revised Version was issued, being a very similar work. It was called the American Revised Version, and Mrs. White made use of it as well, although it too was based on the Wescott and Hort text. A stream of additional translations has followed since 1901, at least 50 in English and many more in other languages, all of them based on modern texts, either of Wescott and Hort or similar. None has used Erasmus' Textus Receptus.

Recently a few Adventists have called for exclusive use of the King James Version (itself last revised in 1769) on the grounds that modern Greek and Hebrew texts have been subjected to possible alteration at the hands of Catholic scholars, whereas Erasmus' Textus Receptus was not. They seem to forget that Erasmus himself was a Catholic scholar. Moreover, the late manuscripts Erasmus used were all drawn from Catholic monasteries, where they had been copied and re-copied over the centuries, so exposing them to very great opportunities to change. Ironically, the most ancient manuscripts used for today's translations were in Catholic hands for 500 years less than Erasmus' manuscripts. One would expect the defenders of the King James Version to take note of this fact if their concern is about possible corruption of the text. These people, although undoubtedly sincere, have failed to take all the evidence into account, and by spreading an alarm about newer versions are doing the cause of Christ a disservice.

There are in fact problems in translations, some significant in the looser "dynamic" translations where translators have taken considerable liberties in departure from a literal reading of the text in order to convey what they believe it really means. Such tactics make these translations suspect as sources for doctrinal belief. Examples of this problem include the New English Bible, Living Bible (actually a paraphrase rather than translation), and Today's English Version, widely distributed by the Bible Societies. But problems with these translations rest not in their Greek and Hebrew base texts, but with renderings into English that do not follow closely the original readings.

Better modern translations include the English and American Revised Versions, Revised Standard Version, New International Version, and New American Standard Bible (itself a revision of the 1901 American Revised Version). The newly-published New King James Version has adopted numerous improvements that occur in other modern translations, but in doing so has departed from sole reliance on Erasmus' Textus Receptus. Bible readers should select a version based on the most ancient manuscript sources, whose translators are committed to a quite literal translation of the text.

Note

Used with permission from the Biblical Research Institute:
Online: http://www.adventistbiblicalresearch.org/documents/Authority%20of%20the%20Bible.htm

Chapter 3

Bible Translations

Gerhard Pfandl

The process of Bible translations began during the third century B.C. with the translation of the Old Testament into Greek. The reason for this translation, called the Septuagint,[1] was the need of a Bible for the Greek speaking Jews in Alexandria who no longer spoke or understood Hebrew.

While the Septuagint was made for Greek-speaking Jews, in the Christian era this translation soon fell out of favor with the Jews, primarily because from the first century onwards the Christians adopted it as their version of the OT [Old Testament] and used it freely in defence of the Christian faith. "Christians came to attach some degree of divine inspiration to the Septuagint, for some of its translations might almost appear to have been providentially intended to support Christian arguments."[2] The Jews, therefore, soon produced other Greek versions.[3]

Other ancient Jewish versions are the Targumim (from the Aramaic *Targōm* "to translate"), which are fairly free translations of the OT text into Aramaic. The Targumim were the product of the official synagogue interpreters who after the Babylonian exile, when Aramaic replaced Hebrew as the spoken language, translated the OT texts into Aramaic during the worship services. These verbal paraphrases were eventually written down and traces of them appear in a few [New Testament] NT texts.[4]

Christian Versions

After the LXX (the scholarly abbreviation for the Septuagint), the oldest and most important translation of the Bible is the Syriac version called the Peshitta or "simple" version. Syriac is an Aramaic dialect that was spoken over a wide area in early Christian times, particularly in western Mesopotamia, where it was used more than Greek. Originally the Peshitta did not include 2 Peter, 2 and 3 John, Jude, and Revelation. These books were added in A.D. 508 when the Syrian-speaking Christians underwent a schism and a new Syriac translation included them.

At the beginning of the Christian era, the churches in the East were Greek-speaking; in the Roman provinces of Africa and Western Europe, however, Latin was the official language. Towards the end of the second century, therefore, we find references to Latin Scriptures in the writings of the church fathers. Because of the tendency of some bishops and priests to make translations of the Septuagint and NT manuscripts into Latin, a number of translations of various Biblical texts began to appear. These fragments were later assembled and became known as the Old Latin text, also called Itala.

In 382, Pope Damasus I (366-384) commissioned his secretary Jerome to produce a new Latin Bible. Jerome first of all revised the Old Latin texts and produced a standard text version of the New Testament. After the death of Damasus, Jerome settled in Bethlehem, where he completed a new translation of the Old Testament from Hebrew in 405. Jerome's Bible became known as the Vulgate (*vulga* meaning "everyday speech"). In 1546, at the Council of Trent, the Vulgate became the official Bible of the Catholic Church. It was the first book to be printed by Johannes Gutenberg in 1456.

English Versions

Ancient Bible versions were of vital importance for taking the Gospel to the pagan nations during the early centuries of Christianity. Similarly, during the time of the Reformation, translations into the vernacular facilitated the spread of Reformation ideas in Europe. Since then, the whole Bible has been translated into 426 languages, the New Testament into another 1,115 languages, and portions of the Bible into still another 862 languages, making a total of more than 2,400 languages.[5]

The first complete English translation is credited to John Wycliffe, a lecturer at Oxford University, in the latter part of the fourteenth century. Wycliffe believed that "if every man was responsible to obey the Bible . . . it follows that every man must know what to obey. Therefore, the whole Bible should be accessible to him in a form that he could understand."[6]

Whether Wycliffe himself took part in the translation is uncertain, but under his influence two English versions of the Latin Vulgate were produced. One hundred fifty years later, William Tyndale, who became proficient in Greek while attending Oxford and Cambridge, translated the Greek New Testament into English. It was published in 1525 in Germany, and was then smuggled in bales of cloth back into England for distribution. Church officials opposed the circulation of his translation; they bought copies and burnt them. Tyndale himself, after being betrayed by a friend, was imprisoned and executed in Belgium in 1536. In 1535, one year before Tyndale's death, Miles Coverdale published another complete translation in English. By that time, Henry VIII had made himself head of the church in England and was ready to accept English translations of the Bible.

After James I became King of England, he authorized a new translation, which since its publication in 1611 has been known as the Authorized or King James Version (KJV). More than fifty scholars, versed in Greek and Hebrew, were responsible for its production. It captured the best of all the preceding translations and far exceeded all of them. It has justifiably been called the "noblest monument of English prose."[7] Based on the best of the earlier English versions, the KJV has remained for over three hundred years "the Bible" *par excellence* wherever the English tongue is spoken. Protestants and Roman Catholics (and Jews also, with respect to the OT) have appreciated its beauty and value. Dr. Alexander Geddes, a great Roman Catholic Biblical scholar at the end of the eighteenth century, stated that "if accuracy and strictest attention to the letter of the text is supposed to constitute an excellent version this is of all versions the most excellent."[8]

Nevertheless, at the end of the 19th century it was felt that a revision was necessary because (1) Knowledge of the Hebrew vocabulary had increased since the beginning of the 17th century (about 1,500 words appear only once in the OT). (2) The Greek text underlying the New Testament was the *textus receptus* (Latin for "received text") which was based on medieval manuscripts, none of them older than about A.D. 1000. The important fourth-and fifth-century manuscript codices Sinaiticus, Vaticanus, and Alexandrinus were not available in 1611. (3) Many English words had become obsolete or archaic; others had changed in meaning. For example, the word "knop" [Exodus 25:31-36] is an archaic word for the bud of a flower or for an ornamental knob or boss."[9] The word "prevent" (1 Thessalonians 4:15) in the seventeenth century meant "to go before," or "precede," rather than "to hinder."

In 1870, the Convocation of Canterbury voted to sponsor a major revision of the King James Version. When the complete Revised Version appeared in 1885, it was received with great enthusiasm, but its popularity was short-lived because most people continued to prefer the Authorized Version.

The King James Version-Only Controversy

In 1516 the Dutch scholar Desiderius Erasmus published the first Greek New Testament in Basel, Switzerland, which became the basis of the *textus receptus*. Unfortunately, none of the Greek manuscripts available to Erasmus was older than about A.D. 1000. The *textus receptus* (a term used for the first time in 1633) preserves a form of the New Testament found in the great majority of Greek manuscripts,[10] most of which were copied between A.D. 750 and 1500, and which show a high level of agreement with one another.

Since the time of Erasmus a number of older Greek manuscripts with variant reading from the *textus receptus* have been discovered. The most important among them are two manuscripts prepared about A.D. 350. One is called Codex Vaticanus because it was found in the library of the Vatican; the other is called Codex Sinaiticus because in 1844 it was discovered in the library of St. Catherine's Monastery on Mount Sinai. By the time of the 19th century, the number of variants among known Greek New Testament manuscripts was estimated to exceed 300,000.[11] In 1881, therefore, two English scholars, Brooke F. Westcott and Fenton J. Hort, published *The New Testament in the Original Greek*, which was based primarily on the ancient codices Vaticanus and Sinaiticus.

It is this Greek New Testament that is attacked by "KJV-only defenders" because most modern translations are no longer based on the *textus receptus*, but rather on the Westcott and Hort and later revisions of the Greek texts. One of the chief arguments of KJV-only defenders is that the King James Bible translators relied on the *textus receptus*, which they believe was providentially preserved through the centuries from scribal mistakes and intentional changes. By contrast, the Westcott and Hort Greek text, it is alleged, is based on manuscripts produced during a period of apostasy in the church and not providentially protected from scribal changes. "Translations based on them are therefore unreliable."[12] While the fourth century certainly was a time in which false teaching entered the church, there is no evidence from the existing New Testament manuscripts that these doctrinal errors affected any of the Greek manuscripts produced during that time.

One of the most frequent criticisms of modern versions is the supposed omission of terms connected with the divinity of Jesus. For example, where the KJV repeatedly has the phrase "Lord Jesus Christ" (Acts 15:11; 16:31; 1 Corinthians 5:4; 2 Corinthians 11:31; etc.), modern versions read only "Lord Jesus." The omission of the word "Christ" in these texts is seen as a denial of Jesus' divinity. Gail Riplinger, a leading proponent of the KJV-only defenders, writes: "Texe Marrs warns, 'New Age leaders believe and will spread the apostasy that Jesus is neither Christ nor God.' New version editors become 'New Age leaders by this definition.'"[13] She completely ignores the fact that the phrase "Lord Jesus Christ" which appears about 80 times in the KJV also appears 36 times in the Revised Standard Version (RSV) and 60 times in the New International Version (NIV). While the *textus receptus* uses this phrase more than 80 times, the older Greek manuscripts only use it about 60 times. But this does not mean that they in any way deny that Jesus was the Christ.

The charge that modern versions minimize the deity of Jesus can be found throughout the writings of KJV-only defenders. However, there are a number of places where modern versions are stronger and clearer on the deity of Jesus than the KJV. One example is John 1:18. The KJV reads, "No man hath seen God at any time; the only begotten Son, which is in the bosom of the Father, He hath declared him." Modern versions like the New American Standard Bible (NASB) read, "only begotten God," and the NIV, "God the One and Only" instead of "only begotten Son."[14]

Two lengthy passages are not found in the earliest manuscripts. One comprises the closing verses of Mark (16:9-20), and the other is the story of the woman taken in adultery (John 7:53 to 8:11). Most modern versions include these passages but indicate their omissions in the ancient manuscripts in various ways. For example, the NIV interrupts the text flow between verses 8 and 9 of Mark 16 with a centered rule (line), followed by a note, "The two most reliable early manuscripts do not have Mark 16:9-20." Because we do not have the original autographs, we do not know whether these stories were lost in the process of transmission or whether they were later additions of oral reports. Whatever the case, their omission in the ancient texts does not warrant the charge that modern versions have changed God's Word.

Modern Versions

The proliferation of new English versions in recent decades has made it necessary to carefully consider which translation one is going to use and for what purpose. First, we need to recognize that there are three basic types of translations: (1) *Formal or literal translations* attempt to translate as close as possible to the original wording, e.g., King James Version (1611), Revised Version (RV, 1885), Revised Standard Version (RSV, 1952), New American Standard Bible (NASB, 1971), etc. (2) *Dynamic equivalency translations* are not so much concerned with the original wording as with the original meaning, e.g. the New English Bible (NEB, 1970), New International Version (NIV, 1978), and Revised English Version (REB, 1989). (3) *Paraphrases of the Bible* seek to restate in simplified but related ways the ideas conveyed in the original language, e.g., The Living Bible (1971), The Message (1993), The Clear Word (2000). Paraphrases are more like commentaries, e.g., in the Message, Colossians 2:9, "For in him dwelleth all the fullness of the Godhead bodily" (KJV) is expanded to, "Everything of God gets expressed in Him, so you can see and hear Him clearly. You don't need a telescope, a microscope, or a horoscope to realize the fullness of Christ, and the emptiness of the universe without Him."

So, which version shall we use? For serious Bible study and preaching it is helpful to consult several good versions. Good modern standard translations are the RSV, the NASB, and the New King James Version (NKJV). For personal and family devotions a paraphrase may be used. Paraphrases, however, should not be used in Sabbath School or in the pulpit.

Ellen White and Bible Versions

Anyone reading the writing of Ellen White soon realizes that she used Scripture profusely. All her articles and books are saturated with Scriptural quotations from the King James Bible. Did she use other version? Yes, but sparingly. Among the modern versions that Ellen White occasionally used were the Revised Version (1885), the American Revised Version (1901), and the translations of Bernard, Boothroyd, Leeser, Noyes, and Rotherham.[15]

Writing in 1931, her son W.C. White stated that "I do not know of anything in the E.G. White writings, nor can I remember of anything in Sister White's conversations, that would intimate that she felt that there was any evil in the use of the Revised Version . . . . When the first revision was published, I purchased a good copy and gave it to Mother. She referred to it occasionally, but never used it in her preaching."[16] The reasons for this was that "there are many persons in the congregation who remember the words of the texts we might use as they are presented in the Authorized Version, and to read from the Revised Version would introduce perplexing questions in their minds as to why the wording of the text has been changed by the revisers and as to why it was being used by the speaker. She did not advise me in a positive way not to use the A.R.V., but she intimated to me quite clearly that it would be better not to do so, as the use of the different wording brought perplexity to the older members in the congregation."[17]

Ellen White did not hesitate to use other versions, but out of concern for those who had heard or read only the King James Version she did not use them in public. However, she never made the use of the King James Version a criterion of orthodoxy. She was aware of the fact changes in the text, nevertheless she could say, "I take the Bible just as it is, as the Inspired Word,"[18] and so should we.

Endnotes

1 The word *Septuagint* comes from the Latin for "seventy" (abbr. LXX). According to a legendary explanation for the name Septuagint, the Greek King Ptolemy II Philadelphus (285-247 B.C) was persuaded by his librarian to secure a Greek translation of the Hebrew Bible for the royal library. The king appealed to the high priest at Jerusalem, who responded by sending seventy-two elders to Alexandria with an official copy of the Law. Over a period of seventy-two days these men made a complete translation of the Torah, working independently during the day and comparing their results in the evening so as to arrive at a rendering that would be satisfactory to all concerned. The rest of the Old Testament was translated in piecemeal fashion over the next one hundred years.

2 F.F. Bruce, *The Books and the Parchments*, rev. ed. (London; Marshall Pickering, 1991), p. 141. In Isaiah 7:14, for example, the LXX uses *parthenos* (virgin) rather than *neanis* (young woman), which is generally used to translate the Hebrew word *almah*.

3 The version of Aquila and Theodotion were named after their translators.

4 For example, the expression "spirit of prophecy" which appears only in Revelation 19:10 is frequently used in the Targumim to describe the gift of prophecy, e.g., Gen. 41:38 "Pharaoh said to his servants, can we find a man like this, in whom is the Spirit of prophecy from before the Lord?"

5 Statistical summary of the United Bible Society of February 14, 2006. See http://www.biblesociety.org/index2.htm

6 F. F. Bruce, *The English Bible* (Oxford: University Press, 1961), p. 13.

7 J.H. Skilton, "English Versions of the Bible," *New Bible Dictionary*, ed. J.D. Douglas et al., (Leicester, England: Inter-Varsity Press, 1962), p. 333.

8 F. F. Bruce, *the Books and the Parchments*, p. 220.

9 R. Bridges and L. Weigle, *The King James Word Book* (Nashville: Thomas Nelson Publishers, 1994), p. 196.

10 About 95% of the 5,400 Greek manuscripts known.

11 None of these variant readings affects any of the teachings of the Bible, however.

12 S. Thompson, "The Great Bible Versions Debate," *Record*, July 22, 1995, p. 5.

13 G.A. Riplinger, *New Age Bible Versions* (Munroe Falls, Ohio: AV Publications, 1993), p. 313.

14 For purposes of exact textual comparison in the immediate instance, we have refrained from our customary practice of clarifying spelling and capitalization while not materially altering original texts. This was commonly done editorially in Ellen White's writings during her life time.—*Ed.*

15 General Conference Committee, *Problems in Bible Translations* (Washington, D.C.: Review and Herald, 1954), pp. 71, 72.

16 Ibid., p. 72.

17 Ibid., pp. 72, 73.

18 Ellen G. White, *Selected Messages*, bk. 1, p. 17.

Note

*Used with permission from Adventists Affirm [*Adventists Affirm *vol. 20(3), 44-50, 2006] and the author Dr Pfandl who is an Associate Director, Biblical Research Institute.*

Chapter 4

Approaching Revelation and Inspiration

Ekkehardt Mueller

The Bible, revelation, inspiration, and Scripture's reliability and authority are hotly debated today, with repercussions for Adventists. In some cases even the possibility of divine revelation and inspiration is totally rejected. In others revelation and inspiration are reinterpreted.[1]

The issues are hot because these topics belong to the most fundamental ones in theology, having a strong impact on the beliefs and the everyday lives of Christians. Although Jesus and salvation through Him form the heart of our theology and experience, it is ultimately only through the Scriptures that we receive necessary information about Him and redemption. There we know Jesus' in His multifaceted ministry on our behalf. How we understand Scripture will shape our perception of Him and our understanding of discipleship.

This article focuses on the methods of studying revelation, inspiration, and authority of Scripture. It will not discuss these biblical doctrines *per se*, but provides limited short definitions.

Definitions

According to the biblical testimony special revelation[2] is an act of God in which He reveals to specific persons (1) Himself, (2) truths of various natures, and/or (3) His will. As a result of God's initiative and action these humans, called prophets, have access to an experience which otherwise is not open to humans, receiving knowledge not otherwise available.

According to Scripture inspiration is God's act in which He enables the prophet to understand and communicate the received message. By this process the proclaimed message becomes words from God and is not just human words. In order to communicate revelation reliably, inspiration is needed. However revelation and inspiration cannot be sharply separated.

Speaking of the authority of Scripture, we believe that Scripture as "the infallible revelation of His will,"[3] is the standard for a Christian life. Everything has to be tested by it. Each doctrine must be founded upon it. Scripture, then, has priority over all human thought, research, and emotion.

Methodology

No scholar or scientist works without certain presuppositions. On this topic, some will overtly deny such things as divine revelation and inspiration. Others claim the opposite. Some hold that there *may* be divine inspiration. Based on these presuppositions some scholars consider the Bible to be merely a human book, or a divine book, a mixture of the two, or a book with both characteristics at the same time. Such preconceived ideas influence the research.

Several approaches present themselves. They are not exclusive but can be combined with one another. One option is to proceed inductively. Another one is to work deductively. In the first instance the researcher can choose to study inspiration by means of extra-biblical sources and draw conclusions which then are applied to the Bible. Another possibility is to create analogies in order to demonstrate how inspiration works and to make deductions. Again the respective approach selected will shape the outcome.

Inductive versus Deductive

The major choice is whether to proceed inductively or deductively. Normally an inductive approach begins with the investigation of biblical phenomena. One reads, for instance, through the Gospels, compares them with each other, and detects differences and so-called discrepancies. One studies Chronicles and Kings and notices gaps and divergence. A comparison of Paul's experience as reported in Acts and in Galatians seems to reveal differences. Supposedly, even his conversion accounts in Acts do not correspond. An inductive approach oftentimes does not allow for harmonization even where it seems to be possible and advisable. It is preoccupied with finding differences rather than agreement and unity. And it always works with only parts of the entire puzzle. Nevertheless, based on this type of collected and interpreted data a doctrine of inspiration is formulated. The problem with this approach is that it largely disregards the self-testimony of Scripture. The starting point is not what Scripture claims to be, but the phenomena of the biblical texts as seen and interpreted by a rational human being of the 20th or 21st century.

A deductive approach begins with the self-testimony of Scripture, that is, the texts which directly or indirectly refer to revelation, inspiration, and authority of Scripture. A doctrine of inspiration, for example, is formulated based on the claims of Scripture and its numerous references to this topic.

Probably, the issue of inductive versus deductive is not simply a matter of either/or. Both approaches are needed. In formulating a doctrine of inspiration one cannot disregard the textual phenomena and one should not discard the self-testimony of Scripture. The Bible must be allowed to speak for itself. Thus, the question is: How do we start? Or, which approach comes first? In a trial, it is only fair to listen to a witness first and to take him or her seriously before one questions his or her statements. To a certain degree, Heinrich Schliemann even took Homer's writings at face value and excavated Troy, a city previously believed to be fiction only.[4] Because the Bible claims revelation and inspiration, it is fair to start from there and to ask oneself how the phenomena can be reconciled with this assertion.[5]

Use of Extra-biblical Sources

Among others, the history of religions school has used extra-biblical sources to interpret Scripture, such as Babylonian myths, Hellenistic mystery cults, and ideas of the Roman Emperor cult.[6] Their views have been read back into the Bible. We would be very hesitant to use such a procedure, since Adventists accept the principle of Scripture being its own interpreter.

However, we must go a step further. To study inspiration in an inspired, non-canonical prophet, for instance in E. G. White, and read the data gathered back into the Bible is—on the basis of the *sola scriptura* principle also not acceptable. The Bible can stand on its own, and a biblical doctrine of inspiration must be derived from the Bible and the Bible alone. Genuine non-canonical prophets may provide helpful information, but to view the Bible through the processes involved in the inspiration of a non-canonical prophet is circular reasoning.[7] In addition, we must ask if by allowing for such an approach a sort of principle of uniformity is at work. Although the Bible does not provide evidence for stages of inspiration, that is, one prophet being more inspired than another, the question remains whether or not inspiration really worked the same way in all prophets. The outcome is equal in so far that revelation, God's message, is passed on faithfully, but the processes are not necessarily identical. Jeremiah's experience in dictating God's message to Baruch while being inspired (Jeremiah 36) is obviously different from Luke's experience in gathering information and under inspiration putting together his gospel.

Use of Analogies

Analogies can be extremely helpful. They are like pictures that bring home a point to the audience. But analogies, like parables, have limitations. They should not be overextended. To create an analogy and make deductions from that analogy may not any longer correspond with reality.[8] Therefore, we need to exercise caution.

One of the most common analogies is the so-called incarnational model. In this case, Scripture is paralleled with Jesus Christ. There are theologians who deny the divine character of Scripture. There are others who omit or underestimate the human factor. The incarnational model stresses both the human and the divine. However, even after accepting the last option, a question remains. Are the human and divine sides complementary, yet separable? Or is there an inseparable unity between the human and the divine?

In the case of Jesus, Christians claim that He was truly God and became also truly man. Human and divine cannot be split apart in Jesus. This seems also to be true for Scripture. 2 Peter 1:21 points to a cooperation between the Holy Spirit and human agents, acknowledging the divine and the human. Yet, Scripture was not created by humans. Through God prophets talked about God. God is the origin and final author of Scripture. Gerhard Maier summarizes this in three points: (1) Men spoke; that is, representatives of normal persons at a particular place and time, not instruments, writing implements, or the like; and they used a normal human language. (2) None of them, curiously enough, spoke from the standpoint of men, but from God; that is sent from Him, empowered, proceeding from His vantage point and bringing across a message from Him that is no less than a divine message. (3) The one who brought about this peculiar state of affairs is the 'Holy Spirit.'[9]

Prophetic messages and prophetic writings are the words of the Lord and are accepted by God as such.[10] Biblical books are the word of the Lord.[11] Thus, the human and the divine in Scripture are not complementary. They are integrated. Consequently, different sets of tools in order to study the human side and the divine side of the Bible cannot do justice to its unified nature, the truly incarnational character of Scripture. And by the way, many tools of scholarship are not just neutral. They are linked to presuppositions so much so that by eliminating these presuppositions the tools themselves have evaporated.[12]

In all these questions, Christians are always referred back to Jesus Christ, their Lord and Savior and their Exemplar. How did Jesus come to grips with Scripture in His time, with issues such as revelation, inspiration, and authority? Jesus made statements about Scripture, and He used Scripture profusely. Certainly, he was not naive or ignorant with regard to the issues we raised. Here is Jesus' position on Scripture:

- Jesus trusted Scripture. For Him the Old Testament (OT), His Bible, is God's word. Through human agents God has spoken.
- Jesus regarded the prophets as reliable communicators of God's words and accepted inspiration on the part of the writers of the OT Scripture contains genuine predictive prophecy. Many of these prophecies He regarded to be fulfilled in Himself.
- Jesus accepted the historical reliability of Scripture, including all the important events in Israel's history as well as creation and [the] flood.

- Jesus considered as author of a book that person who was identified as such in the respective biblical book.
- Divine interventions in history such as miracles posed no problem for Jesus.
- Jesus interpreted Scripture literally and typologically. Critical methods in expounding the Bible were foreign to Him. Although he must have known so-called discrepancies in Scripture He never focused on them and did not even mention them.
- Jesus considered Scripture not only as addressed to the original readers and hearer but also to His generation. Scripture transcends culture.
- Jesus' understanding of God's will and His actions in history are founded on Scripture. Biblical doctrines can be derived from the OT. At the same time, the OT was the standard for His life as well as a justification of His behavior.
- Scripture has practical value. It fosters faith. It can be used as the authority and weapon against temptations.
- Jesus expected His contemporaries to know Scripture.[13]

Suggestions

How then can we handle these issues of revelation, inspiration, and authority of Scripture? Here are some suggestions:

- Start with an attitude of trust instead of a position of doubt. This does not exclude openness.
- Take seriously Scripture's self-testimony.
- Do not deny or underestimate problems in the biblical text. Take care, however, not to overstate them. Be careful with extreme positions on personalized inspiration as well as mechanical inspiration.
- Look for solutions with regard to the biblical phenomena without trying to make them fit artificially and be able to suspend judgment. If you cannot find a solution that does not mean that there is none.[14]
- Use an appropriate interpretive method and suitable exegetical tools that fit the character of God's word.
- Live the word of God.
- Proclaim it, empowered by the Holy Spirit.

References

1 Cf. Wolfhart Pannenberg, "The Revelation of God in Jesus of Nazareth", J. M. Robinson und J. B. Cobb, Jr., Hrsg., in *Theology as History*, New Frontiers in Theology, Bd. 3 (New York: Harper and Row, 1967), 101-133; Gabriel Moran, *The Present Revelation: The Search for Religious Foundations* (New York: Herder and Herder, 1972), 38-40, 130, 227, 299, 341; Gerhard Maier, *Biblical Hermeneutics* (Wheaton, IL: Crossway Books, 1994), 97.

2 Theologians distinguish between general revelation, which, e.g., is found in nature, and special revelation.

3 See the Fundamental Beliefs of Seventh-day Adventists, no. 1, in *Seventh-day Adventist Church Manual,* (Hagerstown, MD: Review and Herald Publishing Association, 1995), 7.

4 Cf. *Encyclopaedia Britannica: Micropaedia* (Chicago: Encyclopaedia Britannica, 1981), VIII: 965.

5 Cf. Peter M. van Bemmelen, *Issues in Biblical Inspiration: Sanday and Warfield* (Berrien Springs, MI: Andrews University Press, 1987), 377-378.

6 These were proposed by Gunkel, Reitzenstein, and Bousset.

7 By means of Biblical criteria a prophet is declared genuine and inspired. Then this very prophet is used to formulate a doctrine of inspiration of the Bible.

8 It may be useful to compare the nature of Scripture with the nature of light. However, to conclude that for these different aspects of light different tools must be used and apply this to Scripture seems to go too far. Scripture may be similar to light, but it is not light in the literal sense. Cf. Richard W. Coffen, "A Fresh Look at the Dynamics of Inspiration: Part 2," *Ministry* February 2000, 20-23.

9 Maier, 102.

10 See Jer. 36:1-6 and Jer. 25:2-8.

11 See Mic. 1:1; Hos. 1:1; Zeph. 1:1.

12 See, e.g., form criticism which investigates the oral stage of material, smallest units that were, for instance, created at a campfire or a funeral procession. No revelation took place. Texts developed along evolutionary lines.

13 References can be found in Ekkehardt Mueller, "Jesus and Scripture in the Gospels," unpublished manuscript, March 1999.

14 See Edwin R. Thiele, *The Mysterious Numbers of the Hebrew Kings* (Grand Rapids: William B. Eerdmans Publishing Company, 1951).

Note

Chapter 5

Methods of Bible Study

General Conference of Seventh-day Adventists Executive Committee

Bible Study: Presuppositions, Principles, and Methods

Preamble

This statement is addressed to all members of the Seventh-day Adventist Church with the purpose of providing guidelines on how to study the Bible, both [for] the trained biblical scholar and others.

Seventh-day Adventists recognize and appreciate the contributions of those biblical scholars throughout history who have developed useful and reliable methods of Bible study consistent with the claims and teachings of Scripture. Adventists are committed to the acceptance of biblical truth and are willing to follow it, using all methods of interpretation consistent with what Scripture says of itself. These are outlined in the presuppositions detailed below.

In recent decades the most prominent method in biblical studies has been known as the historical-critical method. Scholars who use this method, as classically formulated, operate on the basis of presuppositions which, prior to studying the biblical text, reject the reliability of accounts of miracles and other supernatural events narrated in the Bible. Even a modified use of this method that retains the principle of criticism which subordinates the Bible to human reason is unacceptable to Adventists.

The historical-critical method minimizes the need for faith in God and obedience to His commandments. In addition, because such a method de-emphasises the divine element in the Bible as an inspired book (including its resultant unity) and depreciates or misunderstands apocalyptic prophecy and the eschatological portions of the Bible, we urge Adventist Bible students to avoid relying on the use of the presuppositions and the resultant deductions associated with the historical-critical method.

In contrast with the historical-critical method and presuppositions, we believe it to be helpful to set forth the principles of Bible study that are consistent with the teachings of the Scriptures themselves, that preserve their unity, and are based upon the premise that the Bible is the Word of God. Such an approach will lead us into a satisfying and rewarding experience with God.

Presuppositions Arising From the Claims of Scripture

Origin

1. The Bible is the Word of God and is the primary and authoritative means by which He reveals Himself to human beings.

2. The Holy Spirit inspired the Bible writers with thoughts, ideas, and objective information; in turn they expressed these in their own words. Therefore the Scriptures are an indivisible union of human and divine elements, neither of which should be emphasized to the neglect of the other (2 Pet. 1:21; cf. *The Great Controversy*, pp. v, vi).
3. All Scripture is inspired by God and came through the work of the Holy Spirit. However, it did not come in a continuous chain of unbroken revelations. As the Holy Spirit communicated truth to the Bible writer, each wrote as he was moved by the Holy Spirit, emphasizing the aspect of the truth which he was led to stress. For this reason the student of the Bible will gain a rounded comprehension on any subject by recognizing that the Bible is its own best interpreter and when studied as a whole it depicts a consistent, harmonious truth (2 Tim. 3:16; Heb. 1:1, 2; cf. *Selected Messages*, book 1, pp. 19, 20; *The Great Controversy*, pp. v, vi).
4. Although it was given to those who lived in an ancient Near Eastern/Mediterranean context, the Bible transcends its cultural backgrounds to serve as God's Word for all cultural, racial, and situational contexts in all ages.

Authority

1. The sixty-six books of the Old and New Testaments are the clear, infallible revelation of God's will and His salvation. The Bible is the Word of God, and it alone is the standard by which all teaching and experience must be tested (2 Tim. 3:15, 17; Ps. 119:105; Prov. 30:5, 6; Isa. 8:20; John 17:17; 2 Thess. 3:14; Heb. 4:12).
2. Scripture is an authentic, reliable record of history and God's acts in history. It provides the normative theological interpretation of those acts. The supernatural acts revealed in Scripture are historically true. For example, chapters 1-11 of Genesis are a factual account of historical events.
3. The Bible is not like other books. It is an indivisible blend of the divine and the human. Its record of many details of secular history is integral to its overall purpose to convey salvation history. While at times there may be parallel procedures employed by Bible students to determine historical data, the usual techniques of historical research, based as they are on human presuppositions and focused on the human element, are inadequate for interpreting the Scriptures, which are a blend of the divine and human. Only a method that fully recognizes the indivisible nature of the Scriptures can avoid a distortion of its message.
4. Human reason is subject to the Bible, not equal to or above it. Presuppositions regarding the Scriptures must be in harmony with the claims of the Scriptures and subject to correction by them (1 Cor. 2:1-6). God intends that human reason be used to its fullest extent, but within the context and under the authority of His Word rather than independent of it.
5. The revelation of God in all nature, when properly understood, is in harmony with the written Word, and is to be interpreted in the light of Scripture.

Principles for Approaching the Interpretation of Scripture

1. The Spirit enables the believer to accept, understand, and apply the Bible to one's own life as he seeks divine power to render obedience to all scriptural requirements

and to appropriate personally all Bible promises. Only those following the light already received can hope to receive further illumination of the Spirit (John 16:13, 14; 1 Cor. 2:10-14).

2. Scripture cannot be correctly interpreted without the aid of the Holy Spirit, for it is the Spirit who enables the believer to understand and apply Scripture. Therefore, any study of the Word should commence with a request for the Spirits guidance and illumination.
3. Those who come to the study of the Word must do so with faith, in the humble spirit of a learner who seeks to hear what the Bible is saying. They must be willing to submit all presuppositions, opinions, and the conclusions of reason to the judgment and correction of the Word itself. With this attitude the Bible student may come directly to the Word, and with careful study may come to an understanding of the essentials of salvation apart from any human explanations, however helpful. The biblical message becomes meaningful to such a person.
4. The investigation of Scripture must be characterized by a sincere desire to discover and obey God's will and word rather than to seek support or evidence for preconceived ideas.

Methods of Bible Study

1. Select a Bible version for study that is faithful to the meaning contained in languages in which the Bible originally was written, giving preference to translations done by a broad group of scholars and published by a general publisher above translations sponsored by a particular denomination or narrowly focused group.

   Exercise care not to build major doctrinal points on one Bible translation or version. Trained biblical scholars will use the Greek and Hebrew texts, enabling them to examine variant readings of ancient Bible manuscripts as well.
2. Choose a definite plan of study, avoiding haphazard and aimless approaches. [***Editorial Comment:*** The six points mentioned in the original have been omitted. The study plan relevant for our purpose involves book-by-book analysis. The books of Daniel and Revelation contain important parallel ideas.]
3. Seek to grasp the simple, most obvious meaning of the biblical passage being studied. [***Editorial Comment:*** In seeking the plain and obvious sense, care needs to be exercised to identify where figures of speech, allegory, metaphors, similes and other devices are being used.]
4. Seek to discover the underlying major themes of Scripture as found in individual texts, passages, and books. Two basic, related themes run throughout Scripture: (1) The person and work of Jesus Christ; and (2) The Great Controversy perspective involving the authority of God's Word, the fall of man, the first and second advents of Christ, the exoneration of God and His law, and the restoration of the divine plan for the universe. These themes are to be drawn from the totality of Scripture and not imposed on it.
5. Recognize that the Bible is its own interpreter and that the meaning of words, texts, and passages is best determined by diligently comparing Scripture with Scripture. [***Editorial Comment:*** Basing ideas on a single proof-text is not a proper basis for proceeding. There is unity throughout the Scriptures so that a broadly based approach will deliver a sound understanding.]

6. Study the context of the passage under consideration by relating it to the sentences and paragraphs immediately preceding and following it. Try to relate the ideas of the passage to the line of thought of the entire Bible book.
7. As far as possible ascertain the historical circumstances in which the passage was written by the biblical writers under the guidance of the Holy Spirit.
8. Determine the literary type the author is using. Some biblical material is composed of parables, proverbs, allegories, psalms, and apocalyptic prophecies. Since many biblical writers presented much of their material as poetry, it is helpful to use a version of the Bible that presents this material in poetic style, for passages employing imagery are not to be interpreted in the same manner as prose.
9. Recognize that a given biblical text may not conform in every detail to present-day literary categories. Be cautious not to force these categories in interpreting the meaning of the biblical text. It is a human tendency to find what one is looking for, even when the author did not intend such.
10. Take note of grammar and sentence construction in order to discover the author's meaning. Study the key words of the passage by comparing their use in other parts of the Bible by means of a concordance and with the help of biblical lexicons and dictionaries. [***Editorial Comment:*** Sometimes a detailed knowledge of the ancient languages is required in order to gain a proper understanding of the text.]
11. In connection with the study of the biblical text, explore the historical and cultural factors. Archaeology, anthropology, and history may contribute to understanding the meaning of the text. [***Editorial Comment:*** Scholarly articles based on the historical-critical method of analysis may be of little value in understanding the text on account of the presuppositions brought to the task.]
12. Seventh-day Adventists believe that God inspired Ellen G. White. Therefore, her expositions on any given Bible passage offer an inspired guide to the meaning of texts without exhausting their meaning or pre-empting the task of exegesis (for example, see *Evangelism*, p. 256; *The Great Controversy*, pp. 193, 595; *Testimonies*, vol. 5, pp. 665, 682, 707-708; *Counsels to Writers and Editors*, pp. 33-35).
13. After studying as outlined above, turn to various commentaries and secondary helps such as scholarly works to see how others have dealt with the passage. Then carefully evaluate the different viewpoints expressed from the standpoint of Scripture as a whole.
14. In interpreting prophecy keep in mind that:
    a. The Bible claims God's power to predict the future (Isa. 46:10).
    b. Prophecy has a moral purpose. It was not written merely to satisfy curiosity about the future. Some of the purposes of prophecy are to strengthen faith (John 14:29) and to promote holy living and readiness for the Advent (Matt. 24:44; Rev. 22:7, 10, 11).
    c. The focus of much prophecy is on Christ (both His first and second advents), the church, and the end-time. [***Editorial Comment:*** "The Old Testament sheds light upon the New, and the New upon the Old. Each is a revelation of the glory of God in Christ. Christ as manifested to the patriarchs, as symbolized in the sacrificial service, as portrayed in the law, and as revealed by the prophets is the riches of the Old Testament. Christ in His life, His death, and His resurrection, Christ as He is manifested by the Holy Spirit, is the treasure of the New. Both

Old and New present truths that will continually reveal new depths of meaning to the earnest seeker." (Counsels to Parents, Teachers, and Students, pp. 462, 463).]

d. The norms for interpreting prophecy are found within the Bible itself: The Bible notes time prophecies and their historical fulfillments; the New Testament cites specific fulfillments of Old Testament prophecies about the Messiah; and the Old Testament itself presents individuals and events as types of the Messiah.

e. In the New Testament application of Old Testament prophecies, some literal names become spiritual: for example, Israel represents the church, Babylon apostate religion, etc.

f. There are two general types of prophetic writings: non-apocalyptic prophecy as found in Isaiah and Jeremiah, and apocalyptic prophecy as found in Daniel and the Revelation. These differing types have different characteristics:

i. Non-apocalyptic prophecy addresses God's people; apocalyptic is more universal in scope.

ii. Non-apocalyptic prophecy often is conditional in nature, setting forth to God's people the alternatives of blessing for obedience and curses for disobedience; apocalyptic emphasises the sovereignty of God and His control over history. [***Editorial Comment:*** The prophecy of Jonah that he delivered to Nineveh is understood finally to be a conditional prophecy (Jon. 3:10; 4:2), although the initial impression was that it was not (3:4). Other prophecies, such as Isaiah 34, may be understood as conditional on the basis on Jer. 18:7-10.]

iii. Non-apocalyptic prophecy often leaps from the local crisis to the end-time day of the Lord; apocalyptic prophecy presents the course of history from the time of the prophet to the end of the world.

iv. Time prophecies in non-apocalyptic prophecy generally are long, for example, 400 years of Israel's servitude (Gen. 15:13) and 70 years of Babylonian captivity (Jer. 25:12). Time prophecies in apocalyptic prophecy generally are phrased in short terms, for example, 10 days (Rev. 2:10) or 42 months (Rev. 13:5). Apocalyptic time periods stand symbolically for longer periods of actual time.

g. Apocalyptic prophecy is highly symbolic and should be interpreted accordingly. In interpreting symbols, the following methods may be used:

i. Look for interpretations (explicit or implicit) within the passage itself (for example, Dan. 8:20, 21; Rev. 1:20).

ii. Look for interpretations elsewhere in the book or in other writings by the same author.

iii. Using a concordance, study the use of symbols in other parts of Scripture.

iv. A study of ancient Near Eastern documents may throw light on the meaning of symbols, although scriptural use may alter those meanings.

h. The literary structure of a book often is an aid to interpreting it. The parallel nature of Daniel's prophecies is an example.

15. Parallel accounts in Scripture sometimes present differences in detail and emphasis (for example, cf. Matt. 21:33, 34; Mark 12:1-11; and Luke 20:9-18; or 2 Kings 18-20 with 2 Chron. 32). When studying such passages, first examine them carefully

to be sure that the parallels actually are referring to the same historical event. For example, many of Jesus' parables may have been given on different occasions to different audiences and with different wording.

In cases where there appear to be differences in parallel accounts, one should recognize that the total message of the Bible is the synthesis of all of its parts. Each book or writer communicates that which the Spirit has led him to write. Each makes his own special contribution to the richness, diversity, and variety of Scripture (*The Great Controversy*, pp. v, vi). The reader must allow each Bible writer to emerge and be heard while at the same time recognizing the basic unity of the divine self-disclosure.

When parallel passages seem to indicate discrepancy or contradiction, look for the underlying harmony. Keep in mind that dissimilarities may be due to minor errors of copyists (*Selected Messages,* book 1, p. 16), or may be the result of differing emphases and choice of materials of various authors who wrote under the inspiration and guidance of the Holy Spirit for different audiences under different circumstances (*Selected Messages*, book 1, pp. 21, 22; *The Great Controversy*, p. vi).

It may prove impossible to reconcile minor dissimilarities in detail which may be irrelevant to the main and clear message of the passage. In some cases judgment may have to be suspended until more information and better evidence are available to resolve a seeming discrepancy.

16. The Scriptures were written for the practical purpose of revealing the will of God to the human family. However, in order not to misconstrue certain kinds of statements, it is important to recognize that they were addressed to peoples of Eastern cultures and expressed in their thought patterns.

Expressions such as "the Lord hardened the heart of Pharaoh" (Exod. 9:12) or "an evil spirit from God" (1 Sam. 16:15), the imprecatory psalms, or the "three days and three nights" of Jonah as compared with Christ's death (Matt. 12:40), commonly are misunderstood because they are interpreted today from a different viewpoint.

A background knowledge of Near Eastern culture is indispensable for understanding such expressions. For example, Hebrew culture attributed responsibility to an individual for acts he did not commit but that he allowed to happen. Therefore the inspired writers of the Scriptures commonly credit God with doing actively that which in Western thought we would say He permits or does not prevent from happening, for example, the hardening of Pharaoh's heart.

Another aspect of Scripture that troubles the modern mind is the divine command to Israel to engage in war and execute entire nations. Israel originally was organized as a theocracy, a civil government through which God ruled directly (Gen. 18:25). Such a theocratic state was unique. It no longer exists and cannot be regarded as a direct model for Christian practice.

The Scriptures record that God accepted persons whose experiences and statements were not in harmony with the spiritual principles of the Bible as a whole. For example, we may cite incidents relating to the use of alcohol, polygamy, divorce, and slavery. Although condemnation of such deeply ingrained social customs is not explicit, God did not necessarily endorse or approve all that He permitted and bore within the lives of the patriarchs and in Israel. Jesus made this clear in His statement with regard to divorce (Matt. 19:4-6, 8).

The spirit of the Scriptures is one of restoration. God works patiently to elevate fallen humanity from the depths of sin to the divine ideal. Consequently, we must not accept as models the actions of sinful men as recorded in the Bible.

The Scriptures represent the unfolding of God's revelation to man. Jesus' Sermon on the Mount, for example, enlarges and expands certain Old Testament concepts. Christ Himself is the ultimate revelation of God's character to humanity (Heb. 1:1-3).

While there is an overarching unity in the Bible from Genesis to Revelation, and while all Scripture is equally inspired, God chose to reveal Himself to and through human individuals and to meet them where they were in terms of spiritual and intellectual endowments. God Himself does not change, but He progressively unfolded His revelation to men as they were able to grasp it (John 16:12; *The SDA Bible Commentary*, vol.7, p. 945; *Selected Messages*, book 1, p. 21). Every experience or statement of Scripture is a divinely inspired record, but not every statement or experience is necessarily normative for Christian behavior today. Both the spirit and the letter of Scripture must be understood (1 Cor. 10:6-13; *The Desire of Ages*, p. 150; *Testimonies*, vol. 4, pp. 10-12).

17. As the final goal, make application of the text. Ask such questions as, "What is the message and purpose God intends to convey through Scripture?" "What meaning does this text have for me?" "How does it apply to my situation and circumstances today?" In doing so, recognize that although many biblical passages had local significance, nonetheless they contain timeless principles applicable to every age and culture.

Conclusion

In the "Introduction" to *The Great Controversy* Ellen G. White wrote:

"The Bible, with its God-given truths expressed in the language of men, presents a union of the divine and the human. Such a union existed in the nature of Christ, who was the Son of God and the Son of man. Thus it is true of the Bible, as it was of Christ, that 'the Word was made flesh, and dwelt among us.'" John 1:14.

As it is impossible for those who do not accept Christ's divinity to understand the purpose of His incarnation, it is also impossible for those who see the Bible merely as a human book to understand its message, however careful and rigorous their methods.

Even Christian scholars who accept the divine-human nature of Scripture, but whose methodological approaches cause them to dwell largely on its human aspects, risk emptying the biblical message of its power by relegating it to the background while concentrating on the medium. They forget that medium and message are inseparable and that the medium without the message is as an empty shell that cannot address the vital spiritual needs of humankind.

A committed Christian will use only those methods that are able to do full justice to the dual, inseparable nature of Scripture, enhance his ability to understand and apply its message, and strengthen faith.

Editorial Comments

Several comments have been added to the article. These have been clearly identified. In addition, one omission has been identified through an Editorial Comment, as the information was not relevant to the documents being studied in this book.

Notes

The Scripture quotations in this article are from the King James Version.

This statement was approved and voted by the General Conference of Seventh-day Adventists Executive Committee at the Annual Council Session in Rio de Janeiro, Brazil, October 12, 1986.

Used with permission from the Biblical Research Institute. Online: http://www._adventist.org/beliefs/other_documents/other_doc4.html?&template=printer.html

Chapter 6

Ellen G. White and the Interpretation of Daniel and Revelation

Biblical Research Institute

The study of the prophecies of Daniel and Revelation is important to the spiritual dynamics of the Seventh-day Adventist Church. It has always been so. "Ministers should present the sure word of prophecy as the foundation of the faith of Seventh-day Adventists," declared Ellen White. "The prophecies of Daniel and the Revelation should be carefully studied, and in connection with them the words, 'Behold the Lamb of God, which taketh away the sin of the world.'"—*Gospel Workers*, p. 148.

Again she wrote: "When the books of Daniel and Revelation are better understood, believers will have an entirely different religious experience. They will be given such glimpses of the open gates of heaven that heart and mind will be impressed with the character that all must develop in order to realize the blessedness which is to be the reward of the pure in heart."—*Testimonies to Ministers*, p. 114.

Historicist Method of Interpretation

As every reader of the Bible knows, the books of Daniel and Revelation are written largely in symbols. Bible students, consequently, describe them as apocalyptic prophecy to distinguish from straightforward classical prophecy, such as we find in the major and minor prophets of the Old Testament. In these two apocalyptic books God reveals the sweep of the moral controversy which has convulsed our planet, focusing on the ultimate victory of His cause and the final doom of the forces of evil.

From the beginning Seventh-day Adventists have followed the *historical method of prophetic interpretation* to explain the symbols and their meaning. Sometimes this approach is called the historicist method or the continuous historical method.

The historicist method accepts the assumption that the prophecies of Daniel and Revelation are intended to unfold and to find fulfillment in historical time—in the span between the prophets Daniel and John respectively and the final establishment of God's eternal kingdom. The year-day principle (a symbolic day equals a literal year) is an integral part of this method inasmuch as it functions to unroll the symbolic time periods so that we are able to locate the predicted events along the highway of history.

Jesus used the historicist method for interpreting Daniel when He announced, "The time is fulfilled, and the kingdom of God is at hand" (Mark 1:15). In this affirmation of prophetic fulfillment He alluded to Daniel's 70-week prophecy (Daniel 9:24-27) which foretold the appearance of the Messiah. Near the close of His life Jesus again referred to the same prophecy. This time, however, He pointed to another aspect—to "the prince that [should] come [and should] destroy the city and the sanctuary." (vs. 26; see Matthew 24:15; Luke 21:20.) These events were to take place after His death and ascension. Their historical fulfillment occurred in the destruction of Jerusalem and the temple by the Romans in A.D. 70.

The Protestant reformers (from whose roots we spring) likewise employed the historicist method. On this basis they concluded that the Papacy was the focus of several of the prophecies in Daniel and Revelation. Following this method the early Seventh-day Adventist pioneers came to perceive our own times, the twofold ministry of Christ in the heavenly sanctuary, our identity as a people, and our task. Our understanding of Daniel and Revelation became the distinctive frame to hold in place and to highlight the biblical truths we teach as a church.

Preterist and Futurist Methods of Interpretation

Sixteenth century Protestant interpretations of Daniel and Revelation shook the Roman Catholic Church. In response the Catholic Counter-Reformation introduced the initial arguments for two different systems of prophetic interpretation: preterism and futurism. These moves served to deflect the accusing finger of prophecy away from the papal system.

Preterism (from the Latin, *praeter,* meaning "past") argued that these prophetic books met their fulfillment in the pre-Christian past or early centuries of the Christian era. Preterism eventually penetrated Protestant thought in the late eighteenth century and became the standard view of liberal Protestantism. Today, standard historical-critical scholarship places the composition of Daniel in the second century B.C. and sees its alleged prophecies as reflecting the person and times of Antiochus IV Epiphanes, the Seleucid king of Syria. The book of Revelation is restricted to a Roman setting in the first centuries of the Christian era.

Futurism entered Protestant ranks in the first quarter of the nineteenth century. The most prominent form of futurist interpretation today places the fulfillment of the bulk of Revelation (other than chapters 1-3) in a three and one-half year period of tribulation at the end of the age, commencing with a secret rapture of the church to heaven. The seventieth week of the 70-week prophecy of Daniel 9:24-27 is detached from its setting and relocated as the last seven years of the world. Many conservative Protestants have adopted futurism (with additions and variations) as their standard system for interpreting the prophecies of Daniel and Revelation.

Rome shrewdly knew that a change in the method of interpretation would lead inevitably to a change in conclusions. It is easy to see that both preterism and futurism direct the prophetic spotlight away from Rome and her activities. Preterism and present-day historical-critical studies place all fulfillments in the past. Futurism defers the fulfillment of the bulk of Revelation to a future point—at the end of the world after an alleged secret rapture. (Historical-critical scholars also regard Daniel 11:40-45 as a prophecy that failed to materialize.)

Today, Seventh-day Adventists stand virtually alone as proponents of the historicist method of interpreting Daniel and Revelation, the method of Christ, Paul, and the Reformers.

Counter-Reformation "Knocks" at the Adventist Door

In a very real sense the spirit of the Counter-Reformation is knocking today at the door of the Adventist Church and urgently pressing to enter!

Some Adventist Bible students propose that the church seriously consider the preterist and historical-critical positions that would regard these prophetic books either as fulfilled or as having failed in the past. Different approaches are then adopted to make such prophecies meaningful and relevant to the church today.

Preterist variations. For example, some suggest that a prophecy may have *multiple* fulfillments. This approach would argue that the little horn of Daniel 8 could find successive fulfillments (in different ages) in Antiochus IV, pagan Rome, papal Rome, and even (just before the end) in Satan when he impersonates Christ.

Another approach asserts that Daniel's prophecies are not a revelation of God's foreknowledge. Rather, they were intended to be a statement of His purpose and were conditional on Israel's obedience. When Israel failed to accept the Messiah and was rejected by God as His agent, the original intent of Daniel's prophecies failed. Consequently, Daniel has no meaning for today's church unless later inspired writers make a reapplication of a given prophecy. On this basis the *preadvent judgment* scene recorded in Daniel 7:9-10, 13-14 is forced to become the executive *judgment* scene of Revelation 20:11-15 because the latter passage is considered to be John's *reapplication* of Daniel 7!

A third spin-off of the preterist position leads some to take an idealist approach to Daniel and Revelation. This position argues that the books are to be viewed as illustrating (in symbolic form) the Great Controversy between good and evil—between God and Satan—from which only spiritual principles may be drawn. While such a struggle is evident, the idealist chooses to go no further; he is unwilling to make specific application of the symbols to historical realities.

Futurist variations. Other Adventist Bible students (ministers and laity alike) are taking a more futurist-oriented approach. They commonly claim loyalty to the historicist interpretations of Daniel and Revelation which we hold as a people. But there is a deep desire to make these prophecies relevant to current events. While some place certain prophecies after the close of probation for their *primary fulfillment* (such as the seven trumpets), it is more common to opt for a *dual fulfillment* in the end-time of certain selected prophecies in Daniel and Revelation. The only way in which to retain the church's historicist positions, they believe, and at the same time to make certain prophecies relevant, is to employ the *dual fulfillment device.*

But there is no consistency. Only certain chapters are reapplied. For example, some teach that the beasts of Daniel 7 and 8 are currently meeting another fulfillment in the activities of the United States, Russia, Iraq, and Iran. Some argue that the 1260 year time period is to have another fulfillment in the future on a day-for-a-day basis, while others have suggested a dual fulfillment for the 70-week prophecy.

These well-meaning persons who argue for a dual fulfillment of selected prophecies in Daniel and Revelation have one thing in common: *they all believe that Ellen White supports the dual fulfillment theory for the books of Daniel and Revelation.*

Seventh-day Adventists have always recognized from the biblical data itself that certain of the classical prophecies (in the major and minor prophets) give clear evidence in their contexts that a more complete fufillment may be expected after a partial application (for example, Joel's prophecy about the outpouring of the Holy Spirit [Joel 2:28-32] and Malachi's prophecy of an Elijah message [Malachi 4:5-6]).

However, we have never taken such a position on the prophecies of Daniel and Revelation. To give dual and multiple fulfillments to these grand revelations of divine foreknowledge is to give the face of prophecy a nose of wax to be turned this way and that. Dual and multiple fulfillments rob these great prophecies of real significance and evaporate their contribution to our spiritual certainty.

The series on the seven churches is unique (Revelation 1-3). When first written, these messages apparently had a direct application to the local situation (1:11), and they continue to carry lessons for the church in every age. But even in this special instance the Spirit seems to have intended only one true *prophetic* fulfillment. "The names of the seven churches are symbolic of the church in different periods of the Christian Era. The number 7 indicates completeness, and is symbolic of the fact that the messages extend to the end of time, while the symbols used reveal the condition of the church at different periods in the history of the world."—*The Acts of the Apostles,* p. 585.

But is the assertion true that hidden away in the writings of Ellen White we may find the seeds of a new method of interpreting Daniel and Revelation—the dual fulfillment method? Is it possible that Ellen White in fact taught and endorsed the historicist method of interpreting Daniel and Revelation and at the same time inserted statements here and there from which the church could later construct a new method of prophetic interpretation? Let us not forget the valid truth that Rome fully recognized when her Jesuit theologians proposed new methods for interpreting Daniel and Revelation: *A change in method inevitably leads to a change in conclusions.*

In terms of prophetic interpretation the Adventist Church stands at a crossroads. The spirit of the Counter Reformation knocks on the Adventist door. The decision to open the door and to go the way an earlier Protestantism went is one option. In today's ecumenical climate the temptation to go that way is alluring. But there is valid reason why we should remain loyal to the prophetic faith of our pioneer fathers.

Ellen G. White's Historicist Position

There is not the slightest evidence that Ellen White intended for the church to follow any other method of interpreting the prophecies of Daniel and Revelation than the historicist method. In the clearest manner her comments on the book of Revelation present the historicist understanding that the prophecies of Daniel and Revelation unroll in history from the times of Daniel and John until the establishment of the eternal kingdom of God. For instance:

"The book of Revelation opens to the world *what has been, what is, and what is to come;* it is for our instruction upon whom the ends of the world are come. It should be studied with reverential awe. We are privileged in knowing what is for our learning."—Ellen G White Comments, *The SDA Bible Commentary*, vol. 7, p. 954 (emphasis added).

"In the Revelation are portrayed the deep things of God . . . . Its truths are addressed to those living in the last days of this earth's history, as well as to those living in the days of John. *Some of the scenes depicted in this prophecy are in the past, some are now taking place; some bring to view the close of the great conflict between the powers of darkness and the Prince of heaven, and some reveal the triumphs and joys of the redeemed in the earth made new."*—*The Acts of the Apostles*, p. 584 (emphasis added).

In these comprehensive statements Ellen White demonstrates how apocalyptic prophecy was designed by God to find sequential fulfillment as history unfolded. (1) Some of these prophecies have now met their fulfillment in past ages; (2) some of the prophecies are finding fulfillment now; (3) some focus on the final conflict in the controversy and have not as yet met their fulfillment; finally, (4) some portions of the prophecies relate to the new earth estate and Ellen White asserts that the book of Revelation is as important to last-day Christians as it was to Christians in John's day. "Its truths are addressed to those living in the last days of this earth's history." This is not because she is proposing dual fulfillments of those portions of the prophecies already fulfilled. The implication of her statement is clear. The book remains relevant because the fulfillments of some of these prophecies "are now taking place," and others will shortly find fulfillment in "the close of the great conflict between the powers of darkness and the Prince of heaven." Furthermore, the present day Adventist may continue to learn spiritual lessons from past history and prophetic fulfillment. In this manner the prophecies of Daniel and Revelation continue to give encouragement, confidence, and motivation to last-day Christians even though large portions of these books have met complete fulfillment in past ages.

Ellen White does not discuss every portion of Daniel and Revelation in her writings. Her most comprehensive presentations are found in the well-known volume, *The Great Controversy.* For example, she presents a clear interpretation of the little horn (Daniel 7); the dragon (Revelation 12); the leopard beast (Revelation 13); and the related time periods (3 1/2 times=1260 days=42 months=1260 years of papal supremacy; 538-1798) as well as the two-horn beast (Revelation 13) and the final conflict over the Sabbath and God's Law symbolized by the enforcement of the "mark of the beast" by the "image of the beast." (*See The Great Controversy*, pp. 438-450). These views fully endorse the historicist method and the main conclusions and positions arrived at by our pioneers who employed this system. Her divinely guided writings confirm the prophetic foundation (derived from Daniel and Revelation) on which the Seventh-day Adventist Church rests today.

Do the Ellen G. White Writings Teach Another Method of Prophetic Interpretation?

The Adventists who are giving a dual fulfillment application to selected prophecies in Daniel and Revelation generally argue that they find Ellen White's endorsement of this method hidden in certain statements. These alleged keys to a new system of prophetic interpretation are scattered throughout her large corpus of writings and have been brought to light only in recent years. We turn next to examine citations commonly used without attempting to be exhaustive:

Exhibit 1

"The world is stirred with the spirit of war. The prophecies of the eleventh of Daniel have almost reached their final fulfillment."—*Review and Herald*, Nov. 24, 1904, p. 94.

Argument: Emphasis is put on the phrase, "final fulfillment." It is suggested that if a prophecy has a *final* fulfillment, it must have had previous fulfillments.

Answer: There is no hidden dual or multiple fulfillment principle here. Ellen White is simply noting that the *last portion* of this long prophecy is about to meet its fulfillment. *Daniel 11 is about to be completed.* That this is the true sense of the passage can be seen by comparing her restatement of the same point five years later in an article entitled, "The Last Crisis." It reads: "The world is stirred with the spirit of war. *The prophecy of the eleventh chapter of Daniel has nearly reached its complete fulfillment."—Testimonies*, vol. 9, p. 14 (published 1909 emphasis added).

Exhibit2

"We are standing on the threshold of great and solemn events. Many of the prophecies are about to be fulfilled in quick succession. Every element of power is about to be set to work. *Past history will be repeated;* old controversies will arouse to new life, and peril will beset God's people on every side. Intensity is taking hold of the human family. It is permeating everything upon the earth. *Study Revelation in connection with Daniel, for history will be repeated."—Testimonies to Ministers*, p. 116 (emphasis added).

"The prophecy in the eleventh [chapter] of Daniel has nearly reached its complete fulfillment. *Much of the history that has taken place in fulfillment of this prophecy will be repeated."*—Letter 103, 1904 (MR 1077 emphasis added).

Argument: A repetition of the historical events which fulfilled a given prophecy indicates that the prophecy itself will have a dual fulfillment.

Answer: Ellen White uses the expression, "history will be repeated," a number of times. But history and prophecy are two different matters. It does not follow that a repetition of a historical experience also means a repetition of the same prophecy. Such a conclusion distorts her meaning.

Ellen White is counselling us to study the prophetic fulfillments of the past—to study the principles involved—because similar issues will rise again, and God's people will have to meet them. "Old controversies will arouse to new life." We prepare ourselves for such issues by understanding the challenges involved in those past events. *History* will, indeed, be repeated, but not the same, specific prophecy that has already met its fulfillment in the past.

For example, Daniel 7:25 and Revelation 13:7 are two prophecies that deal with the persecution of God's people during the 1260 years of papal dominance in Europe. We know that persecution against God's people will be repeated in the closing era of human history because another prophecy says it will (Revelation 13:15-17). But this repetition of persecution (repeated history) does not involve the repetition of the prophecies of Daniel 7:25 and Revelation 13:7. Studying the lives of the faithful and the issues they met in their times—and how they met them—can strengthen us to meet persecution in our own times should we face it.

Exhibit 3

"The light that Daniel received from God *was given especially for these last days.* The visions he saw by the banks of the Ulai and the Hiddekel, the great rivers of Shinar, are *now* in process of fulfillment, and all the events foretold will soon come to pass."—*Testimonies to Ministers*, pp. 112-113 (emphasis added). This statement is linked to the angel Gabriel's explanation to Daniel after he had seen the vision recorded in chapter 8: "Understand, O son of man: for at *the time of the end*" (Daniel 8:17).

Argument: Ellen White died in the first part of this century. Like Gabriel she is evidently pointing us to a future event beyond her time.

Answer: In citing this paragraph by itself (lifting it out of the context of her writings and evident beliefs), we may make it appear that Ellen White is here supporting a dual fulfillment of Daniel 8. In the chapter Gabriel specifically mentions the kingdoms of Medo-Persia and Grecia as the fulfillments of the symbolic ram and goat respectively (Daniel 8:20-21). This is now past history. Yet Ellen White appears to say that the visions Daniel saw in chapter 8 "are now in process of fulfillment," and since Gabriel also said the fulfillment would take place in the "time of the end," it would seem that a current or dual fulfillment of Daniel 8 is to be expected. However, such a conclusion ignores the historical setting in which Ellen White wrote the above as well *as the particular aspect of the vision* to which she referred when she said it was "now in the process of fulfillment."

Ellen White, along with the Adventist Church in general, believed that the period of papal oppression, the 1260 years, extended from 538 B.C. to A.D. 1798. This prophetic period is mentioned in both Daniel and Revelation under three different time symbols: (1) three and one-half times—Daniel 7:25; 12:7; Revelation 12:14; (2) 1260 days—Revelation 11:3; 12:6; (3) 42 months—Revelation 11:2; 13:5. Accordingly, *Ellen White and the pioneers believed that the period of time which extended from 1798 to the close of human probation was to be designated as "the time of the end"—the period spoken of by the angel Gabriel.* The preadvent (investigative) judgment would take place in this period and would be announced on earth by the first angel's message (Daniel 7:9-10, 13-14; Revelation 14:6-7). Note Ellen White's clear statements on this point: "Daniel stood in his lot to bear his testimony *which was sealed until the time of the end, when the first angel's message should be proclaimed to our world.*"–*Testimonies to Ministers*, p. 115 (emphasis added).

"Since 1798 the book of Daniel has been unsealed, knowledge of the prophecies has increased, and many have proclaimed the solemn message of the judgment near."–*The Great Controversy*, p. 356.

"The message of Revelation 14, proclaiming that the hour of God's judgment is come, *is given in the time of the end.*"–*Selected Messages*, book 2, p. 107 (emphasis added).

"The prophetic visions of Daniel and John foretell a period of moral darkness and declension; *but at the time of the end, the time in which we are now living* the vision was to speak and not lie."–*Testimonies*, vol. 5, pp. 9-10 (emphasis added).

In the light of the above remarks it is evident that when Ellen White said that the visions Daniel saw (chapter 8) "are now in process of fulflillment" *she was referring to the great preadvent investigative judgment (Daniel 7-8) that was going on in heaven in her day, and which will continue until the close of human probation.* She was not disclosing a hidden principle to lead the church to discover a dual fulfillment for the ram, he-goat, four horns, and little horn. The *aspect* of the vision which Daniel saw by the banks of the Ulai that is still in the process of being fulfilled pertains to Christ's Most Holy Place ministry of judgment prior to His reception of the eternal kingdom and His second coming. On earth the messages of the three angels (Revelation 14:6-14) continue to announce to global populations the urgency of the times: "the hour of his [God's] judgment is come" (Revelation 14:7).

Exhibit 4

"The Sabbath question will be the issue in the great conflict in which all the world will act a part. [Revelation 13:4-8, 10 quoted.] *This entire chapter is a revelation of what will surely take place* [Revelation 13:11, 15-17 quoted]."–Ellen G White Comments, *The SDA Bible Commentary*, vol. 7, p. 979 (emphasis added).

Argument: This passage is cited as "the clincher" to prove that Ellen White endorsed a dual fulfillment of the prophecies, and, in this instance, a replay of the 1260 year prophecy. The reader is asked to observe that Ellen White quotes Revelation 13:4-8, in this passage. The text portrays the papal power under the symbol of a leopard beast with seven heads and ten crowned horns. The passage also includes the time element of its supremacy before its wounding: 42 prophetic months or 1260 prophetic days. The reader's attention is then directed to the statement following the Scripture passage: "This *entire chapter* is a revelation of what will surely take place" (emphasis added).

From this two-point sequence the following position is reasoned: The 1260 year career of the papacy is past. But *now* Ellen White tells us that this "entire chapter"—including the 42 month time element—will [future tense] surely take place. Here is a clear-cut proof for employing a dual fulfillment principle to interpret Daniel and Revelation in a manner to render them relevant to our times.

Answer: This Ellen White statement needs only to be read in its setting to see that it provides no basis for a dual fulfillment of Revelation 13:1-10 or its time period. If the commentary volume is available, the reader is invited to follow along as we sketch the contents of this two-paragraph selection printed as a comment on Revelation 14.

The context of the alleged "clincher" begins in a preceding paragraph in which Ellen White first quotes Revelation 14:9-10, the third angel's warning against the mark of the beast and its image. She then makes her point: "It is for the interest of all to understand what the mark of the beast is, and how they may escape the dread threatenings of God. *Why are men not interested to know what constitutes the mark of the beast and his image?* (emphasis added). it is in direct contrast with the mark of God" She then cites Exodus 31:12-17 which states that the Sabbath is God's "sign" or mark, thus implying that the "mark of the beast" is something that is just the opposite of the Sabbath. She continues:

"The *Sabbath question* will be the issue in the great conflict in which all the world will act a part" (emphasis added). At this point she cites Revelation 13:4-8, 10. This passage provides the information by which one can identify the beast: its origin/power derived from the dragon; its special rule for 42 prophetic months; its persecution of the saints in that time; its blasphemy against Heaven; its captivity; and the fact that the world will worship and follow its lead again. On the basis of this data one can determine that the beast is the papal power. This puts the reader in a position to identify the mark and image of the beast as she urged him to do in the first paragraph of her statement.

After citing Revelation 13:4-8, 10 (providing the information for identifying the beast), Ellen White says, "This entire chapter is a revelation of what will surely take place." She then immediately quotes (*by way of explanation*) Revelation 13:11, 15-17. These verses foretell the rise of the two-horn beast (vs. 11) and the institution of the image of the beast and the enforcement of the mark of the beast under penalty of boycott and death.

Thus, it is quite clear that when Ellen White says, "This entire chapter is a revelation of what will surely take place," she is not saying that Revelation 13:4-8, 10 is going to have a dual fulfillment. To force such a meaning is to wrest the statement from its context.

Her *topic is not a dual fulfillment of Revelation 13:1-10, or of its time period. Rather, her subject is "the mark of the beast" and its end-time enforcement.* That is the thrust of both paragraphs of this selection. The only purpose for citing Revelation 13:4-8, 10 is so the reader may identify the beast. If he can identify the beast, he is in position to identify its mark which, she says, is just the opposite of God's sign. Thus with the beast and its mark in place, she points to the prophetic forecast dealing with the image of the beast and the enforcing of the mark and the crisis that will surround that issue in the future.

Exhibit 5

[The exhibit contains] statements pertaining to Christ's discourse in Matthew 24. The following items are usually noted: "When He referred to the destruction of Jerusalem, His prophetic words reached beyond that event to the final conflagration."–*The Desire of Ages*, p. 628. "But this prophecy was spoken also for the last days."–*The Desire of Ages*, p. 631. "This prophecy will again be fulfilled"–*The Desire of Ages*, 633. "The prophecies that received a partial fulfillment in the overthrow of Jerusalem have a more direct application to the last days."–*Thoughts from the Mount of Blessing*, pp. 120-121.

Argument: It is inferred from these statements that Christ's prophecy regarding the destruction of Jerusalem will find a second fulfillment in the destruction of the world. Thus, it is claimed that, according to this exhibit, Ellen White really taught dual fulfillments of apocalyptic prophecy.

Answer: Here is the setting for the several citations from *The Desire of Ages and Thoughts from the Mount of Blessing* regarding our Lord's Olivet discourse (Matthew 24): "Jesus did not answer His disciples by taking up separately the destruction of Jerusalem and the great day of His coming. *He mingled the description of these two events.* Had He opened to His disciples future events as He beheld them, they would have been unable to endure the sight. In mercy to them *He blended the description of the two great crises, leaving the disciples to study out the meaning for themselves.* When He referred to the destruction of Jerusalem, His prophetic words reached beyond the event to the final conflagration in that day when the Lord shall rise out of His place to punish the world for their iniquity, when the earth shall disclose her blood, and shall no more cover her slain. This entire discourse was given, not for the disciples only, but for those who should live in the last scenes of this earth's history."–*The Desire of Ages*, p. 628 (emphasis added); see also p. 631.

It should be noted at the outset that Ellen White clearly understood that our Lord's discourse *dealt with two distinct events.* One event had to do with the destruction of Jerusalem, and one had to do with the Second Coming and the end of the world. He blended His description of the two because the two judgments had similarities. Because these two events are blended in the one discourse, the prophecy has value for us in the end-time of the world as well as for the disciples then. There is no principle of repeated fulfillments being enunciated here. Each event which our Lord discusses has its own one-time fulfillment in its own time slot—the fall of Jerusalem, and later at the end of the age, the fall [of the nations].

Thus we may say that both the contents of our Lord's course and the comments of Ellen White in *The Desire Ages and Thoughts from the Mount of Blessing* indicate plainly that Matthew 24 is *not* a single prophecy with a dual fulfillment. *Rather, it is a twofold prophecy dealing with two distinct events (one event viewed as a symbol of the other, due to certain similarities), each event to be fulfilled at its respective time.* Consequently, neither Matthew 24 nor the Ellen White comments on it provide a sound basis from which to derive a principle of dual fullfilment for the prophecies of Daniel and Revelation.

Exhibit 6

"The great work of the gospel is not to close with less manifestation of the power of God than marked its opening. The prophecies which were fulfilled in the outpouring of the former rain at the opening of the gospel are again to be fulfilled in the latter rain at its close."–*The Great Controversy*, pp. 611-612.

Argument: The prophecy of the early rain (Pentecost) to have a dual fulfillment in the outpouring of the latter rain.

Answer: Ellen White comments on the outpouring of the Holy Spirit are similar to her comments on Matthew 24. Immediately preceding the paragraph cited above, Ellen White quotes Hosea 6:3 and Joel 2:23. Both passages predict *two events:* a former and a latter rain, just as the natural rainy seasons occur in Israel from which the biblical imagery is taken. Thus, these prophecies which she cites met a fulfillment at Pentecost (early rain) and will naturally meet another fulfillment (latter rain) as the work of the gospel comes to its finale.

Summary: These six exhibits give a fair sampling of the kind of statements some Adventist Bible students are using in an endeavor to find Ellen White support for a dual fulfillment principle. Honesty and a sense of fairness should prevent us from wresting the writings of one who stands as a strong exponent of the historicist method to teach a contrary theory of dual or multiple fulfillments. As we have seen, when the alleged statements are fairly examined, we find there is no dual or multiple fulfillment principle present to be used as a tool to explain the apocalyptic prophecies of Daniel and Revelation.

Ellen White and Dual Fulfillment Proponents

In our day as in Christ's day, there may be a misreading and misinterpreting of the Scriptures. [Notice]: "There are those who are searching the Scriptures for proof that these messages are still in the future. They gather together the truthfulness of the messages, *but they fail to give them their proper place in prophetic history.* Therefore such are in danger of misleading the people in regard to locating the messages. They do not see and understand the time of the end, or when to locate the messages."–*Evangelism*, pp. 612-613 (emphasis added).

"I have not been able to sleep since half past one o'clock. I was bearing to Brother T a message which the Lord has given me for him. *The peculiar views he holds are a mixture of truth and error . . . . The great waymarks of truth, showing us our bearings in prophetic history, are to be carefully guarded, lest they be torn down, and replaced with theories that would bring confusion rather than genuine light . . . .*

There have been one and another who in studying their Bibles thought they discovered great light, and new theories, but these have not been correct. The Scripture is all true, but by misapplying the Scripture men arrive at wrong conclusions . . . . Some will take the truth applicable to their time, and place it in the future. *Events in the train of prophecy that had their fulfillment away in the past are made future,* and thus by these theories the faith of some is undermined.

From the light that the Lord has been pleased to give me, *you are in danger of doing the same work presenting before others truths which have had their place and done their specific work for the time, in the history of the faith of the people of God. You recognize these facts in Bible history as true, but apply them to the future.* They have their force still in their proper place, in the chain of events that have made us as a people what we are today, and as such, they are to be presented to those who are in the darkness of error.

The leadings of the Lord were marked [to our pioneers], and most wonderful were His revelations of what is truth. Point after point was established by the Lord God of heaven. That which was truth *then* [author's emphasis], is truth today. But the voices do not cease to be heard—'This is truth. I have new light.' But these new lights in prophetic lines are manifest in misapplying the Word and setting the people of God adrift without an anchor to hold them."–*Selected Messages*, book 2, pp. 101-104 (emphasis supplied).

Conclusions

In this survey on Ellen White and the interpretation of the prophecies of Daniel and Revelation three points and out:

1. Ellen White clearly endorses the historicist method for interpreting the prophecies of these two important books.

2. The Ellen White writings contain no dual fulfillment principle hidden in random paragraphs to support the current practice of reapplying certain prophecies in Daniel and Revelation to the present scene.

3. Ellen White disavows attempts to give such prophecies a dual fulfillment. "Events in the train of prophecy that had their fulfillment away in the past are made future, and thus by these theories the faith of some is undermined."–*Selected Messages*, book 2, p. 102.

Seventh-day Adventists recognize that we are living in "the time of the end," the closing era of human probation. In harmony with the historicist method, we, along with Ellen White, have traced the unrolling of the prophetic scrolls of Daniel and Revelation. The prophecies which have been fulfilled in the past give us a firm confidence that God will fulfill the few remaining portions. These focus primarily on the final conflict between Heaven and the powers of darkness over the seal of God and the mark of the beast. What mistaken zeal would constrain us now to alter our method of prophetic interpretation? What is the nature of the impulse which prompts some among us to speculate how certain prophecies must be replayed again with fulfillments that are considered more important than the "first" fulfillment to which such persons continue paying lip service? We believe such speculation, if followed, will ultimately leave "the people of God adrift without an anchor to hold them."–*Selected Messages*, book 2, p. 104.

In the light of this survey we may be sure that if Ellen White were alive today, she would deplore the strained interpretations being urged upon the church as a result of employing the dual fulfillment concept. Furthermore, we may be sure she would request that her writings not be used to support such an error. And we may be sure that she would add: If you want to know what the Lord has revealed to me regarding Bible prophecy, don't try to deduct a hidden principle from a paragraph here and a line there. Rather, read my volume, *The Great Controversy*, where the major lines of Daniel and Revelation are treated. Here is the prophetic truth for our times.

Note

The Scripture quotations in this article are from the King James Version.

Used with permission from the Biblical Research Institute, which prepared the document, May 1988. Online: http://www.adventistbiblicalresearch.org/documents/WhiteInterDanielandRev.htm

Chapter 7

Great Controversy Theme and Prophecy

Warren A. Shipton

An appreciation of prophecy must always be incomplete without an understanding of the fundamental place of the struggle between good and evil. The cosmic battle between good and evil and the triumph of the star of the drama, Christ, saturates the pages of the Bible. The text, "Surely the Lord GOD does nothing, unless He reveals His secret to His servants the prophets (Amos 3:7), emphasises the central place of Christ in communicating with His servants and encouraging them concerning the righteousness of His principles (cf. John 5:39).

Conflict in Perspective

The conflict with God began in heaven when the created being Lucifer, the principal angel in heaven, became dissatisfied with the position and duties allocated to him (Isa. 14:12; Ezek. 28:14; Rev. 12:7-9). He wished to be like God (Isa. 14:12-14) and particularly to be included in the counsels of heaven. Pride dominated his thinking and he began a campaign for promotion above Christ. This movement began in secrecy and ended in the public domain with the deception of a great host of his fellow angels (Rev. 12:4). The progress from innocence to evil outcomes was gradual, long and without excuse. The remonstrance of the angels who were not convinced of Lucifer's claims failed to impact on those sympathising with him and finally God determined to expel from heaven those unhappy with the principles of His kingdom. They were cast down to the earth (Rev. 12:7-9). At this point Lucifer became known as Satan, the devil (Rev. 12: 9).

God's creative activities did not cease on account of controversy with Satan over the insistence that he should be involved in planning this world. Neither did God cease His creative activities even though He knew that the emergence of evil would involve an incredible sacrifice in pursuit of the claim that the principle of love (*agape*) was able to ensure the perpetuity of His kingdom throughout eternity. The creation of the human race was a judgment on Satan and, in fact, proclaimed that good would triumph over evil. However, before this outcome could be secured, a trail of suffering and misery punctuated with faith and hope would burst upon the human race. The first step down this trail commenced soon after the creation of mankind, when the progenitors of the race (Adam and Eve) fell. Eve was deceived and believed the devil's lies. In doing so she doubted God's integrity and chose to disobey His direct instructions. Adam, on the other hand, was unable to see a future without his companion and began to doubt God's abilities too (Gen. 3:1-7). Satan, by this act of deception in the Garden of Eden, became known as the "prince of this world" (cf. John 14:30, KJV)

In the process of time, Satan succeeded in bringing such wickedness on the world that God destroyed all but a remnant in the great flood (Gen. 7:17-23). Despite this judgment, many of the descendants of the survivors did not remain faithful. This was illustrated by the rebellion at the tower of Babel that was an act of disbelief, defiance and an expression of resentment concerning the flood (Gen. 9:1, 11; 11:1-4). The rebellion continued through the long ages to follow and climaxed in the crucifixion of Christ who was sent to save the race (Matt. 21:33-44).

Now the Bible presents Satan's rebellion as focussing on this earth as the one blighted spot in the universe. It also presents this world as the testing place where God's servants demonstrate their loyalty to Him (Job 1:6 to 2:1-7). All heaven is interested in the outcome (1 Cor. 4:9).

Issues in the Controversy

The basis of God's kingdom is love (*agape*). This principle is given a central place in the Decalogue (Matt. 22:36-39). Now love speaks of a relationship and when this relationship is broken, then men and women feel free to disobey God's will as expressed in His law (John 14:15). The lawless state found in this world is on account of transgressing this code (1 John 3:4).

God's throne is based on mercy and justice (Pss. 85:10; 89:14), which are simply expressions of the *agape* principle. Satan alleged from the beginning that there was a fault in God's character, and this was evident in His law, a claim that he still pursues strongly. He not only claimed that a fault existed in God's law, but that it was not possible for the human race to keep it. These claims were and are made in an attempt to both discredit and overthrow God's government. Christ, in response while on earth, held firm to the word of God; He trusted the righteousness of His Father's character and undertook to obey His will (Matt. 4:4). Furthermore, He depended on the exercise of faith to deliver a singular victor at Calvary. There He stated in triumph: "'Now the prince of this world [Satan] will be driven out'" (John 16:11, NIV).

Even though victory was gained at the cross, the controversy continues. The Bible, the Decalogue and Christ's provisions of salvation are all under attack. This controversy impacts on each individual, for all must answer the question: "'But who do you say that I am?' And Simon Peter answered and said, 'You are the Christ, the Son of the living God.' Jesus answered and said to him, 'Blessed are you, Simon Bar-Jonah, for flesh and blood has not revealed this to you, but My Father who is in heaven'" (Matt. 16:15-17).

Strategies Pursued

Questions about philosophical issues dealing with human existence, purpose and appropriate ways of acting are answered generally in today's world without reference to the principles outlined by God in the Bible. Satan has steadfastly attacked the credibility of God's word and has promoted the superiority of human reason. Doubts about the Scriptures originate with pride of intellect, which is the same commencing point for the rebellion in heaven that started with Satan (Isa. 14:12-14). Such thinking has led to a steady decline in appreciation of the character of God, an increase in human arrogance and to a host of shameful outcomes that flow from a rejection of ethical principles.

Truth has been sought in opposition to God by appeals to human wisdom (Prov. 14:12; 16:25), nature or the universe (e.g., Acts 17:18–Stoics and pantheism; religious authorities and critical scholars—Dan. 7:25; Mark 7:9, 13; 2 Pet. 3:16; and the occult—Isa. 8:19). While limited truth may be associated with some of these sources, truth cannot be assessed apart from God's word (John 14:6).

The magnitude of Satan's influence is well expressed by the apostle Paul: "We do not wrestle against flesh and blood, but against principalities, against powers, against the rulers of the darkness of this age, against spiritual hosts of wickedness in the heavenly places" (Eph. 6:12). The agencies he uses are revealed more explicitly in prophecy. God has promised to stand by those faithful to His cause and to give them a sure reward (Rev. 14:1-4).

The history of the struggle between good and evil from Eden until Judah was taken into captivity is related in the Old Testament. The history of the church and the major influences that impacted on it until well after the Jewish nation was rejected by God are related more explicitly in Daniel's prophecies. In the long ages to follow the ascension of Christ, John the Revelator fills in some vital details, which serve to warn and encourage the church to be faithful. The advice is for all believers to be watchful and to lean continually on Christ for help (Eph. 6:13-18). The assurance is that if we exercise faith in Christ we can be "more than conquerors" (Rom. 8:37).

The Cross Highlighted

Satan was cast down at the cross when mercy and justice kissed (Ps. 85:10; cf. 89:14). On the basis of that victory following the resurrection, Christ is carrying out the last phases of the atonement in heaven and will soon return to execute judgment. At the end of the millennium, Satan finally will be consigned to oblivion (Rev. 20:10), for it will be evident to all that the principles of his kingdom are utterly destitute of credibility. He is the author of sin and suffering. The principles of his government have been shown to be flawed and to be antagonistic to the development of peaceful and harmonious relationships. He and his followers will be forever destroyed. Sin and suffering will not arise the second time (Nah. 1:9).

The Remnant

The Great Controversy theme has embedded in it the concept of the remnant. This concept carries with it a note of certainty that God will be victorious and that a people will be saved who value His friendship and the principles of His kingdom. Throughout the history of the controversy, God has always had a remnant group to preserve His name and righteous principles. For example, Abraham was called to stand apart and enter into covenant relationship with God (Gen. 17:1, 2). He worshipped the living creator God rather than idols. His faith was proverbial (Heb. 11:8-10; 17-19); he kept God's ways faithfully (Gen. 18:19). Again, the church of the Thyatira period (A.D. 538 to Reformation) was condemned on account of its apostasy, but even here there was a faithful remnant (Rev. 2:24, 25). Those in God's remnant are sanctified through the truth (John 17:17). It is only through the life, death, resurrection and ministry of Christ that the remnant is assured an eternal future. Christ defeated the "cosmic forces of evil" at the cross and will come soon as our victorious king.

Satan has been active throughout history to frustrate God's plans and destroy those who have put faith in Him. Revelation 12 pictures a time in history when religious forces cooperated with civil powers of earth to impose religious views on the people. This led to great difficulty and suffering. However, a remnant stood firm. Again, just before the close of earth's history, God will have a visible remnant on earth that will uphold the truths of God's word. Seventh-day Adventists believe that their church champions the characteristics portrayed in Revelation (14:6-12), which outlines the features of the end-time remnant. These include holding fast to the Commandments of God through faith, honouring the Creator on the Sabbath, valuing the gifts of the Spirit (including the prophetic gift), giving centrality to the life and teachings of Jesus, and rejecting man-made worship systems. These individuals are counted among the remnant as they wait patiently for Jesus return.

The remnant is characterized by having a clear view of their world-encompassing mission. This includes giving widespread voice to the everlasting gospel in the context of God's judgment of this world, holding fast to the belief in a creator God who fashioned this world in seven days and left a memorial day (the Sabbath) for mankind to worship Him on. This group also holds fast to the ethical and moral principles of Scripture amidst widespread apostasy in the world. They not only identify the elements of mankind's departure from God's ideals, but give a certain and clear call to come back to the truths of His word and be saved. Many will respond to these appeals and come out of spiritual Babylon to be part of the final remnant people.

Every individual in God's remnant will have a vibrant, personal relationship with Christ. They all will have experienced the following: "and this is eternal life, that they may know You, the only true God, and Jesus Christ, whom You have sent" (John 17:3). It is clearly understood by Adventists (as expressed in *Seventh-day Adventists Believe* 1988, 152) that "The universal church is composed of all who truly believe in Christ." This means in the context of our discourse that God has many earnest, faithful and sincere followers in other Christian groups. These He is calling out of confusion to take a stand with His faithful people today in preparation for the soon coming of Christ.

Resources Used

Goldstein, C. 1994. *The Remnant.* Boise: Idaho: Pacific Press Publishing Association; Ministerial Association. 1988. *Seventh-day Adventists Believe: A Biblical Exposition of 27 Fundamental Doctrines.* Chapter 8–The Great Controversy, pp. 98-105 and chapter 12–The Remnant and Its Mission, pp. 152-169. Hagerstown, Maryland: Review and Herald Publishing Association; Mueller, E. 2000. The end time remnant in Revelation. *Journal of the Adventist Theological Society*, vol. 11(1/2), 188-204; Rodriquez, A. 2010. The remnant. *Record*, vol. 115(6), 14-16; White, E. G. 1947. *The Story of Redemption.* Washington, D. C.: Review and Herald Publishing Association; White, E. G. 1950. *The Great Controversy between Christ and Satan.* Mountain View, California: Pacific Press Publishing Association.

Chapter 8

Introduction to Daniel

Warren A. Shipton

In order to facilitate the discussion of prophecy, it may be classified according to content (ethical messages—Elijah, Jeremiah; or predictions with an ethical component—Isaiah, Jeremiah, Daniel); form (literal, figurative or symbolic, enacted or prophetic parables); range (immediate or short range versus long range—Ezek. 4:5 versus Dan. 2:44; predictions of single events or double applications—Isa. 45:1 versus Gen. 17:7, 16/Gal. 3:16); fulfillment of predictions of divine purpose (Christ's sacrifice—Isa. 40:3-5; Dan. 9); predictions of divine foreknowledge (betrayal and crucifixion of Christ—Ps. 22:12-18, cf. Dan. 9:26); or predictions of divine reward or punishment (Jer. 17; Dan. 7:10, 14, 26, 27; 8:25; 9:27). The writings of Daniel, on detailed analysis, will be seen to contain poetry, narratives, prayers as well as predictions of divine purpose and end time predictions.

Conditional and Unconditional Prophecy

The prophecies of Daniel commence with a brief account of the Jewish captivity (Dan. 1:1-4). Now, the prophecy of the captivity was conditional. The kingdom of Judah was taken into captivity on account of disobedience (2 Chron. 36:14-17), but this might have been avoided if they had noted Jeremiah's warning messages (Jer. 17:21-27). Even yet, their national disgrace might yet be avoided, the prophets stated, if they learnt from the experience and entered into a new covenant relationship with God (Jer. 31:31-34; 32:36-41; Ezek. 37:19-28). This new relationship simply stated meant that God invited the captives and their descendants to accept the provisions of His salvation through faith (gospel).

The promises of restoration were partially fulfilled in that the captives returned from Babylon (Ezra 1:3; 6:14, 15; 7:11-26) and the Messiah came during the time of the Roman Empire and sacrificed His life (or was 'cut-off' as Daniel expressed it—Dan. 9:25, 26). "It was God's design that the whole earth be prepared for the first advent of Christ, even as today the way is preparing for His second coming" (White 1943, 703, 704). But Israel failed to accept her King and was rejected (Matt. 23:28-38) and finally was destroyed (Dan. 9:27; Matt. 24:15-20). The actual descendants of Abraham were replaced by the spiritual children of Abraham (Rom. 9:6, 8, 25; Gal. 3:29), so that generations of God's chosen people would continue and would enable God's purposes to be fulfilled. God always has preserved a remnant to fulfil His purposes.

The major prophecies of Daniel are located sequentially in time and are confirmed several times (Dan. 2, 7, 8, 12) or the ethical message is repeated (Dan. 3, 6, etc.). The book is concerned primarily with significant approaching events and the end of time and these are not conditional in nature. The end of the Great Controversy between Christ and Satan is the theme of all Scripture and moves to an inexorable climax. This means we find that God's triumph is emphasized throughout the book (Dan. 2:44; 7:14, 27; 8:25; 11:45; 12:1, 2, 13).

Confirmation of Meaning

Jesus' name "Son of Man" is based on Daniel 7, verse 13. He clarified some of the aspects of Daniel's prophecies when He spoke of the destruction of Jerusalem and the end of the world (Matt. 24:15-31). By this means He gave insights into the fulfillment of prophecy from the Roman era onwards to the end of time. The apostles also applied the prophecies of the kingdom to the church of the Christian era. This means that we do not wait for ultimate fulfillment of the Old Testament prophecies in the Jewish nation but rather in those who honour God's gift of love.

Approach to Interpretation

Seventh-day Adventists hold to the historicist approach to interpretation of prophecy. The prophets or seers utterances are viewed in the stream of historical events from the time they were given down to the close of human history. In taking this approach, the ideas of all prophecy being related to past events (preterist approach) or future events (futurist approach) are rejected. Adventists also hold to a premillennial view. This position holds that the second coming of Christ is heralded by the resurrection of the saints amidst cataclysmic events. Then a period of 1000 years (millennium) follows that ends with the second resurrection (the unjust) and the establishment of Christ's kingdom on earth. By contrast the postmillennial position holds that the second coming of Christ comes after the millennium.

In seeking to understand the text, the reader must give due consideration to the culture and language of the prophet's time. Appropriate respect needs also to be given to both the implicit and explicit meanings of the text and to gain understandings relevant to our time. The idea that prophecies have many applications (apotelesmatic approach) is not part of the scheme adopted. Where multiple applications are intended by the text, this should be clearly evident from either the author's own witness or from that of other biblical authors.

Structure of the Book

The book of Daniel is believed to have been written in the sixth century B.C. Chapter 1 serves as an introduction to the book. The book is organised into the historical section (chapters 2-6) and the prophetic section (chapters 7-12) and emphasises, as Doukhan (1987, p. 6) puts it, "judgment, waiting and war."

The structure of the book may be represented pictorially using a number of approaches. One example featuring concentric parallels is given by Doukhan (1987, 6) and is illustrated in Figure 1.

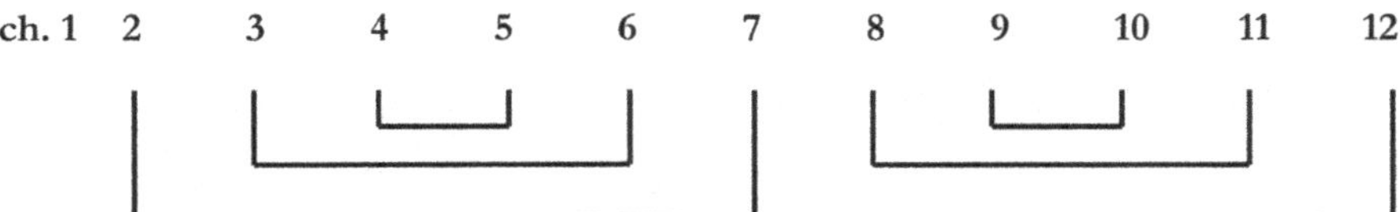

Figure 1. Schematic diagram of thought relationships found among the chapters in the book of Daniel.

For example, parallels are found in chapters 3 and 6 that deal with the rescue of God's faithful servants. An emphasis in chapters 4 and 5 is that God is in control; He is the universal sovereign (Dan. 4:25, 35; 5:23). Chapter 7 with its emphasis on judgment by the Son of Man joins the historical and prophetic sections of the book. Chapters 2, 7 and 12 are connected in respect to judgment and the coming of the Son of Man (Michael) and this theme is seen also in chapters 9 and 10. Historical interpretations in chapters 2 and 7 (also 8 and sections of 11) follow similar patterns. Chapters 9 and 10 also give insights into the person and ministry of Christ.

On account of the pattern of connections throughout the book, it has a unique unity that testifies to a single author. This claim is made throughout the book (chapters 1:1, 2, 21; 2:1, 14; 7:1, 2; 8:1; 9:1, 2; 10:1, 12:4, 5). The book shows increasing complexity as the reader progresses from chapter 2 to chapters 7, 8, 9 and 10-12. The over-riding emphasis is on God being in control of world events, which move inexorably to the second coming of Christ that marks the end of time (i.e., Dan. 2:41-45; 7:24-28; 8:23-26; 11:5-45; 12:1-13). The book is full of hope and assurance.

Daniel chapter 1 begins with the exile of 605 B.C. and ends with reference to Cyrus and was probably written around 536/535 B.C. All the revelations of the book represent the word of God—"for prophecy never came by the will of man, but holy men of God spoke as they were moved by the Holy Spirit" (2 Pet. 1:21).

Resources Used

Doukhan, J. B. 1987. *Daniel: The Vision of the End.* Berrien Springs: Andrews University Press; Holbrook, F. B. Ed. 1986. *Symposium on Daniel.* Washington, D.C.: Biblical Research Institute; Paulien, J. 2006. The end of historicism? Reflections on the Adventist approach to biblical apocalyptic—part two. *Journal of the Adventist Theological Society* 17(1), 180-208; Knight, G. R. Ed. 2003. *Questions on Doctrine,* annotated edition. Question 22: Basic principles of prophetic interpretation, pp. 173-197; Question 38: Varied concepts of the millennium, pp. 365-380. Berrien Springs, Michigan: Andrews University Press; White, E. G. 1943. *The Story of Prophets and Kings.* Mountain View, California: Pacific Press Publishing Association.

Chapter 9

Studies in Daniel

Warren A. Shipton & Ebenezer A. Belete

9.1 Exiled to Babylon

Introduction

The Babylonian Empire introduced in the book of Daniel can be traced to Nimrod's time when he built the Tower of Babel (Genesis 11). This city state experienced varying fortunes throughout the centuries and reached prominence in Hammurabi's time (around 1800 B.C.) but eventually found itself part of the Assyrian Empire. This empire also experienced changing fortunes and around 626 to 612 B.C., the king of Babylon known as Nabopolassar established a new Babylonian Empire (Neo-Babylonian Empire). It was under the reign of his son Nebuchadnezzar II that the empire reached great prominence. The Neo-Babylonian Empire was one of the players in Middle East politics along with Egypt, Lydia and Media, but in Nebuchadnezzar's lifetime his empire dominated.

It was during one of the disputes between Babylon and Egypt that Daniel and his friends were taken captive. The kingdom of Judah sought to gain protection from Babylon by allying itself with Egypt (2 Chron. 36:1-4). However, this scheme came unstuck in 605 B.C. when the king of Babylon gained control of Jerusalem and made Jehoiakim the king sign a treaty with him instead of Egypt. At this time the Babylonians took captives and spoil from the magnificent temple in Jerusalem that had been built by Solomon.

Judah was not very faithful to the treaty signed with Babylon and continued to flirt with Egypt. This resulted in two more visits by the Babylonian armies—in 597 B.C. and 586 B.C. The last visit was disastrous for the city as Nebuchadnezzar raised it and destroyed the temple and took most of the remaining people captive (2 Kings 24:10-15).

Throughout all this misery of captivity, the Jewish people remembered the words of Jeremiah the prophet (Jer. 29:10) that after 70 years the captives would be able to return to their homeland. This time would be fulfilled in 538/537 B.C. that was the first year of King Cyrus (Dan. 1:21). When the ability to return to Jerusalem was given to the captives, Daniel was already too old to take advantage for he is thought to have been taken captive in his late teens and would then have been in his late eighties.

The Study

Read chapter 1 then the notes and Bible texts below in answer to the questions posed.

1. Who was the king of Judah reigning in Jerusalem when the city was besieged by the Babylonian armies?

Daniel 1:1 In the third year of the reign of Jehoiakim king of Judah, Nebuchadnezzar king of Babylon came to Jerusalem and besieged it.

Note: The invasion of Judah by Nebuchadnezzar in 605 B.C. has been established from astronomical data. The kingdom of Judah was subdued on account of the fact that the people chose to put other things before God and were not particular about obeying Him. The kingdom of Judah was in the south. Of the two kingdoms (Israel and Judah) that separated after the time of King Solomon, Judah was the last to apostatize, but when it did it exceeded the rebellion of its sister kingdom in the north.

2. Who is identified as allowing the kingdom of Judah to be taken captive?
Daniel 1:2 And the Lord gave Jehoiakim king of Judah into his [Nebuchadnezzar's] hand.

Note: God is in overall control of the affairs of nations. He had chosen the Israelites to be a special witness to the nations to bring them the knowledge of salvation, but they failed to do this (Acts 13:46-48). The special status of the people had begun with the Exodus from Egypt (Deut. 32:9), but it was not long before the spirit of rebellion was revealed. After the Israelites reached the Promised Land, their lack of cooperation with God continued. Now the nation was divided into two kingdoms, Israel and Judah, after King Solomon's time. The kingdom of Israel rebelled and took on pagan practices (1 Kings 12:25-33) and was finally given to the Assyrian's (722 B.C.). Judah was to suffer a similar fate for essentially the same reasons (Jer. 9:14-16; 17:19-27; 22:1-5; 28). Although such a fate pained God (Hos. 11:8), He was unwilling to tolerate evil in His representatives any longer (2 Chron. 36:15-17). The captivity was a judgment on Judah in fulfillment of the prophecies of Isaiah and Jeremiah (Isa. 39:5-7; Jer. 20:5).

3. Who else besides the king was taken captive?
Daniel 1:3 Then the king instructed Ashpenaz, the master of his eunuchs, to bring some of the children of Israel and some of the king's descendants and some of the nobles.

Note: According to the practice of the times, members of the royal household and representatives of the nobility and prominent citizens were taken as captives. These individuals were educated and used in the service of the country. They could not be used in this manner under the age of 17 years. We learn further that "Among those who maintained their allegiance to God were Daniel and his three companions—illustrious examples of what men may become who unite with the God of wisdom and power. From the comparative simplicity of their Jewish home, these youth of royal line were taken to the most magnificent of cities and into the court of the world's greatest monarch" (PK 480).

4. What items of treasure were taken from Jerusalem and where were they placed?
Daniel 1:2 And the Lord gave Jehoiakim king of Judah into his hand, with some of the articles of the house of God, which he carried into the land of Shinar to the house of his god; and he brought the articles into the treasure house of his god.

Note: Treasures were taken from the temple at this time (605 B.C.) and on the two successive occasions (597 and 586 B.C.–2 Kings 24:13; 25:8-15). This leads us to the conclusion that the most valuable items would have been taken on the first visit to be used in the temple of Marduk, the chief god of Babylon. The Babylonians considered the treasures that were taken from God's temple as an evidence for the superiority of their god over the God of Israel. However, the almighty God already had planned to give them the evidence of His superiority through His children, Daniel and his friends, by giving them wisdom to interpret mysteries (PK 480). God is always ahead of His enemies.

5. What special talents did the captives possess who were selected to be trained for the king's service?
Daniel 1:4 [The master of the eunuchs choose] young men in whom *there was* no blemish, but good-looking, gifted in all wisdom, possessing knowledge and quick to understand, who *had* ability to serve in the king's palace, and whom they might teach the language and literature of the Chaldeans.

Note: Besides being physically sound, the youth taken were from the most educated and gifted segments of society. The scholars of Babylon were required to be proficient in the sciences, including astronomy (and astrology), and in languages. Daniel is thought to have been proficient in Akkadian, Aramaic, Hebrew and Sumerian.

6. What special privileges did a group of four freshmen request from the court officer?
Daniel 1:12 "Please test your servants for ten days, and let them give us vegetables to eat and water to drink."

Note: The foods offered to the trainee courtiers were rations specified in the royal household (vs. 5) and were luxurious in character (CD 31). Daniel and his companions were determined to live by the principles they had learnt in their childhood and youth. The meat and wine diet specified by the king represented some type of acceptance of the Babylonian culture and religion in the form of devotion to the king (as a god).

7. Why did Daniel and his companions make the unusual request to eat simple food and drink?
Daniel 1:8 But Daniel purposed in his heart that he would not defile himself with the portion of the king's delicacies, nor with the wine which he drank.

Note: Rejecting the king's food was a serious matter (vs. 10). However, by their demeanour Daniel and his friends had gained favour with a court official (vs. 9). The flesh diet offered to the young men contained unclean meat and was not prepared in the kosher manner, which meant that the blood was not drained from the carcass properly (CD 30; cf. Lev. 17:14, 15). There is some thought too that a token portion of the animals may have been offered to idols (cf. Acts 15:29). Overall, it was the intention of the young men to follow the ideal diet specified by God in Eden so as to keep them mentally and spiritually alert (YI Aug. 18, 1898).

8. After eating the vegetarian diet what outward signs of good health were evident?
Daniel 1:15 And at the end of ten days their features appeared better and fatter in flesh than all the young men who ate the portion of the king's delicacies.

Note: God's special blessing was showered on these men in recognition of their resolve to follow the instructions given in Eden and in recognition of the warnings given to the sons of Aaron about the conduct of those who sought to serve God acceptably (cf. Lev. 10:9; 1 Sam. 2:12-17, 22, 30). "The Lord will bless those who make every effort to keep themselves free from disease and lead others to regard as sacred the health of the body as well as of the soul" (6T 302). The scientific world now understands that a vegetarian diet not only supplies adequate nutrition but also enables the individual to live a healthier and even an extended life.

9. What was the outcome of the examination at the end of the training of the young men?
Daniel 1:20 And in all matters of wisdom *and* understanding about which the king examined them, he found them ten times better than all the magicians *and* astrologers who *were* in all his realm.

Note: The remarkable outcome achieved was on account of the previous stand taken by these youth to remain faithful to God's instructions. They were careful to diligently apply their talents (cf. PK 486, 487; PP 214). A broad range of knowledge was learnt in the Babylonian courts by those studying there; we have no idea whether specialization in various fields was permitted. We should not assume that Daniel and his companions believed in the system of magic or astrology taught even if they undertook to take lessons in this area. Just as in modern scientific circles, those who study in a particular branch of science understand the prevailing theories but may have no philosophical attachment to these theories, so too with Daniel and his friends. They were not moved from their grounding philosophy.

10. What special skills besides knowledge and wisdom were shown by Daniel?
Daniel 1:17 As for these four young men, God gave them knowledge and skill in all literature and wisdom; and Daniel had understanding in all visions and dreams.

Note: Chapter 1 stands apart from the remainder of the book and is thought to have been written after the event as indicated by the mention of Cyrus made in verse 21 whose activities came near the end of the exile (2 Chron. 36:22, 23). Daniel related in verse 17 that God gave him special understanding above his faithful companions. However, there was no exultation in this special gift for he understood, as his companions did, that each had received their gifts from God (cf. 1 Cor. 4:6, 7).

11. What names were given to Daniel and his companions and why?
Daniel 1:7 To them the chief of the eunuchs gave names: he gave Daniel *the name* Belteshazzar; to Hananiah, Shadrach; to Mishael, Meshach; and to Azariah, Abed-Nego.

Note: The assignment of names was not an unusual practice and indicated the acceptance of the young men by the court. Daniel's name was given in honour of the king's god, Bel (Dan. 4:8), which was another name for Marduk, the chief god. The origin of the other names mentioned seems to be involved with heathen deities. Every effort was taken to surround the captives with heathen influences and make them identify fully with the religion and culture of their captors.

Assigning Daniel a name in honour of Bel must have been especially disturbing to him. This god was none other than the Babylonian's creator god. Bel represented the spring sun and a great eleven day festival was held to commemorate the coming of spring. All the other gods were assembled at the temple of Bel-Marduk in Babylon for this event.

Hebrew parents used to give names to their children as a reminder of a character trait they wished to see in them (PK 480). The names Daniel and his friends were given by their parents were intended to continually impress God's character upon their lives. Satan was working behind the chief of the eunuchs attempting to destroy the influence of the Hebrew names upon their character.

12. What answer can be provided to the question of why the righteous captives were to suffer along with the wicked ones?
Jeremiah 20:12 But, O LORD of hosts, You who test the righteous, a*nd* see the mind and heart, let me see Your vengeance on them; for I have pleaded my cause before You.

Note: The life of Jeremiah the prophet, who lived to see the conquest by Babylon, illustrates that God is anxious always to provide the greatest opportunity for those in error to see and acknowledge His ways. Jeremiah suffered in order to encourage others to repent and follow the ways of righteousness (PK 410-413). In allowing the righteous to be taken captive to Babylon with those who did not care for His ways, it was God's purpose for them to witness to His ways and character (PK 480, 487). This Daniel and his companions did untiringly.

13. Daniel chapter 1 commences with exile of selected inhabitants of Jerusalem in Babylon and ends with a hint at their release under Cyrus (vs. 21). Throughout the Bible what significance is given to the idea that Babylon will eventually be overthrown and God's people triumph?
Jeremiah 51:7 Babylon *was* a golden cup in the LORD's hand that made all the earth drunk. The nations drank her wine; therefore the nations are deranged.

Revelation 18:21 Then a mighty angel took up a stone like a great millstone and threw it into the sea, saying, "Thus with violence the great city Babylon shall be thrown down, and shall not be found anymore.

Revelation 19:1 After these things [the fall of Babylon] I heard a loud voice of a great multitude in heaven, saying, "Alleluia! Salvation and glory and honor and power belong to the Lord our God!

Note: The city of Babel was the place where the ancient city builder Nimrod rebelled against God (Gen. 10:8-10; 11:1-9). In the time of Jeremiah, Babylon was represented by a golden cup containing contents that deranged the nations. This theme will be developed when we study the book of Revelation. The system of religion held by her priests was based on ideas inspired by Satan and that perverted the truths delivered to mankind by God. The city was known as the "gate of the gods" (Horn 1960, 103), in recognition of the city's attempt to reject and rival the principles of the God of heaven by promoting alternative worship arrangements even in the time of Nebuchadnezzar. The symbol of Babylon is used in the Scriptures as representing religious systems opposed to God (cf. Isa. 21:9; Jer. 50:28, 29).

The Scriptures recognize just two religious systems (e.g., Matt. 13:37-43; 25:31-34). The one ordained by God and spoken about kindly in the Scriptures is the authentic version. Anything that deviates from this model, or incorporates human tradition into the practices that oppose God's revealed will, is ultimately inspired by the arch deceiver, Satan. The Bible takes Babylon as an example of false systems of worship. This is connected to Nimrod's activities at Babel after the great flood where he showed defiance of and contempt for God's revealed will. He erected altars to the gods of the heavens in ziggurats and started a rival system of worship that centred on the worship of the heavenly bodies. These worship forms were taken on by the kingdom of Babylon and were embellished there by traffic in religious ideas from surrounding people groups.

9.2 A Spectacular Dream

Introduction

During the second year of Nebuchadnezzar's reign, he had a spectacular dream but when he awoke he could not remember the vital details. In his dilemma he called for the wise men to help by telling him both the dream and the interpretation of it, but they could not oblige. They protested at the request, but the king ordered Arioch (captain of the guard) to execute them. Evidently not all the wise men had been called so when Daniel heard of this, he requested time from the king to consider the matter. Now Daniel asked for time because he was a man of prayer. He understood the power of prayer, for "Prayer moves the arm of the omnipotence" (5T 452).

The king extended the time available. In answer to the prayers of Daniel and his companions, God gave Daniel both the dream and its interpretation. Arioch was informed of this breakthrough and immediately arranged an audience with the king. The dream he related was to reveal the history of the nations that would impact significantly on God's faithful people right down to the end of probationary time.

God can see ahead and tell what is going to happen. "In the annals of human history, the growth of nations, the rise and fall of empires, appear as if dependent on the will and prowess of man; the shaping of events seems, to a great degree, to be determined by his power, ambition, or caprice. But in the word of God the curtain is drawn aside, and we behold, above, behind, and through all the play and counter play of human interest and power and passions, the agencies of the All-merciful One, silently, patiently working out the counsels of His own will . . . ." (CC 250).

The kingdom of Babylon holds a central place in the history of God's church. A majority of earth's inhabitants rebelled after the universal flood and their arrogance and disloyalty came to prominence in the city of Babel. In fact, they invented their own religious practices and promoted these in the region and also devised the first system of writing, which enabled them to convey their thoughts more effectively. In the time of Daniel's witness, their system of religion had been modified and refined even to the point of having their own creator and saviour god. Around this period, in the region of Mesopotamia and in other parts of the world novel systems of philosophy were emerging under notable leaders, namely, Confucius and Lao Tze in China, Buddha in India, Pythagoras in Greece and Zoroaster in Iran. Some of these ideas evolved and took root in succeeding civilizations and have influenced Christianity. In particular Zoroaster's concepts are thought by some to have contributed to the Roman religion known as Mithraism. This belief system would impact significantly on Christianity in the time of the Roman Empire.

The Study

Read chapter 2 then the notes and Bible texts below in answer to the questions posed.

1. What time period elapsed between the end of Daniel's training session recorded in chapter 1 until the spectacular image was seen in a dream by Nebuchadnezzar?

Daniel 2:1 Now in the second year of Nebuchadnezzar's reign, Nebuchadnezzar had dreams; and his spirit was *so* troubled that his sleep left him.

Note: The second year of Nebucchadnezzar's reign was 603 B.C. In Babylonian society, dreams were reasonably common and were heralded as divine messengers. The king was anxious to learn the meaning of the dream since he had been so privileged. The God of heaven by this means had chosen to speak to the king through an avenue that he appreciated.

2. What type of court environment existed in Babylon during the time Daniel was in the king's service?
Daniel 2:2 Then the king gave the command to call the magicians, the astrologers, the sorcerers, and the Chaldeans to tell the king his dreams. So they came and stood before the king.

Note: The Chaldeans were skilled at divination, magic, astrology and similar practices. They were mainlining into occult practices. By means of such devices as animal sacrifices, inspection of the entrails and body organs, looking at signs in heavens and by following set numerical formulas, based on their magic squares, the practitioners came to a settled opinion about the future.

3. What type of impact did the king's dream have upon him?
Daniel 2:3 And the king said to them, "I have had a dream, and my spirit is anxious to know the dream."

Note: In verse 1 the text indicates that the king dreamt "dreams" that suggests to some that the dream we are about to study may have been repeated several times. Nebuchadnezzar was convinced of the divine origin of the dream.

4. What procedure was adopted by the king of Babylon when he experienced dreams or wished to have guidance about the future?
Daniel 2:2 Then the king gave the command to call the magicians, the astrologers, the sorcerers, and the Chaldeans to tell the king his dreams. So they came and stood before the king.

Note: Babylon is considered to have been the birth place of astrology. The Babylonians taught that everything was dependent upon the stars. In the time of Nebuchadnezzar, it was also a place where the creator god, Marduk was worshipped. This god had links to the sun, for he is shown with the rays of the sun arising from him. Here and at other places the sun god was worshipped as the leading deity.

The belief that the stars exerted a controlling influence on individuals, their characters and their affairs is of ancient origin. The Sumerians and Babylonians were some of the earliest known exponents of the art of astrology. The heavenly bodies (sky gods) held various levels of significance in the theological systems of the ancients. In these cultures, the sun and moon were the recipients of high veneration. In the Assyrian Empire the sun god (Ashur) rose to full glory, so that all other deities were subservient. We notice that the influence of the sun god remained strong in the independent Neo-Babylonian Empire that overthrew the Assyrian Empire under the leadership of Nabopolasser in 626 B.C. In the Neo-Babylonian period, Nebuchadnezzar II (reigned 605-562 B.C.) and Nabonidus spent lavishly to refurbish the temple of the sun at Sippar, not far from the capital, Babylon. So we find that the sun god increased with the brilliance of her kings and their unified rule and system of justice.

The link between spiritualism (an important idea held is that "the soul of man is a spiritual substance"–Pace 1912) and Babylon, even when spoken about symbolically in either Daniel or Revelation, is an important point that we should not miss. Astrology is at the base of all occult practices. In the Babylonian system the stars were regarded as the resting place of departed spirits. The devil's lie spoken in Eden, namely, "You will not surely die" (Gen. 3:4), underscored this system of worship and many others that deviate from God's authentic pattern. Hence, we find that in the Old Testament there is explicit instruction to avoid any contact with occult practices and worship of celestial bodies (Exod. 20:3-5; Isa. 8:19) and, in the book of Revelation, God reiterated that those who call themselves His people should disassociate themselves from everything connected with the worship of the sun or celestial bodies. This call still comes to us today. In the book of Daniel, God chose to reveal His mysteries to His servant

Daniel. They were hidden from the Chaldeans because they promoted a system of worship antagonistic to the authentic article.

5. Was the king confident and complementary about the predictions and interpretations of events offered by the court officials?

Daniel 2:9 [The king said] "If you do not make known the dream to me, *there is only* one decree for you! For you have agreed to speak lying and corrupt words before me till the time has changed. Therefore tell me the dream, and I shall know that you can give me its interpretation."

Note: The king told the court officials only that he had dreamt a "dream" and did not tell them of his repeated forgetful state. By the beliefs of the times, dreams needed to be interpreted quickly because appropriate actions may be demanded at auspicious moments in the near future. The repeated requests made by the Chaldeans for more information raised the king's suspicions that they were trying to prepare "lying and corrupt words" for his ears (vss. 8, 9). By their own words (vs. 11), they admitted that their skills depended on the right technique, not on account of their connection with the gods, the supposed origin of dreams. This may not have been the first time the king had such poor thoughts about them and this idea is strengthened by his subsequent treatment of Daniel's request for time (vs. 16).

6. Was the king renowned for his patience with his counselors?

Daniel 2: 13 For this reason [that the wise men began to reason and argue with the king about the impossibility of his request—vss. 10, 11] the king was angry and very furious, and gave the command to destroy all the wise *men* of Babylon.

Note: The practices of the times were severe. The undertaking of the king to cut the Chaldeans to pieces and destroy their houses (vs. 5) is attested by history as no idle threat. The action he threatened would certainly be carried out. On the other hand too, it seems that Nebuchadnezzar was not the most patient of individuals (cf. Dan. 3:13). In his position as a god, his commands were to be obeyed.

7. Daniel was received differently by the king. What was one possible reason for this?

Daniel 2:16 So [after a courteous request was made to the king—vss. 14, 15] Daniel went in and asked the king to give him time, that he might tell the king the interpretation.

Note: Daniel's approach to the king's representative was both wise and tactful. When Arioch brought his request to the king, one can only imagine that the good favour expressed by the king towards Daniel and his friends previously (Dan. 1:18-20) was remembered. Daniel had built a network of good relationships in the court and was known as a person of principle (Dan. 1:8-12). Indeed, at this time, he might have sought to distance himself from the other wise men, but he identified with them and was willing to speak on behalf of their lives as well as his own (Dan. 2:13-15, 24). Daniel and his friends did not forget how God had led them in the past. "In times of perplexity and danger they had always turned to Him for guidance and protection, and He had proved an ever-present help" (PK 393).

8. What assistance did Daniel seek in attempting to avert the general death sentence delivered against the wise men?

Daniel 2:17, 18 Then Daniel went to his house, and made the decision known to Hananiah, Mishael, and Azariah, his companions, that they might seek mercies from the God of heaven concerning this secret, so that Daniel and his companions might not perish with the rest of the wise *men* of Babylon.

Note: Daniel's training in the court practices had not altered his devotion and trust in God. He well knew that human wisdom was inadequate to deliver him from the situation in which he found himself.

9. In response to being shown the nature of the king's dream in a vision by night, did Daniel take any credit to himself?
Daniel 2:23 "I thank You and praise You, O God of my fathers; You have given me wisdom and might, and have now made known to me what we asked of You, for You have made known to us the king's demand."

Daniel 2:28 "But [Daniel answered the king concerning his skills] there is a God in heaven who reveals secrets, and He has made known to King Nebuchadnezzar what will be in the latter days."

Note: Daniel gave all the credit to God for revealing both the dream and its interpretation (vss. 20-23). There is more power than we realize in thanksgiving. Daniel no doubt understood that "If the loving-kindness of God called forth more thanksgiving and praise, we would have far more power in prayer" (5T 317). Daniel reminded Nebuchadnezzar that he served a living God who was interested in the affairs of men in contrast to the gods of the realm. The king was about to learn that the God of Daniel also controls history.

10. What did the king see in his dream?
Daniel 2: 31-33 "You, O king, were watching; and behold, a great image! This great image, whose splendor *was* excellent, stood before you; and its form *was* awesome. This image's head *was* of fine gold, its chest and arms of silver, its belly and thighs of bronze, its legs of iron, its feet partly of iron and partly of clay."

Note: The king had seen a human image made of different metals that was supported on legs of iron and clay. Such an image was not an unusual way in which to depict the destiny of nations in the times of the prophet. We notice carefully that the head was composed of the most precious metal and this was followed by silver, bronze and finally iron, which represented metals of decreasing value.

11. What spectacular event climaxed the dream?
Daniel 2:35 "Then the iron, the clay, the bronze, the silver, and the gold were crushed together, and became like chaff from the summer threshing floors; the wind carried them away so that no trace of them was found. And the stone that struck the image became a great mountain and filled the whole earth."

Note: A supernatural event climaxed the dream in that a stone not prepared by human hands (Dan. 2:45) struck the base of the image so that no trace remained. The stone in turn filled the whole earth. In other words, it occupied much more space than all the other components of the image combined.

12. What interpretation was placed on the image seen in vision by Daniel and the head of gold in particular?
Daniel 2:37, 38 "You, O king, *are* a king of kings. For the God of heaven has given you a kingdom, power, strength, and glory; and wherever the children of men dwell, or the beasts of the field and the birds of the heaven, He has given *them* into your hand, and has made you ruler over them all—you *are* this head of gold."

Note: This text clearly indicates that the head of gold represented the kingdom of Babylon under the rulership of Nebuchadnezzar. This kingdom blossomed from 605-539 B.C. and was characterized by the abundant use of gold in its temples and palaces (cf. Isa. 14:4).

13. What would happen to the Babylonian kingdom and subsequent kingdoms including the fourth?

Daniel 2:39-41 "But after you shall arise another kingdom inferior to yours; then another, a third kingdom of bronze, which shall rule over all the earth. And the fourth kingdom shall be as strong as iron, inasmuch as iron breaks in pieces and shatters everything; and like iron that crushes, *that kingdom* will break in pieces and crush all the others. Whereas you saw the feet and toes, partly of potter's clay and partly of iron, the kingdom shall be divided . . . ."

Note: Proof of the identity of the kingdoms spoken about will be given as we proceed through the book of Daniel. Each kingdom had its allotted time on the world stage. The remaining parts of the body represented successive kingdoms as follows: Silver—Medo-Persia (539-331 B.C.); Bronze—Greece (331-168 B.C.); Iron—Rome (168 B.C.–A.D. 476). Silver was the currency of the Persian Empire, bronze was commonly used in the armor of the Greeks and iron in the Roman army. The Roman Empire gave way to the divided kingdoms of Europe represented by the mixing of iron and clay. The disintegration of the Western Roman Empire commenced in A.D. 476 and the Eastern portion finally disintegrated in A.D. 1453 under pressure from the Turks. No matter how powerful these successive kingdoms were during their time, they fell apart. " . . . the strength of nations, as of individuals, is not found in the opportunities or facilities that appear to make them invincible; it is not found in their boasted greatness. It is measured by the fidelity with which they fulfill God's purpose" (PK 502).

14. What unusual event happened to the fourth or iron kingdom?

Daniel 2:40, 41 "And the fourth kingdom shall be as strong as iron, inasmuch as iron breaks in pieces and shatters everything; and like iron that crushes, *that kingdom* will break in pieces and crush all the others. Whereas you saw the feet and toes, partly of potter's clay and partly of iron, the kingdom shall be divided; yet the strength of the iron shall be in it, just as you saw the iron mixed with ceramic clay."

Note: The Western section of the Roman Empire gave way to various European kingdoms. The list produced differs somewhat among authorities. Some have attempted to identify the ten kingdoms represented by the ten toes of the image (Dan. 2:42), but disagreements have emerged. Perhaps the comment made by Doukhan (2000, 105) on this issue is sufficient. He said the meaning of the number ten (in the time of the prophet) "represents a number beyond which it is impossible to count" (cf. Gen. 18). Attempts to reunite Europe since Rome disintegrated have been uniformly unsuccessful (Charlemagne, Charles V, Louis XIV, Napoleon, Kaiser Wilhelm, and Adolf Hitler). After the fall of the Western section of the Empire of Rome the pattern in Europe has been one of strong nations interacting with weaker elements.

Up to this point, it is considered that the metals mentioned referred to political powers. Now we have clay or a different type of power introduced. Some commentators believe that the reference to clay infers that a religious element would become significant in the history of the European nations. This has proven to be correct.

15. What kingdom was represented by the stone (vs. 34) that demolished the divided kingdoms of the world?

Daniel 2:44 "And in the days of these kings the God of heaven will set up a kingdom which shall never be destroyed; and the kingdom shall not be left to other people; it shall break in pieces and consume all these kingdoms, and it shall stand forever."

Note: The choice of a stone to represent God's kingdom indicates permanence (vs. 44; cf. Exod. 24:12). The coming of the kingdom owed nothing to the preceding nations. The coming of God's kingdom of glory is spoken about in the New Testament. Christ spoke of taking His followers to be with Him (John 14:1-3). This kingdom will last forever (Rev. 11:15). The coming of Christ the king will not be occur in secret; it will be a spectacular event (Matt. 24:24-31). Christ's kingdom will be finally established on the earth (Rev. 21:1-5).

16. Do you think the prophecy of the parade of kingdoms contains conditional elements?
Daniel 2:45 "The great God has made known to the king what will come to pass after this. The dream is certain, and its interpretation is sure."

Note: The progress of nations noted in Daniel's prophecy establishes the certainty of the final act. The prophecy makes certain statements on the successive rise and fall of kingdoms reflecting God's foreknowledge. "In the history of nations the student of God's word may behold the literal fulfillment of divine prophecy" (PK 502). Christ will come to put an end to sin in fulfillment of the unconditional prophecy given in Genesis 3:15.

17. Only a few nations are mentioned in this great prophecy that attempts to map history until Christ returns. Why is no mention made of China or India, for example?

Note: Some might argue that Daniel's prophecy should have commenced with the Assyrian Empire, which was borne out of Nimrod's kingdom. This, we remember, was the first kingdom established after the great flood (Gen. 10:8-10; Mic. 5:6). However, the religious practices and perversions of authentic worship introduced by this kingdom were taken on rather boldly by Babylon, making such an application unnecessary. The histories of the nations presented by the prophet Daniel have a focused interest on the fortunes of authentic worship and those who choose to follow its tenets. Its purpose was to reveal the nature of the forces that would impact most significantly on the understanding and expression of authentic worship.

The principles of God-ordained worship were given in Eden and were practiced by Noah. However, various people groups chose to invent alien practices. These ideas have impacted significantly on the understanding of the authentic article and have been copied by other groups or have arisen independently. How this process may have worked is illustrated by the short discourse to follow centring on the Middle East, the Mediterranean basin and Europe.

The Garden of Eden and the resting place of Noah's ark are both considered to have been located in north-east Iran/Kurdistan. After the great flood, the people descended from the mountain regions to the plains of Mesopotamia. At that time the plains were very fertile, hence the name *The Fertile Crescent.* The Scriptures clearly indicate that the first city builder was Nimrod and that two of his cities were Babel and Nineveh (in today's Iraq). The historical record goes back at least 23 centuries before the present era. It is evident that already there was an elaborate system of polytheistic worship that centred on the worship of the celestial gods. Elaborate stepped structures called ziggurats were constructed, which contained a shrine to the principle god. For example, the temple at Babylon was for Marduk, the creator god, and is thought to have been greater than 90 metres high. The patron god of Nineveh was Ishtar, the goddess of love.

Astrology actually commenced among the Assyrians (an empire in existence before Nebucchadnezzar's kingdom and from which ideas were taken) and involved the study of the heavenly bodies which they believed controlled the affairs of men. The chief star in their system of worship was the sun. The position of the stars, particularly the seven planets, and their movement through the zodiacal belt, was significant. Indeed, the sky was divided into 12 houses (three rooms each) with a star, representing a god, to rule over it. Each god was given a characteristic number. Inserted into these religious practices was the use of a system of magic squares that were used to calculate future events from the movement of the stars. The phases of the moon were also of considerable interest in determining the omens, for it was believed that these determined which days were lucky or unlucky in relation to other life events.

A development of great significance in world history was the creation of the art of writing. This occurred several centuries before 3000 B.C. in Sumer (southern Iraq). It eclipsed the achievements of any other people group and allowed the effective transmission of learning and the construction of a strong administrative system. As these developments were occurring there was a growing confidence in astronomical observations and calculations. These interests were developed later by the Greeks who gave greater emphasis to mathematical astronomy. Their philosophies also were to become fundamentally importance in modes of thinking even into the present era.

The *Fertile Crescent* is also renowned as the place where plants and animals were first domesticated. This provided the opportunity for intensive agriculture to develop and the possibility to support large populations. The benefits of domestication could be shared with surrounding peoples. This occurred quickly as the geography of the region allowed domesticated plants to be grown widely. The ecological barriers found in other parts of the world were not present. The advantages presented to the people of this region through these developments meant that they had great potential to influence social development in the region and beyond.

The flow of ideas was not unidirectional. The development of astrological ideas in Babylon was influenced by ideas coming from Iran. In turn these ideas infiltrated eastward across Asia, south to Africa and north west to Europe as people moved away from the centre following migration or trading pathways or following in the train of the fortunes of conquest. The fourth kingdom in Daniel's dream, Rome, rather avidly took on elements of Babylon's worship (in the form of Mithraism). This finally led to a spectacular clash of ideas with Christianity in the time of Constantine. Christianity seemingly triumphed, but in reality paganism had entered the church to remain. Until the present time, such alien religious ideas and practices have clouded the minds of many about authentic worship. Nothing developed in other parts of the world has rivalled this impact. Hence, it was not necessary for the prophet to mention other great nations that would come upon the scene of action. Daniel's messages apply equally to any other philosophical systems, for they all contain elements that do not agree with the word of God.

9.3 Death Sentence Proclaimed

Introduction

King Nebuchadnezzar had been impressed by the dream that Daniel related to him and he bowed and offered worship (Dan. 2:46, 47) in recognition that God had seen fit to honour him and give such a clear message concerning the future. In his thanks and praise Nebuchadnezzar initially acknowledged that Daniel's God was superior to Marduk, the "lord of gods" (vs. 47). However, at the opening of chapter 3 we find that the king was determined to rewrite history and he erected a golden image to indicate his determination for the kingdom of Babylon to continue without end. "The prosperity attending his reign filled him with pride. In time he ceased to honor God and he resumed his idol worship with increased zeal and bigotry" (PK 504).

The plain on which the image was constructed is thought to have been at a site 4.8 kilometres south of Babylon and the meeting organized there was designated as a worship event. The king now demanded adoration (Dan. 3:2, 3), which he had so willing given to Daniel a little time earlier. Some have noted the parallels between the activities surrounding the tower of Babel (Gen. 11:1, 2) and the events on the plain of Shinar in the province of Babylon (Dan. 3:1). In ancient Babel the people gathered to make a name for themselves (Gen. 11:4). In the parallel passage in Daniel, the king gathered his subjects to give honour to him and the chief god, Bel-Marduk.

"Accustomed as they were to magnificent representations of their heathen deities, the Chaldeans had never before produced anything so imposing and majestic as this resplendent statue, threescore cubits in height and six cubits in breadth"(PK 505). The choice of an image that towered to 60 cubits (approx. 31.4 metres) high was because the number symbolised the concept of unity. In this particular instance, it represented one eternal kingdom (Babylon) where all were meant to worship in unity. The outcome of Nebuchadnezzar's attempt to enforce uniform worship demands on his subjects is the topic of this chapter.

The Study

Read chapter 3 then the notes and Bible texts below in answer to the questions posed.

1. After Daniel's interpretation of the dream experienced by Nebuchadnezzar, what honours were given to the four Hebrew captives highlighted in chapter 1?
Daniel 2:49 Also Daniel petitioned the king, and he set Shadrach, Meshach, and Abed-Nego over the affairs of the province of Babylon; but Daniel *sat* in the gate of the king.

Note: The chief actors in the drama recorded in chapter 3 are Daniel's friends who had been elevated to posts of responsibility at Daniel's request after the king had honoured him following the interpretation of the dream in chapter 2. Daniel, now a governor, was not part of this episode being perhaps either ill or on important business elsewhere.

2. What unusual activity did King Nebuchadnezzar engage in which brought important people together from throughout his realm?
Daniel 3: 1, 2 Nebuchadnezzar the king made an image of gold, whose height *was* sixty cubits *and* its width six cubits. He set it up in the plain of Dura, in the province of Babylon. And King Nebuchadnezzar sent *word* to gather together the satraps, the administrators, the governors, the counsellors, the treasurers,

the judges, the magistrates, and all the officials of the provinces, to come to the dedication of the image that King Nebuchadnezzar had set up.

Note: On reflection the king was disappointed with the idea that his kingdom would disappear and he sought to signal his intention to change the course of history by constructing an image purely of gold. Pride began to control his activities. He was attempting to recapture the glory of Babel that had suffered a set-back through the confusion of languages. He spared no effort to make sure all the significant people of the realm were in attendance (vs. 3).

3. What planned event was about to bring about a challenge to King Nebuchadnezzar's authority?
Daniel 3:4, 5 Then a herald cried aloud: "To you it is commanded, O peoples, nations, and languages, *that* at the time you hear the sound of the horn, flute, harp, lyre, *and* psaltery, in symphony with all kinds of music, you shall fall down and worship the gold image that King Nebuchadnezzar has set up."

Note: Music accompanied the event (vs. 5) and was designed to lead to a state of devotion and compliance. No expense was spared to make this gathering a spectacular event. Even some foreign musical instruments were used.

4. What threat did the king make to anyone who failed to worship the image of gold?
Daniel 3:11 [The decree issued by the king stated—vs. 10] "and whoever does not fall down and worship shall be cast into the midst of a burning fiery furnace."

Note: The dedication of the image spoken of in verse 2 was in actual fact an act of homage offered to the king and the gods of the realm. The threat to burn those who did not bow down to the image was made clear (vs. 6). Furnaces were commonly used in the region to prepare bricks and the practice of burning people alive for disobedience was not unknown (Jer. 29:21, 22). Indeed, Hammurabi (1728-1686 B.C.), who was a king in the first Babylonian dynasty, codified the procedure and it was practiced reasonably widely in the region. Nebuchadnezzar's statement was no idle threat as all subjects of the realm knew.

5. What did some of the Chaldeans accuse Daniel's friends of failing to do?
Daniel 3:12 "There are certain Jews whom you have set over the affairs of the province of Babylon: Shadrach, Meshach, and Abed-Nego; these men, O king, have not paid due regard to you. They do not serve your gods or worship the gold image which you have set up."

Note: The sudden elevation of these three youths to prominence gave rise to envy. Their rivals forgot that their lives were saved by the prayer of these young men. "Envy is not merely a perverseness of temper, but a distemper, which disorders all the faculties" (5T 56). In many nations, there is perhaps a resistance to foreigners and their cultural and religious practices. Clearly, these foreign individuals had failed to obey the king's command and those who reported the event may have been hoping for some reward.

6. Were these Hebrews acting from principle or had they elevated meaningless traditions to a place of importance?
Exodus 20:4, 5 [God said] "You shall not make for yourself a carved image—any likeness *of anything* that *is* in heaven above, or that *is* in the earth beneath, or that *is* in the water under the earth; you shall not bow down to them nor serve them. For I, the LORD your God, *am* a jealous God, visiting the iniquity of the fathers upon the children to the third and fourth *generations* of those who hate Me."

Note: The clearest instruction on appropriate ways of behaviour was delivered to mankind at Mount Sinai when God both spoke (Exod. 20:1) the Decalogue and then wrote it on tables of stone. Then the LORD said to Moses (recorded in Exod. 24:12), "Come up to Me on the mountain and be there; and I will give you tablets of stone, and the law and commandments which I have written, that you may teach them." The understanding of these principles is still held firmly in the Christian church (Rev. 22:14).

7. What response did the Jewish captives make to King Nebuchadnezzar's offer of another chance and the promise to consign them to a burning furnace if they did not worship his image (vss. 14, 15)?

Daniel 3:16-18 Shadrach, Meshach, and Abed-Nego answered and said to the king, "O Nebuchadnezzar, we have no need to answer you in this matter. If that *is the case,* our God whom we serve is able to deliver us from the burning fiery furnace, and He will deliver *us* from your hand, O king. But if not, let it be known to you, O king, that we do not serve your gods, nor will we worship the gold image which you have set up."

Note: The king received the response recorded in our verses in answer to his commands. Nebuchadnezzar was sure of either destroying these youths or inducing compliance, for he had dismissed already the possibility that any god could deliver one thus threatened (vs. 15). The Hebrews did not reply arrogantly but calmly assured the king that they did not need to reconsider their settled opinions. They claimed that their God was able to save them, but they willingly gave their lives into His hands and keeping (cf. Jer. 26:20-23). In this way they highlighted the difference between the false religion of the Chaldeans—obey or perish now—with that of the Jews who believed in a gracious, personal God in charge of the future.

8. Was the king true to his promise?

Daniel 3:19 Then Nebuchadnezzar was full of fury, and the expression on his face changed toward Shadrach, Meshach, and Abed-Nego. He spoke and commanded that they heat the furnace seven times more than it was usually heated.

Note: The now furious king ordered the furnace to be heated to its limits and for the three Hebrews to be thrown into the furnace immediately. This was done and those who carried out the task were struck dead by the heat (vs. 22).

9. What phenomenon brought the king from a state of rage to one of astonishment?

Daniel 3:24, 25 Then King Nebuchadnezzar was astonished; and he rose in haste *and* spoke, saying to his counsellors, "Did we not cast three men bound into the midst of the fire?" They answered and said to the king, "True, O king." "Look!" he answered, "I see four men loose, walking in the midst of the fire; and they are not hurt, and the form of the fourth is like the Son of God."

Note: The king was the first to notice that something unusual had happened. The three men had been thrown bound into the furnace and had fallen down on impact. Now they were walking around but four people were visible. It became evident to the king that the extra person was divine. None of his gods appeared among men, for none showed such interest in the welfare of their subjects. Clearly the Hebrew youth worshipped a personal and loving God.

10. The miracle of deliverance from the fiery furnace was evident to all the officials looking on and closer examination revealed additional evidence. What was the nature of this?

Daniel 3:27 And the satraps, administrators, governors, and the king's counsellors gathered together, and they saw these men on whose bodies the fire had no power; the hair of their head was not singed nor were their garments affected, and the smell of fire was not on them.

Note: The careful examination by the officials and the king simply confirmed what they saw. The extraordinary nature of the miracle was evident to all. Without a doubt some present had witnessed similar execution attempts, but now it was evident that the Hebrew youth believed in a God who had saved in a remarkable manner. "In the presence of the Lord of heat and cold, the flames lost their power to consume" (PK 509).

11. What immediate change of attitude was demonstrated by the king?
Daniel 3:28, 29 Nebuchadnezzar spoke, saying, "Blessed be the God of Shadrach, Meshach, and Abed-Nego, who sent His Angel and delivered His servants who trusted in Him, and they have frustrated the king's word, and yielded their bodies, that they should not serve nor worship any god except their own God! Therefore I make a decree that any people, nation, or language which speaks anything amiss against the God of Shadrach, Meshach, and Abed-Nego shall be cut in pieces, and their houses shall be made an ash heap; because there is no other God who can deliver like this."

Note: The king by making these statements admitted personal defeat and the existence of powers far superior to those known by the Chaldeans. Truly here was a god who could save from death. He was the genuine creator God, not like Bel-Marduk. Faith in the living God of heaven had saved the Hebrew youth.

In response to this miracle, the king said that his subjects should not speak against such a powerful person as the Hebrew God. Freedom of religious expression had been achieved, although the king did not publically declare any change of heart in his own worship practices.

12. What positive outcome for the Hebrew youth occurred?
Daniel 3:30 Then the king promoted Shadrach, Meshach, and Abed-Nego in the province of Babylon.

Note: The king through this act of promotion recognized the value of character in those attending to the affairs of his kingdom. "The Hebrew captives filling positions of trust in Babylon had in life and character represented before him the truth. When asked for a reason of their faith, they had given it without hesitation" (PK 509). Faithfulness gets the attention of the Almighty. God rewards those who are faithful to the principles of His kingdom (Ps. 23:5).

13. The death penalty inflicted on the Hebrew youth was on account of their refusal to worship the creator god of Babylon. Does this theme recur in the writings of the apostle John?
Revelation 13:15 He [lamb-like beast] was granted *power* to give breath to the image of the beast, that the image of the beast should both speak and cause as many as would not worship the image of the beast to be killed.

Note: The story of the Hebrew worthies is an account of a minority of bright captives who chose to suffer death rather than relinquish their beliefs in the creator God. They were singularly honoured by Jesus Christ. The interesting observation that we can make that is relevant to the story is the concept of a faithful remnant. This theme recurs throughout the Bible. In every age, groups of individuals have been found who will stand firm to God's principles whatever the cost.

The interesting text quoted above will be studied in more depth when we get to the book of Revelation. The concept that we wish to develop is that worship will be the great issue at the end of time. The demand then will be made that the peoples of the world must worship according to human-inspired ideas or perish. However, a remnant group chooses not to worship and will be delivered by God (Rev. 14:1-5, 12).

The end-time repeat performance of the events on the plain of Dura will involve worship of the creator God, Christ, on His memorial day (Saturday) rather than worship on a day of that proclaims its pagan origin. In John's revelation of Jesus Christ the information is given that the forces against God in the end time are identified by the mystic number 666 (Rev. 13:18). This is the same number that defined the Sun-god in the Babylonian mysteries. Now the ancient Sun-god's day was Sunday and a memorial to him was created when religious leaders in times past transferred the sanctity of God's day to Sunday.

Satan's contention always has been against the Creator and His law. It was no different on the plain of Dura. Worship was demanded to the image of the king's creation, honouring Babylon and Bel-Marduk, in defiance of God's command not to worship any images or likenesses to things created. The same great test will come to earth's inhabitants at the end of time. Whether believers are successful in this test will be determined by their relationship with the Creator.

"As in the days of Shadrach, Meshach, and Abednego, so in the closing period of earth's history the Lord will work mightily in behalf of those who stand steadfastly for the right. He who walked with the Hebrew worthies in the fiery furnace will be with His followers wherever they are. His abiding presence will comfort and sustain. In the midst of the time of trouble (trouble such as has not been since there was a nation), His chosen ones will stand unmoved. Satan with all the hosts of evil cannot destroy the weakest of God's saints. Angels that excel in strength will protect them, and in their behalf Jehovah will reveal Himself as a 'God of gods,' able to save to the uttermost those who have put their trust in Him" (PK 513).

9.4 Pride Brings a Fall

Introduction

The account given in Daniel chapter 4 represents a different Nebuchadnezzar. His testimony is recorded after recovery from mental illness over a period of seven years. His statements also foster the idea that he had been converted through this experience (PK 521). The text itself gives some clues to his changed state of mind in that the discourse commences with the words: "I thought it good to declare the signs and wonders that the Most High God has worked for me" (vs. 2).

The king continued with an outpouring of praise for the goodness of God. He acknowledged the reality that God's kingdom is indeed everlasting (vs. 3), which represented a repudiation of his claims made in chapter 2. Nebuchadnezzar looked for God's rulership.

His praises were preceded by a vivid dream, an explanation offered by Daniel, and an almost immediate fulfillment. The dream was of a magnificent tree with beautiful leaves, fruit that provided rest and food for the beast and birds. Then an angel came from heaven and ordered that the tree be chopped down and the stump bound with bands. The dream then changed and the stump took on the nature of a person. This individual was to act as a beast of the field for seven years.

The dream was fulfilled when the king declared with pride that he had done great things in Babylon by his own power. His reason immediately left him and he was excluded from power for a time. His full reason returned when he acknowledged the need for God's salvation; his kingdom was restored to him and his honour was multiplied.

The Study

Read chapter 4 then the notes and Bible texts below in answer to the questions posed.

1. The revelation of the Son of Man in the fiery furnace impressed Nebuchadnezzar and he responded positively. However, he still had a struggle. What temptation still plagued him?
Daniel 4:30 The king spoke, saying, "Is not this great Babylon, that I have built for a royal dwelling by my mighty power and for the honor of my majesty?"

Note: Archaeological evidence (Grotenfend cylinder) supports the claim made by the text that Nebuchadnezzar was the builder of the new Babylon. The original city was destroyed by Sennacherib, the Assyrian king, in 689 B.C. Nebuchadnezzar subsequently built walls and large city gates besides palaces, temples, channels and dams. In this way he created an impressive inner city, about 8 kilometres in circumference, and through this city the river Euphrates ran. There was also an outer wall that protected the city. This city was the pride of the king. It was a symbol of his worldly greatness. Nebuchadnezzar was exalted to the pinnacle of worldly honour. He was acknowledged even in the Bible (Ezekiel 26: 7) as 'a king of kings' (PK 514).

2. Nebuchadnezzar's second dream is recorded as a personal testimony of gratitude to God. What amazing confession did he make?
Daniel 4:2, 3 I thought it good to declare the signs and wonders that the Most High God has worked for me. How great *are* His signs, and how mighty His wonders! His kingdom *is* an everlasting kingdom, and His dominion *is* from generation to generation.

Note: Pride was Nebuchadnezzar's basic problem (vs. 37), which he had demonstrated amply in chapter 2. It also was the basic problem that Lucifer had displayed in heaven and that led to his removal (Isa. 14:13, 14). Pride has ever been the most dangerous foe for created beings. "The sin that is most nearly hopeless and incurable is pride of opinion, self conceit" (7T 199). However, when Nebuchadnezzar understood the compassion and character of God and the kingdom He intended to establish, the king was willing to acknowledge his sin and humble himself. "Pride and self-importance, when compared with lowliness and humility, are indeed weakness" (3T 477).

3. What strange dream was seen that ultimately led to this confession of confidence in God?
Daniel 4:10 "These *were* the visions of my head *while* on my bed: I was looking, and behold, a tree in the midst of the earth, and its height was great."

Verse 14 [Near the end of the dream the king heard an onlooker speak and] He cried aloud and said thus: "Chop down the tree and cut off its branches, strip off its leaves and scatter its fruit. Let the beasts get out from under it, and the birds from its branches."

Note: The tree was great indicating the significance of the person symbolized and the importance of Babylon in the world of religious developments. A similar symbol was used by the prophet Ezekiel to represent Assyria (Ezek. 31:3-9) at a somewhat later date in the history of Judah. In the account in Daniel, the height of the tree represented the pride of the nation (vs. 10). In similar fashion, we might take the vision of Daniel chapter four to mean that Nebuchadnezzar was exceedingly proud. It is conceivable that the king suspected that the tree represented himself. As a lover and planter of trees, he must have been distressed by the vision before him. To lose such a magnificent tree was a tragedy.

4. This vision (chapter 4) had a disturbing twist to it. What did the king hear the onlooker say?
Daniel 4:15, 16 "Nevertheless leave the stump and roots in the earth, b*ound* with a band of iron and bronze, in the tender grass of the field. Let it be wet with the dew of heaven, and *let* him graze with the beasts on the grass of the earth. Let his heart be changed from *that of* a man, let him be given the heart of a beast, and let seven times pass over him."

Note: A disturbing element is revealed in the verses above. The great tree was to be cut down, but preserved. Then it was to take on the likeness of the beasts of the field and experience the natural world from their perspective. Amazingly, the tree also took on some characteristics of a human being. This state was to continue for seven times. The meaning of this text will be developed later.

5. From what source did this order proceed and for what ultimate purpose?
Daniel 4:17 'This decision *is* by the decree of the watchers, and the sentence by the word of the holy ones, in order that the living may know that the Most High rules in the kingdom of men, gives it to whomever He will, and sets over it the lowest of men.'

Note: The watchers no doubt referred to the angels. The clear intention of this passage was to remind the king that God watches over the affairs of mankind. However, in the mind of the king it is possible that this revelation may have had a different level of significance. In the religion of the kingdom of Babylon, four watchmen were understood to be at the four corners of the earth and these were considered to regulate astral movements.

The text is also instructive in that it informs us that God controls the affairs of the nations. On account of this, the apostle Paul advised readers that they should pray for and respect those in high positions (1 Tim. 2:1, 2). He added in the book of Romans that it is the duty of believers to obey authorities (Rom. 13:1-5); that is, where their requirements do not clash with God's express will and command (Acts 5:29).

6. Who did the king turn to in his distress?
Daniel 4:7 Then the magicians, the astrologers, the Chaldeans, and the soothsayers came in, and I told them the dream; but they did not make known to me its interpretation.

Verse 18 "This dream I, King Nebuchadnezzar, have seen. Now you, Belteshazzar, declare its interpretation, since all the wise *men* of my kingdom are not able to make known to me the interpretation; but you *are* able, for the Spirit of the Holy God *is* in you."

Note: The king's first recourse was to the magicians, astrologers and Chaldeans, but he found no practical help from this source. Although the dream was apparently vivid and self-explanatory, no one could decipher it. Only those who love and fear God can understand the mysteries of the kingdom of heaven (PK 516). At last, he consulted the one person who he had previously declared was connected with the holy gods (Dan. 2:47).

7. Initially Daniel was troubled. What was the reason for his difficulty?
Daniel 4:19 Then Daniel, whose name *was* Belteshazzar, was astonished for a time, and his thoughts troubled him. *So* the king spoke, and said, "Belteshazzar, do not let the dream or its interpretation trouble you." Belteshazzar answered and said, "My lord, *may* the dream concern those who hate you, and its interpretation concern your enemies!"

Note: Daniel understood the dream but was in a difficult situation. He was embarrassed or perhaps perplexed about how he could relate the dream acceptably.

8. Who sent the message to Nebuchadnezzar?
Daniel 4:24 [Daniel said] "this is the interpretation, O king, and this is the decree of the Most High, which has come upon my lord the king."

Note: Daniel always gave clear credit to God for revealing secrets to him. This instance is no exception. Daniel's promptness to give credit to God was the secret of his wisdom. A humble person is always God's choice to send His message. Today we find that "God will move upon men in humble positions to declare the message of present truth" (7T 6).

9. What disturbing interpretation was offered?
Daniel 4:25, 26 "They shall drive you from men, your dwelling shall be with the beasts of the field, and they shall make you eat grass like oxen. They shall wet you with the dew of heaven, and seven times shall pass over you, till you know that the Most High rules in the kingdom of men, and gives it to whomever He chooses. And inasmuch as they gave the command to leave the stump *and* roots of the tree, your kingdom shall be assured to you, after you come to know that Heaven rules."

Note: The seven times are best interpreted as years. Perhaps a strong reason for suggesting that "times" in verse 25 represents years is that an Aramaic phrase rendered "at the end of that time" is used to introduce the 12 month period spoken of in verse 29 and the expression "time" in verse 34 (Doukhan (2000, 71). In these passages, the only unit of time specified is the year. Indeed, the Septuagint version of the Scriptures (oldest Greek version of the Hebrew Scriptures completed in the second century B.C.) inserts this meaning and other ancient sources agree with the idea. In one cuneiform text located in the British Museum there is tantalizing suggestions confirming Nebuchadnezzar's madness.

10. Daniel pled with the king to turn to righteousness (vs. 27), but twelve months later what happened to the king?
Daniel 4:30 The king spoke, saying, "Is not this great Babylon, that I have built for a royal dwelling by my mighty power and for the honor of my majesty?"

Note: Daniel tried to convey to the king the idea that God would change the decree if the king was willing to repent of his sins and live righteously (vs. 27). This did not happen and twelve months later in the act of boasting about his accomplishments, the prophecy was fulfilled.

It is true that the king had built extensively in Babylon and had erected lavish palaces, temples and other sections so that the size of the city had been more than doubled during his rulership. "In the intervals between his wars of conquest he gave much thought to the strengthening and beautifying of his capital, until at length the city of Babylon became the chief glory of his kingdom, 'the golden city,' 'the praise of the whole earth.' His passion as a builder, and his signal success in making Babylon one of the wonders of the world, ministered to his pride, until he was in grave danger of spoiling his record as a wise ruler whom God could continue to use as an instrument for the carrying out of the divine purpose" (PK 515). The famous hanging gardens were also his creation.

11. What did the king hear?
Daniel 4:31 While the word *was still* in the king's mouth, a voice fell from heaven: "King Nebuchadnezzar, to you it is spoken: the kingdom has departed from you!"

Note: A voice from heaven put an end to the king's proud thoughts just as had happened in the city of Babel (Gen. 11:5-7). The king had failed both to learn from the events of history and he had failed to take Daniel's advice seriously.

12. How long did it take for this sentence to be carried out?
Daniel 4:33 That very hour the word was fulfilled concerning Nebuchadnezzar; he was driven from men and ate grass like oxen; his body was wet with the dew of heaven till his hair had grown like eagles' *feathers* and his nails like birds' *claws.*

Note: Nebuchadnezzar's disgrace is not recorded in history precisely, but there is a suggestion that at some point in the king's life his existence was not meaningful to him, as indicated above. Psychiatric cases similar to that spoken of as applying to the king have been recorded elsewhere, even in recent history. Suffers are reported to imagine themselves as animals. Perhaps Nebuchadnezzar imagined himself as an ox (a condition known as boanthropy).

13. What was the turning point in Nebuchadnezzar's captivity?
Daniel 4:34 And at the end of the time I, Nebuchadnezzar, lifted my eyes to heaven, and my understanding returned to me; and I blessed the Most High and praised and honored Him who lives forever: For His dominion *is* an everlasting dominion, and His kingdom *is* from generation to generation.

Note: Even during his madness, periods of lucidity came to the king, as is reported in modern cases where people regard themselves as animals. When he "lifted his eyes to heaven" in repentance and requested help, his sanity returned to him. His immediate response was to thank God and acknowledged the nature of His greatness.

Nebuchadnezzar had just won the toughest battle of his life by surrendering his will to God (TMB 141). "Meekness and lowliness of heart are the conditions for strength and victory" (7T 747).

14. When the time specified was fulfilled, Nebucchadnezzar was restored to his kingdom. What final response did he offer?
Daniel 4:37 Now I, Nebuchadnezzar, praise and extol and honor the King of heaven, all of whose works *are* truth, and His ways justice. And those who walk in pride He is able to put down.

Note: The intent of this experience from God's viewpoint was to rescue Nebuchadnezzar from destruction and to fit him for His kingdom (cf. Luke 19:10). However unpromising an individual may seem to us, we should remember the experience of King Nebuchadnezzar and God's patience with him. As a result of his experience in the fields with the beasts, his reputation was actually enhanced for the text says "excellent majesty was added to me" (vs. 36). The king ended his prayer with praise and acknowledgment of the salvation and greatness of God and the dependence of mankind on His mercy and justice. "This public proclamation, in which Nebuchadnezzar acknowledged the mercy and goodness and authority of God, was the last act of his life recorded in sacred history" (PK 521).

9.5 Toasting Disaster

Introduction

The contrast between Daniel chapters 4 and 5 is remarkable. Nebuchadnezzar ended his testimony in chapter 4 in praise of the God of heaven. In contrast, Belshazzar despised the memory of his grandfather and had no need of God. The events recorded in chapter 5 took place some 23 years after the death of Nebuchadnezzar. His strong rule of more than forty years was followed by a succession of weak rulers. Finally, Nabonidus reigned and then he moved to the city of Tema and his eldest son Belshazzar carried out the royal duties in Babylon. Belshazzar's mother is thought to have been the daughter of Nebuchadnezzar so that he was regarded by the custom of the times as being his father (in actual fact he was his grandfather—PK 522).

On the fateful night recorded in our story, Belshazzar was feasting with his lords and desecrating the articles taken from the temple of God in Jerusalem. There seemed to be a deliberate effort on his behalf to ignore the information given to the kingdom through Nebuchadnezzar. He attempted to defy history. He had all the privileges to learn from his grandfather's experience that God's approach is preferable. These opportunities he ignored and received a pronouncement of doom from God (PK 524).

Cyrus the Persian was about to remind him of Nebuchadnezzar's dream recorded in Daniel chapter 2 when he conquered Babylon in 539 B.C. Belshazzar was enjoying a session of revelry with his lords and praising the gods of the realm when a mysterious hand began to write on the wall. Memory flooded back and he became very anxious and called for an explanation. The story of the discovery of the meaning of the mysterious writing is the subject of chapter 5. Belshazzar was to pay with his life for his frivolity and arrogance.

The Study

Read chapter 5 then the notes and Bible texts below in answer to the questions posed.

1. Belshazzar did not share Nebuchadnezzar's confidence in and praise of God. How did he demonstrate his attitude of defiance?

Daniel 5:1, 2 Belshazzar the king made a great feast for a thousand of his lords, and drank wine in the presence of the thousand. While he tasted the wine, Belshazzar gave the command to bring the gold and silver vessels which his father Nebuchadnezzar had taken from the temple which *had been* in Jerusalem, that the king and his lords, his wives, and his concubines might drink from them.

Note: Belshazzar was commemorating the victory of his grandfather over the kingdom of Judah and ultimately the triumph of the Babylonian gods over the God of Israel (cf. vs. 4). The fact that he chose to hold this feast while the armies of Medo-Persia were outside the city was an act of foolishness borne of arrogant pride and disregard for all the warnings God had given to his grandfather Nebuchadnezzar.

2. What act of sacrilege did Belshazzar commit?

Daniel 5:3, 4 Then they brought the gold vessels that had been taken from the temple of the house of God which *had been* in Jerusalem; and the king and his lords, his wives, and his concubines drank from them. They drank wine, and praised the gods of gold and silver, bronze and iron, wood and stone.

Note: The main point of his command to bring the vessels taken from the temple in Jerusalem was to praise the victory of Babylon and its gods over Jerusalem and the God of Israel. The selection of vessels of gold, silver, bronze, iron, wood and stone from the collection held indicates that the king was deliberately rejecting the idea that Babylon would be replaced by kingdoms of silver, bronze, iron, iron and clay and stone. This represents in microcosm the Great Controversy through the ages and is a theme that will be expanded later in Daniel's book and especially in Revelation.

Belshazzar's judgment was further numbed by drinking. Princes and statesmen drank wine like water and took delight under its maddening influence (PK 523). Alcohol, even in the name of social drinking destroys reason. In fact, "Moderate drinking is the school in which men are receiving an education for the drunkard's career" (5T 357). Such an act of sacrilege might be expected to be ignored by God, if we look at the acts of sacrilege occurring in the world around us. However, this act of defiance was answered directly by God.

3. What ghostly event happened to remind the king of his irreverent act?
Daniel 5:5 In the same hour the fingers of a man's hand appeared and wrote opposite the lampstand on the plaster of the wall of the king's palace; and the king saw the part of the hand that wrote.

Note: The unnerving sight of the fingers of a hand writing deliberately on a wall would not be something to inspire confidence in anyone. The king grew pale and his knees shook and in fact he could not stand properly (vs. 6). He cried to his helpers for assistance (vs. 7). His confidence and arrogance were destroyed in a moment by the vision.

4. The king called for the usual group of astrologers, Chaldeans and soothsayers. What did they tell him about the writing?
Daniel 5:8 Now all the king's wise *men* came, but they could not read the writing, or make known to the king its interpretation.

Note: Evidently the hand disappeared yet the writing remained. Those given to revealing mysteries were powerless and the next verse reminds us that this had the effect of making the king "greatly troubled." Meanwhile the astrologers were perplexed (vs. 8). No doubt the king was beginning to remember more clearly the stories about his grandfather and his difficulties with the astrologers.

5. Who reminded the king of the skills of the aged Daniel?
Daniel 5:10, 11 The queen, because of the words of the king and his lords, came to the banquet hall. The queen spoke, saying, "O king, live forever! Do not let your thoughts trouble you, nor let your countenance change. There is a man in your kingdom in whom *is* the Spirit of the Holy God. And in the days of your father, light and understanding and wisdom, like the wisdom of the gods, were found in him; and King Nebuchadnezzar your father—your father the king—made him chief of the magicians, astrologers, Chaldeans, *and* soothsayers.

Note: An analysis of the background data has led scholars to conclude that the queen referred to here was the king's mother (cf. PK 527). This is conceivable as the ability of this lady to come to the banquet hall unannounced was permissible for the king's mother, but was not an acceptable practice even for his wife (cf. Esth. 4:11, 16). The king's mother came suddenly to the banquet hall. She had no hesitation in reminding the king of Nebuchadnezzar's chief advisor, Daniel, and the "Holy God" he served (vs. 11). She went on to recommend that since Daniel had remarkable skill that he be called to interpret the writing (vs. 12). Before the assembled nobles and on account of the inability of the astrologers to help, the king did not have much option but to ask Daniel to come. Evidently, Daniel had been removed from his post as chief adviser.

6. After some preliminary comments, what request did the king make of Daniel and what reward did he offer?
Daniel 5:15, 16 "Now the wise *men,* the astrologers, have been brought in before me, that they should read this writing and make known to me its interpretation, but they could not give the interpretation of the thing. And I have heard of you, that you can give interpretations and explain enigmas. Now if you can read the writing and make known to me its interpretation, you shall be clothed with purple and *have* a chain of gold around your neck, and shall be the third ruler in the kingdom."

Note: Belshazzar welcomed Daniel by asking whether he was indeed the captive brought from Judah by Nebuchadnezzar and offered the suggestion that he had heard of his understanding and wisdom under the blessing of God (vss. 13-–16). This was not an overly warm welcome for he deliberately reminded Daniel that he was an alien by using his Jewish name and by emphasizing the fact that he was brought to Babylon as a captive. It has been noted by some that the king omitted the use of the term "holy" used by the queen (vs. 11) in referring to the origin of Daniel's reported unusual skills (vs. 14). The king had been put in a hard place by the sudden arrival of the aged queen in response to receiving word of the handwriting on the wall (vs. 10). One might imagine that he was almost sarcastic or acted in an aloof fashion in response to this embarrassment.

7. How did Daniel commence his explanation of the writing?
Daniel 5:17 Then Daniel answered, and said before the king, "Let your gifts be for yourself, and give your rewards to another; yet I will read the writing to the king, and make known to him the interpretation."

Note: The world generally appreciates people who have moral backbone, an integrity that cannot be flattered, bribed, or terrified (5T 297). Daniel was one of these individuals. He did not commence with pleasantries. He commenced his speech by reminding the king that he was not interested in his promised gifts. Then he launched into a reprimand in the following verses.

Daniel was an individual who worked according to principle, as described by one author. "The greatest want of this age is the want of men,—men who will not be bought or sold; men who are true and honest in their inmost souls; men who will not fear to call sin by its right name, and to condemn it, in themselves or in others; men whose conscience is as true to duty as the needle to the pole; men who will stand for the right, though the heavens fall" (ST May 4, 1882).

8. What main point did Daniel draw from the experiences of Nebuchadnezzar and what lesson did he indicate Belshazzar might have gained from these stories?
Daniel 5:18 "O king, the Most High God gave Nebuchadnezzar your father a kingdom and majesty, glory and honor."

Verse 22 "But you his son, Belshazzar, have not humbled your heart, although you knew all this."

Note: The main points raised in Daniel introductory remarks (vss. 18-24) are as follows: God controls the nations, He gives rulers abilities to conquer, manage, nourish and judge as long as there is some sentiment of responsiveness to the idea that there is a higher power and that the talents possessed have been given.

The ascendancy of pride over reason leads to disaster. Belshazzar was reminded that Nebuchadnezzar's experience was there for him to profit and build upon, but he had refused to be instructed. "God does not send judgments upon His people [or on others] without first warning them to repent. He uses every means to bring them back to obedience and does not visit their iniquity with judgments until He has given them ample opportunity to repent" (4T 179).

9. What particular sins did Daniel slate to Belshazzar's account?
Daniel 5:23 "And you have lifted yourself up against the Lord of heaven. They have brought the vessels of His house before you, and you and your lords, your wives and your concubines, have drunk wine from them. And you have praised the gods of silver and gold, bronze and iron, wood and stone, which do not see or hear or know; and the God who *holds* your breath in His hand and owns all your ways, you have not glorified."

Note: Daniel penetrated the purpose of the king and reminded him that he had failed not only to profit through the experiences of Nebuchadnezzar but had deliberately set himself against the God of heaven by claiming the greatness of Babylon was due to the gods of the realm. The God who held his life in the balances was unrecognized and not honoured. His forgetfulness through pride was about to be rewarded. He was to be judged for his ill advised actions. This carries a message of warning to all to the end of time (MS 13, 1895).

10. Who did Daniel identify as the source of the writing and what did it say?
Daniel 5:24, 25 "Then the fingers of the hand were sent from Him, and this writing was written. And this is the inscription that was written: MENE, MENE, TEKEL, UPHARSIN."

Note: It is thought by some that the writing, which was in Aramaic, may have been written without a space between the words, making the task of reading difficult. However, the still more difficult task was to decipher the meaning of the words.

11. What was the meaning of the words?
Daniel 5:26-28 "And this is the inscription that was written: MENE, MENE, TEKEL, UPHARSIN. This is the interpretation of each word. MENE: God has numbered your kingdom, and finished it; TEKEL: You have been weighed in the balances, and found wanting; PERES: Your kingdom has been divided, and given to the Medes and Persians."

Note: The plain meaning of the words has been suggested as follows: Mene—literally *a mina* (50 shekels) from the verb "to number." Tekel—literally *a shekel* from the verb "to weigh." Upharsin—literally *and half-shekels* from the verb "to divide." God had numbered and weighed (judged Belshazzar) and his probation and that of Babylon was about to close.

Belshazzar's initial terror at the writing on the wall was fully justified as its meaning was made known. God is the judge of the earth. He has known us from the moment of our conception; He has created us all for a purpose and knows our thoughts and actions. We cannot hide from His presence (Ps. 139:1-24).

12. What reward did Daniel receive?
Daniel 5:29 Then Belshazzar gave the command, and they clothed Daniel with purple and *put* a chain of gold around his neck, and made a proclamation concerning him that he should be the third ruler in the kingdom.

Note: Daniel was not interested in the reward offered but received it anyhow (cf. verse 17). He knew that the Babylonian kingdom would end that night and that any favours promised would be fleeting. God honoured Daniel in the presence of the lords and nobles by giving him understanding (Dan. 5:26-29).

13. What reward did Belshazzar receive?

Daniel 5: 30 That very night Belshazzar, king of the Chaldeans, was slain.

Note: Within a short time of the honours being showered on Daniel, Belshazzar was dead. History records that the "impious king" was slain immediately (Rollin 1836, 129-131). On the other hand, Nabonidus, his father, surrendered some time later and his life was spared. The armies of Cyrus had approached the city and entered by way of the river Euphrates. The seemingly impregnable city had been taken by stealth for Cyrus had diverted the waters of the river thereby lowering the water level and allowing his troops to enter the city through the stream bed that flowed through it. When they came to the gates leading down to the river, they were open just as prophecy had foretold (Isa. 45:1). They quickly entered and subdued the defenders.

Darius the Mede reigned in Babylon as governor for a little over a year. He is thought by some to have been "Gobryas of Xenophon" who became "Satrap of Babylonia" (Burn 1984, 55, 56). Cyrus, the founder of the Persian Empire, entered the city three days after its fall. This was in 539 B.C. He retained its splendour and added to its grandeur and security.

The fall of the kingdom of Babylon anciently speaks to the ultimate fall of the spiritual Babylon written about in Revelation (Rev. 18:21). We will deal with this subject at a later point in our studies.

9.6 Prayer Brings Trouble

Introduction

Daniel had just survived the overthrow of the Babylonian Empire. On the night of Belshazzar's extravagant feast recorded in chapter 5, Darius the Mede and his companions stormed the city of Babylon through way of the river; the king of Babylon was killed. Now in chapter 6, we find him setting up his government and establishing the rule of law.

Perhaps surprisingly Daniel was given a place of honour and soon was proposed as the first president. This act led to a plot being devised among the other presidents and princes to dispose of Daniel. They thought of a clever plan that on the surface promised to honour the new king. He fell for the scheme in which worship could be performed only by the king for the next thirty days on pain of death. Daniel who was accustomed to regular worship continued this practice and in consequence was sentenced to death by mauling from lions. Miraculously, he was delivered by God in answer to his prayers of faith. As a result, Darius praised God as did Nebuchadnezzar before him.

Chapter 6 is a thrilling story of this desperate encounter and how the conspirators were punished. It also represents the end of the first section of the book of Daniel. The remainder of the book is concerned, not with current events in the lives of people, but with distant and dramatic events.

The Study

Read chapter 6 then the notes and Bible texts below in answer to the questions posed.

1. Daniel had been brought briefly from retirement by Belshazzar on his last evening as ruler of Babylon. When Darius took over the reins of government, who did he appoint to an important post?
Daniel 6:2 And over these [120 satraps Darius set], three governors, of whom Daniel *was* one, that the satraps might give account to them, so that the king would suffer no loss.

Note: Daniel was perhaps chosen in the first instance as a governor because he had just been appointed the third ruler of the kingdom of Babylon (Dan. 5:29) and he was thoroughly familiar with the province through serving for over 70 years. An additional reason suggested is that he was an alien and hence less prone to be engaged in national political arguments and sensitivities.

2. What qualities were observed in Daniel that led to his proposed elevation to the position of first president of the kingdom?
Daniel 6:3 Then this Daniel distinguished himself above the governors and satraps, because an excellent spirit *was* in him; and the king gave thought to setting him over the whole realm.

Note: Daniel's exceptional personal characteristics convinced Darius to consider him as the leader of his administrative team.

3. Jealousy soon arose among the top administrators and whom did they seek to displace from office?
Daniel 6:4 So the governors and satraps sought to find *some* charge against Daniel concerning the kingdom; but they could find no charge or fault, because he *was* faithful; nor was there any error or fault found in him.

Note: No doubt many of these governors and satraps would have been familiar with Daniel's reputation over the past decades. The coolness with which he was received by Belshazzar on the night of the kingdom's fall was perhaps reflected in the attitude of these leaders too. They well knew that he was a former captive, displayed strange behaviours and beliefs and that through his skills he could expose the shortcomings of others.

4. What offense did the top administrators find in Daniel and in what area of activity did they seek to find fault?

Daniel 6:5 Then these men said, "We shall not find any charge against this Daniel unless we find *it* against him concerning the law of his God."

Note: The majority leaders of the administrative team selected had no time for Daniel and his righteous principles and planned his downfall on account of his religious practices. His attention to principle offended and inhibited their scope of activities.

5. The presidents and princes laid a plot (chapter 6:6) and approached Darius with a proposal hoping to convince him they wished to honour the king. What was the nature of the request made to the king?

Daniel 6:7 "All the governors of the kingdom, the administrators and satraps, the counsellors and advisors, have consulted together to establish a royal statute and to make a firm decree, that whoever petitions any god or man for thirty days, except you, O king, shall be cast into the den of lions."

Note: The scheme laid by the conspirators was ostensibly to honour the king. This was perhaps to elevate him to a position above the people to rival the importance of a god. The practice was not unknown around this time. We note at this point that intolerance is the mark of a false religion. The governors of the Medo-Persian Empire showed their prejudices by their proposed actions under the cloak of royal devotion.

6. What was Darius' reaction to the proposal made by his leading officials? What did Daniel's do when he learnt that worship to any god was forbidden for 30 days?

Daniel 6:9, 10 Therefore King Darius signed the written decree. Now when Daniel knew that the writing was signed, he went home. And in his upper room, with his windows open toward Jerusalem, he knelt down on his knees three times that day, and prayed and gave thanks before his God, as was his custom since early days.

Note: The king was evidently flattered by the prospect of the decree and signed it into law.
Daniel soon became aware of the decree, but it did not interfere with his prayer habits. The practice of making intercession three times a day was common in Jewish circles (at the 3, 6 and 9th hours) and the suppliants faced Jerusalem on their knees. The first and last prayer sessions corresponded with the evening and morning sacrifices (1 Chron. 23:30, 31). Since the times when Daniel was likely to pray were probably well known, there was no difficulty in observing his now illegal behaviour. Daniel would not stop praying because he knew that prayer was the breath of his soul (Mar, 85). Daniel's prayer consisted of thanks (vs. 10) and requests (vs. 11) to God. He perfectly understood the essence of true prayer. "Prayer is the opening of the heart to God as to a friend. Not that it is necessary in order to make known to God what we are, but in order to enable us to receive Him. Prayer does not bring God down to us, but brings us up to Him" (SC 93).

7. The presidents and princes harboured a grudge against Daniel. What was the nature of their complaint to the king against him?
Daniel 6:13 So they answered and said before the king, "That Daniel, who is one of the captives from Judah, does not show due regard for you, O king, or for the decree that you have signed, but makes his petition three times a day."

Note: The conspirators show their prejudice against Daniel by their remarks concerning his foreign origin and religion and they couched their comments in terms of Daniel's supposed disrespect for the king.

Now consider that Daniel might have prayed three times a day at other than his usual place and might have prayed standing (cf. 1 Sam. 1:26). However, he decided that he would not change his practices on principle. He would witness for religious freedom and as an expression of his utmost faith in God. His example is a challenge to all to set aside a place and time for regular prayer in times of peace as well as times of difficulty. We understand "That prayer which comes forth from an earnest, believing heart is the effectual, fervent prayer that availeth [accomplishes] much" (4T 531).

8. How did the king react to the realization that he had been deceived and what did he finally do?
Daniel 6:14 And the king, when he heard *these* words, was greatly displeased with himself, and set *his* heart on Daniel to deliver him; and he labored till the going down of the sun to deliver him.

Verse 16 So the king gave the command, and they brought Daniel and cast *him* into the den of lions. *But* the king spoke, saying to Daniel, "Your God, whom you serve continually, He will deliver you."

Note: The king had been duped and was very angry that his vanity had been appealed to the detriment of his beloved governor. The law of the Medes and Persians apparently could not be changed (vss. 12, 15). The king valiantly tried to find a legal loophole but could not. He had no alternative but to carry out the decree. Daniel was delivered to die (vs. 16).

9. How secure was the lion's den made against any rescue attempt?
Daniel 6:17 Then a stone was brought and laid on the mouth of the den, and the king sealed it with his own signet ring and with the signets of his lords, that the purpose concerning Daniel might not be changed.

Note: The den was made secure with a stone and with the king's seal so that none of the lords might kill Daniel secretly or the king and his agents release him. The king's parting words to Daniel were: "Your God, who you serve continually, He will deliver you" (vs. 16).

10. How did the king spend the night and how anxious was he to find out whether Daniel had survived the experience?
Daniel 6:18, 19 Now the king went to his palace and spent the night fasting; and no musicians were brought before him. Also his sleep went from him. Then the king arose very early in the morning and went in haste to the den of lions.

Note: The king had developed a genuine affection and concern for Daniel. His fast and night vigil speaks to the gentler side of his nature and to his religious leanings (cf. Dan. 10:3). The king was at the den very early in the morning hoping that Daniel had been delivered.

11. What outcome was evident in the morning? Was a similar outcome experienced by the conspirators?
Daniel 6:21, 22 Then Daniel said to the king, "O king, live forever! My God sent His angel and shut the lions' mouths, so that they have not hurt me, because I was found innocent before Him; and also, O king, I have done no wrong before you."

Verse 24 And the king gave the command, and they brought those men who had accused Daniel, and they cast *them* into the den of lions—them, their children, and their wives; and the lions overpowered them, and broke all their bones in pieces before they ever came to the bottom of the den.

Note: Daniel gave immediate praise to God for His mercy and deliverance through the ministry of His angel. Deliverance comes from God in answer to the prayer of faith of the righteous. Ellen White has advised, "You must pray as though the efficiency and praise were all due to God, and labor as though duty were all your own" (4T 538).

The manner in which the lions dispatched with the conspirators removed all doubt about the genuineness of the miracle.

12. How did Darius honour God?
Daniel 6:25-28 Then King Darius wrote: To all peoples, nations, and languages that dwell in all the earth: peace be multiplied to you. I make a decree that in every dominion of my kingdom *men must* tremble and fear before the God of Daniel. For He *is* the living God, and steadfast forever; His kingdom *is the one* which shall not be destroyed, and His dominion *shall endure* to the end. He delivers and rescues, and He works signs and wonders in heaven and on earth, Who has delivered Daniel from the power of the lions. So this Daniel prospered in the reign of Darius and in the reign of Cyrus the Persian.

Note: Darius responded to this dramatic example of God's deliverance by calling the attention of all people throughout the realm to show awe and respect to the Almighty, the "living God" of Daniel who saves and does not change. Darius then continued his decree and in essence acknowledged the reality of the vision of Daniel 2 and the fact that God will establish an enduring kingdom. He gave assurance to his subjects that signs and wonders may be evident in both the heavens and the earth and testify to the existence of Almighty God; miracles after the kind observed are divine in origin and sometimes are shown in the lives of those who pray to and exercise faith in God.

13. What role did faith play in Daniel's escape from death?
Hebrews 11:33, 40 [All the examples of heroes given] who through faith subdued kingdoms, worked righteousness, obtained promises, stopped the mouths of lions . . . should not be made perfect [rewarded] apart from us.

Note: The experience of Daniel is alluded to in the above verses by the apostle Paul. Daniel had indeed escaped death through the power of faith in the living God. In the story of Daniel found in chapter 6 there are parallels with the story of Jesus sentence to death by those jealous of His righteous deeds and character. He arose victorious and broke the seals of the Roman governor. Jesus is the world's only hope and we may grasp the reality through faith. It may take a while but eventually God's people will overcome false accusations. "Truth is stronger than error. Righteousness will prevail over wrong" (3T 572).

14. How long did Daniel's prosperity last?
Daniel 6:28 So this Daniel prospered in the reign of Darius and in the reign of Cyrus the Persian.

Note: Daniel's deliverance and the mention of Darius (he began to reign in the autumn of 538 B.C.) introduces the thought that God was about to deliver the Jews from their Babylonian captivity. The time had almost come for Jeremiah's prophecy to be fulfilled when the exiles would return to Jerusalem (Jer. 29:10). In similar vein the children of God near the end of earth's history will be delivered from death and ushered into God's eternal kingdom, the New Jerusalem. Indeed, the promise was later given to Daniel that he would be given an honoured place in that kingdom (Dan. 12:13).

9.7 Wild Beasts Parade as Nations

Introduction

In the second half of the book Daniel takes us back in time to Belshazzar's reign. Indeed this vision took place in the first year of the king or about 550 B.C. and already Daniel could see the possible successor of Babylon arising in the person of Cyrus who had just been victorious over the king of the Medes. Daniel was living some fifty years after the great vision of Daniel, chapter 2. He immediately would have recognized that the vision he was now receiving had some links to this information, but the fresh vision introduced new and disturbing elements.

In this pivotal chapter 7 the idea of a judgment day is highlighted. This topic will be further expanded in chapters 8 and 9 and in the book of Revelation.

The Study

Read chapter 7 then the notes and Bible texts below in answer to the questions posed.

1. What were the main features that Daniel saw in his vision?

Daniel 7:2, 3 Daniel spoke, saying, "I saw in my vision by night, and behold, the four winds of heaven were stirring up the Great Sea. And four great beasts came up from the sea, each different from the other."

Note: The vision was cast in language that made it evident that what was about to happen would impact a wide segment of the world. Indeed, the four winds of heaven were involved, which conveyed the idea that no section of the world would be unaffected by the powers identified. Their deeds, philosophies and inventions would become known to and influence the nations of the world. The beasts in Daniel's vision represented human kingdoms that would rule the world with physical power. In contrast, Christ will abolish all coercive human kingdoms and establish His kingdom of love to uplift fallen humanity (4BC 1171).

2. What were the main characteristics associated with the beasts Daniel observed and how do these contrast with those he saw previously in chapter 2?

Daniel 2		Daniel 7	
Symbol	Kingdom	Symbol	Kingdom
Gold head (vss. 37, 38)	Babylon	Lion (vs. 4)	First king
Silver chest (vs. 39)	Second kingdom	Bear (vs. 5)	Second king
Bronze thighs (vs. 39)	Third kingdom	Leopard (vs. 6)	Third king
Iron legs (vs. 40)	Fourth kingdom	Fourth beast (vss. 7, 19, 23)	Fourth king
Iron and clay feet (ten toes) (vss. 41–43)	Divided kingdoms	Ten horns among which arose a little horn (vss. 7, 8, 20, 24)	Ten kings and another (little horn) arising after them
Stone (vss. 34, 44, 45	God's eternal kingdom	Final everlasting kingdom (vss. 19, 27)	Most High's kingdom

Table 1. Some characteristics associated with the powers (beasts) described in Daniel chapters 2 and 7.

Note: The characteristics associated with the powers described are summarized in Table 1. It should have been immediately evident to Daniel that the lion-like beast represented Babylon. The winged lion was emblazoned on the glazed tiles of the city, there was a stone statue of a lion in the palace courtyard, and the prophet Jeremiah had used this symbol to represent the kingdom (Jer. 49:19, 22). The winged lion suffered the indignity of having its wings removed and made docile like a man (vs. 4). This imagery reminds the reader about the vision of the tree and of Nebuchadnezzar's madness.

The identity of the second and third kingdom was to be given by the angel later (Dan. 8:20, 21). Suffice it to say here that they are identified as Medo-Persia and Greece. The kingdom of the Medes and Persians was represented by the bear, which had a cruel nature (cf. 2 Sam. 17:8; Prov. 28:15). The raising of the animal on one side (vs. 5) can be considered to represent both its readiness to fight and the unequal nature of the partnership between the two groups with the Persians ultimately attaining ascendency. Its ability to "devour much flesh" represented by three ribs in its mouth draws attention to the kingdoms it would destroy in its rise to greatness, namely Lydia, Babylon and Egypt.

The kingdom of the Greeks is represented by the leopard-like beast. This identification is made clear in the following chapter (Dan. 8:20). It had four heads and four wings (vs. 6). The possession of wings conveyed the thought of speed in conquest (cf. Hab. 1:8) and the number four pointed to the widespread nature of its influence. Indeed, even today Greek thought is still widespread in the Western world. The four heads also can be understood to indicate that when the first king (Alexander) died, four leading generals would divide the kingdom among themselves. However, the dominance of the Greek Empire did not continue.

We do not need to know a great deal of history to understand that the fourth kingdom was the iron kingdom of Rome. Following a long and brilliant history spanning vast areas, this power finally was weakened and the Western Empire disintegrated into the kingdoms of Europe. From the embers of the Western Empire arose the prominent little horn or papal power (we will address this phenomenon in later questions and lessons).

3. What did the messenger from heaven say the beasts represented?
Daniel 7: 16, 17 "I [Daniel] came near to one of those who stood by, and asked him the truth of all this. So he told me and made known to me the interpretation of these things: 'Those great beasts, which are four, *are* four kings *which* arise out of the earth.'"

Note: The angel gave Daniel to understand that he was seeing in vision four successive kingdoms represented by their prominent kings. No doubt Daniel immediately remembered his vision recorded in chapter 2 that gave details of the kingdoms that would arise after Babylon and exert widespread influences on the prosperity of God's kingdom on earth. This accounts for his particularly interest in the identity and activities of the fourth beast (vs. 19) in contrast to the others.

4. The fourth beast was unusual and possessed horns. What interpretation does the Bible say is to be given to this symbol?
Daniel 7:7 "After this I saw in the night visions, and behold, a fourth beast, dreadful and terrible, exceedingly strong. It had huge iron teeth; it was devouring, breaking in pieces, and trampling the residue with its feet. It *was* different from all the beasts that *were* before it, and it had ten horns."

Verse 24 first part "Thus he [the angel] said: 'The ten horns *are* ten kings w*ho* shall arise from this kingdom.'"

Note: The fourth terrible kingdom is not identified in the book of Daniel. Having identified the three kingdoms before it, there is really no difficulty in retrospect in identifying this kingdom as the iron kingdom of Rome. It remained dominant from 168 B.C. until over four centuries into the Christian era. This constitutes a remarkable record. The historian Gibbon (chapter 38) described it as the "iron monarchy of Rome." Eventually, it fell into decay and from the embers of the Western Empire a number of nations arose and some still continue as the nations of modern Europe. The exact identity of these nations is not the significant issue and it is not a valuable pastime to argue on this point.

5. The ten horns that owed their origin to the fourth beast or nation gave rise to a little horn that was to achieve great prominence. This power arose after the ten kingdoms coming from the disintegration of the great fourth world kingdom. What destructive activities were associated with the little horn's birth?

Daniel 7: 24 [The angel continued to say to Daniel] 'The ten horns *are* ten kings w*ho* shall arise from this kingdom. And another shall rise after them; he shall be different from the first *ones,* and shall subdue three kings.'

Note: The little horn was to be different in that it was to be established around the representation of a man with prominent eyes and mouth (vs. 8). It arose after the disintegration of the Western Roman Empire. It is primarily represented as a religious power (papal). This becomes evident in the next chapter where it challenges God (Dan. 8:9-11). It would enforce its mandates through political connections. However, in order to gain prominence it first needed to displace three existing kingdoms.

History records that in order to make the old seat of the Roman Empire in Rome, Italy, secure three powers needed to be destroyed or displaced (Heruli—A.D. 493, Vandals—A.D. 534 and Ostrogoths—A.D. 538). These powers were antagonistic to the church's spiritual aims (they held Arian beliefs). All these Christian powers held to a variant form of belief in the divinity of Christ (the Arians believed that Christ was a created being) and this was opposed by the church. When the last Arian power was expelled from the city of Rome, the papacy had greater ability to grow in strength and to become a dominating power. The period of prophetic time spoken about in the next verse commenced in A.D. 538, the year the Ostrogoths were displaced from the city of Rome.

6. The little horn power turned out to be a persecuting power. How long would it continue these activities?

Daniel 7:25 [The angel continued to say to Daniel] 'He shall speak *pompous* words against the Most High, shall persecute the saints of the Most High, and shall intend to change times and law. Then *the saints* shall be given into his hand for a time and times and half a time.'

Note: The little horn power is identified as a persecuting power that would continue for a period of time. We understand that this power was to exercise its persecuting activities in the area of religious thought for it spoke "pompous words against the Most High"; to these activities the saints objected. The spirit energizing ancient Babylon to resist God, spoken about in Daniel chapter 3, re-emerged in this power. Its pride even extended to attempts to alter the words of God expressed in His law.

The prophetic period spoken about in terms of "a time and times and half a time," or 1260 years, commenced in A.D. 538 and ended in 1798 when the pope was taken captive in the Vatican by General Berthier of Napoleon's army. In A.D. 538 a previous decree made by Emperor Justinian (ruling out of Constantinople) became effective. This decree made the pope the head of the churches. At the end of the time period indicated, the papacy indeed received a deadly wound (1798), but its power was to be restored, as we will learn in the book of Revelation.

7. What is the basis for understanding the time symbolism used as years?
Ezekiel 4:4-6 "Lie also on your left side, and lay the iniquity of the house of Israel upon it. *According* to the number of the days that you lie on it, you shall bear their iniquity. For I have laid on you the years of their iniquity, according to the number of the days, three hundred and ninety days; so you shall bear the iniquity of the house of Israel. And when you have completed them, lie again on your right side; then you shall bear the iniquity of the house of Judah forty days. I have laid on you a day for each year.

Numbers 14:34 [The Lord said] "'According to the number of the days in which you spied out the land, forty days, for each day you shall bear your guilt one year, *namely* forty years, and you shall know My rejection.'"

Note: The year-day principle has been recognized by scholars for many years—from the third century A.D. in fact. The above examples illustrate the application of this principle in two circumstances involving the children of Israel. Importantly, Ezekiel was a contemporary of the prophet Daniel. Since the prophecies encountered in the book of Daniel stretch to the end of time, the time periods noted are given in symbolic language.

8. Is there any other evidence found in Scripture that might confirm the interpretation offered for the time element given in Daniel chapter 7, verse 25 (refer to Question 6)?
Revelation 12:14 But the woman was given two wings of a great eagle, that she might fly into the wilderness to her place, where she is nourished for a time and times and half a time, from the presence of the serpent.

Verse 6 Then the woman fled into the wilderness, where she has a place prepared by God, that they should feed her there one thousand two hundred and sixty days.

Note: "Times" is calculated to represent a minimum of two days and "time" as one day. This means that the total period represented is 720+360+180 or 1260 days. This understanding has been held for many centuries by Bible scholars. This is confirmed in verse 6 where it is noted that the same time period is spoken about as 1260 days. The 1260 days are also referred to as 42 months (42×30=1260; Rev. 11:2, 3). In practical terms, a prophetic day is equated with a literal solar year of 365 days. This means that a symbolic day in prophecy is taken as a literal year. The events spoken of in the book of Daniel are taken up in the book of Revelation in a more systematic manner. It is primarily there that the following information is provided relating to the same persecuting power (Table 2).

Time description used	Reference
A time times and half a time	Dan. 7:25; 12:7; Rev. 12:14
Twelve hundred and sixty days (prophetic days or literal years)	Rev. 11:3; 12:6
Forty two months	Rev. 11:2; 13:5

Table 2. Expressions used in the books of Daniel and Revelation to refer to the 1260 years of special difficulty for God's church.

The prophecy spoken about in Daniel 7 (vss. 24, 25) and in Revelation 12 (vss. 6, 14) commenced in A.D. 538, which is the year when the city of Rome was freed from the rule of the Ostrogoths. It was then that the decree issued by Justinian in A.D. 533 conferring great authority on the Church at Rome could go into full effect. In this decree he made the pope head of all the churches.

9. Why is the judgment scene placed in the middle of Daniel's vision? What are the main ideas that can be learnt from this account?
Daniel 7:9, 10, 13, 14—Read.

Notes: In verses 9 and 10 the reader is asked to consider that the heavenly judgment scene involves the "Ancient of Days" or God the Father. The court scene described is both grand and orderly and many heavenly beings are seen in attendance. Books of record are brought to the court scene. Indeed, "There is an unerring register kept of all sins committed. All man's impiety, all his disobedience to Heaven's commands, is written in the books of heaven with unerring accuracy. The figures of guilt rapidly accumulate, yet the judgments of God are tempered with mercy, until the figures have reached their appointed limit" (MS 17, 1906).

In verse 13 the reader's attention is drawn to the fact the Son of Man or Christ is involved in the judgment (cf. Matt. 26:64). He stands in place of His people, for He has earned the right to represent them (John 5:27). In verse 14, at the end of the court proceedings, authority is given to Christ to establish His eternal kingdom.

The idea that God will judge recurs throughout Daniel. This is indeed appropriate for Daniel's name means "my judge [is] God." We first noticed the judgment in chapter 1 (vs. 2). In chapter 7, the judgment scene indicates that the court will declare its findings before God's eternal kingdom is established (cf. vss. 26, 27). It will be impartial but will vindicate those who support God's principles and rule against those who promote ideas of human devising.

10. What categories of activities did/does the little horn participate in and what warnings has God given us about such involvements?
Activities:

1. Speaks pompous word against God (vss. 8, 20, 25).
2. Attempts changes to God's nominated times and laws (vs. 25).
3. Persecution (vss. 21, 25).

Warnings:

1. "You shall not take the name of the LORD your God in vain, for the LORD will not hold *him* guiltless who takes His name in vain" (Exod. 20:7).
2. God alone is empowered to change times (Dan. 2:21; cf. Exod. 20:8-11).
3. Those who use the sword of persecution will perish violently (Matt. 26:52).

Note 1: Speaking words against God can now be practiced with seeming impunity, but a day of reckoning is coming. Those who change God's ordinances and place the traditions of men (Mark 7:9, 13; Rev. 22:18) in their place are setting themselves up for the destroying fires of God's wrath. Daniel 7, verse 25, implies that Satan, using human agents, will try to turn the signpost contained in the law of God around (by changing it) so that it leads on a path to destruction. The law of God was given to lead hearers to the path of happiness though obedience (RH April 17, 1900).

We are assured in Daniel 7, verse 26, that those who have persecuted the true followers of Christ will be given their just rewards in the following words uttered by an angel: "'But the court shall be seated, and they shall take away his dominion, to consume and destroy *it* forever.'"

Note 2: The idea that any power can speak pompous words against God with impunity is dispelled by the judgment scene. A "fiery stream issued" from the presence of God (vs. 10) conveying the idea that He will avenge His reputation (Ps. 18:9-14; 97:3). Books of record are held (vs. 10), from which unambiguous proof may be gained of all the deeds of the children of men. God will remember and reward appropriately. At the end of the judgment, Jesus is shown coming in grandeur to establish His eternal kingdom of glory (vss. 13, 14). The location of this scene in the middle of the book is fitting for judgment is one of the principle messages of the book.

11. How will the saints finally be rewarded after withstanding the little horn power?
Daniel 7:22 [Daniel looked in vision] "Until the Ancient of Days came, and a judgment was made *in favor* of the saints of the Most High, and the time came for the saints to possess the kingdom."

Verse 27 'Then the kingdom and dominion, and the greatness of the kingdoms under the whole heaven, shall be given to the people, the saints of the Most High. His kingdom *is* an everlasting kingdom, and all dominions shall serve and obey Him.'

Note: The good news is that despite appearances, those standing firm for God's principles will receive an eternal reward. The judgment is made in favour of the saints (cf. Rom. 8:15-17), for God is love. We will visit the judgment scene again in Revelation chapter 14 where we will discover the important issues that will feature in this event.

12. How did Daniel react to the vision?
Daniel 7:28 "This *is* the end of the account. As for me, Daniel, my thoughts greatly troubled me, and my countenance changed; but I kept the matter in my heart."

Note: The history revealed to Daniel showed peoples and systems rebelling against God. This rebelling spirit will continue but finally God will set up His kingdom after judging the nations. The activities of the little horn power and its dominance troubled the prophet, but Daniel would have to wait for some time before enlightenment came.

9.8 King of Universe Judges Nations

Introduction

The vision recorded in Daniel chapter 8 was set in the third year of the reign of king Belshazzar of Babylon. Thus it occurred two years after the previous one (551 B.C.). The vision commenced with a picture of two animals fighting vigorously. These were identified in the vision as Medo-Persia and Greece. Babylon was no longer mentioned as the chapter focussed more particularly on the emergence of the little horn power, its activities, and the scope and duration of its dominion.

Daniel was discomfited by the vision recorded in chapter 8 just as he was by the revelations about this power recorded in the previous chapter (cf. Dan. 7:28 and 8:27).

The Study

Read chapter 8 then the notes and Bible texts below in answer to the questions posed.

1. Again Daniel observed animals in conflict but this time a ram and a goat were seen. In the struggle between these animals which one prevailed?
Daniel 8:6 Then he [the goat] came to the ram that had two horns, which I had seen standing beside the river, and ran at him with furious power.

Note: The vision described here began in verse 3 where the prophet observed a ram with two horns pushing westward, northward and southward and becoming great (vs. 4). Soon this power was to meet a rival—a goat power. This power possessed a significant horn, it came from the west and proceeded with lightning speed (vs. 5) and confronted the ram.

2. The male goat became powerful, but its single large horn was broken. What appeared in its place?
Daniel 8:8 Therefore the male goat grew very great; but when he became strong, the large horn was broken, and in place of it four notable ones came up toward the four winds of heaven.

Note: The goat power moved with rage against the ram and led to its disappearance (vs. 7). The goat power then became "very great." This contrasted with the lesser greatness of the nation it displaced. However, just after the goat had attained its great power, its notable horn was broken and four new ones grew as replacements.

3. Suddenly Daniel saw something spectacular. A little horn power appeared in vision from one of the four horns sprouted by the goat. In contrast to the other powers, how great was the little horn to become?
Daniel 8:9 And out of one of them came a little horn which grew exceedingly great toward the south, toward the east, and toward the Glorious *Land.*

Note: This power was to become "exceedingly great." Naturally, Daniel's interest was focused on this last horn, for it was to have the greatest influence on the affairs of the nations.

4. Did Daniel understand the meaning of any of the symbols he saw?
Daniel 8:15, 16 Then it happened, when I, Daniel, had seen the vision and was seeking the meaning, that suddenly there stood before me one having the appearance of a man. And I heard a man's voice between *the banks of* the Ulai, who called, and said, "Gabriel, make this *man* understand the vision."

Note: Daniel may have understood some of the meaning of the vision, but additional details were given that he had not encountered before. His queries were to be answered partially by the angel Gabriel who stood in the very presence of God (Luke 1:19).

5. Gabriel was sent to explain the prophecy to Daniel but what was the ultimate purpose of such an act?
Daniel 8:19 And he said, "Look, I am making known to you what shall happen in the latter time of the indignation; for at the appointed time the end *shall be."*

Note: Gabriel's appearance signaled the vital importance of the information about to be given. This angel has played a significant role in bringing crucial messages in the unfolding episodes of the Great Controversy. Notice, "It was Gabriel, the angel next in rank to the Son of God, who came with the divine message to Daniel. It was Gabriel, 'His angel,' whom Christ sent to open the future to the beloved John; and a blessing is pronounced on those who read and hear the words of the prophecy, and keep the things written therein. Rev. 1:3" (DA 234).The prophecies of Daniel focus on significant events from the time of the prophet until the time of the end, just before the coming of the Lord in glory. They help us to identify the nature of the Great Controversy that will be waged on this earth and that will impact on the lives of all believers.

6. What did the ram with the two horns represent? What possible meaning can be given to the observation that one horn was higher than the other?
Daniel 8:3 Then I lifted my eyes and saw, and there, standing beside the river, was a ram which had two horns, and the two horns *were* high; but one *was* higher than the other, and the higher *one* came up last.

Verse 20 [Gabriel said] "The ram which you saw, having the two horns—*they are* the kings of Media and Persia."

Note: The two horns represented the kingdom of the Medes and Persians. The Persians were not initially dominant but quickly became the stronger force thus fulfilling the details mentioned in the prophecy. We remember that the last horn to appear eventually becoming higher than the first horn. Indeed, it was Cyrus the Great, the Persian, who conquered Babylon in 539 B.C.

7. What power did the swiftly moving male goat with one prominent horn represent?
Daniel 8:5 And as I was considering, suddenly a male goat came from the west, across the surface of the whole earth, without touching the ground; and the goat *had* a notable horn between his eyes.

Verse 21 [Gabriel said] "And the male goat *is* the kingdom of Greece. The large horn that *is* between its eyes *is* the first king."

Note: The united kingdom of Greece (Macedonian Empire) prospered under Alexander the Great who swept suddenly onto the scene of action. He defeated Darius the third and final time in 331 B.C. His conquests took place with lightening speed and extended as far as to the Indus Valley (India).

It is interesting to note that when he died, Buddhism was given opportunity to flourish in India. King Asok founded the Indian Empire after he defeated the Greek forces. He also was converted to Buddhism and as "the head of 'Church' and State . . . [he converted the belief of Buddhism] to a world religion" (Humphreys 1958, 46).

8. Where did the little horn power come from?
Daniel 8:8, 9 Therefore the male goat grew very great; but when he became strong, the large horn was broken, and in place of it four notable ones came up toward the four winds of heaven. And out of one of them [one wind or direction of the compass] came a little horn which grew exceedingly great toward the south, toward the east, and toward the Glorious *Land* [or Judea/Palestine].

Verses 22, 23 [Gabriel commented] "As for the broken *horn* and the four that stood up in its place, four kingdoms shall arise out of that nation, but not with its power. And in the latter time of their kingdom, when the transgressors have reached their fullness, a king shall arise, having fierce features, who understands sinister schemes."

Note: Alexander the Great was the brilliant commander represented by the prominent horn. He was able to conquer great nations at a very young age. He was good at military governance but could not control himself when it came to drinking alcohol. "The government of self is the best government in the world" (4T 348). He died at the age of around 32 and four leading generals ultimately shared the spoils.

The Septuagint version of the Bible says that at the end of these kingdoms, the little horn arose from one of the winds or directions of heaven. We might infer from the text that the power did not arise from the east or south. History records that Rome, the next great power to arise, came from the west and occupied Judea, Egypt and Syria in fulfillment of this prophecy.

9. Before we proceed further, how does the overall message of the vision fit into the basic structure already established in chapter 7?
Daniel 8:6-26—Read texts and refer to Table 3.

Daniel 7		Daniel 8	
Symbols	Meaning	Symbols	Meaning
Lion (vs. 4)	First king	No symbol	
Bear (vs. 5)	Second king	Ram (vss. 6, 20)	Medo-Persia
Leopard (vs. 6)	Third king	Goat (vss. 7, 21)	Greece
Fourth beast (vss. 7, 19, 23)	Fourth king	Four notable horns arise (vss. 8, 22)	Four kingdoms
Ten horns (vss. 7, 8, 20, 24)	Ten kings	No representation	
Little horn (vss. 8, 20, 24)	Special religio-political power with great influence	Little horn (vss. 9, 23–26)	Powerful religious and political entity
Judgment and destruction of little horn (vss. 9, 10, 13, 14, 22, 26)	End time judgment of God	Sanctuary will be cleansed (vss. 13, 14)	End time judgment of God
Final everlasting kingdom (vss. 18, 27)	Most High God's kingdom	Little horn broken (vs. 25)	Divine intervention happens

Table 3. Parallels found in Daniel 7 and 8 regarding the rise of significant political powers.

Note: The parallels illustrated in Table 3 should be kept in mind as we proceed.

10 What additional features were shown to Daniel in vision that helps to identify the little horn power?
Daniel 8:9-25—Read texts and refer to Table 4.

Identifying features of the little horn	Textual reference in Daniel
Followed Medo-Persia, Greece and the next four kingdoms	8:20–23
Became "exceedingly great"	8:9
Has some connection with the fourth beast. It would "cast down, trample, destroy" (cf. 2:40; 7:7, 19, 23—breaking, crushing, trampling, shattering, devouring)	8:9, 24
Has no respect for God's holy people. It destroys them "fearfully"	8:24
"Exalted [itself] as high as the Prince of hosts," opposes God's heavenly ministry and the truths of His word	8:11, 12, 25
Feature possessed are that he is "fierce, sinister, cunning," proud and deceitful and beyond all "mighty" and highly successful	8:23–25
Works through external powers to achieve aims	8:24
Would continue unchecked for 2300 evenings-mornings (prophetic days or literal years)	8:13, 14

Table 4. Features of the little horn power described in Daniel chapter 8.

Note: The details presented in Table 4 are significant, for they make it evident that this power would have a determining influence on the fortunes of God's people. In the book of Revelation it will be shown that the power operates until the coming of the Lord in glory.

The little horn power represented Rome in both its pagan and papal phases. When Constantine the Great moved his capital to Constantinople (now Istanbul), the power of the bishop of Rome effectively was increased. The Roman Empire began to decay, particularly in the west, and foreign people groups began to occupy the former Roman territories. Rome was also occupied by the Ostrogoths and it was not effectively regained until A.D. 538 by armies directed by the Emperor located in Constantinople. When this happened the pope emerged as the most prominent leader in the city of Rome (the capital of the Ostrogoths was located in the north—at Ravenna—where the capital of the Western Roman Empire had been since A.D. 402). It was then that we might say that pagan Rome was replaced by papal Rome. This also is the date when the 1260 year prophecy began (refer to lessons 9.7, 9.12).

11. While Daniel was considering this power one angel spoke to another about the time period over which the little horn would exercise its exceeding great power. What details were given?
Daniel 8:13, 14 Then I heard a holy one speaking; and *another* holy one said to that certain *one* who was speaking, "How long *will* the vision *be, concerning* the daily *sacrifices* and the transgression of desolation,

the giving of both the sanctuary and the host to be trampled underfoot?" And he said to me, "For two thousand three hundred days; then the sanctuary shall be cleansed."

Note: A time period is mentioned but no starting point is given. We will have to wait until the next chapter to discover the starting date.

12. What meaning can be given to the statement that "by him [little horn power] the daily sacrifices were taken away"?

Daniel 8:11 He even exalted *himself* as high as the Prince of the host; and by him the daily *sacrifices* were taken away, and the place of His sanctuary was cast down.

Hebrews 9:24 For Christ has not entered the holy places made with hands, *which are* copies of the true, but into heaven itself, now to appear in the presence of God for us.

Hebrews 8:1, 2 Now *this is* the main point of the things we are saying: We have such a High Priest, who is seated at the right hand of the throne of the Majesty in the heavens, a Minister of the sanctuary and of the true tabernacle which the Lord erected, and not man.

Note: The Hebrew word "tamid" has been translated above as "daily sacrifices." This fails to convey the meaning intended. The word "tamid" was used extensively when referring to the ministry of the priests in the earthly sanctuary. This was deliberately done to convey the idea that their ministry was continual as represented by the continual sacrifices, the continual presence of the bread, and the continual burning lights and incense (e.g., Exod. 27:20; 29:42; 30:8; 2 Chron. 2:4).

The important lesson conveyed by these symbols was that God's provisions of mercy were continually available to mankind. Furthermore, now Jesus Christ is mediating for us continually in the heavenly sanctuary (Heb. 7:21-25); we do not need the aid of intermediary agents to approach Him. The papal or little horn power makes different claims. It proclaims that it has the ability to forgive sins and to attribute merit. It has discovered other ways in which to nullify the effects of Christ's sacrifice and ministry such as insisting that Christ is present bodily in the emblems at the Mass and that the saints and Mary are available to assist the believers in approaching God. The church goes on to assert that tradition has an equal place alongside Scripture in determining acceptable behavior. This means that God's words are placed on an equal basis with those of men. The little horn power, through these means, has attempted to change the provisions of the gospel to which the sanctuary witnessed.

13. In our study of Jesus ministry today, what significant point should we always bear in mind?

1 Timothy 2:5 For *there is* one God and one Mediator between God and men, *the* Man Christ Jesus.

Hebrews 7:25 Therefore He [Jesus Christ] is also able to save to the uttermost those who come to God through Him, since He always lives to make intercession for them.

1 John 2:1 My little children, these things I write to you, so that you may not sin. And if anyone sins, we have an Advocate with the Father, Jesus Christ the righteous.

Note: No human intermediaries are required to represent believers before God. Christ alone is our advocate. There is no need for the activities of an earthly priestly office in order to hear the confessions of parishioners nor is the assistance of saints needed to make their prayers effective. Because of the sacrifice Jesus made in lowering Himself by sharing our human nature, it is only Christ who can bring us back to God and grant us forgiveness. "As we approach God through the virtue of the Redeemer's merits, Christ places us close by His side, encircling us with His human arm, while with His divine arm He grasps the throne of the Infinite" (8T 178).

14. Did Gabriel offer any further explanation about the long time prophecy of 2300 days? When would the explanation of its starting point be given?
Daniel 8:17 But he said to me, "Understand, son of man, that the vision *refers* to the time of the end."

Verse 26 "And the vision of the evenings and mornings which was told is true; therefore seal up the vision, for *it refers* to many days *in the future.*"

Note: The emphasis given in chapter 8 was that this prophecy would be fulfilled in the distant future, or after "many days" from the time at which Daniel was writing. Its message applied to the time right up to the point where probationary time would end—"the time of the end." A time for the commencement of this prophecy was not given. We will address this issue in the next lesson.

The expression "evenings and mornings" has confused some. In fact, the language of Genesis (1:5, 8, etc.) is expressed in a similar fashion—in terms of evenings and mornings and it is clearly noted that the reference is to a day (Gen. 1:5 says "God called the light Day, and the darkness He called Night. So the evening and the morning were the first day."). No one chooses to interpret this verse and others like it as though they refer to half days. Certainly, the Jewish scholars who worked on the Greek translations of the Old Testaments had a clear understanding that days were being referred to.

However, some still wish to make verse 26 read as half days and thus calculate a period of 1150 days or years (2300 divided by two) and try and apply this prophecy to Antiochus Epiphanes IV (c. 215-164 B.C.). The prophecy does not fit, for his reign lasted only 1080 days! In addition, his kingdom never became great, let alone "exceedingly great" as demanded by the prophecy (Dan. 8:9). It is not surprising that his reign does not fit the prophecy; the prophet clearly indicated that the fulfillment was in the far distant future. Despite this obvious misfit, many attempt to avoid the message of the prophecy by insisting that Antiochus was the king referred to by Daniel.

15. Did Gabriel explain what would happen when the long time prophecy began to be fulfilled? In other words, did he explain the meaning of the words "then the sanctuary shall be cleansed"?
Daniel 8:14 And he said to me, "For two thousand three hundred days; then the sanctuary shall be cleansed."

Hebrews 9:23 *Therefore it was* necessary that the copies of the things in the heavens should be purified with these [Christ's sacrifice], but the heavenly things themselves with better sacrifices than these.

Note: The concept behind the word "cleansed" can be understood by studying the meaning of the root word. This is explained in Frank Holbrook's book (1986, 200). The thought being conveyed by this word is that at the end of the time period specified the sanctuary (heavenly) would be "restored" or "vindicated" or "have its rights restored" as a result of Christ's sacrifice on Calvary.

16. Where would we look in the Bible to find out more details about the cleansing of the heavenly sanctuary?

Leviticus 16:15-21—Read texts.

Note: The parallels between the account of the Day of Judgment (Dan. 7:9, 10, 13, 14), Daniel 8, verse 14, and the Day of Atonement in Leviticus are significant. On that day of affliction and judgment (cf. Lev. 16:29; 23:29, 30) the sanctuary was returned to its rightful state and God was vindicated as the record of confessed sins was transferred to their source (Azazel or the devil—"Azazel was firmly identified with Satan in Jewish apocryphal sources"–Shea 2002, 8). The people were cleansed as their sins were no longer symbolically present before the Lord. "Since Satan is the originator of sin, the direct instigator of all the sins that caused the death of the Son of God, justice demands that Satan shall suffer the final punishment. Christ's work for the redemption of men and the purification of the universe from sin will be closed by the removal of sin from the heavenly sanctuary and the placing of these sins upon Satan, who will bear the final penalty. So in the typical service, the yearly round of ministration closed with the purification of the sanctuary, and the confessing of the sins on the head of the scapegoat" (PP 358).

The activities on the Day of Atonement represented the purification of the entire camp of the Israelites and pointed forward to the day of the Lord's coming. The ceremony conveyed the idea that God's work on earth will be finished on this day (cf. Exod. 40:33), just as it was at creation (Gen. 2:2). It has been observed by Doukhan (2000, 130-132) that the affinity to creation alluded to here is reflected in Daniel's choice of words "evenings and mornings." These words are applied to the cleansing event. In this context we find that "judgment is synonymous with creation." This means that at the end of time God's justified people are ready for a new beginning. Their hope and faith is about to be rewarded. They are about to be transformed and translated to heaven (cf. 1 Cor. 15:52; 1 Thess. 4:13-18).

17. What was the overall effect of the vision on Daniel?
Daniel 8:27 And I, Daniel, fainted and was sick for days; afterward I arose and went about the king's business. I was astonished by the vision, but no one understood it.

Note: Daniel would begin to understand this vision in chapter 9. However, the explanatory vision would be given after some years of waiting. His patience would have to extend from 551 until 538 B.C.

9.9 The Coming of the Messiah

Introduction

A startling prophecy about the coming of the Messiah was to Daniel in chapter 9. After the depressing news of the domination and destructive activities of the little horn power for 2300 years spoken about in the previous chapter, Daniel was left to wonder, pray and seek an explanation. Now 13 years later (538 B.C.) we find him considering the prophecies of Jeremiah, which indicated that the Babylonian exile was about to end. In chapter 9 he prayed about the matter and confessed his own sins and those of his people and pled with God to act in mercy to bring honour to His name. Suddenly the angel Gabriel appeared and commenced to unravel the riddle of the activities of the desolating power that was to reign during and after the Messiah had come. The exceptionally good news of Christ's coming overshadowed all the uncertainty that Daniel had experienced until this time.

The Study

Read chapter 9 then the notes and Bible texts below in answer to the questions posed.

1. At the opening of chapter 9, what issue do we find Daniel pondering over?
Daniel 9:2 In the first year of his [Darius's] reign I, Daniel, understood by the books the number of the years *specified* by the word of the LORD through Jeremiah the prophet, that He would accomplish seventy years in the desolations of Jerusalem.

Jeremiah 25:11, 12 [Jeremiah reported that the Lord said] 'And this whole land shall be a desolation *and* an astonishment, and these nations shall serve the king of Babylon seventy years. Then it will come to pass, when seventy years are completed, *that* I will punish the king of Babylon and that nation, the land of the Chaldeans, for their iniquity,' says the LORD; 'and I will make it a perpetual desolation.'

Note: Daniel chapter 8 ended with the prophet not understanding the vision of the 2300 years (vs. 27). Now, in the first year of the reign of Darius, that is 538 B.C., we find Daniel considering the words of his fellow prophets. He had decided to reexamine the prophecies of Jeremiah regarding the return of the Jews to Jerusalem. The Jews had been taken into captivity in 605 B.C.; it was now 538 B.C. The time for the fulfillment of the prophecy was about to be experienced. There were several years remaining, but Daniel could observe a few encouraging signs to indicate how this might happen.

2. How did Daniel approach the problem of understanding Jeremiah's prophecy?
Daniel 9:3 Then I set my face toward the Lord God to make request by prayer and supplications, with fasting, sackcloth, and ashes.

Note: The description given by Daniel is a good example of how persons in ancient times and this Eastern culture showed repentance. "Daniel knew that the appointed time for Israel's captivity was nearly ended; but he did not feel that because God had promised to deliver them, they themselves had no part to act. With fasting and contrition he sought the Lord, confessing his own sins and the sins of the people" (RH Feb. 9, 1897).

3. What can we learn from the high points of Daniel's prayer?
Daniel 9:4-19—Read texts.

Note: Daniel remembered first God's promise to save (covenant) and the clear expression of His will (vs. 4). Then he identified with his people in their rebellion against God's servants and His principles and the confusion this had brought to the witness of God's people to the nations (vss. 5-11; YI Jan. 18, 1894). His prayer then changed to observe that as a result of departing from God. His blessings had been removed because the people no longer put their trust in the righteousness of God (vss. 12-14). After reciting the justness of God's actions, he pled with Him to restore His people to Jerusalem so that the name of the God of Israel would not be held in reproach and that the sanctuary might be restored (vss. 15-18). Daniel pled for God's mercies and blessings, not because of the merits of the people but because God is abundant in mercy. His further request was that God would not delay (vs. 19). "Thus, while those who had remained loyal to God in the midst of Babylon were seeking the Lord and studying the prophecies foretelling their deliverance, God was preparing the hearts of kings to show favor to his repentant people" (RH March 21, 1907).

4. Was direct help offered to Daniel in answer to his prayer about the return of the Jews to Jerusalem?

Daniel 9:21-23 Yes, while I *was* speaking in prayer, the man Gabriel, whom I had seen in the vision at the beginning, being caused to fly swiftly, reached me about the time of the evening offering. And he informed *me,* and talked with me, and said, "O Daniel, I have now come forth to give you skill to understand. At the beginning of your supplications the command went out, and I have come to tell *you,* for you *are* greatly beloved; therefore consider the matter, and understand the vision."

Note: Daniel had seen Gabriel previously during the giving of the 2300 year vision. The explanation of that vision had not been completed. It was now time to indicate its starting date. The vision about to be given would also answer Daniel's prayer that God in mercy might still honour His people, His name and sanctuary.

5. What questions did Gabriel help Daniel to understand? What are we to understand by the term "determined"?

Daniel 9:24 first part "Seventy weeks are determined for your people and for your holy city."

Note: Gabriel indirectly answered the question about the return of the exiles by speaking of the coming of the Messiah. More importantly, he helped Daniel to understand the starting point of the 2300 year prophecy. The word "determined" simply means to "cut-off." This is the only place in Scripture that the Hebrew word is used. At the time of writing the book of Daniel (6th century B.C.), the meaning of the word was "to cut," "dissect," "sever" or "divide" (Tolhurst 1983, 6, 7, 14). The angel was seeking, by using this unusual word, to indicate that the starting point of both the Messianic and 2300 year prophecies was the same. How we visualize this is illustrated in Figure 2.

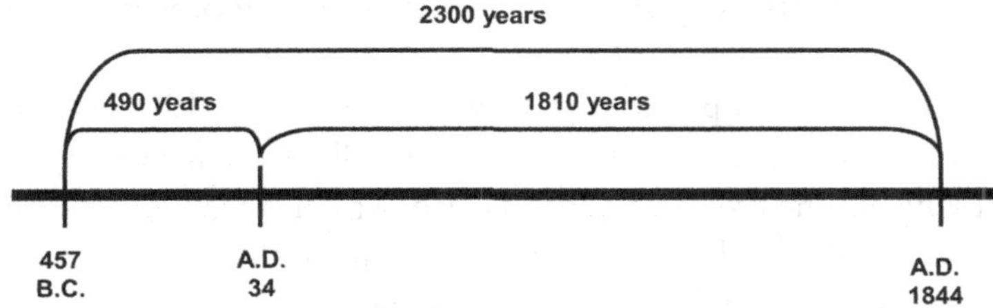

Figure 2. Schematic representation of the 70 weeks or 490 year prophecy in relation to the 2300 year prophecy.

6. In Gabriel's explanation of Daniel 8, verse 13, and in answer to the prophet's question about the return of the exiles, how much time would be given to the Jews to make the most of their opportunities?
Daniel 9:24 middle section [Seventy weeks of years are set aside] "For your people and for your holy city, to finish the transgression, to make an end of sins, to make reconciliation for iniquity, to bring in everlasting righteousness, to seal up vision and prophecy . . . ."

Note: The explanation given made it abundantly clear to Daniel that the exiles would return and that additional opportunities would be given to them to become good ambassadors for God. Almost 500 years were being allocated to them.

7. What would happen after 490 years came to an end?
Daniel 9:24 last part "And to anoint the Most Holy."

Note: During the period of this prophecy, the most glorious event in the history of the world would occur; the Messiah would come and be proclaimed! His anointing would not be at the hands of men. God would announce this event Himself (Luke 3:21, 22).

Now the anointing of Christ had parallels with the anointing of Aaron the High Priest (cf. Exod. 29:42-44) and indicates to us that we should be looking for parallels in the heavenly sanctuary (Heb. 9:8-12) for the application of the 2300 year prophecy.

8. When did this period of opportunity for the Jewish nation commence?
Daniel 9:25 "Know therefore and understand, *that* from the going forth of the command to restore and build Jerusalem until Messiah the Prince, *there shall be* seven weeks and sixty-two weeks; the street shall be built again, and the wall, even in troublesome times."

Note: The prophecy would commence with the decree to restore and rebuild Jerusalem. The historic records indicate that three successive decrees were issued by Cyrus, Darius, and Artaxerxes Longimanus (Ezra 6:14; 7:11-26). It has been observed by commentators that the third decree issued by Artaxerxes was the most complete and was the first "involving both the reconstruction of the Temple and the reestablishment of the political and administrative structures of Jerusalem," so as to give near autonomy under authority of the Persian Empire (Doukhan 2000, 143). The prophet Ezra understood the fulfillment of prophecy in this decree in his acknowledgement of God's intervening work (Ezra 7:27, 28). This decree took effect in the seventh year of the king, which was 457 B.C. (the decree was given "in the winter of 458/457 B.C., the departure [occurred] in the spring of 457 B.C."–Shea 2001, 90). There should be no question in anyone's mind that the time period indicated must be in weeks of years if for the only reason that the rebuilding process would take much longer than 70 literal weeks.

The practice of counting prophetic days as years is established by reference first to Numbers (14:34). In this example, the Israelites were punished in the wilderness for forty years in response to the forty days they spent spying out the Promised Land. They had given a faint-hearted and faithless approach to God's invitation to occupy the land. Hence, they were sentenced to a wilderness stay equivalent of a year for each day spent spying the land. The same principle was used by the prophet Ezekiel (4:5, 6). It is also significant to notice that the Bible uses the term days and years interchangeably in a number of verses (e.g., Job 10:5; Ps. 77:5; Isa. 61:2).

9. The prophetic time period of 490 years was broken into three sections. What details were given? Daniel 9:25, 27

7 weeks—49 years to rebuild Jerusalem.

62 weeks—434 years. Messiah would appear after 49+434 or 483 years (A.D. 27).

1 week—7 years. After the 490 years the favoured status of the Jewish nation would finally cease (A. D. 34). Figure 3 illustrates the texts.

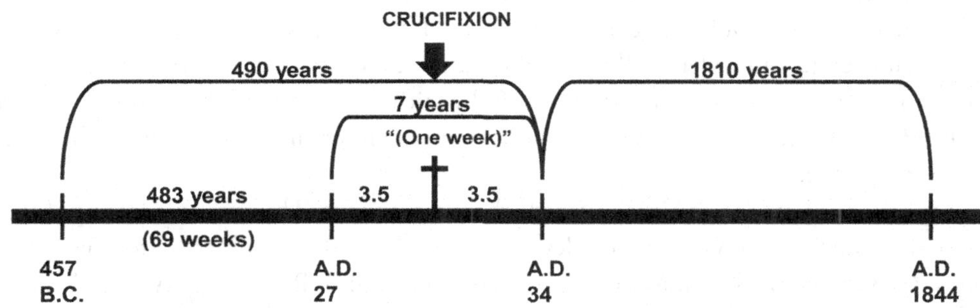

Figure 3. Schematic representation of the details of the 70 weeks or 490 year prophecy and their relation to the 2300 year prophecy.

Note: Daniel understood that the time period referred to in our texts was weeks of years (7×70=490 years). This is indicated by his carefulness to distinguish the time period mentioned here from ordinary time spoken of in chapter 10, verse 2. In this last verse he spoke of "weeks of days" (cf. Young's Literal Translation). The understanding that 490 years is spoken about in this prophecy has been held since well before the present era. The Protestant Reformation arose in response to such understandings.

True to the prophecy the rebuilding activities in the city of Jerusalem took 49 years to complete (408 B.C.). The anointing of the Messiah would occur 483 years after the decree went forth (in A.D. 27—we must remember that in changing from B.C. to A.D. there is no year zero. This means that 1 B.C. was followed immediately by A.D. 1). The anointing took place in the fifteenth year of Tiberius Caesar (Luke 3:1, 22, 23). Both John the Baptist and Jesus understood and declared that prophecy was being fulfilled at this time (Mark 1:3, 15). At Jesus' baptism the words were uttered by God the Father in acknowledgement: "This is My beloved Son, in whom I am well pleased" (Matt. 3:17).

10. When precisely, according to this time prophecy, would Christ be sacrificed for the sins of the world?

Daniel 9:26, 27 first sections "And after the sixty-two weeks [refer to Question 9] Messiah shall be cut off, but not for Himself. . . . Then he shall confirm a covenant with many for one week; but in the middle of the week He shall bring an end to sacrifice and offering."

Note: The covenant is none other than the good news of God's saving grace. The promises of salvation made first to Adam and Eve and all those other believers during the intervening ages would now be made sure. Jesus was about to die for the human race, the just for the unjust. The use of the indefinite article "a" before the covenant should not be misunderstood.

God only has one covenant or agreement to save—"For by grace you have been saved through faith, and that not of yourselves; it is the gift of God" (Eph. 2:8; 6T 392). The first promise was made in Genesis to Adam and Eve after the couple sinned (Gen. 3:15). The apostle Paul tells us clearly that there is one everlasting covenant or gospel and John the Revelator adds his voice of witness (Heb. 13:20; Rev. 14:6).

Some Christians are confused about the old and new covenant talked about in Scripture. God's plan of salvation was revealed progressively commencing with the announcement of His merciful offer in the Garden of Eden after the Fall (Gen. 3:15; cf. Heb. 2:14). God subsequently made undertakings with Noah, Abraham and Moses. The plan of salvation was made sure by the death and resurrection of Christ many centuries later. Now the covenant with the children of Israel at Sinai basically was a reiteration of the agreement to save humanity made with Abraham (Exod. 2:24; 19:5, 6). God sought to educate the Israelites after their long years of bondage and gave them clear precepts to follow, stated His law and gave them the sanctuary services in order to illustrate the meaning of the covenant. However, Israel showed a general failure to enter into the covenant relationship by faith and to follow the example of Abraham (cf. Exod. 32:1-6 informs readers that Israel broke the agreement almost immediately after the covenant was made; see also Acts 7:53).

The apostle Paul called the Sinai covenant the old covenant. This was on account of the fact that the special relationship between God and the Jews ceased at the cross and after the stoning of Stephen the gospel went to the Gentile world (cf. Matt. 27:51; Acts 7; Heb. 9:1). Paul's allegory recorded in Galatians (4:23-31) illustrates rather well that the Israelites, with few exceptions, attempted to save themselves by works—this is the old covenant experience characteristic of pagan religions (Exod. 19:8; 24:7; DA 35, 36). The new covenant was ratified by the blood of Christ after the old covenant was established with Israel at Sinai (cf. Heb. 9:18-20), hence it is called the new or ever new covenant. Salvation has always been by faith and not by works. This is the essence of God's everlasting agreement (Hab. 2:4; Luke 7:50; Rom. 1:17; Eph. 2:8).

Now let us go back to our text in verse 26. This text in Daniel's account indicates that Christ would be "cut-off" but this is more precisely expressed as "cut down"—a term that usually indicated "a person condemned to death" (Doukhan 2000, 148). The violence of the act is thus indicated. This idea is echoed by the prophet Isaiah in a well known passage that says (Isa. 53:6, 7)—"And the LORD has laid on Him the iniquity of us all. He was oppressed and He was afflicted, yet He opened not His mouth; He was led as a lamb to the slaughter, and as a sheep before its shearers is silent, so He opened not His mouth."

Christ confirmed or made the existing covenant sure for half a week or three and a half years by living a righteous life and then dying on mankind's behalf. "Christ was treated as we deserve, that we might be treated as He deserves. He was condemned for our sins, in which He had no share, that we might be justified by His righteousness, in which we had no share. He suffered the death which was ours, that we might receive the life which was His" (DA 25).

The cutting down represented Jesus' crucifixion. This happened in A.D. 31. There is reasonable agreement on this date, although some sources put it a year or two later.

11. What happened in A.D. 34 that represented the end of the seventy weeks prophecy?
Daniel 9:27 first section "Then he shall confirm a covenant with many for one week; but in the middle of the week He shall bring an end to sacrifice and offering."

Acts 7:59 And they stoned Stephen [after he witnessed about God's dealings with Israel and the leaders' murder of Jesus Christ] as he was calling on *God* and saying, "Lord Jesus, receive my spirit."

Note: The text in verse 27 represents the last section of the 490 year prophecy. It is important for readers to remember that this prophecy is presented as a complete unit (it was cut-off from the 2300 year prophecy—Dan.

9:24). The verse may be interpreted as follows. The special promises to the Jewish nation extended beyond the time of Christ's crucifixion (that occurred in the middle of the week or A.D. 31). Three and a half years after this event (A.D. 34), the Jews rejected the special arrangements God had made with them.

There is no text that pinpoints the stoning of Stephen as the time when this prophecy ended. However, at this time it is held by scholars that the powerful ruling body in Israel rejected the covenant relationship with God by their responses to Stephen (Acts 7:51-54). Saul's (Paul) conversion experience began from this point and soon he became the apostle to the Gentiles. Following this line of thought, it is interesting to note that Paul's conversion occurred in A.D. 34. The date can be calculated with reasonable accuracy. Paul tells us that his first visit to Jerusalem as a Christian was three years after his conversion and the second was 14 years later (Gal. 1:18; 2:1). Shortly after this he visited Corinth and appeared before the proconsul Gallio under accusation of wrongdoing (Acts 18:12). Since Gallio functioned only in A.D. 51 according to historical evidence, then Paul's conversion must have occurred in A.D. 34 (or 51–17=34).

It is important to note that Stephen's conflict with the priests reached the climax when he started asserting that Jesus Christ was the Messiah in his summary of the Plan of Redemption. "When he connected Christ with the prophecies and spoke as he did of the temple, the [high] priest, pretending to be horror-stricken, rent his robe. To Stephen this act was a signal that his voice would soon be silenced forever" (AA 100).

12. Gabriel also indicated that the city of Jerusalem and the sanctuary would be destroyed. Why was this to happen?

Daniel 9:26 (NIV) "The people of the ruler who will come will destroy the city and the sanctuary. The end will come like a flood: War will continue until the end, and desolations have been decreed."

Matt. 27:25 And all the people [Jewish people] answered and said [to Pilate], "His blood *be* on us and on our children."

Note: The children of Israel rejected the Messiah as a nation and thus accepted the consequences of this act. True to their undertaking and the prophecy, which Jesus affirmed (Matt. 24:2, 15), the Roman army stormed the city and it was destroyed by Titus in A.D. 70. The Romans destroyed Jerusalem because Judea had rebelled. The Jewish people caused their own destruction through their rebellious acts. Titus' triumphal arch in Rome shows the trophies of the sanctuary/temple being carried away. The temple structure itself was destroyed by fire.

13. Daniel's prophecy indicated that both the Messianic prophecy and the 2300 year prophecy could begin to be understood when a starting date was supplied. When would the 2300 year prophecy be fulfilled and what would happen then?

Please refer again to the diagram given under Question 9 above.

Hebrews 9:24 For Christ has not entered the holy places made with hands, *which are* copies of the true, but into heaven itself, now to appear in the presence of God for us.

Note1: Using the common starting date of 457 B.C., the 2300 year prophecy would reach to 1844. The prophecies of Daniel 8 and 9 have a common theme, namely, salvation and the fulfillment of God's rescue plan. It is interesting to note that before the fulfillment of this prophecy in the nineteenth century other scholars understood that about this time significant events were about to happen according to the heavenly schedule. These included people of many Christian faiths as recorded in the book *Questions on Doctrine* (Knight 2003, 247-251).

Note 2: Daniel chapter 9 introduces Christ's sacrificial atonement and Daniel 8 has to do with His mediatorial atonement. The book of Hebrews bridges the gap between the Old Testament types and informs us what Christ is doing today. These two phases of salvation are explained as follows: Atonement for sins cannot be made without the shedding of blood (Lev. 17:11; Heb. 9:22), for sin brings death. Christ's blood was shed on Calvary in fulfillment of the requirements of the sacrificial atonement. His sacrifice was both perfect and complete. Let us look at the details a little more closely:

i. *Sacrificial atonement.* When an animal (representing Christ) was sacrificed for sin in the Old Testament sanctuary system, its spilt blood was regarded as making atonement (Exod. 29:36). When this system of worship was initiated, the offerings were made in the courtyard of the sanctuary signifying that Christ would suffer and die on this earth (Isa. 53:4, 5). Christ's sacrifice was all sufficient (Heb. 10:12). This is expressed by one author as follows: "Christ's words on the mountainside were the announcement that His sacrifice on behalf of man was full and complete. The conditions of the atonement had been fulfilled; the work for which He came to this world had been accomplished" (DA 819). When we come to Christ in faith, we are released from the guilt of sin and are regarded as if we had never sinned; we are justified (Rom. 5:1; 1 John 1:9).

The sacrificial atonement was followed by Christ's needful ministry in heaven. This is the time period during which He undertook and still undertakes His mediatorial work.

ii. *Mediatorial atonement.* Following the sacrifice of the animal victim by the penitent believer, the priest performed a work of mediation on behalf of the believer. The Scriptures clearly state that the priest (representing Christ) "made an atonement" (Lev. 4:20, 26, 31, 35; 5:6, 10, 13, 18; 6:7; 7:7). Since the priest did not participate in slaying the victim, we must conclude that the priest's work was additional to the sacrificial atonement. This phase of the atonement was essential and took place in the first apartment of the earthly sanctuary. It consisted of sprinkling the blood of the sacrifice before the veil in front of the Most Holy Place (Lev. 4:5-7, 16, 17). This signified that the priest was mediating on the sinner's behalf. The priest became a sin-bearer in type, again representing Jesus.

These services represented Christ's work in the heavenly sanctuary that He was able to undertake by virtue of His death. Christ is hence represented as having a work of mediation in the first apartment of the heavenly sanctuary subsequent to His death on the cross (Acts 2:33; 1 John 2:1). The apostle Paul in the epistle of Hebrews informs us also that Christ has a work to perform in the heavenly sanctuary for us (Heb. 9:24). Indeed, we notice that "Jesus is our High Priest in heaven and what is He doing? He is making intercession and atonement for His people who believe in Him. Through His imputed righteousness, they are accepted of God as those who are manifesting to the world that they acknowledge allegiance to God, keeping all His commandments" (TM 37). He has promised to give us help in time of need as we plead with Him (Heb. 4:14-16). The sanctifying influence of the Spirit of God in the life will transform believers and make them like Christ in character (Acts 26:18; Rom. 12:2; 2 Cor. 4:6). The righteousness of Christ will be imparted to us as we live day-by-day by faith.

14. What special manifestations were observed in the religious world around the year 1844 that indicated heaven had a special interest in informing the inhabitants of earth that the last phase of Jesus' mediatorial atonement had commenced?

Note: After the capture of the pope by the French armies in 1798, the papacy went into a period of decline. There was recognition in many quarters that the second coming of the Lord was indicated by the prophecies of Daniel. This interest spanned across the churches and in various places Roman Catholic, Jewish and Protestant clergy and lay people took up the theme. In Scandinavia even little children preached on the subject of the soon return of Christ. In remote places of the world, such as Papua New Guinea, there are stories in folklore that people saw angels in the clouds of heaven proclaiming the good news of Jesus soon return. From an historic viewpoint, there was considerable interest in both prophecy and the coming of Christ.

The predictions that Jesus would come in the mid 1840s met with disappointment, but then scholars realized that Christ was entering into the last phase of His heavenly ministry preparatory to coming the second time.

9.10 Praying for Understanding

Introduction

The vision introduced in Daniel chapter 10 takes us about two years beyond the events recorded in chapter 9. Daniel had lived to see the political movements that would give rise to the commencement of the prophecy leading up to the Messiah's coming. The first of the commands had been given already relating to Jerusalem (538 B.C.) and some exiles had returned. Soon a comprehensive decree would be proclaimed to restore and rebuild Jerusalem. Daniel was bound to be joyful at this news.

However, the returning exiles found their neighbours hostile. They sought to frustrate the work of the Jews and they even sent messages back to the Persian king making false accusations about them. They sought by this means to prejudice the ruler against the returned exiles and their rebuilding efforts. Indeed, they were successful in stopping the work for a time (Ezra 4:1-24; Neh. 6:5-8).

It was with these thoughts in mind that Daniel received the vision of chapter 10 to 12. This was Daniel's last recorded vision. We will analyse it chapter by chapter, but remember that the chapter headings are an artificial, later addition to God's word and are not inspired.

The Study

Read chapter 10 then the notes and Bible texts below in answer to the questions posed.

1. Daniel was now near the end of his life and was about to receive his fourth great vision. When did this take place?

Daniel 10:1 In the third year of Cyrus king of Persia a message was revealed to Daniel, whose name was called Belteshazzar. The message *was* true, but the appointed time *was* long; and he understood the message, and had understanding of the vision.

Note: Daniel was about 18 when he went into captivity (4T 570) and now the seventy years of captivity had been completed. He was around ninety years of age. The vision he was about to receive was given in 536/535 B.C.

2. What possible reasons can be given for Daniel's distressed state of mind?

Daniel 10:2 In those days I, Daniel, was mourning three full weeks.

Ezra 4:4, 5 Then the people of the land tried to discourage the people of Judah. They troubled them in building [rebuilding Jerusalem after the return of the Babylonian captives], and hired counsellors against them to frustrate their purpose all the days of Cyrus king of Persia, even until the reign of Darius king of Persia.

Note: The Babylonian exiles had just returned under Zerubbabel but they were encountering great difficulty from the Samaritans and those remaining in the land. These people sought to hinder their building activities under the guise of helping. They also sent false reports back to Cyrus (Ezra 4:1-24). One of the principle opponents, Sanballat, even wrote an open letter saying that the rebuilding work was going forward quickly because the Jews actually had plans to rebel and that Nehemiah intended to proclaim himself king. Furthermore, Sanballat alleged that Nehemiah had appointed prophets to say good things about his coming reign in Jerusalem (Neh. 6:5-8; PK 571, 572).

3. In his distress what unusual behaviour did Daniel engage in?

Daniel 10:3, 4 I ate no pleasant food, no meat or wine came into my mouth, nor did I anoint myself at all, till three whole weeks were fulfilled. Now on the twenty-fourth day of the first month [that is the Passover season or March/April], as I was by the side of the great river, that *is,* the Tigris [a messenger was sent to me—vss 5, 6].

Note: The time when Daniel's fasting took place was during the time set aside for Passover and the taking of unleavened bread (Exod. 12:2-6; 13:3-8). His unusual abstinence from food and wine during the time specifically set aside to commemorate the Exodus experience and to partake of the emblems associated with the experience (prefigured Christ providing an escape for doomed humanity) simply highlights Daniel's anguish about the interruption to the work of rebuilding the Temple. His fasting in a time of extreme distress is similar to that recorded for Queen Esther (Esth. 4:16). As soon as the fasting period ended, Daniel's vision commenced. Fittingly, it pointed to the final exodus of the saved from this corrupted earth.

4. While praying and fasting, what happened to Daniel?

Daniel 10:5, 6, 7 I lifted my eyes and looked, and behold, a certain man clothed in linen, whose waist *was* girded with gold of Uphaz! His body *was* like beryl, his face like the appearance of lightning, his eyes like torches of fire, his arms and feet like burnished bronze in color, and the sound of his words like the voice of a multitude. And I, Daniel, alone saw the vision, for the men with me did not see the vision . . . .

Note: At this time Daniel received an important vision. The "certain man" referred to in our text was latter (vs. 13) identified as Michael. We will give proof that this individual represented the Son of Man or Christ later in our study.

5. The vision that Daniel received from the "certain man" might be compared to that seen by John the Revelator. Who did Daniel and John see?

Daniel 10:5, 6; Revelation 1:13-16—Read texts.

Note: One interesting individual participated in giving both Daniel and John their visions. This is evident, as he displayed similar features. These included a golden band around middle, flaming eyes, feet like burnished bronze and a magnificent voice. "This description [given to Daniel] is similar to that given by John when Christ was revealed to him upon the Isle of Patmos. Our Lord now comes with another heavenly messenger to teach Daniel what would take place in the latter days" (RH Feb. 8, 1881). The individual seen was none other than the Son of God.

6. The Great Controversy theme is opened more fully before Daniel in this vision. What struggle of temporal powers had delayed a response from the angel Gabriel to Daniel's prayer (vs. 12)? And what task would Gabriel engage in after his visit?

Daniel 10:13 "But the prince of the kingdom of Persia withstood me [Gabriel] twenty-one days; and behold, Michael [Christ], one of the chief princes, came to help me, for I had been left alone there with the kings of Persia."

Verse 20 [Then he said] "Do you know why I have come to you? And now I must return to fight with the prince of Persia; and when I have gone forth, indeed the prince of Greece will come."

Note: These verses illustrate the intensity of the struggle that goes on in the unseen world. The Great Controversy between Christ and Satan is intense. The discourse between the angel Gabriel and Daniel indicates that God's agents are active to direct world events and ensure that His plans are fulfilled on earth. Daniel struggled in prayer while Gabriel and Christ worked to ensure events in the Persian court followed the grand purpose of God. "It is God's purpose to carry forward His work in correct lines, in ways that will advance His glory. But Satan is ever trying to counterwork God's purpose. Only by humbling themselves before God can God's servants advance His work. Never are they to depend on their own efforts or on outward display for success" (Letter 201, 1899).

7. What additional information does the Bible give that would indicate the reality and intensity of the struggle between the forces of good and evil?
Revelation 12:7, 8 And war broke out in heaven: Michael and his angels fought with the dragon; and the dragon and his angels fought, but they did not prevail, nor was a place found for them in heaven any longer.

Job 2:1, 2 Again there was a day when the sons of God came to present themselves before the LORD, and Satan came also among them to present himself before the LORD. And the LORD said to Satan, "From where do you come?" So Satan answered the LORD and said, "From going to and fro on the earth, and from walking back and forth on it."

Ephesians 6:10-12 Finally, my brethren, be strong in the Lord and in the power of His might. Put on the whole armor of God, that you may be able to stand against the wiles of the devil. For we do not wrestle against flesh and blood, but against principalities, against powers, against the rulers of the darkness of this age, against spiritual *hosts* of wickedness in the heavenly *places.*

Note: The struggle that commenced in heaven when Lucifer rebelled was continued on earth. He intended to question and destroy the principles of God's government. When he was excluded from the inner courts of heaven, he was determined to use the newly created human race to achieve his ends. Satan intended to use them as accomplices to gain access to the tree of life so that he could live forever in rebellion in the beautiful planet earth (SR, 28). He misled the human pair, but failed in his other objectives. However, he has not given up the struggle. Occasionally the Bible gives us a glimpse of how this struggle impacts on human existence. The story of Job's experience is very informative in this respect and illustrates the idea that God forms a wall of protection around His children (Job 1:6-19; 2:1-7). Like Daniel, our struggles in prayer ultimately will be answered; sometimes the answer is to wait patiently on the Lord. "The prayer of faith is never lost; but to claim that it will be always answered in the very way and for the particular thing we have expected, is presumption" (1T 231).

8. What specific task did Gabriel come to address?
Daniel 10:14 "Now I have come to make you understand what will happen to your people in the latter days, for the vision *refers* to *many* days yet *to come.*"

Note: The messages of Daniel 10-12 are primarily meant for a time period far in the future from Daniel's day. From the phraseology used elsewhere in the book, this can be understood to be well after of the coming of the Messiah.

9. The scope of the vision about to be given went beyond the 2300 year prophecy and extended to the coming of Christ. Perhaps this is the time for us to look more closely at some of the disturbing

aspects associated with the visions in Daniel chapters 7 and 8 so that we can link them to the vision about to be given. Daniel, you will remember, was disturbed about the identity and activities of the little horn power. What prominent and disturbing activities would this power engage in until the coming of Christ?

Comments: On analysis of the evidence so far, we can say briefly that the little horn power would seek to change people's perception of the principles of God's government and actually present the changes as being God's will. Textual evidence along these lines is given in the following list. As we look at this, it is apparent that the power would strike at the very foundation of God's throne (cf. Ps. 85:10; 89:14). The textual evidence is borne out by the events of history. Refer to the relevant texts below:

a. Exalt himself as high as Christ (Dan. 8:11, 25).
b. Take away the pathway of continual access to Christ's forgiving power as illustrated in the earthly sanctuary (Dan. 8:11, 12).
c. Seek to change times and law (Dan. 7:25).
d. Cast truth to the ground (Dan. 8:12).
e. Persecute the saints for their obedience to God's revealed will (Dan. 7:25; 8:10, 13, 24, 25).

For the next several questions, we will explore briefly some of these issues mentioned under point c.

10. In looking at changes to God's law, which specific principles in the Decalogue might be tampered with by the little horn power to most effectively change attitudes concerning both God's nature and the salvation He offers?

Idol/image worship/veneration allowed (second commandment)

Exodus 20:4, 5 "You shall not make for yourself a carved image—any likeness *of anything* that *is* in heaven above, or that *is* in the earth beneath, or that *is* in the water under the earth; you shall not bow down to them nor serve them. For I, the LORD your God, *am* a jealous God, visiting the iniquity of the fathers upon the children to the third and fourth *generations* of those who hate Me."

Assuming the prerogatives of God (third commandment)

Revelation 13:1, 2 Then I stood on the sand of the sea. And I saw a beast rising up out of the sea, having seven heads and ten horns, and on his horns ten crowns, and on his heads a blasphemous name. Now the beast which I saw was like a leopard, his feet were like *the feet of* a bear, and his mouth like the mouth of a lion. The dragon gave him his power, his throne, and great authority.

Sabbath changes championed (fourth commandment)

Ecclesiastes 12:13, 14 Let us hear the conclusion of the whole matter: Fear God and keep His commandments, for this is man's all. For God will bring every work into judgment, including every secret thing, whether good or evil.

Revelation 14:12 Here is the patience of the saints; here *are* those who keep the commandments of God and the faith of Jesus.

Daniel 7:25 middle section "And [the little horn] shall intend to change times and law."

Notes:

Idols/images. The nations of Israel and Judah had succumbed already to the beguiling religious practices of surrounding nations. When the exiles came to Babylon, there was only a remnant who stood firm in the great test given on the plain of Dura (Dan. 3: 12). There would be no immediate reason for Satan to give up on such a successful strategy. Indeed, in the book of Revelation, we will discover in a later study that human-inspired religious practices from past civilizations infiltrated the Christian churches. Such practices performed in these churches still blunt their influence. Adoration of images or icons is inherently dangerous. Simple remembrance quickly is transformed into praying and giving obeisance to the person identified, as can be seen readily among those who today worship pagan deities.

Blasphemy. The Bible clarifies one meaning of blasphemy in John 10. Jesus was about to be stoned for claiming to be one with the Father (vs. 30). The Jews who were going to kill Him said, "For a good work we do not stone You, but for blasphemy and because You, being a Man, make Yourself God" (vs. 33). These texts inform us that it is blasphemy for a man to claim near equality/equality with God and to claim the prerogatives of God. One of the prerogatives of God is to forgive sins as noted in Mark 2, verse 7–"Why doth this man thus speak blasphemies? Who can forgive sins but God only?"

Notice the tendency to make such claims, as indicated in the Catholic Catechism. "For the Roman Pontiff, by reason of his office as Vicar of Christ, and as pastor of the entire Church has full, supreme, and universal power over the whole Church, a power which he can always exercise unhindered" (paragraph #882) and "By Christ's will, the Church possesses the power to forgive the sins of the baptized and exercises it through bishops and priests normally in the sacrament of Penance" (paragraph #986). Perhaps the clearest quote is: "The Pope is of so great dignity, and so exalted that he is not a mere man, but as it were God, and the vicar of God" (Ferraris' *Prompta Bibliotheca*, etc., vol. V, col. 1823).

Sabbath sanctity. The Sabbath is the memorial of creation and salvation, "a golden clasp that unites God and His people" (6T 351). The children of Israel had added to their accumulated sins by desecrating the Sabbath (Ezek. 22:8; 23:37, 38). This was one of the reasons that they found themselves in exile (Ezek. 22:8; 23:37, 38). Perhaps, surprisingly, not long after the return of the exiles, Sabbath sanctity came under pressure again (Neh. 13:15-18). Daniel's discourse continually reminds the reader of the creation/ re-creation aspects of God's activities. This is no mere coincidence. We notice this emphasis briefly as shown in Table 5.

Creation		Salvation	
Theme	Reference	Theme	Reference
Diet at creation–cf. Gen. 1:29	Dan. 1:8, 12	Saved from fire	Dan. 3:27, 28
Stone fashioned without human hands–cf. Pss. 104:30; 148:5; Isa. 45:12	Dan. 2:35, 45	Saved from madness and ignorance–cf. Ps. 51:10	Dan. 4:36, 37
Daniel saved amidst chaos–cf. Gen. 1:2	Dan. 5:30, 31	Saved from wild beasts	Dan. 6:22, 23
Makes everlasting kingdom	Dan. 7:27	Cleansing of sanctuary–cf. Gen. 3:15; Heb. 9:6–15, 28	Dan. 8:14
Resurrection of just and unjust	Dan. 12:2, 13	Salvation secured by Christ's sacrifice	Dan. 9:26, 27
–	–	Passover time inferred	Dan. 10:3
–	–	Holy covenant mentioned–cf. Rev. 14:6	Dan. 11:30

Table 5. Creation and salvation ideas highlighted in the book of Daniel.

The pages of history faithfully record the concerted and successful efforts made by various philosophical systems to alter God's will. This means that even many with a Christian heritage continue to disregard both the second and fourth commandments of the Decalogue (we will deal with these aspects in greater depth in our study of Revelation). Notice the following information about the little horn power: "The papacy has attempted to change the law of God. The second commandment, forbidding image worship, has been dropped from the law, and the fourth commandment has been so changed as to authorize the observance of the first instead of the seventh day as the Sabbath. But papists urge, as a reason for omitting the second commandment, that it is unnecessary, being included in the first, and that they are giving the law exactly as God designed it to be understood. This cannot be the change foretold by the prophet. An intentional, deliberate change is presented: "He shall *think* to change the times and the law." The change in the fourth commandment exactly fulfils the prophecy. For this the only authority claimed is that of the church. Here the papal power openly sets itself above God."

"While the worshipers of God will be especially distinguished by their regard for the fourth commandment,—since this is the sign of his creative power, and the witness to His claim upon man's reverence and homage,—the worshipers of the beast will be distinguished by their efforts to tear down the Creator's memorial, to exalt the institution" (GC 446).

11. What are some prominent religious practices, coming principally from the Babylonian and Medo-Persian Empires, that have influenced Christian worship and belief?

2 Thessalonians 2:7 For the mystery of lawlessness [iniquity] is already at work; only He [or he] who now restrains *will do so* until He [or he] is taken out of the way.

Note: Tracing the history of ideas is a difficult task as the records are incomplete. However, there have been two streams of thought almost from the beginning of human existence (Gen. 4:2-8). One stream has carried authentic truth; the other stream has carried polluted waters. Even from the early years of civilization some rejected God's will outright in favour of man-made ideas; others attempted to modify His instructions.

As we look at the Babylonian and Medo-Persian Empires, it is evident that several practices have come from these civilizations to influence behaviours in the Christian church. By making this association we are not ultimately claiming that the thoughts originated with the above empires, but they certainly gained strong support from their thought leaders. We highlight a number of practices.

Sunday sacredness and celebration of Christ's birth on December 25 has come to the majority in the Christian church from Mithraism that had strong roots in Persia. There is clear evidence that the pagan day of light and of the sun (Sunday) was accepted and promoted in some Christian circles around A.D. 260-340, particularly in centres such as Rome and Alexandria. The title *pontifex maximus* (bridge builder), used for the popes, also came from that source.

Others, such as the scholar Hislop, have noticed that the concept of Easter appears to owe something to the Babylonians who held elaborate celebrations to honour the resurrection of Tammuz (agricultural deity), the lover of the moon goddess (Ishtar—Queen of Heaven). Other people groups held similar festivals to commemorate the rebirth of their fertility goddesses and the sun god in the spring. Now in Christian circles Easter is held in celebration of the resurrection of Jesus Christ and is based on the cycles of the moon. Its celebration commenced in the second century in the Christian church. There are no biblical injunctions that promote its observance.

12. What assurance was given to Daniel and to all true believers about the triumph of the principles of God's kingdom?

Daniel 10:19 And he said, "O man greatly beloved, fear not! Peace *be* to you; be strong, yes, be strong!" So when he spoke to me I was strengthened, and said, "Let my lord speak, for you have strengthened me."

Note: The assurance given to Daniel is to each believer. Daniel was assured that in order for God's will be achieved on earth Christ Himself is willing to lend divine assistance to human beings. Indeed, the thrilling promise is made by the apostle Paul: "No temptation has overtaken you except such as is common to man; but God *is* faithful, who will not allow you to be tempted beyond what you are able, but with the temptation will also make the way of escape, that you may be able to bear *it*" (1 Cor. 10:13). We also find that "Those who are earnestly seeking a knowledge of the truth and are striving to purify their souls through obedience, thus doing what they can to prepare for the conflict, will find, in the God of truth, a sure defense. 'Because thou hast kept the word of my patience, I also will keep thee' (vs. 10), is the Saviour's promise. He would sooner send every angel out of heaven to protect His people than leave one soul that trusts in Him to be overcome by Satan" (Mar 207).

9.11 Battles Engulf the World

Introduction

The angel Gabriel now gave Daniel a detailed view of unfolding world events. The section of the vision we are about to address is the most difficult in the book of Daniel. It is amazing that at an advanced age Daniel could remember the details. As we proceed past the first section of the vision, commentators tend to disagree markedly on the meaning, so we will confine this study to a consideration of the general features emphasized when we come to the difficult sections.

Remember that chapters 10-12 constitute the last vision recorded by Daniel. The vision proper is recorded in chapters 11:2 to 12:4. The language used in chapter 11 is not like that used in chapters 2, 7 and 8. It tends to be phrased in literal language rather than symbolic language. However, there are symbolic elements. The wealth of information given in such a condensed form makes it difficult to interpret. Perhaps it is fair to say that no entirely satisfactory explanation for the chapter has been made. However, it should be evident from the discourse that God is aware of and involved in guiding His disciples throughout the complex political events until His coming in glory. The conflict between good and evil is intense, but God will prevail. He is in control.

The Study

Read chapter 11 then the notes and Bible texts below in answer to the questions posed.

1. In this section of the vision, Daniel was taken back to the time of Darius. What did the angel show Daniel about the future rulers of the Persian Empire?

Daniel 11:2 "And now I will tell you the truth: Behold, three more kings will arise in Persia, and the fourth shall be far richer than *them* all; by his strength, through his riches, he shall stir up all against the realm of Greece."

Note: At the time of the vision Darius was reigning in Babylon as a co-regent with Cyrus. The kings to follow were Cambyses (530-522 B.C.), Darius I Hystaspos (522-486 B.C.), Xerxes (486-465 B.C.) and Artaxerxes I (465-423 B.C.). Many commentators put the False Smerdis or Bardiya (522 B.C.) into the list and omit Artaxerxes. He reigned for only a few months, so perhaps he should not be placed in the group. Now the last king in our list was responsible for the comprehensive decree to restore and rebuild Jerusalem, which marked the starting point of the Messianic prophecy. He is also known from history on account of his wealth. These details help us to include his name among the four kings considered in our text.

2. What additional details were given about the Grecian kingdom?

Daniel 11:3, 4 "Then a mighty king shall arise, who shall rule with great dominion, and do according to his will. And when he has arisen, his kingdom shall be broken up and divided toward the four winds of heaven, but not among his posterity nor according to his dominion with which he ruled; for his kingdom shall be uprooted, even for others besides these."

Note: There is no missing the identity of the "mighty king" mentioned in our text. He represented none other than Alexander the Great. When he died at an early age, the leading four generals divided the kingdom. Their identity was as follows: Lysimachus (north or Asia Minor), Cassander (west or Greece), Seleucus (east or Syria) and Ptolemy (south or Egypt).

3. From the previous pattern of prophecy studied in the book of Daniel, we would now expect to see the iron kingdom of Rome mentioned. How is its rise described?

Daniel 11:4 "And when he [Alexander] has arisen, his kingdom shall be broken up and divided toward the four winds of heaven [or taken over by four leading generals], but not among his posterity nor according to his dominion with which he ruled; for his kingdom shall be uprooted, even for others besides these [different from the four generals; a transition to Rome is indicated]."

Note: The text says that ultimately the kingdom would pass to "others besides these." Some interpret this to mean it would pass to those not connected with the Greek empire. In this obscure manner, some believe that the kingdom of Rome is introduced. One commentator (Doukhan 2000, 169), who takes this line of argument, notices the following parallels with Daniel, chapter 8 (Table 6).

Sequence of events/powers	
Daniel chapter 8	**Daniel chapter 11**
Medo-Persia, vss. 3, 4	**Medo-Persia, vs. 2**
Greece, vss. 5–8	**Greece, vss. 3, 4**
Rome, vss. 8, 9	**Rome, vs. 4**
Little horn, vss. 9–12	**North-South conflict, vss. 5–39**
Time of the end, vss. 13, 14, 17, 25	**Time of the end, vss. 40–45**

Table 6. Parallels noted in Daniel chapters 8 and 11 in the sequence of events and powers.

Others are more comfortable with the idea that Rome is introduced in verse 14 or later. For example, commentator Maxwell sees Rome coming on the scene of action in the words "Also, violent men [literally sons of breakage] of your people shall exalt themselves in fulfillment of the vision, but they shall fall" (vs.14). This can be seen as a possible reference the activities of the fourth beast of Daniel 7 that broke in pieces (vss. 7, 23). Further parallels can be found in relation to the same idea developed in Daniel 2 and 8 (2:40; 8:10, 13, 24). Whatever view is taken, the assurance is that the power spoken about will fall.

If Rome is indicated in verse 14, then verse 5-13 can be applied to events happening principally between the Greek successors of Ptolemy in Egypt and the successors of Seleucus in Syria. Such an explanation is traditionally offered within Seventh-day Adventist circles. The details are quite intense and we do not intend to record them here.

4. From the security of the first section of chapter 11, we move into the more complex sections of the vision. What is one interpretation that can be placed on the identity of kings from the North and the South (refer to Table 7)?

Daniel 11: 6 first part "And at the end of *some* years they [kings of North and South] shall join forces, for the daughter of the king of the South shall go to the king of the North to make an agreement."

Note: It has been observed by Doukhan (2000, 169) that there are many parallels between the king of the North and the little horn power. We notice these in Table 7. There are substantial similarities shown by this analysis making it tempting to accept the explanation. Reference to the Glorious Land (vss. 16, 20—Jerusalem or Judea/Palestine) in a symbolic sense is meant to convey the idea that the power spoken about will seek to change the perception of the truths of God that are seen as emanating from the temple. These truths relate particularly to perceptions of God's mercy (gospel) and law that stand at the foundation of His throne (Ps. 89:14).

Little horn power		King of North power	
Features	**Reference (Dan.)**	**Features**	**Reference (Dan.)**
Originates in north	8:9	Originates in north	11:6
Against Prince of princes	8:10, 11	Speak against God of gods	11:36
Casts down sanctuary	8:11	Desecrates sanctuary	11:31
Takes away daily sacrifice (associated with covenant)	8:11	Attacks holy covenant	11:28, 30
Grows towards the "Glorious Land" (Jerusalem or Palestine) and destroys the holy people	8:9, 24	Against the "Glorious Land" or Jerusalem/Palestine	11:16, 20
Broken, consumed	7:26; 8:25	Dies without help	11:45

Table 7. Parallels noted between the little horn and king of the North powers.

To some Bible students, the initial verses of chapter 11 (vss. 5-15) appear to refer to the traditional powers lying to the north and south of Judah, namely Syria with its province of Babylon to the north and Egypt to the south. This identification means that the wars featured between these powers are most likely pointing to the Seleucids to the north and Ptolemies to the south. So the question arises: How can these differences be resolved? We will follow through one suggestion (Shea 2005, 246-266) in the following questions. Before we do that, we just mention that the new power, Rome, is indicated clearly as appearing in verse 16. Then by verse 22, Christ's crucifixion is mentioned and in the next verse the activities of papal Rome come to prominence.

5. If we accept the reference to the king of the North as being symbolic in the latter part of the chapter, what additional meaning can we read into the verses mentioning this force?
Isaiah 14:13, 14 "For you have said in your heart: 'I will ascend into heaven, I will exalt my throne above the stars of God; I will also sit on the mount of the congregation on the farthest sides of the north; I will ascend above the heights of the clouds, I will be like the Most High.'"

Note: When speaking about the spiritual forces of evil, Isaiah chose, under inspiration, to feature the king of Babylon (vs. 4) as coming from the north. He then went on to reveal (vs. 12) that the power behind Babylon was, in actual fact, that of Lucifer the great deceiver who was expelled from heaven. The allusion to Babylon as being spiritually antagonistic to God is the story of the Bible from Genesis 10 and 11 until the last book, Revelation. Spiritual Babylon is anxious to set itself in opposition to God and His ways. Specifically, it is against the covenant, the truths of the sanctuary and ultimately those who believe in the truths of God's word. It is primarily a spiritual force operating through temporal powers.

6. If we accept the reference to the king of the South as being symbolic in the latter part of the chapter, what additional meaning can we read into the verses mentioning this force?
Isaiah 31:1 Woe to those who go down to Egypt for help, a*nd* rely on horses, who trust in chariots because *they are* many, and in horsemen because they are very strong, but who do not look to the Holy One of Israel, nor seek the LORD!

Verse 3 Now the Egyptians *are* men, and not God; and their horses are flesh, and not spirit. When the LORD stretches out His hand, both he who helps will fall, and he who is helped will fall down; they all will perish together.

Note: The forces from the South characteristically put their faith in material things. This means that these forces relied on the wisdom of man (reason—characteristic of Egypt, cf. Exod. 5:2) and the help of man (Isa. 31:1). There is no future in the philosophies of purely human devising (humanism). God wishes to bring His people far from such influences (cf. Ezek. 20:6). He wishes us to be aware of the assaults of humanistic and materialistic ideas on our religious experience. The experiences of the French Revolution vividly illustrate where "unbelief and defiance" of God and "philosophical materialism, atheism, and moral relativism" lead (Miller 2005, 83; GC 269).

It has been observed by some commentators that the king of the South actually operated in the "time of the end" or after 1798 by verse 40 (see question 8). This leads us to the conclusion that it could not refer to literal Egypt. Consequently, this creates a real problem for those who wish to interpret everything as applying to the Ptolemies. One who has made a deep study of these verses suggests that at the beginning of chapter 11 the king of the South "referred to Egypt from which the Ptolemies came. But here at the end of chapter 11 the identification seems to be more spiritual than political. Thus just as the king of the north has become the papacy and is no longer a territorial king in the literal sense in which chapter 11 presents him at the beginning, so the king of the south is also a spiritual entity here in these last verses of the chapter" (Shea 2005, 264). This interpretation allows us to see the activities of many nations contributing to the fulfillment of end time prophecy.

7. Commentators generally accept that the little horn power is actively represented in Daniel's vision we are studying. What are we to understand by several phrases describing this power's activities? These phrases are as follows (highlighted by bolding).
Daniel 11:30 last part, 31 "[The king of the North will] return in rage against the **holy covenant, and do *damage*.** So he shall return and **show regard for those who forsake the holy covenant**. And forces shall be mustered by him, and they shall **defile the sanctuary fortress**; then they shall **take away the daily *sacrifices*,** and place *there* the abomination of desolation."

Daniel 11:36 "Then the king shall do according to his own will: he shall **exalt and magnify himself above every god**, shall **speak blasphemies against the God of gods**, and shall prosper till the wrath has been accomplished; for what has been determined shall be done."

Notes:
Damage the covenant. The covenant has been mentioned before in Daniel's prophecies (9:27 and 11:22). The covenant refers to the plan of salvation made sure by Christ's death and resurrection and that is accepted by faith. The damage done to the covenant may be highlighted at two levels. The first is the confusion between the old and new covenants and the second is the insistence that the Decalogue was replaced under a new arrangement following Christ's death.

The apostle Paul makes it abundantly clear that the old covenant instituted at Sinai was based on types, symbols and ceremonies connected with the earthly sanctuary that pointed to Christ's coming (Heb. 9:1-11). Associated with the sanctuary we find the law of the covenant or Decalogue. It was given in God's own handwriting. The old covenant was ratified by animal sacrifices and based on promises; the new covenant is based on reality. The new covenant is permanent for Christ's blood now has been shed. Hence, forgiveness is certain and our assurance firm.

The covenant has been damaged by the insistence that the "Law of the Gospel" actually "surpasses" the "Old Law" (*Catechism of the Catholic Church*, paragraph #1967). The apostle Paul talking of the Mosaic law (Deut. 31:26 located in the side of the ark of the covenant; cf. 1 Kings 8:9) insisted that changes were needed (Heb. 7:12), but he was clearly talking of the ceremonies and undertakings associated with the sanctuary services (Heb. 10:1). The principles of the Decalogue are as valid under the new as under the old covenant (Jer. 31:33; Heb. 8:10; 1 John 5:3). In order to make this point abundantly clear, the apostle John was shown the ark of the covenant in heaven (Deut. 4:13; Heb. 9:4; Rev. 11:19). Latter verses in the book make it clear that the Decalogue still is considered holy by God (Rev. 14:12; 22:14, 15). This means that the sanctity of the seventh-day has not been transferred to Sunday as insisted upon by the 'universal' church. God's intentions are clear; it is part of His perpetual covenant (Exod. 31:16). "The Sabbath is a golden clasp that unites God and His people" (6T 351).

Regards those who forsake the holy covenant. This means that those who honour God's covenant will do badly in the religious and political turmoil described. The persecution of the saints was mentioned previously in Daniel's prophecies (Dan. 7:25; 8:24). The history of the persecution of the Waldenses, Hussites, Huguenots, Lutherans and other Protestant groups in Europe and elsewhere at the hand of the Inquisition should suffice to illustrate that standing firm for God's covenant was taken at the cost of life. On the other hand, those who forsook the covenant were safe from the hand of the persecutor.

Defile the sanctuary and take away the daily. Two sanctuaries are spoken about in the Scriptures. The one on earth (Exod. 25:9, 40) was patterned after the heavenly sanctuary (Heb. 8:1-6). The earthly sanctuary was destroyed in A.D. 70, but even before that time God had signaled that the services there would be no longer relevant (Matt. 23:37-39; 27:50, 51). Jesus' ministry in heaven commenced after His resurrection and now He is carrying out the second phase of His reconciliation ministry. By losing sight of Jesus' ministry and replacing it with traditions and practices of human devising, human agents are defiling the heavenly sanctuary. Christ's daily ministry in heaven, which all can access freely, has been taken away by religious systems that insist that the priests and the church hold the key of access to salvation.

Some of the principle aspects of the earthly sanctuary service that have been modified by human agencies are illustrated in Table 8.

Magnify and blaspheme against God. The offering that Christ made on Calvary was sufficient once and for all (Heb. 10:10). Nowhere in Scripture is information given to suggest that in the celebration of the Eucharist or Mass Christ offers Himself again in an "unbloody manner" (*Catechism of the Catholic Church*, paragraph #1367). The claims made by the Catholic Church that it possesses the means and its offices are necessary for salvation are not supported in Scripture. Yet these are the claims made unambiguously by it. Taking the believers mind off the continual ministry of our Advocate in heaven is one way in which it is possible to magnify the human instrument almost equal to the divine and thereby to bring discredit on God's name. We are free to come to Christ by faith by going directly to Him in prayer. He is the rightful mediator between us and God because of the sacrifice He made.

Worship form represented	Sanctuary symbolism targeted		
	Most Holy Place	Holy Place	Outer court
Authentic	Times and law specified in Decalogue held sacred for all time	Continual (tamid) intercession of Christ represented in emblems	Penitents enter facing west Penitents come confessing sins over lamb or substitute (representing Christ)
False	Times and law not held sacred Changes have been made to the Decalogue or it is ignored	Prayers assisted by human intermediaries Human traditions are used to replace divine emblems	Enter worship experiences using or bearing symbols of the rising sun (east– cf. Ezek. 8, especially vs. 16) Claims universal church can forgive sins Bring tokens of own merits to offer

Table 8. Sanctuary symbolism highlighted in Scripture and subsequently targeted by human agencies.

"As we approach God through the virtue of the Redeemer's merits, Christ places us close by His side, encircling us with His human arm, while with His divine arm He grasps the throne of the Infinite" (8T 178).

The claim that the pope is infallible and is God's vicar on earth constitutes an extravagant claim that is unsupported by the Scriptures.

8. For how long would the little horn power continue?
Daniel 11:33 "And those of the people who understand shall instruct many; yet *for many* days they shall fall by sword and flame, by captivity and plundering."

Verse 35 "And *some* of those of understanding shall fall, to refine them, purify *them,* and make *them* white, *until* the time of the end; because *it is* still for the appointed time."

Note: Persecution would moderate by the "time of the end." This expression will be expanded as we come to our study of the book of Revelation. At this juncture it is understood by Seventh-day Adventists to represent the time period when the 1260 year prophecy terminated, namely 1798. The great period of religious oppression spoken about in these verses was finished at that time for it was then that General Berthier captured the pope. However, persecution will be used by those opposed to God's people until the end of time (cf. Rev. 13).

9. Which power, North or South, eventually wins?
Daniel 11:40 "At the time of the end the king of the South shall attack him; and the king of the North shall come against him like a whirlwind, with chariots, horsemen, and with many ships; and he shall enter the countries, overwhelm *them,* and pass through."

Note: The clear indication is that the king of the North will overrun the king of the South (or power that represents those who are "amoral, individualistic, without judgment, and tending towards lawlessness and moral breakdown"–Miller 2005, 84). This is the same message given in Revelation chapter 13. The king of the North represents those powers that are intolerant of civil and religious liberties (the North represents a "moralistic, absolutist, judgmental, and oppressive" system—Miller 2005, 84).

10. In Daniel chapter 2 we asked the question why only a few world empires (and their accompanying philosophies) are emphasized in Scripture. Now that we are about to end our tour through the book, what general principles can we establish about the critical areas where departures from authentic worship would take place until the end of human history?
Psalm 89:14 Righteousness and justice *are* the foundation of Your throne; mercy and truth go before Your face.

Note: The Scriptures lay down general principles that can be applied widely. It is not a comprehensive history book. Looking at the broad sweep of philosophies present in the world they may be classified as supporting the concept of a creator God or denying it. Denial of the existence of God is one devise that effectively closes the door to personal salvation. Polytheistic belief systems reject the idea that there is a personal, creator god who is dedicated to their salvation and who operates by a sophisticated code of justice. Their worldview may be complex and tends to change over time but salvation through the acquisition of merit is high on the agenda. Monotheistic systems of religion (Christianity, Judaism and Islam) have a simpler worldview and promote clearer ideas about God and His will.

Daniel's prophecies focus principally on attempts to contaminate peoples' minds about the reality and relationships of mankind with the unseen world. Ideas drawn from polytheistic religions and humanistic philosophies misdirect peoples' attention from God's will for their lives. The two areas Satan seeks to attack intensely are identified by Daniel as follows:

1. *Destroying the foundations of God's throne.* As our text reminds us, God's throne is founded on the dual principles of mercy (love—*agape* type) and justice. Powers are revealed by the prophet that dispute aspects of divine mercy and the sinners access to it (e.g., Dan. 8:11, 12) and the principles of divine justice (e.g., Dan. 7:25, 8:12; SR 59). In explanation of the latter point, justice demands the existence of law and a law that is changeable indicates the existence of an imperfect and fickle individual. Any changes in the concepts of mercy and justice will hence alter our perceptions of God. It helps us to gain a clearer idea of the significance of the law given by God when we read that it is as "sacred as God Himself" (SR 48). God's law was given that we might live in harmony with Him, other men and nature itself. "Obedience to God's law is the greatest incentive to industry, economy, truthfulness, and just dealing between man and man" (8T 199).

2. *Sitting on God's throne or a throne like His.* In the beginning of the Great Controversy, it was Satan's studied plan to be like God and to place his throne above that of Christ (Isa. 14:12-14). Assuming a role like God's on earth (e.g., Dan. 7:25; 8:25) is equivalent to sitting on a throne like God's. This type of activity may be illustrated by reference to the claim made on behalf of Mithras of old (Mithraism was a Roman religion) that he was a mediator between heaven and earth. A related belief came into the Christian church after paganism entered its doors in the time of Constantine. Then, in addition, some of the early Muslim caliphs claimed to be God's deputy. Hence, we find that a number of groups have attempted to usurp God's authority through their religious practices.

9.12 Blessings Pronounced on the Overcomer

Introduction

The long vision that commenced in Daniel chapter 10 is concluded in chapter 12, verse 4. Remember that this vision experienced by Daniel began in 536/5 B.C., after the exiles had returned to Jerusalem. Daniel had lived to see the commencement of the prophecy that would end in the Messiah's coming to this earth. His joy was no doubt blunted by the realization that following Christ's ministry long ages of political and religious turmoil would ensue and that the truths of God's word would be severely damaged.

Chapter 12 commences with Michael standing up. This infers that something dramatic was about to be revealed. After the vision was finished, Daniel heard two heavenly messengers talking. What they discussed is the subject of the remaining verses in the chapter. Actually, the events about to be explained concern each reader.

The Study

Read chapter 12 then the notes and Bible texts below in answer to the questions posed.

1. As Daniel was viewing the turmoil among the powers in the world, what Supreme Being intervened?

Daniel 12:1 "At that time Michael [Christ] shall stand up, the great prince who stands *watch* over the sons of your people; and there shall be a time of trouble, such as never was since there was a nation, *even* to that time. And at that time your people shall be delivered, everyone who is found written in the book."

Note: There is a great deal of information in this text. First, we need to talk briefly about the identity of Michael. Then in our following questions, we will begin to tease the text apart.

The word Michael means "who is like God" (Doukhan 2000, 183). Immediately our minds go to John 1, verse 1, which says "In the beginning was the Word, and the Word was with God, and the Word was God." John goes on to clarify that the "Word" is indeed Christ (vs. 14). We have observed already that "Messiah the Prince" (Dan. 9:25) is also spoken of elsewhere by the prophet as "Prince of the host" and "Prince of princes" (Dan. 8:11, 25). This means that "Michael your prince" (Dan. 10:21) and "Michael . . . the great prince" (Dan. 12:1) should not be difficult to identify. They all represent one and the same person and that person is Christ, as we will discover again in the next question.

The time of trouble spoken of in the text is a time of deliverance for God's people. This occurs after the finalization of the judgment spoken about in Daniel chapter 7. The judgment results in a favourable outcome for the righteous and an unfavourable one for the wicked (Dan. 7:26, 27). We will address this topic more fully latter.

2. What connection is there between Michael standing up in chapter 12, verse 1, and the judgment scene shown in Daniel 7?

Daniel 12:1 first part "At that time Michael [Christ] shall stand up, the great prince who stands *watch* over the sons of your people."

Daniel 7:9 first part "I watched till thrones were put in place, and the Ancient of Days was seated."

Verse 13 "I was watching in the night visions, and behold, *One* like the Son of Man [Christ], coming with the clouds of heaven! He came to the Ancient of Days, and they brought Him near before Him."

Note: The term "Son of Man" is used extensively in the New Testament and was Jesus' favourite term to refer to Himself (e.g., Matt. 8:20; 26:2). Jesus came as the second Adam to redeem mankind (Rom. 8:3). He did not come in a make believe human form. He was of human flesh and blood (Heb. 2:14, 17). Humanity and divinity were combined. This means that He rose by the power within Himself (John 2:19; cf. Rom. 8:11; Gal. 1:1) and He forever bears the marks of the crucifixion in His body (John 20:25-28). Indeed, He has given Himself to the human race forever. The Son of God could not have shown greater condescension than He did; He could not have stooped lower (7T 29).

Christ is presented in Scripture as the intercessor between God the Father and man (Heb. 7:25). Daniel chapter 7 is informing us of this fact; there Christ is shown sitting down and commencing His work. Daniel 12 is a continuation of the judgment scene. In this chapter we are informed that a time will come when Christ's work of reviewing the records of people's lives in the books of heaven will be completed (He will stand up) and the final phases of the Great Controversy will commence. The last great struggles with the forces of darkness then will begin. This recounting of Christ's ministry means that we are led to conclude that both names, Michael and the Son of Man, represent Jesus Christ.

3. What is the nature of the time of global trouble spoken about in Daniel 12?
Daniel 12: 1 first part "At that time Michael shall stand up . . . and there shall be a time of trouble, such as never was since there was a nation, *even* to that time."

Revelation 13:15 He [lamb-like beast] was granted *power* to give breath to the image of the beast, that the image of the beast [image made to the leopard like beast or little horn power] should both speak and cause as many as would not worship the image of the beast to be killed.

Verse 17 [Further, the lamb like beast establishes conditions] that no one may buy or sell except one who has the mark or the name of the beast, or the number of his name.

Note: The time of trouble spoken about by the prophet Daniel is elaborated on by the apostle John. When God's Spirit is withdrawn from the world, a time of persecution and restriction of liberties will descend as the dominant political and religious powers attempt to sway the consciences of men and women to follow their policies (CC 68). These are in direct contradiction to the will of God. Those dedicated to following God's principles will not be able to buy or sell and they will be in danger of their lives. The antagonistic spirit manifested against the three worthies on the plain of Dura and against Daniel will be repeated on a global scale when the forces of evil gather in the last great assault on those who choose to honour God. Satan uses different strategies to attack children of God. Those whom he can deceive are an easy prey. "And those whom he cannot lead into sin he will persecute" (5T 295).

4. The book spoken about in verse 1 contains the names of those who will be delivered from the power of the oppressor. Does the Bible enlighten us about this matter?
Daniel 12:1 last part "And at that time your people shall be delivered, everyone who is found written in the book."

Exodus 32:32 [Moses said] "Yet now, if You will forgive their sin—but if not, I pray, blot me out of Your book which You have written."

Revelation 20:12 And I saw the dead, small and great, standing before God, and books were opened. And another book was opened, which is *the Book* of Life. And the dead were judged according to their works, by the things which were written in the books.

Note: We are here looking at the final judgment scene. Judgment has been made and the names of the saved and unsaved have been recorded. Daniel chapter 7 introduced the court scene. There we learnt that books of record existed and were being used (7:10). Elsewhere in Scripture books are spoken about. Moses, who we mentioned in our text above, was aware that God entered and deleted names from His record books. The apostle John spoke about books and specifically the Book of Life. He clearly informs us that our deeds are assessed using these records. Now, "The book of life contains the names of all who have ever entered the service of God" (GC 480).

Nothing done in secret will be missed, whether good or evil (Eccles. 12:14). "The secret purposes and motives appears in the unerring register; for God 'will bring to light the hidden things of darkness, and will make manifest the counsels of the hearts.' [1 COR. 4:5.]"–GC 481). We will be held accountable for our actions with due consideration being given to our background and opportunities to know the will of God (Ps. 87:6). It is important to have our names written in God's book and to praise Him for it (COL 299). There is no future in worshipping a false god (Rev. 13:8).

5. What miraculous event takes place at the deliverance of the living saints?

Daniel 12:2 "And many of those who sleep in the dust of the earth shall awake, some to everlasting life, some to shame *and* everlasting contempt."

2 Thessalonians 2:8 And then the lawless one will be revealed, whom the Lord will consume with the breath of His mouth and destroy with the brightness of His coming.

Note 1: A time will arrive when God comes to take the living saints back to heaven with Him. However, just before this event He also raises the righteous dead so that both the living and the resurrected saints might ascend in glory to heaven (1 Thess. 4:13-17). The wicked dead are raised at a later time prior to receiving their rewards.

The text in Daniel affirms that the dead are asleep in the grave awaiting their reward. The idea that on death the righteous go to heaven is a concept that has crept into the Christian church. Ancient pagan religious beliefs such as the immortality of the soul came in unaltered form first into Judaism and finally into the Christian church (GC 551). The assault on the Christian church began to bear fruit around the end of the second century A.D. The concept of the immortality of the soul was promoted along with the idea of the eternal punishment of the wicked and today we find that most Christians believe in both these ideas. The Bible contends that God alone is immortal (1 Tim. 6:15, 16); making claims about the immortality of the soul is blasphemous.

The teachings of Jesus, when on earth, reaffirmed that death is a sleep (John 11:11). The dead do not have consciousness neither do they praise God (Ps. 6:5; Eccles. 9:5). Immortality is given at Christ's coming (1 Cor. 15:51-54). This was the truth taught by Justin Martyr (died A.D. 165) who wrote: "Why do we any longer endure those unbelieving and dangerous arguments [that the resurrection of the body is not possible], and fail to see that we are retrograding when we listen to such an argument as this: that the soul is immortal, but the body is mortal, and incapable of being revived? For this we used to hear from Pythagoras and Plato before we learned the truth."

Note 2: At Christ's coming, all injustice, corruption, cruelty and unpleasantness will come to an end. The standard used in judgment is clearly outlined in Scripture—the law of God (Deut. 32:4; Eccles. 12:13, 14; Rom. 2:5-12). The great mystery of iniquity has run its course (2 Thess. 2:2, 3). Those who have led out in the deceptions concerning the principles of God's kingdom will be destroyed by Christ's coming (2 Thess. 2:8).

6. What advice was given to believers in preparation for the coming of Christ?
Daniel 12:3 "Those who are wise shall shine like the brightness of the firmament, and those who turn many to righteousness like the stars forever and ever."

Note: Christian believers are motivated to share with others the love that God has showered on them. A sharing faith is a faith that is alive, as the apostle James reminds readers (Jas. 2:14-26). Sharing is the basis of growth for a Christian. "He whose life consists in ever receiving and never giving, soon loses the blessing. If truth does not flow forth from him to others, he loses his capacity to receive. We must impart the goods of heaven if we desire fresh blessings" (6T 448).

7. Will the coming of Christ be recognized easily?
Matthew 24:30 "Then the sign of the Son of Man will appear in heaven, and then all the tribes of the earth will mourn, and they will see the Son of Man coming on the clouds of heaven with power and great glory."

Acts 1:9-11 Now when He had spoken these things, while they watched, He was taken up, and a cloud received Him out of their sight. And while they looked steadfastly toward heaven as He went up, behold, two men stood by them in white apparel, who also said, "Men of Galilee, why do you stand gazing up into heaven? This *same* Jesus, who was taken up from you into heaven, will so come in like manner as you saw Him go into heaven."

Note: The coming of Christ will be personal and visible (Matt. 24:27; Acts 1:9-11). He will be accompanied by the heavenly hosts (Matt. 16:27). Everyone will see this spectacular event (Matt. 24:30; Rev. 1:7). Christ prophesied that attempts would be made to suggest that His coming will be a secret affair. He advised His followers to reject such claims (Matt. 24:26). Christ's appearing will be accompanied by shouts and acclamation from the heavens associated with heavenly music. The event will be announced in an explicitly audible fashion (1 Thess. 4:16). This world-wide event will end with the righteous being caught up to meet the Lord in the air (1 Thess. 4:16, 17). Christ does not touch the ground or wander around among the people; there will be no secret rapture. The coming of Christ the second time is the blessed hope of the Christian (Tit. 2:13).

This scene contrasts with Satan's upcoming plans. "As the crowning act in the great drama of deception, Satan himself will attempt to personate Christ. The church has long professed to look to the Saviour's advent as the consummation of her hopes. Now the great deceiver will make it appear that Christ has come. In different parts of the earth, Satan will manifest himself among men as a majestic being of dazzling brightness, resembling the description of the Son of God given by John in the Revelation. The glory that surrounds him is unsurpassed by anything that mortal eyes have yet beheld. The shout of triumph rings out upon the air, 'Christ has come! Christ has come!'" (TA 273).

8. As Daniel was thinking on the many aspects of his last vision, what did the angel suddenly tell him to do?

Daniel 12:4 "But you, Daniel, shut up the words, and seal the book until the time of the end; many shall run to and fro, and knowledge shall increase."

Note: What this meant was that the words of the prophecy would begin to be understood near the time of the end (vss. 9, 10). The book of Daniel began to be understood at the Protestant Reformation and later the Bible Societies began to do their work of placing the word of God in peoples' hands. Unfortunately, now we find that there is a great fascination in the Protestant world to use the preterist approach to prophecy. This means that many of Daniel's prophecies are applied to Antiochus Epiphanes of the second century B.C. and their true meaning has been obscured. However, with the vast flood of archaeological and other information now available, the prophecies of Daniel can be understood and appreciated as God designed. As a result of detailed study of this information, faith can be increased in God's word (John 14:29).

9. As Daniel continued to ponder the vision, he heard heavenly messengers speaking about the time it would take to conclude the wonders just seen (vs. 6). What information of interest did Daniel then hear?

Daniel 12: 7 last part [The heavenly messenger said] that *it shall be* for a time, times, and half *a time;* and when the power of the holy people has been completely shattered, all these *things* shall be finished.

Note: In the previous chapter (11), the work of the little horn power was the focus of attention. The angel messengers now focus on its activities rather than the coming of Christ, for nobody knows when this will happen (Matt. 24:36). The time period identified here is the same as previously revealed to Daniel, namely, the 1260 years of papal dominance and persecution (Dan. 7:25) that commenced in 538 and ended in 1798. At the end of this period, a time of relative peace and religious enlightenment would come to the world focusing on the commencement of the last phase of God's mediatorial judgment in heaven.

10. Daniel was puzzled and asked for further information (vs. 8). What further time periods were mentioned that confirmed the emphasis was on the time after 1798?

Daniel 12:11, 12 "And from the time *that* the daily *sacrifice* is taken away, and the abomination of desolation is set up, *there shall be* one thousand two hundred and ninety days. Blessed *is* he who waits, and comes to the one thousand three hundred and thirty-five days."

Note: It is significant to notice that the 1290 day prophecy is linked to the daily sacrifices that were previously spoken about (Dan. 8:11; 11:31), so this does not represent another long time prophecy projecting into the future. The usual explanation for these events is that in A.D. 508 the king of the Franks, Clovis, helped the Latin or Catholic Church to stabilize its fortunes by defeating the Visigoths who believed differently to the Church (they held to Arian beliefs at this time). An historian has said that the conversion of Clovis (referred to as the "new Constantine") was "an event of major historical importance for the future of the papacy" for it "provided the papacy with a platform from which it was able to deploy its own governmental schemes safely" (Ullmann 2003, 37). During the time from 508 to 1798, many changes were introduced into the church, which led to Christ's ministry in the heavenly sanctuary being obscured.

Commencing at the same date of 508, the 1335 days bring us to the year 1843 when there was a great awakening under the Millerite movement regarding the final phases of Christ's ministry preparatory to His coming again. This was a time of testing when many studied the word of God and understood the prophecies relevant to our time. Students of prophecy made a mistake and set the date for the cleansing of the sanctuary at 1843. This soon was rectified on closer examination and it was then placed as occurring in 1844 (EW 232). Interest in the Messiah's activities was shown not only by Christians, but groups of Jews and Muslims also shared in the excitement.

11. What were the last words of assurance given to the prophet Daniel about his place in God's kingdom?

Daniel 12:13 "But you [Daniel], go *your way* till the end; for you shall rest, and will arise to your inheritance at the end of the days."

Note: With Daniel we wait for our inheritance at the end of time. Our assurance of salvation rests in acceptance of Jesus forgiveness and His promise of empowering us through the Spirit. He expressed the simplicity of this proposal in the following words: "For God so loved the world that He gave His only begotten Son, that whoever believes in Him should not perish but have everlasting life. For God did not send His Son into the world to condemn the world, but that the world through Him might be saved" (John 3:16, 17).

Chapter 10

Ten Keys for Interpreting the Book of Revelation

Edwin Reynolds

The Book of Revelation is at once one of the most important books of the Bible for many Christians, yet one of the most difficult books to understand. It holds a unique place in biblical interpretation.

Ten keys should aid the interpreter of Revelation in coming to terms with its unique nature: (1) the genre of the book; (2) the purpose of the book; (3) the structure of the book; (4) the roots of Revelation in Old Testament theology and prophecy; (5) the essential unity of the book; (6) the ethical dualism of the book, especially in the Great Controversy theme; (7) the important theological themes; (8) the book's sanctuary emphasis; (9) the distinctions between the symbolic and the literal, with particular attention to numerology; and (10) the message of Christ, as opposed to a schematization of history.

1. The Genre of Revelation

Revelation claims to be a prophecy. In its prologue, a blessing is pronounced upon the one who takes to heart the words of "this prophecy" (1:3). Again, in the epilogue, a similar saying is pronounced by Jesus Himself: "Blessed is he who keeps the words of the prophecy in this book" (22:7). An angel tells John in 22:10, "Do not seal up the words of the prophecy of this book." This same angel apparently regards John as among the prophets, because he speaks in verse 9 of "your brothers the prophets." And Revelation is called a prophecy twice more in 22:18, 19.

To say Revelation is a prophecy, however, is to tell only part of the story. It is a very special kind of prophecy. Not only is it the only book of the New Testament that deals almost exclusively with the future, but it is also the most thorough-going example of biblical apocalyptic prophecy. It is the book from which the genre "apocalypse" takes its name. Though it was not the first apocalyptic work, it is the most characteristic and well known of all. The very first word of the book is *apokalypsis*, meaning an unveiling, uncovering, or revealing of something previously hidden. From this word we get the name *Revelation*. Many things that were previously hidden regarding the future are now revealed in this book.

Revelation also has elements of an epistle. Following the preamble in 1:1-3, there is a typical introduction in verses 4 and 5, following a style similar to that of the Pauline epistles. First, the name of the writer is given, followed by the identification of the addressees. Finally, there is a salutation, wishing grace and peace to the recipients from the triune Deity. In the subsequent vision of 1:9-3:22, seven letters are dictated by the glorified Christ to John, to be sent to the seven churches named in 1:11. Each of these letters, in turn, follows a slightly modified epistle form in which the recipients are named before the author identifies Himself. Instead of a salutation at the beginning, Jesus moves directly to the point: "I know your deeds," but ends with an individual appeal and promise to each church. The book itself also ends with a close composed of appeals and promises and a final benediction: "The grace of the Lord Jesus be with God's people. Amen" (22:21).

The genre of Revelation, complex as it may be, nevertheless offers us some keys for its interpretation in harmony with the function of each aspect of the genre. As a prophecy, it can be expected to speak prophetically, bring a message direct from God. This is the substance of the first three verses of the book, assuring us that the message is from God, sent via His own appointed channels of revelation, and that there is a blessing in properly receiving it.

John designates it as "the word of God and the testimony of Jesus Christ" (1:2), signifying that it carries the twofold witness that ensures its authority and veracity. We cannot afford to neglect it. Many today prefer not to consider its claims to prophetic authenticity as valid. Yet it has stood the test of time, and we ignore its claims to our own detriment. We will never be able to interpret the book correctly if we begin by denying the claims it makes to speak prophetically.

Second, the nature of its prophetic character is explicitly oriented toward the future. It represents that aspect of prophecy that reveals things to come. If Revelation is not accepted as actually foretelling the future, one will see only a feeble attempt at prophecy after the fact, which makes it a book of history that has little relevance for later generations.

Third, because Revelation is apocalyptic prophecy, we need to recognize that it differs in a number of significant ways from classical prophecy. Its primary purpose is not to deal with local, contemporary issues, but with the sovereignty of God in history and His broad, historical plan for the redemption of His covenant people and final judgment on their enemies. Apocalyptic is known for its cosmic sweep and emphasis on end time, among other things. This means we should not look for a narrow, local fulfillment of its visions, but should see the broad outlines of history from the time of John until the return of Christ to render judgment on sin and sinners, gather His covenant people, and establish His eternal kingdom. All history is moving toward this end and should be seen from this perspective. The Great Controversy between Christ and Satan is a major theme of Revelation, and a striking ethical dualism is apparent. The symbolism is extensive and composite, challenging us to understand it at a figurative level, but one consistent with established biblical criteria and practice.

Finally, the epistolary aspects of the genre remind us that, as with other New Testament epistles, there is both a theological and a hortative [advisory] purpose to the book. The theological elements serve as a foundation for the hortative elements. The appeal is very personal.

2. The Purpose of Revelation

The Book of Revelation has both an explicit and an implicit purpose. The explicit purpose is clearly stated in the very first verse of the book: "The revelation of Jesus Christ, which God gave him to show his servants what must soon take place."[1] According to this verse, God gave to Jesus a revelation to pass along to His servants to show them what must soon take place. This explicit purpose makes plain the future orientation of the prophetic contents of this book. At the same time, it conveys a sense of the imminence of coming events, for it states that these events "must soon take place." Verse 3 adds that those who take to heart the words of this prophecy are blessed "because the time is near." This clause, "the time is near," is expressed again in 22:10.

In 4:1, at the beginning of the section of the book often considered historical in focus, John is invited by Christ, "Come up here, and I will show you what must take place after this." Again the future is a key aspect of the prophecies of the book. The sense of imminence is also conveyed explicitly and repeatedly, keeping expectation alive in readers' minds. At the end of the book, the recipients are told three times by Jesus Himself, "I am coming soon!" (22:7, 12, 20).

Besides this explicit purpose of revealing the future as imminent expectation, an implicit purpose seems to coincide in the repeated calls for endurance and faithfulness on the part of the readers and hearers. Apocalyptic prophecy is given to meet the needs of those facing adversity. The precise nature of the adversity faced by the readers of Revelation has been debated by scholars, but there is little question that the book seems to have been written especially for those facing difficult times, including persecution. Jesus appeals to believers to hold fast till He comes, even unto death, so they will not lose their crown of life (2:10, 25; 3:11). There are further calls for patience and faithfulness on the part of the saints who face the persecuting beast in 13:10; 14:12. Many promises are made to those who overcome, despite obstacles, by the blood of the Lamb and by the word of their testimony. This suggests the hortative purpose of the book, to encourage those facing trials and persecutions to be faithful until the end, in light of God's sovereignty, the victory of the Lamb, and the promises of coming vindication and reward for the saints and judgment on their enemies.

3. The Structure of Revelation

Though there is little scholarly consensus on the overall structure of Revelation, most agree on a few key structural elements for any careful study of the book.

Probably the most important structural element is the division of the book into two main parts, one emphasizing primarily salvation's historical events and the other emphasizing primarily eschatological [end of the world] events. Most scholars divide the book between chapters 11 and 12. However, a number of Seventh-day Adventist scholars follow Kenneth Strand's chiastic structure, which places the division between chapters 14 and 15.[2] In reality, chapters 12-14 constitute a unit containing a mix of both historical and eschatological events, making it difficult to assign it exclusively to either section. Chapters 12-14 could be called the Great Controversy vision, which points all the way back to the beginning of rebellion in heaven and points forward to the glorified redeemed standing victorious with the Lamb on Mt. Zion. In any case, chapters 1-11 fall in the historical section and chapters 15-22 fall in the eschatological section. Contents of these sections must be interpreted accordingly. The vision of chapter 1-11 deals primarily with events that would occur between John's day and the Second Coming, while the visions of chapters 15-22 deal primarily with events that take place at the end time and beyond. Since the historical visions generally cover events up to the end time, obviously there will be eschatological events found at the end of those visions in particular. It is hazardous for the interpreter to stray from this structural guideline.

A second important structural element is the explicit use of groups of seven throughout the book: seven letters, seven seals, seven trumpets, and seven bowls. Some authors have attempted to structure the whole book according to groups of seven, but this may be going beyond the self-evident, although evidence for some others has been frequently cited. The explicit groups of seven form literary units that should be held together. Each of these literary units has an introduction that, except the first, reveals events taking place in the heavenly sanctuary while the events of the respective groups of seven are taking place on earth. These introductions cover the whole period represented by the respective groups, not just its beginning. Taken together with their introductions, they cover most of the Book of Revelation, leaving only the prologue, chapters 12-14, chapters 17-22, and the epilogue unaccounted for. If chapters 12-14 constitute a unit, as noted above, then only chapters 17-22 remain to be structured. Various proposals have been made, none of which is decisive. But we can know that they deal with final events and the judgment on God's enemies and the final reward of the saints.

Other important structural features include the prologue and epilogue, which include an epistolary introduction and conclusion and manifest remarkable similarities; recurring parallel themes and symbols that tie the book together as a unit; possible chiasms; and recapitulation of the historical visions, each covering the period from John's day to the Second Coming, in different ways, for different purposes.

4. The Relation of Revelation to the Old Testament

No other book of the New Testament draws on the Old Testament as heavily as does the Book of Revelation. Unless one appreciates this fact, one cannot fully grasp the meaning of the book. John is heavily indebted to the Old Testament for much of the theology, vocabulary, and symbolism of Revelation, although it is always Christologically informed. This is not to suggest that John did not receive his messages in visions, as he claims. Rather he saw things remarkably similar to those shown to Old Testament prophets and found it convenient to describe them by utilizing familiar Old Testament language and thought forms brought forcibly back to mind by his own visions. The extent of this indebtedness has been shown well in the significant work by Hans K. Larondelle, *How to Understand the End-Time Prophecies of the Bible.*[3]

John's prophecies are rooted in the Old Testament prophecies, particularly those of the major and apocalyptic prophets. Revelation cannot be understood apart from its constant references to the Old Testament. Yet even here one must exercise caution, for John does not merely transfer Old Testament concepts to Revelation; he transforms them for his own purposes.

Interestingly, there are no direct quotations, or even citations, of the Old Testament in Revelation, only backgrounds to which John seems to allude indirectly. These Old Testament backgrounds can be evaluated fairly objectively following a methodology established by Jon Paulien. Based on verbal, thematic, and structural parallels, he suggests ways of evaluating the certainty with which texts may be deemed to function as allusive backgrounds in Revelation.[4]

5. The Unity of Revelation

In the early 20th century, a few proposals disputed the unity of the Book of Revelation. Most scholars today, however, agree on its unity. The complexity of the structure, interconnected as it is, is one of the compelling arguments for its unity.

One portion of the Book of Revelation is frequently interpretable by recourse to another, simply by cross-referencing the imagery or language. For example, the mention of the beast that comes up from the abyss in 11:7 and the great city spiritually called Sodom and Egypt in verse 8 may seem somewhat obscure in that context until one compares the language with chapter 17, where the great city and the beast that comes up from the abyss are more fully described and explained. Many similar examples exist throughout the book. Thus, the unity of Revelation permits it to interpret itself in many areas, supplemented, of course, by Old Testament allusive backgrounds, guided by verbal, thematic, and structural parallels to various Old Testament texts and contexts.

6. The Ethical Dualism of Revelation

One of the prominent characteristics of Johannine literature is its ethical dualism. This is no less characteristic of Revelation than it is of John's Gospel or his Epistles.

Ethical dualism refers to the clear and essential contrast between good and evil, no matter in what ways it is manifest or characterized. In Revelation this dualism appears in the Great Controversy motif, centered in chapter 12. It begins with the war in heaven between Michael and the dragon, and continues in the struggle on earth between the dragon-beast, including his heads and horns (earthly civil powers that accomplish his purposes), and the pure woman and her offspring, first the male Child (the messianic Lamb Himself), then the rest of her offspring. The pure woman is also shown in contrast to a great harlot, a religio-political power reigning over the kings of the earth and responsible for the blood of the saints and prophets. The symbol of the pure woman, in the end time age, is transformed into the bride of the Lamb by whose blood her children have overcome the dragon. The two women are also depicted as two cities in Revelation: The harlot is the great city variously characterized as Sodom, Egypt, and Babylon; while the bride is the Holy City, the New Jerusalem. The dragon, the beast (from the sea), and the false prophet (the beast from the earth) seem to form a triumvirate on earth (16:13) that constitutes a counterpart of the heavenly Trinity.

This ethical dualism is far-reaching in Revelation. There is little room for any middle ground. Most things belong to either one camp or the other. Any rational being, at least, cannot be neutral. One may be temporarily identified with the wrong camp (e.g., 2:2, 9, 13, 20; 3:9; 18:4), but one belongs innately to one or the other. The reader or hearer of the book can quickly identify which is the right side to be on and what needs to be done to be on that side. Once the two sides are clearly identified, it remains for the reader to choose which side to be identified with and to be faithful to that decision until the end.

7. Important Theological Themes in Revelation

The Book of Revelation is primarily concerned with a few theological issues: (1) God's sovereignty, (2) God's justice, (3) the process of salvation, (4) the role of Christ in salvation history, (5) the role of the church in God's salvific plan, (6) the role of revelation and prophecy in communicating what is essential for salvation, (7) the role of personal decision in preparation for the judgment. These issues are closely inter-twined in the book.

One cannot truly understand the issue of God's justice independently of His sovereignty. He is sovereign because His is Creator of all things (4:11). He is before all else, greater and more powerful than all else, wiser than all else, and holier than all else (1:8; 4:8; 6:10; 15:3, 4). No one can question the infinite wisdom of His judgments, because He sees the end from the beginning and judges righteously. When He has completed His judgments, He is declared just and true in light of the equity with which He judges. Then He sets up His eternal kingdom, free from all unrighteousness.

Another reason for the proclamation of His justice, or righteousness, is that He has provided salvation as a free gift to the believer through the blood of Christ, the Lamb. The process of salvation is described at several points in the book, beginning in 1:5, 6. It is clear that it centers on the figure of the Lamb, making it Christologically oriented. The Christology of Revelation is extensive, particularly in the variety of titles and functions given to Christ in the book. Besides His function as sacrificial Lamb, Christ also functions as the promised Child of the woman (12:4, 5), as Lord of the church (1:10 to 3:22), as Intercessor in the heavenly sanctuary and the One who effects the covenant (5:6 to 11:19), as Judge of the nations (6:16, 17; 14:10; 19:11-15), as returning Son of man (14:14-16; 22:7, 12, 20) and conquering King of kings and Lord of lords (17:14; 19:16), and finally, as Shepherd of His redeemed people (7:17) and the One who shares with God the worship of the redeemed hosts on the throne of the universe (22:3), among other things.

The people of God, or the church, also play a significant role in salvation history. This becomes evident from the very beginning, where the glorified Son of man is revealed to John as walking in the midst of seven golden candlesticks, which represent the churches and as holding in His right hand seven stars, which represent the angels, or spiritual leaders, of the churches. The messages that Christ delivers to the churches make their role abundantly clear. The churches, and the spiritual leaders of the churches, are the designated recipients of the message of Christ to His people. It is within the churches that Christ and His Spirit work for the salvation of His elect. That the whole book is addressed to God's people in the context of the church becomes self-evident in 1:4 and 22:16. The pure woman at the heart of the book represents the corporate people of God in both the old and new dispensations. She is Christ's beloved, who is transformed into the bride of Christ, represented by the holy city, New Jerusalem, in 19-22. The church militant becomes finally the church triumphant.

The whole book is designated a revelation and a book of prophecy, as well as the word of God and the testimony of Jesus (1:1-3). This is not merely a designation of genre, but a theological assertion regarding the essential connection between communication of objective truth from God and the process of salvation. The expression, "the word of God and the testimony of Jesus," which reappears throughout the book, is rooted in the legal concept of the twofold witness as essential for establishing truth. This is made more graphic in the case of God's two witnesses in chapter 11, who prophesy for 1260 prophetic days and are martyred for their witness in the Great City. The two witnesses represent the word of God and the testimony of Jesus, or the witness of the prophets, Jesus, and the apostles in the Old and New Testaments. All revelation is in harmony. Jesus Himself initiates the prophetic witness to the churches in Revelation. And he is called the Faithful and True Witness (3:14), as well as the Word of God (19:13). The revelation itself is in fact the revelation of Jesus Christ (1:1). At the same time, Christ speaks to His churches by His Spirit (2:7, 11, 17, 29; 3:6, 13,22), and 5:6 shows the intimate relation that exists between Christ and the Spirit, so that it would be a mistake to overlook the important role of the Holy Spirit in the prophetic revelation of God to His people. The testimony of Jesus is the spirit of prophecy (19:10).

As readers of the book respond to the prophetic witness calling them to salvation and steadfast faithfulness, they become prepared for the coming judgment. Everything in Revelation is to be understood in light of this impending judgment. The sense of imminence and urgency is everywhere communicated, from the very first verses (1:2, 3) to the very last verses (22:6, 7, 10, 12, 20). Appeals to respond are also found repeatedly in the book, from 1:3 to 22:17. Blessings and promises are offered as incentives to accept the messages of the book and prepare for an eternal dwelling with God in a re-created heaven and earth, where sin, pain, sorrow, and death are no more. The path may be strewn with hardships, suffering, even death, but the one who overcomes and endures to the end will receive the crown of life. This inheritance is worth every sacrifice. The redeemed will dwell with God and He with them.

8. The Sanctuary in Revelation

Another of the important keys to understanding the Book of Revelation is a realization of the extent to which the sanctuary functions as a framework for the work of Christ in our salvation. On one level, John repeatedly mentions the temple as well as various articles of Sanctuary furnishings, like seven lamps burning before the throne (4:5), golden bowls full of incense (5:8) and golden censers full of incense (8:3-5), unidentified altars (6:9; 11:1; 16:7), the golden altar before the throne (8:3, 5; 9:13), and the ark of the covenant (11:19). There are also individuals who are designated as priests, and some who seem to be dressed and function like priests. On a second level, John refers to the performance of some of the sanctuary rituals (8:3-6). The repeated reference to the Lamb and the blood of the Lamb is itself explicit sanctuary imagery. On a third level, careful research has shown that the Book of Revelation seems to follow the cycle of annual feasts associated with the Hebrew cultus.

The extent of these references and the interconnections among them make it unreasonable to consider interpreting the Book apart from the centrality of the sanctuary theme, particularly the work of Christ in the heavenly sanctuary from the Cross to the Second Coming. Much more attention needs to be given to this aspect of the theology of the book than has generally been done.

9. Symbolism and Numerology in Revelation

The Book of Revelation is replete with symbolism and numerology. Extensive symbolism is one of the characteristics of apocalyptic. Numerology is also frequently used in apocalyptic, because numbers may have symbolic value. The symbolic value of a number does not necessarily mean it has no literal value. Some numbers are purely symbolic, while others seem to have a literal value, though perhaps also carrying some symbolic value. The key is to know when something is to be taken literally and when symbolically. This is no easy task.

Richard Davidson has suggested what may be a valuable insight into solving this problem in the Book of Revelation, at least with reference to sanctuary imagery, which comprises a significant part of the book. It has to do with the eschatological substructure of New Testament typology. He notes that "in the time of the church the earthly antitypes in the spiritual kingdom of grace find a spiritual (non-literal), partial (non-final), and universal (non-geographical/ethnic) fulfillment, since they are spiritually (but not literally) related to Christ in the heavenlies. Thus, we should expect that when sanctuary/temple imagery in Revelation is applied to an earthly setting in the time of the church, there will be a spiritual and not literal interpretation, since the temple is a spiritual one here on earth."[5]

Conversely, he observes that "during the time of the church, the earthly spiritual kingdom is overarched by the literal rule of Christ in the heavenlies. Consistent with this New Testament perspective, the sanctuary typology of Revelation, when focused upon the heavenly sanctuary, partakes of the same modality as the presence of Christ, that is, a literal antitypical fulfillment."[6]

If this system of interpretation is consistently followed, many problems seem to be resolved in deciding what should be taken literally and what symbolically. Nonetheless, numbers still may have symbolic value, even in heavenly scenes that would be otherwise literally interpreted according to the above method. To determine what various numbers stand for requires careful cross referencing of Scripture.

Traditionally, three has often been considered the number of God, or unity, while four has been considered the number of earth, or creation, but this is largely without biblical precedent. The numbers three and four have no clear symbolic meaning in Scripture, though some would suggest that symbolic meanings may be inferred from the emphasis given in various texts. John Davis argues that seven is the only number that can be clearly shown to have a symbolic use in Scripture[7]. Seven, the sum of three plus four, represents completeness or perfection throughout Scripture, and is the most important number in Revelation. Ten is a number used primarily as a factor in multiplication, to create large round numbers. It appears as a unit in Revelation only in the 10 horns, with respect to which the number may have more literal than symbolic value. If it has any symbolic value, it is probably as a whole or round number, representing a basic mathematical unit of general nature. Twelve, incidentally the product of three and four, is widely understood to be the kingdom number, though this is inferential only, used as it is for the people of God who make up the kingdom, represented by the 12 tribes in the time of Israel and the 12 apostles in the time of the church. The numbers one thousand, ten thousand, and multiples thereof are generally used in Revelation to signify very large numbers, not exact figures.

The primary basis for interpreting either symbolism or numerology in Revelation is from within Scripture. Doing a concordance study is very useful, but one should focus particularly on those passages in which the image or number seems to have a symbolic value in the context. One may also learn what certain symbols or numbers represented in extra-biblical literature, but should exercise caution in allowing such information to outweigh or contravene the biblical evidence. Kenneth Strand [refer to reference 2] has made some very practical suggestions for interpreting the symbolism within Revelation, to which the student of Revelation is referred.

10. The Message of Christ in Revelation

Reserved for last is probably the most important key to interpreting Revelation. One needs to begin from the right assumptions. What is it that the book is trying to communicate? Some readers of Revelation believe John was writing about events taking place in his own day, as well as events in the very near future. These interpreters ignore John's own claims about what he is recording and why. They fail to accept John's claim that he received visionary revelations from God that pertain exclusively to the future, especially to the time pertaining to the end-time judgment and the setting up of Christ's eternal kingdom. They see only the beginning of Christian history, but not the middle or the end. Nor do they see the message of Christ to His people in every age.

Other readers believe John is writing only about the final events of history and the establishment of the kingdom of God on earth. They fail to see that John includes much historical activity before he gets to the end: seven churches, six seals, six trumpets, during which events continue on Earth. It is only in the days when the seventh trumpet sounds that the mystery of God is finished (10:7). These futurist interpreters see the end of Christian salvation history, but not its beginning or its struggle through the long ages that intervene before the end. Nor do they see the message of Christ for His people in every period.

Still other readers believe John is writing primarily about history, setting forth a detailed scheme of history by which we can reconstruct the past and predict yet future events if we will but decode the symbols correctly. The results are a vast diversity of opinions about the meaning of the many symbols and the resulting reconstructions of history past, present, and future. These historicist interpreters may be correct in seeing a rough outline of history afforded by the prophecies of Revelation, but they are often overzealous in attempting to define every detail of the symbolism in their scheme of history, resulting in speculative confusion and a tendency to keep changing the interpretation as extended time makes old interpretations invalid. Such a focus on history draws away the reader's attention from the main message of the text, which would have been of spiritual benefit and blessing if applied as intended.

Even those idealist readers who, wrongly, believe Revelation is not about history—either past, present, or future—risk missing the true message of Christ to the reader by losing the perspective of the message, which is rooted in and tied to the progress of Christian salvation history.

Only a balanced approach to the interpretation of the book, keeping in mind the true object of the revelation, will yield satisfactory results. The revelation was given not only for John and for the seven churches in the Roman province of Asia, but for God's servants (1:1), who would live in the interim before the final judgment, to prepare them for the coming events. It was not preserved in the canon of Scripture as a history textbook, but as a message from Christ to His people, with the object of preparing them spiritually for what would lie ahead. Unless one reads the book with the intention of discerning this message from Christ, he or she has missed the most important content of the book. What happened in the past serves only as a witness to the trustworthiness of the revelations concerning the future. What will happen in the future is only a promise, dimly understood, of what we may expect, depending on the choices we make in the present. It is to our present choices that the book constantly appeals.

The most meaningful part of the book for our experience is the letters of Christ to the seven churches. Here Christ speaks personally to every individual in every age. The seven churches represent the complete cross section of the church in every age, as well as the various experiences that any individual Christian may have at any given time. That this is true may be seen from the injunction, repeated seven times: "Let anyone who has an ear listen to what the Spirit is saying to the churches" (2:7, 11, 17, 29; 3:6, 13, 22 NRSV). The appeal is individual, and the message to each church is applied to all churches.

If one takes a similar approach to each of the visions of Revelation, seeking for the personal message from Christ to the reader, understood within the historical context to which the vision pertains and in light of the development of events described in the vision, with a view to personal application and present decision making, the blessing of 1:3 and 22:7 will accrue to the reader. That should be the goal of the study of the Book of Revelation. That alone will prepare the reader for what yet lies ahead.

References

1 All Scripture quotations in this article are from the New International Version unless otherwise noted.

2 Kenneth A Strand, "The Eight Basis Visions in the Book of Revelation," *Andrews University Seminary Studies* (AUSS) 25 (1987), pp. 107-121; C. Mervyn Maxwell, God Cares, vol. 2, *The Message of Revelation for You and Your Family* (Bosie, Idaho: Pacific Press Publ. Assn., 1985), pp. 55-62; "Issues in Revelation: DARCOM Report," in *Symposium* 1, p. 177.

3 Hans K. LaRondelle, *How to Understand the End-Time Prophecies of the Bible* (Sarasota, Fla.: First Impressions, 1997).

4 Jon Paulien, *Decoding Revelation's Trumpets: Literary Allusions and Interpretations of Revelation* 8:7-12, Andrews University Seminary Doctoral Dissertation Series, vol. 11 (Berrien Springs, Mich.: Andrews University Press, 1988), 165-194; idem, "Interpreting Revelation's Symbolism," *Symposium* 1, pp. 83-92.

5 Richard M. Davidson, "Sanctuary Typology," in *Symposium* 1, p. 109.

6 Ibid., p. 111.

7 John J. Davis, *Biblical Numerology* (Grand Rapids: Baker, 1968), pp. 116, 124.

Note

Dr Reynolds is now at Southern Adventist University, Tennessee. The article appeared in the Journal of the Adventist Theological Society, *11(1-2), 261-276, 2000. It is used with the author and journal's permission.*

Chapter 11

Studies in Revelation

Warren A. Shipton & Ebenezer A. Belete

11.1 The Revelation of Secrets

Introduction

The book of Revelation was written by the apostle John who was also the writer of the gospel of John and is known as the beloved disciple of Jesus. The well known church figures in the centuries following John's death had no question that he was the author. At the time of writing (last decade of the first century), John was the last of the apostles (7BC 953). The Jewish leaders were outraged at John's clear testimony on behalf of Christianity and determined that he should be silenced. He was brought before Emperor Domitian and seemed set to join his companion disciples in martyrdom. His defense on behalf of his faith was both powerful and eloquent. The Emperor enraged by his testimony, determined that he would be cast into a vat of boiling oil. When he was saved from this horrible death by the hand of God, he was banished for life to the Isle of Patmos (AA 569, 570). This is where he wrote the book of Revelation. What his enemies did not understand was that "they could not put him in any place where his Lord and Saviour Jesus Christ could not find him" (7BC 954). From the rocky and barren island in the Aegean sea, off the coast of modern Turkey, John had time to reflect and pray and it is here that the most terrifying and sublime themes were presented to the apostle. John may have been released on the death of the Emperor to live his last days in the city of Ephesus.

The book is a Revelation of Jesus Christ, for it shows Him as the High Priest in the heavenly sanctuary, the Judge and the King of kings. It shows Him as the one caring for His flock on earth and as the Lamb among His redeemed subjects in the earth made new; it also shows Him triumphant over Satan and His hosts as He ushers in the age of eternal harmony. This record shows that the principles of God's government are superior to any other conceived by men or angels.

The book is John's parting message to each reader. It comes with the words ringing in the ears of each hearer that it actually reveals things "which shortly must take place" (Rev. 1:1). Today, standing almost two millennia beyond the initial events portrayed, it is evident that the book is now speaking of events near the close of time.

The Study

Read chapter 1 then the Bible texts and notes below in answer to the questions posed.

1. Daniel's later prophecies were not to be understood immediately (Dan. 12:4). By contrast, what instruction was given to the prophet John?

Revelation 1:3 Blessed *is* he who reads and those who hear the words of this prophecy, and keep those things which are written in it; for the time *is* near.

Revelation 22:14 Blessed *are* those who do His commandments, that they may have the right to the tree of life, and may enter through the gates into the city.

Note: Those who read, earnestly seeking to understand the book of Revelation, will receive a blessing. The honest in mind will also seek to keep the principles outlined in the prophecies. God will reward them with His everlasting friendship. While many of Daniel's prophecies were for future generations of believers, the first text noted above tells us that John's writings were immediately applicable. Indeed, the prophet Amos (3:7) indicated that God's plans for His church would be known to His people through the prophets so that they would be encouraged.

2. The book of Revelation is a book of disclosures. What or who particularly is the book disclosing?

Revelation 1:1 The Revelation of Jesus Christ, which God gave Him to show His servants—things which must shortly take place; and He sent and signified *it* by His angel to His servant John.

Note: The book reveals Jesus in His various phases of ministry after His resurrection. He is revealed serving in the heavenly sanctuary, acting as the Judge of the universe and coming as King. He is also revealed as the Creator and Redeemer, the one actively engaged in keeping authentic truth alive on the earth, and planning for the second coming and the construction of homes in the new earth for those who accept His claims by faith. "Jesus Christ is the great trustee of divine revelation. It is through Him that we have knowledge of what we are to look for in the closing scenes of this earth's history. God gave this revelation to Christ, and Christ communicated the same to John" (7BC 953).

3. The book of Revelation is a book of blessings. How are these blessings gained?

Revelation 1:3 Blessed *is* he who reads and those who hear the words of this prophecy, and keep those things which are written in it; for the time *is* near.

Note: The action words are "reads," "hear" and "keep." This message is repeated throughout the visions. Later there is a blessing pronounced on the person who "watches and keeps his garments" (Rev. 16:15), and on the ones who are "called to the marriage supper" (19:9), "keeps the words of the prophecy" and "do His commandments" (22:14). This is not a book for the faint-hearted or the casual reader. The book had relevance to those just beyond John's day and continues to have relevance to the end of time, a point already conveyed in verse 1.

4. What particular features did John immediately begin to highlight about Jesus' character and activities in chapter 1?

He was sacrificed for humanity (vs. 5).
He was resurrected (vss. 5, 18).
The second coming is a scheduled event (vs. 7).
The triumph of good over evil is certain (vs. 7).
All disciples' are given a sense of value, dignity and purpose (vs. 6).

Note: The basis of authentic belief is active faith in a personal God who died for our sins. He is living and is now ministering in heaven. Christ's resurrection is the guarantee that believers will live again and that death will be defeated. Other religious leaders who have arisen through history do not make this claim. Even if they did, they do not have the witness of history that the mighty empire of Rome with its professional soldiery could not keep Jesus in the tomb. Nor could the enemies of Christianity find the alleged stolen body of Jesus. His resurrection guarantees that He will come again and triumph over the forces of evil. His victory at the cross gives each person value and allows each believer to be a dignified ambassador for Christ. Indeed, "The Lord is disappointed when His people place a low estimate upon themselves. He desires His chosen heritage to value themselves according to the price He has placed upon them. God wanted them, else He would not have sent His Son on such an expensive errand to redeem them. He has a use for them, and He is well pleased when they make the very highest demands upon Him, that they may glorify His name. They may expect large things if they have faith in His promises" (DA 668).

5. John declared that Jesus was the "faithful witness" (vs. 5). What witness might John have been referring to in these words?

Unity of the Godhead—the Father

John 14: 10, 11 "Do you not believe that I am in the Father, and the Father in Me? The words that I speak to you I do not speak on My own *authority;* but the Father who dwells in Me does the works. Believe Me that I *am* in the Father and the Father in Me, or else believe Me for the sake of the works themselves."

Note 1: John in his previous writings faithfully recorded Jesus' revelation of the Father. Jesus established that there was unity of purpose with His Father (John 14:1, 6, 7). When Jesus was on earth as a man, He could claim that He spoke by the authority of the Father, but then He went on to say that they acted as one. The Father was and is involved in the plan of salvation (John 14: 2). Both the Father and the Son operate by moral law and hold to the same principles of government (John 14:15, 21, 24). The moral law is based on the principle of altruistic love (*agape*), which originates with God (John 14:23, 31; 15:9; 16:27; 1 John 4:7—look at the Greek in a comprehensive concordance to establish this point; 7 BC 952). Both the Father and Son cooperate in judgment (John 15:1, 2).

Unity of the Godhead—the Holy Spirit

John 14:26 "But the Helper, the Holy Spirit, whom the Father will send in My name, He will teach you all things, and bring to your remembrance all things that I said to you."

Note 2: The Holy Spirit was revealed by Jesus. He is the person of the Godhead sent to operate in Jesus' name on earth and to teach and faithfully remind the disciples of the truths Jesus has revealed (John 14:26; 15:26). His role is to convict the world of sin, righteousness and judgment, and guide into new truths and understandings of the prophecies (John 16:8-13). These revelations indicate the unity of purpose among the members of the Godhead.

Witness of Scriptures

Luke 24:25-27 Then He said to them, "O foolish ones, and slow of heart to believe in all that the prophets have spoken! Ought not the Christ to have suffered these things and to enter into His glory?" And beginning at Moses and all the Prophets, He expounded to them in all the Scriptures the things concerning Himself.

Note 3: The text was spoken as Jesus walked with the disciples to Emmaus just after His resurrection. Christ upheld the Scriptures and in particular the Old Testament, which was the only document prepared while He was on earth. The Scriptures reveal Christ (John 5:39); their pages are saturated with truths about Him. Hence it is perhaps not surprising that twenty six of the thirty nine books of the Old Testament are quoted from or alluded to in the book of Revelation.

Foundation principle of God's kingdom and character
John 14:23, 24 Jesus answered and said to him, "If anyone loves Me, he will keep My word; and My Father will love him, and We will come to him and make Our home with him. He who does not love Me does not keep My words; and the word which you hear is not Mine but the Father's who sent Me."

Note 4: The integrity of God's word is structured around the principle of love (*agape*). God's moral law is based on this principle (Matt. 22:36-40). The law is as holy as God Himself (SR 19), and any interference with these precepts detracts from the completeness, certainty and beauty of God's character. The Great Controversy is being waged on the proposition made by Satan and his devotees that there is a defect in God's law (or God's character—SR 18).

Certainty of the Great Controversy outcome
Revelation 1:6, 7 And has made us kings and priests to His God and Father, to Him *be* glory and dominion forever and ever. Amen. Behold, He is coming with clouds, and every eye will see Him, even they who pierced Him. And all the tribes of the earth will mourn because of Him. Even so, Amen.

John 16:22 "Therefore you now have sorrow; but I will see you again and your heart will rejoice, and your joy no one will take from you."

Note 5: The certainty of God's salvation offered to all is indicated by these verses. The theme was taken up by Jesus with confidence early in His pre-crucifixion speech with the disciples (John 10:27-30). Satan could find no answering cord in Jesus mind; it was a lost cause for him. In the book of Revelation, the certainty of the victory is given in the first chapter and is a recurring theme.

Christ carefully assured believers of the certainty of their salvation as they exercised faith in His sacrifice (Rev. 1:5) and depended on the Holy Spirit's enabling power (John 15:4, 5; 1 Cor. 2:4, 5; Gal. 3:14).

6. Jesus spoke to John. What did He say and what important points should we take from this?
Revelation 1:8 "I am the Alpha and the Omega, *the* Beginning and *the* End," says the Lord, "who is and who was and who is to come, the Almighty."

Note: Mention of Christ being the Beginning (Alpha) refers to Christ's omniscient and omnipotence demonstrated by His creative ability (Isa. 41:4; John 1:1-4, 14). Reference to Him being the End (Omega) indicates His preeminence in the plan of salvation and highlights the soundness of His ultimate claim as victor in the Great Controversy. The use of the title, "I am" and the use of the words "is," "was" and "is to come" points to Christ's constancy, unchangeable and eternal nature.

7. As John meditated on the Sabbath day, what additional words did he hear from Jesus?

Revelation 1:10, 11 I was in the Spirit on the Lord's Day, and I heard behind me a loud voice, as of a trumpet, saying, "I am the Alpha and the Omega, the First and the Last," and, "What you see, write in a book and send *it* to the seven churches which are in Asia: . . . ."

Note: The Holy Spirit is revealed in this verse as working with Christ to reach John with the messages recorded in the book of Revelation. The seven churches mentioned in Asia were well known in John's day. The information in the letters was relevant to them but had greater applications, as we will learn in the next chapters.

The first message to John was given on the Sabbath day (7BC 955). John did not recognize Sunday sacredness, as this idea was not developed until the second century. The Lord sanctified the seventh-day (Gen. 2:2, 3; Exod. 16:23, 29); human agents changed the sanctity of the seventh day to the first day in defiance of God's command.

8. In John's vision, he saw a person walking among candlesticks. He described this individual as "like the Son of Man" (vs. 13). What special significance might we attach to the term "Son of Man"?

Matthew 24:29, 30 "Immediately after the tribulation of those days the sun will be darkened, and the moon will not give its light; the stars will fall from heaven, and the powers of the heavens will be shaken. Then the sign of the Son of Man will appear in heaven, and then all the tribes of the earth will mourn, and they will see the Son of Man coming on the clouds of heaven with power and great glory."

Note: In answer to questions asked by Jesus' disciples on the Mount of Olives: "Tell us, when will these things be? And what will be the sign of Your coming and the end of the age?" (Matt. 24:3), Jesus gave the answer in our texts above. In this manner, Christ identified with humanity as a personal God. In Revelation 1, verse 7, there is an allusion to the fact that the marks of His crucifixion will be visible when He returns, just as they were evident after His resurrection (John 20:25-27). Christ identifies Himself with humanity throughout eternity and gives deep meaning to the expression "He will dwell with them" in the world made new (Rev. 21:3).

9. The Son of Man is shown having the keys to something highly significant. What do these keys open?

Revelation 1:18 "I *am* He who lives, and was dead, and behold, I am alive forevermore. Amen. And I have the keys of Hades and of Death."

Note: Jesus holds the keys to the unseen realms and to death. This verse gives us the assurance that Christ has risen. No other founder of a religion claims this power. If the Romans could have shown that Christ had not risen, this would have helped their purpose. The Jews were frantic for this proof. It could not be found, because Christ rose and many witnesses testified to this fact (Matt. 28:4-15; John 20:19-29; 21:1). On account of Jesus' power over death, He will be able to bring an end to suffering and death when the author of death, Satan, is destroyed (Rev. 20:10, 14; 21:1:4).

10. How was it possible for Christ to acquire the keys to the grave and death?

Hebrews 4:15 For we do not have a High Priest who cannot sympathize with our weaknesses, but was in all *points* tempted as *we are, yet* without sin.

Hebrews 9:27, 28 And as it is appointed for men to die once, but after this the judgment, so Christ was offered once to bear the sins of many. To those who eagerly wait for Him He will appear a second time, apart from sin, for salvation.

Note: Before sin entered the universe, Christ had a plan to contend with the threat (Eph. 1:4; 1 Pet. 1:18-20; Rev. 13:8). Through His sinless life, Christ showed that the requirements of God were not unjust and that, through faith in God, it was possible to live above sin. By means of His life here on earth, His cruel death on the cross and His resurrection, Christ demonstrated the justice and mercy of God and the inadequacy and cruelty of Satan's government. By this means He won the right to destroy Satan and sinners and confirm His government for eternity (Rev. 20:11-15).

11. What process is involved in Christ's deciding who will live with Him forevermore?
Daniel 7:9, 10 I watched till thrones were put in place, and the Ancient of Days was seated; His garment *was* white as snow, and the hair of His head *was* like pure wool. His throne *was* a fiery flame, its wheels a burning fire; a fiery stream issued and came forth from before Him. A thousand thousands ministered to Him; ten thousand times ten thousand stood before Him. The court was seated, and the books were opened.

Note: The process of judgment was taught simply in the Old Testament through the earthly sanctuary. The earthly sanctuary was a pattern of the heavenly, and gives us significant insights into the principles of its operation (Ps. 77:13; Heb. 9:23, 24). Let us notice some relevant details about the act of judicial atonement. On the Day of Atonement it is clear from chapter 16 of Leviticus that one task on this special day was a work of judgment (vss. 29, 30). The destinies of the people were settled on that day (Lev. 23:28-30). This represented the closing work of atonement for the people by Christ. It was a time when the high priest made final intercession for all those who by their actions and attitudes signified that they wished to be identified with God's people. The people may have sinned ignorantly; these sins were also represented before the Lord on this day. The work on the Day of Atonement involved sprinkling the blood of the Lord's goat on and before the mercy seat (Lev. 16:15). By this it was signified that the just demands of the law were satisfied by the shedding of the blood of the Lord's goat, which represented Christ.

In the heavenly sanctuary, Christ entered into this final phase of ministry in 1844 (antitypical Day of Atonement or Judgment) to make final atonement for all who might be benefited by His ministry and for the sins that the people have committed in ignorance (Dan. 8:14; Heb. 9:7; EW 253; GC 480). However, He does not cease His intercession on mankind's behalf during this phase (Heb. 7:25). Jesus' intercession on behalf of sinners (Rev. 3:5) ensures that the justice demanded by the law is satisfied by God's mercy. Thus, the salvation of mankind is assured, and the safety of the universe is secured against sin arising the second time (Ps. 85:9, 10; Nah. 1:9; ST Feb. 13, 1893).

The final act of getting rid of sin (spoken of by some as eradicatory atonement) is to place the record of sins, which Satan has caused God's people to commit, to his account. He bears this record into the lake of fire (Ps. 7:14-16; Rev. 20:10, 14). The universe will then be in a state of perfect harmony or unity (at-one). In the Old Testament sanctuary service, the high priest symbolically placed the record of confessed sins on the scapegoat (representing Satan), which was then sent into the land of oblivion or separation from the congregation (Lev. 16:10). As presented in the type, "so [at the end of the pre-advent judgment] Satan will be banished to the desolate earth, an uninhabited and dreary wilderness" and "the sins of those who are redeemed by the blood of Christ will at last be rolled back on the originator of sin, and he must bear their punishment . . . ." (GC 658).

12. What is the outstanding and overarching message of the book of Revelation?
Revelation 1:17 And when I saw Him, I fell at His feet as dead. But He laid His right hand on me, saying to me, "Do not be afraid; I am the First and the Last."

Note: "These are wonderfully solemn and significant statements. It was the Source of all mercy and pardon, peace and grace, the self-existent, eternal, unchangeable One, who visited His exiled servant on the isle that is called Patmos" (MS 81, 1900). John the Revelator, who was a close friend of Jesus on earth, presented Him still as a person of flesh and blood who is intensely interested in believers' daily lives and in their personal salvation. The second significant message in the book of Revelation is that Christ is with His children; He is in charge. Hence, we should not be afraid or discouraged. The comforting assurance is that "No temptation has overtaken you except such as is common to man; but God is faithful, who will not allow you to be tempted beyond what you are able, but with the temptation will also make the way of escape, that you may be able to bear it" (1 Cor. 10:13).

11.2 Guiding the Churches

Introduction

The vision about the churches commenced in Revelation chapter 1. We noticed there that Christ is pictured as moving gracefully among the lamp stands. This brings to our minds the details of the earthly sanctuary and more specifically of the Holy Place. By the time John wrote, the temple at Jerusalem had been destroyed by Titus and the candle sticks located in the temple had been carried to Rome. Their images still may be observed on the triumphal arch of Titus. Thus, the prophecy is directing our attention to the ministry of Christ in the heavenly sanctuary.

Christ is shown in shining brilliance (Rev. 1:14-16) indicating that there is no further need for a sanctuary on earth. He is the light of the world (John 8:12). Indeed, an allusion is made to the Passover (Rev. 1:18), which commemorates the sacrifice of Christ, and gives the assurance that, as Christ rose from the tomb, we may experience a rebirth/recreation. It is thus no coincidence that the vision was given on the Sabbath or Lord's Day (vs. 10). John thus connects the ideas of God's creative activity with His re-creative abilities. Our God is fully able to save us.

The letters to the churches had relevance to the churches already existing in the locations named, but these letters also must be seen in terms of the future. The text gives this information if we analyze it carefully. For example, there are indications that various events were already happening. Phrases such as: "you have left your first love" (Rev. 2:4) or "you . . . have kept My word" (3:8) tell us that John was speaking to congregations in his day. The letters also contain predictive elements. For example, "the devil is about to throw some of you into prison" (2:10) and "I also will keep you from the hour of trial which shall come upon the whole world" (3:10).

There is also a symbolic element to the letters. They symbolized the seven great eras in church experience from John's day until the end of time. The use of the number seven, which Doukhan (2002, 27) tells us stands for "totality and perfection," is an indication of this deep symbolism. Indeed, we notice that the churches named were not the only ones in Asia (Col. 1:2; 4:13). Readers of the text have long understood that the letters to the churches were indicative of the experience through which the church as a whole would pass. This interpretation will be applied in the lesson to follow. The dates suggested for each church period are derived from significant historical events that seem to correspond to the descriptions given in the text.

The Study

Read chapters 2 and 3 then the Bible texts and notes below in answer to the questions posed.

1. In the first vision recorded in Revelation, John saw Christ holding seven stars and walking among seven lamp stands. What do these symbols represent?

Revelation 1:13 [I, John, saw] . . . in the midst of the seven lampstands *One* like the Son of Man, clothed with a garment down to the feet and girded about the chest with a golden band.

Verse 16 He [Christ] had in His right hand seven stars, out of His mouth went a sharp two-edged sword, and His countenance *was* like the sun shining in its strength.

Verse 20 [Christ said] "The mystery of the seven stars which you saw in My right hand, and the seven golden lampstands: The seven stars are the angels of the seven churches, and the seven lampstands which you saw are the seven churches."

Note: The apostle John here reminds readers that although the temple at Jerusalem had been destroyed and the candlesticks had been taken by Titus to Rome, God was still interested in authentic believers and that He tenderly cared for their eternal interests. The seven stars represented the angel messengers to the churches throughout the varied phases of the history of the Christian church. "He [Christ] is represented as 'walking' among them, thus illustrating His constant diligence in behalf of His church" (Letter 4, 1908). By this means Jesus was assuring the prophet that His continual watchcare would be over God's church and He would guide it to a safe haven. The attention that Christ gives to the churches is not always complimentary. This is inferred by the reminder that He possessed a "sharp two-edged sword." The sword in the mouth of Jesus represents the word of God (Heb. 4:12). This both convicts, under the influence of the Holy Spirit, and is the standard used in judgment.

2. What churches were specifically named and where were they located? Was the advice given limited to the churches at the time of writing or does the vision have a broader significance?

Revelation 1:11 last part "What you see, write in a book and send *it* to the seven churches which are in Asia: to Ephesus, to Smyrna, to Pergamos, to Thyatira, to Sardis, to Philadelphia, and to Laodicea."

Note: Even in John's time the number of churches was greater than seven in number and so any application of the messages given to these churches must be more than of local significance. Indeed, in the text the word/phrase "churches" or "all the churches" are used to confirm this interpretation (Rev. 2:7, 11, 17, 23, 29: 3:6, 13, 22).

3. What features are noted in the letter to the church at Ephesus?

Revelation 2:1-7—Read.

The church at Ephesus (meaning "desirable"–Anderson 1978, 15) is considered to represent the experience of the Christian church in the first century of the present era. The prophet is given commendations, observations, recommendations and promises that are faithfully recorded for the actual church at Ephesus, but for other churches as well. Ephesus was an important sea port city and the centre of worship of the goddess Artemis or Diana (Acts 19:28)—location at the modern town of Selçuk in present-day Turkey. Superstition and crime were rife and the efforts of Satan to confuse the church were intense.

Notes:

Commendations: The heavenly record applauds the exemplary labour and patience of the church and its attempts to maintain doctrinal purity. It rejected the teaching and deeds of the Nicolaitans (Rev. 2:2, 3, 6). The Nicolaitans maintained that the body and the mind were separate entities. This allowed doctrines to be taught that the body might be treated harshly or even indulged through depraved activities yet the soul could be saved. This group maintained that the soul possessed an element of the divine. They also had rejected principles contained in the books of Moses.

Observation: A note is made by the angel that the church had left its first love (Rev. 2:4). By this is meant that the missionary fervour of the early disciples had been lost in part and their love for each other had declined. The apostle Paul spent a number of years in the city (Acts 19:8-10; 20:31) and others labored in this pagan religious centre. The efforts were so successful that the trade of the silversmiths was reduced substantially (Acts 19:23-41). However, success and the prosperity of the church eventually led to a loss of vision and responsibility. "God will accept nothing less than the whole heart. Happy are they who from the commencement of their religious life have been true to their first love, growing in grace and the knowledge of our Lord Jesus Christ" (7BC 956).

Recommendations: The simple remedy to the problem identified was for the church to acknowledge the reproof given, repent and return to its first love (Rev. 2:5).

Promise: The overcomers were promised that they would eat of the tree of life in Paradise (vs. 7). In this plain statement, the angel affirms the reality of the physical domain—the saints would "eat" and by referring the readers to the "tree of life" the faithfulness of the words of Moses, spoken of in Genesis, also are upheld.

4. What features are noted in the letter to the church at Smyrna?
Revelation 2:8-11—Read.
The beautiful ancient city of Smyrna (meaning "sweet smelling"—Anderson 1978, 19—today's Izmir in Turkey) was commercially prosperous. The period over which the advice given to this church is considered to apply is approximately from A.D. 100 to 313. This represented the period of persecutions beginning soon after the apostle John died and ending with Diocletian and Galerius' reigns.

Notes:
Commendations: The angel noted that this church was rich on account of the trials they were withstanding, although they were poor in earthly goods. This was on account of their works of faith and their rejection of evil speaking against God (blasphemy), an activity engaged in by some (Rev. 2:9).

Observation: The angel warned that a time of special testing was about to come (vs. 10). Indeed, the city is known especially on account of the martyrdom of Polycarp, bishop of Smyrna, who was burnt to death. The city also was visited by the bishop of Antioch, Ignatius, on his way to Rome where he suffered martyrdom in A.D. 109. They were not the only Christians to suffer persecution and death because they would not revile Christ. Now, this difficulty had come because the emperor demanded that his subjects worship him.

A special period of 10 years intense persecution was seen during the reigns of Diocletian and Galerius that answers to the "tribulation" spoken about in verse 10. The decree of A.D. 303 called for the destruction of churches and the dissolution of Christian communities. The massacre of an entire village is attributed to the persecutions of this period. Persecution extended until 312 and came to an end officially in 313 when the Emperor Constantine began to reign and issued the Edict of Milan.

Recommendations: The encouragement was not to fear but continue to be faithful (vs. 10). Since the voice of the martyrs was strong, believers did not falter. Polycarp is recorded as saying: "I bless thee that thou hath thought me worthy of the present day and hour, to have a share in the number of the martyrs in the cup of Christ" (Anon. 1835, 15).

Promise: The encouraging promise to the overcomers was that they would receive a crown of life and were assured that they would not be subjected to the second or eternal death (vss. 10, 11).

5. What features are noted in the letter to the church at Pergamos?

Revelation 2:12-17—Read.
The famous city of Pergamum or Pergamon (meaning "height" or "elevation"–Anderson 1978, 22) in Asia occupied an elevated position (near the modern city of Bergama in Turkey) giving it comparative security. It was a cultural centre and the site of a number of important temples dedicated to the worship of the emperors. The period of church history covered by this angel is considered to be from A.D. 313 to 538. The period of persecutions had ceased and Christians had become accepted members of society.

Notes:
Commendations: The praise given was that this church held fast to God's name and exercised faith and performed appropriate deeds even at the threat of martyrdom (Rev. 2:13).

Observations: Even though the angel approved of much that was being done in the church, various problems were identified. The members did not have correct views of some doctrines and tolerated some of those in the congregation who should have been expelled (vss. 14, 15). The Nicolaitans are singled out for mention again and also Balaam. The latter was responsible for leading God's people to compromise truth with error (Num. 22; 25:1-5). Now, the Emperor Constantine was the master of compromise and was instrumental in smoothing the way for many pagan practices to come into the Christian church. The Church was filled with the insincere, the self serving, and the politically motivated. This is explained in the following lines. "When Christianity conquered Rome the ecclesiastical structure of the pagan church, the title and vestments of the *pontifex maximus*, the worship of the Great Mother and a multitude of comforting divinities, the sense of super sensible presences everywhere, the joy or solemnity of old festivals, and the pageantry of unmemorial ceremony, passed like maternal blood into the new religion, and captive Rome captured her conqueror. The reins and skills of government were handed down by a dying empire to a virile papacy . . . the revolting provinces, accepting Christianity, again acknowledged the sovereignty of Rome" (Durant 1944, 671, 672).

Some of the changes are more explicitly evident. As we peruse this period of church history, we notice that many pagan ideas entered into Christian practice that we still recognize today. The acceptance of December 25 as the day to commemorate Christ's birth coincided with the pagan festival of *Brumalia* at the winter solstice and was, incidentally, also the birthday of Mithras, a representation of the sun. The celebration of the resurrection of Christ at Easter, the burning of candles and the substitution of Sunday as the holy day instead of the Sabbath constitute additional parallels with pagan sun worship. Other doctrinal adoptions are seen in the concept of hell, the immortality of the soul, and the elevation of the Madonna.

Recommendations: The only remedy for such departures was to repent deeply (Rev. 2:16) and return to the ways of the Scriptures. This process would begin in earnest during the Protestant Reformation.

Promises: The overcomer will be given rewards including the "hidden manna" and a new name (vs. 17). The manna is a clear reference to God's watchcare during the wilderness wanderings of the children of Israel. Today, this means feeding on God's word and contemplating His character. When we see the beauty of Christ's character and by faith follow Him, we are given a new name (cf. Gen. 17:5; 32:28).

6. What features are noted in the letter to the church at Thyatira?
Revelation 2:18-29—Read.

The city of Thyatira (meaning "sacrifice of contrition"–Anderson 1978, 29) was close to Pergamum and was inferior to it (its modern name is Ak-hissar). The period of church history encompassed by the message of the angel to this church is considered to be from 538 until 1517 (October 31, 1517 is called by some the "birthday of the Protestant Reformation"–Stanton & Hyma 2000, 376). It has been said that "Two pre-eminent revolutions have passed over Europe since the beginning of the Christian era. The one struck the Rome and rule of emperors; the other struck the Rome and rule of the popes. The one brought the Dark Ages; the other ended them." Now, "Martin Luther was the chief instrument and embodiment of the second" (Seiss 2007, 14). This church covered the period marked by great darkness and witnessed the Inquisition and the Crusades.

Notes:

Commendations: The church was commended for its works, love, service, faith and patience (Rev. 2:19). The place of works was noted as being predominant (vs. 19). During this period of history the Christian church was involved in establishing schools, universities and hospitals.

Observations: The angel commented specifically on practices showing accommodation with the world that were continuing to creep into the congregation (vs. 20). These are identified as originating with "Jezebel" who induced those following her to commit amoral acts and to eat food offered to idols. In as much as Jezebel was the wife of the king of Israel, Ahab (1 Kings 16:31), the verse is saying that the apostasy seen in the church would be promoted by the leaders of the institution. Like Jezebel, who took authority belonging to God and introduced Baal worship, so the church would take both political and religious power and exert it over the people and lead them deep into apostasy.

Recommendations: The only remedy for departures from God was to repent; however, few would heed the warning (Rev. 2:21). Even among the general departures from authentic faith some goodness remained and those who had truth were admonished to hold fast to it (vs. 25). During the latter part of this church period, reformation was beginning to break the power of darkness.

Promises: The overcomer was promised power over the nations and "the morning star" (vss. 26, 28). This is none other than a reference to Christ (Num. 24:17) and a promise that the overcomer would be able to walk with Him in glory. Christ has power over the nations and will rule them forever ["with a rod of iron" (Rev. 19:15)—symbolizing his rulership and his authority to meter out punishment for sin]. The assurance is given that the saints will reign with Christ (Rev. 20:4).

7. What features are noted in the letter to the church at Sardis?

Revelation 3:1-6—Read.

The name Sardis meant "that which remains"–Anderson (1978, 33). The ancient city was perched on a mountain height making it appear impregnable. However, the enemy opened the gates while the inhabitants slept in their supposed security. The once great city was brought to sudden ruin (now the site of the modern city of Sart in Turkey).

The period covered by the church of Sardis is considered to be from the period of the Protestant Reformation (1517) until the beginning of the first sign marking the "time of the end." Martin Luther published his famous theses in 1517 that crystallized the religious discussion and signaled revolt from the Catholic Church and culminated in protest movements in many countries. These developments led the formation of separate religious organizations. The first sign heralding the "time of the end" was given in 1755 when the Lisbon earthquake struck (see study 11.4–Opening the Seals).

Notes:

Commendation: The angel's advice was to strengthen the few good things that remained (Rev. 3:2). Historically, we find that the effect of the theses posted by Luther "was rapid and powerful" (Scott 1832, 17). The Reformation made great advances for a short time following this event. However, as the movement developed the churches constructed creeds, often became state religions, and unfortunately continued to hold onto non-biblical practices. The insincere joined the popular movement and fanaticism raised its ugly head. Some Protestant groups developed an intolerant attitude towards others of different faiths and did not hesitate to exterminate non-believers.

Towards the end of this period a movement was beginning to develop that would result in the eventual abandonment of strict ideas of right or wrong; the concept that there were absolutes began to disappear. The seeds of rationalism or modern humanism were being developed in the very country where the Reformation shone the brightest. The insidious results of this movement have paralyzed the churches of our day.

Observations: The angel observed that in Sardis there were a few who walked righteously before God, but there was great danger that even these would cease to exist (vss. 2, 4). One problem the church suffered from was quibbling and quarrelling over little things that do not have eternal value. Arguing over matters that are not given by God as tests of faith may get intense and eventually lead to separation (RH Aug. 10, 1905). The tendency to make personal principles a requirement or a standard for other members is a weapon Satan enjoys using.

Recommendations: The advice of the angel was to hold fast to the truth that had been given and repent (vs. 3). God wished this church to recognize the great light and opportunities it had been given and to seek to redeem the time by acting wisely.

Promises: God promised the overcomer a special place next to Him in Paradise. There the saints will be clothed in white and walk with Christ (vss. 4, 5).

8. What features are noted in the letter to the church at Philadelphia?

Revelation 3:7-13—Read.

The church of Philadelphia lay in the midst of a volcanic region and was the centre of Greek culture in Asia (present day Alaşehir in Turkey is the site of this ancient city). Its name meant "brotherly love" (Anderson 1978, 37) to reflect the love between two prominent brother kings in the ancient world (King Eumenes II of Pergamon and Attalus II who would succeed him). In the church era it represented, Philadelphia demonstrated an outstanding expression of brotherly interest, sacrifice and love in the salvation of others.

The church period covered by the angel's message is placed in the period 1755 until 1844. This was the period during which great evangelistic efforts were made in various parts of the world. Following the American and French Revolutions, great missionary outreach endeavours engulfed Africa, India, China and other countries. This religious enthusiasm and emphasis led up to an awakening concerning Christ's second advent culminating in the great disappointment of 1844.

Notes:

Commendation: The church in this period is commended for keeping God's word, upholding His name and performing works of faith (Rev. 3:8, 10). The deeds of the great missionaries such as William Carey in India, Robert Moffat and David Livingstone in Africa, Robert Morrison in China and William Miller in the United States represent just some who pushed back the frontiers of ignorance. Bible societies flourished and the Sunday school movement was popular.

Observations: The one note of concern recorded is that the church possessed but little strength. However, this was counterbalanced by the spirit of loyal perseverance (vss. 8, 10).

Recommendations: Whenever a religious revival takes place, Satan is there to hinder its progress. Thus the advice of the angel to believers was to hold firm and not allow anyone to cheat them of eternal life. This was the time when the cry was heard that Christ would soon come (vs. 11). Indeed, history records that across the Americas, in Australia, Europe, Scandinavia and other parts of the world great interest and excitement was shown in the soon coming of Christ. This interest was fermented by the spectacular falling of the stars in 1833 (Leonid shower) and by the heightened interest in the prophecies of Daniel surrounding the 1260 year and 2300 year prophecies in particular (see Daniel Chapters 7 and 8).

Promises: The overcomers were promised a position and titles of honour in God's eternal city (vs. 12). Like the pillar that withstood the great earthquake in Philadelphia in A.D. 17, so those who remained loyal to Christ were promised a permanent place in God's eternal kingdom.

9. What features are noted in the letter to the church at Laodicea?
Revelation 3:7-22—Read.
Ancient Laodicea was affluent and self sufficient and renowned for its trade in medicinal eyesalve. The name meant "judging of the people"–Anderson (1978, 41). The ruins of the city are found near Denizli in Turkey.

Following the sequence already established, the Laodicean church represents the last church on earth before Christ's coming. This idea is conveyed in verse 14, which introduces the author as "the Amen," who is none other than the Creator! This church's history commenced in 1844, the year when Christ's final phase of ministry commenced in the heavenly sanctuary. This is the church of today!

The general religious awakening of the early nineteenth century came to a premature end in 1844 when the anticipated return of Christ failed to materialize. In response, many abandoned their faith in the Advent message and some descended into fanaticism. The churches retreated into formality and lacked vision (EW 107, 108). Almost coincidental with these developments, Darwin's fascinating evolutionary theory burst upon the scene (1859) and began to capture the minds of men and women and blunt the impact of God's word. The seeming progress of mankind apart from God fastened the minds of people in its mesmerizing grip.

Notes:
Commendation: No specific commendations are mentioned. However, as we will discover later many will choose to believe and obey and will be saved even though they will pass through an especially difficult time just before Christ returns.

Observations: The angel rebuked the church because it was filled with proud, self sufficient individuals who were content with their knowledge, accomplishments, status and acceptance by the world. The members generally failed to discern that they were in a very undesirable condition from God's perspective. He was about to disassociate Himself from them because they were and still are lukewarm (vss. 15-17).

Recommendations: The counsel of the "true witness" is to be zealous and repent and then to buy gold, white garments and eye ointment (vss. 18, 19). Now the gold represents faith that works through love under the testing trials all believers experience (Job 23:10; Gal. 5:5, 6). The white garments are a symbol of purity and represent the righteous deeds of the saints done through exercising faith in Christ's merits (Isa. 61:10; Jer. 23:6; Rev. 19:7, 8). The righteousness that is offered believers comes wholly from Christ; they do not manufacture it through their good works (DA 323, 324). The eyesalve represents the convicting power of the Holy Spirit (John 16:8-10). In reality, these Bible verses paint a picture of the Laodicean believers trying to function acceptably without a vital connection with the vine (John 15:5) and relying on human wisdom and institutions.

The following statement catches our attention: "To be without the graces of the Spirit of God is sad indeed; but it is a more terrible condition to be thus destitute of spirituality and of Christ, and yet try to justify ourselves by telling those who are alarmed for us that we need not their fears and pity. Fearful is the power of self-deception on the human mind! What blindness—setting light for darkness and darkness for light! The True Witness counsels us to buy of Him gold tried in the fire, white raiment, and eyesalve. The gold here recommended as having been tried in the fire is faith and love. It makes the heart rich; for it has been purged until it is pure, and the more it is tested the more brilliant is its lustre. The white raiment is purity of character, the righteousness of Christ imparted to the sinner. This is indeed a garment of heavenly texture that can be bought only of Christ for a life of willing obedience. The eyesalve is that wisdom and grace that enables us to discern between the evil and the good, and to detect sin under any guise. God has given His church eyes, which He requires them to anoint with wisdom that they may see clearly; but many would put out the eyes of the church if they could; for they would not have their deeds come to the light, lest they should be reproved. The divine eyesalve will impart clearness to the understanding. Christ is the depositary of all graces. He says: 'Buy of Me'" (4T 88, 89).

Promise: The overcomer was and is promised the privilege to sit with Christ on His throne (vs. 21). There can be no greater reward than this. The remarkable feature about the message to the Laodicean church was and still is that Christ personally knocks at the door of understanding, seeking recognition (vs. 20).

10. What characteristics of God are particularly emphasized in the messages to the churches?
Revelation 2:1, 8, 12, 18—Read. Notice first Christ's walking and caring activities, then the fact that He is the resurrected Lord, that He carries a sharp sword and possesses flaming or discerning eyes.

Revelation 3:1, 6, 13, 22—Read. The Spirit's cooperative work is emphasized; Christ is presented as the keeper of the truth, the ruler of the nations and the faithful and true witness. Again He is presented as the resurrected Lord.

Note: As the angels speak about the care of the Lord for the churches, they reveal a progression of intimacy. In the message to Ephesus, Jesus was shown as walking among the candlesticks (Rev. 2:1). For Smyrna He was emphasized as the one who died for them (Rev. 2:8). For the next churches He was presented as the one who will come (Rev. 2:16, 25; 3:3, 11. Jesus is the one who "searches the minds and heart" (2:23) and finally, in the message to the Laodicean church, He is the one standing at the door wishing to eat with the believers (Rev. 3:20).

11. From the practical advice given to the seven churches, what cautions might the churches in Australia, India, China, Southeast Asia and elsewhere exercise today?

If we forget the lessons of history, then we may very well be forced to relearn them through sad experience. The falling away of the churches from the purity shown by the apostolic church happened gradually. Failure to maintain a personal relationship with Christ, dependency on others to explain the word of God, mingling philosophical ideas from the world into the fabric of belief, doubting the word of God, taking on customs and practices from other religions (and sanctifying them by practice) and allowing error to flourish unchecked are some of the experiences of the church through the ages. These are being repeated today. In addition, we find that the historical-critical approach to understanding Scripture (reject the idea of miracles and supernatural events—refer to chapter 5) has well nigh obliterated enthusiastic belief in miracles and God's guidance through the ages and thus has blunted the witness of the church.

11.3 Honouring the Redeemer

Introduction

The contrast between the previous chapters in Revelation and those that we will now focus upon is substantial. Christ has been featured as walking among the churches in chapters 1-3. Now the prophet is invited to look into the throne room in heaven. The intention is to lead the reader to recognize that above all principalities and powers encountered here on earth there sits in heaven one whose throne is above all others. This is most appropriate for as we proceed in our study of the book of Revelation it appears that the powers of this world are about to triumph over the people of God.

Our study in chapters 4 and 5 is situated in the sanctuary in heaven. This is a topic that some wish to neglect, but from the time of the Exodus of Israel from Egypt God has used the imagery of the sanctuary to convey eternal truths. Moses built the earthly sanctuary after the model shown him in heaven (Exod. 25:8, 9), for the specific purpose of conveying the idea that God is intimately involved in the affairs of mankind. Now at the end of the Bible this important message is reiterated except that now the heavenly sanctuary is featured. God is not distant and uninvolved in the events on earth. As the sanctuary on earth was a meeting place for God and His children, the heavenly sanctuary maintains the same purpose through the presence of Christ who is "the great ordinance by which man and God are united and commune together" (7BC 967).

The chapters we are studying here complement somewhat the vision seen by the prophet Daniel (7:9, 10, 13, 14). In chapter 7 of Daniel, the Father is shown presiding in judgment while the Son is seen as the deciding judge. Jesus confirmed this when He said: "Therefore whoever confesses Me before men, him I will also confess before My Father who is in heaven" (Matt. 10:32). Some of the scenes in the book of Revelation specifically deal with judgment and the close of the Great Controversy.

The Study

Read chapters 4 and 5 then the Bible texts and notes below in answer to the questions posed.

1. Chapter 4 opens with a scene showing somebody seated upon a throne. Who is represented in the vision and what proceeds from the throne?

Revelation 4:2, 3 Immediately I was in the Spirit; and behold, a throne set in heaven, and *One* sat on the throne. And He who sat there was like a jasper and a sardius stone in appearance; and *there was* a rainbow around the throne, in appearance like an emerald.

Verse 5 And from the throne proceeded lightnings, thunderings, and voices. Seven lamps of fire *were* burning before the throne, which are the seven Spirits of God [or the Holy Spirit—symbolism represents His perfection and completeness].

Note: This scene is reminiscent of the one described by the prophet Daniel (chapter 7) and represents a scene from the heavenly sanctuary, perhaps at the inauguration of Christ. John is not shown the nature of the throne or given a great deal of information regarding the person sitting on it. The first things we notice are the three stones (jasper, sardius and emerald). This immediately brings our minds back to the earthly sanctuary and the breastplate of judgment that contained these precious stones in the first, second and fourth rows (Exod. 28:17-20). The stones chosen have interesting meanings attached to them. The jasper stone related to the tribe of Naphtali that was noted for being "full of the blessing of the LORD"

(Deut. 33:23) because "hope pervaded his daily life and lifted his heart to heavenly places." Gad was represented by the sardony stone that was a "symbol of the saving, soothing grace of God's Spirit" and "purity and sacrifice." The emerald stone stood for the tribe of Zebulun that combined wealth and good character. This tribe "played his part in the cause of God without striving for financial gain" (Hardinge 1991, 321, 326, 335).

The mention of the rainbow casts our mind back immediately to the great flood and to the promises of God. It reflects on both God's grace and mercy and reminds us that both proceed from Him; these attributes reflect aspects of His glorious character (Ezek. 1:28). Emanating from the presence of God there was a stream of glory and fire accompanied by voices and echoing sounds.

2. What similarities can be noticed between the description of the throne room in the present chapter (refer to the previous question) and that described in Daniel chapter 7?

Daniel 7:9, 10 "I watched till thrones were put in place, and the Ancient of Days was seated; His garment *was* white as snow, and the hair of His head *was* like pure wool. His throne *was* a fiery flame, its wheels a burning fire; a fiery stream issued and came forth from before Him. A thousand thousands ministered to Him; ten thousand times ten thousand stood before Him. The court was seated, and the books were opened.

Note: Both visions defy human description. However, there is the impression of grandeur, power, majestic excellence and the smallness of mankind. The vision is of a remarkable God against whom the whole race has rebelled.

3. Twenty four elders are spoken about. Who do they represent and what duties do they have?

Revelation 4:4 Around the throne *were* twenty-four thrones, and on the thrones I saw twenty-four elders sitting, clothed in white robes; and they had crowns of gold on their heads.

Revelation 5:8 Now when He had taken the scroll, the four living creatures and the twenty-four elders fell down before the Lamb, each having a harp, and golden bowls full of incense, which are the prayers of the saints.

Note: As the description of the throne environment unfolds, we are given the remarkable information that Christ does not sit there alone. The individuals shown ministering with Him are evidently from among the redeemed. How do we know this? The "white robes" of the elders and their crowns are evidence that this must be the case. They wear Christ's robe of righteousness bought at an incredible price and the crowns they wear indicate they were soul winners. The number of the elders is 24, which refers the reader's mind back to the 24 divisions of priests in the earthly sanctuary (1 Chron. 24:1-19) and the 24 divisions of singers who praised the Lord there (1 Chron. 25:1-31). We might conclude then that the elders assist in ministering in the heavenly sanctuary and bring honour to the Lord as trophies of His victory over Satan (Matt. 27:52, 53; cf. Eph. 4:8). Taking our cue from the earthly sanctuary, we do not have to consider these beings as heavenly angels, for priests ministered in the earthly sanctuary as representatives of Christ.

The identity of the four living creatures is a little more difficult to pin point. We will address this question later.

4. What special feature of Christ's activities do the elders highlight?

Revelation 4:11 [The twenty-four elders say] "You are worthy, O Lord, to receive glory and honor and power; for You created all things, and by Your will they exist and were created."

Note: It is significant to note that the emphasis is on Christ's creatorship. This is the one activity on which all others rest for His creatorship indicates His access to absolute power and infinite wisdom. In this very language of creation, heaven proclaims that the Lord is both Creator and Redeemer and is to be honoured throughout eternity on the seventh-day Sabbath (EW, 217). The world is very bold in proclaiming the naturalistic origin of the universe and, too often, Christians are weakly accepting of this explanation. In this manner they blaspheme God's name and deny His power.

This verse is a reminder that the Great Controversy originated over the creation of this universe and the principles that regulate its operation. One author (Bauer 2009, 227, 228) has expressed the significance of the creation theme thus:

"But if Darwinism is accepted as factual, then the lack of teleology [design] means there can be no divine design for morality, just as there was none for creation. Why would God avoid design in creation only to have design in morals? [Now] . . . designless theism . . . would have to eliminate the Ten Commandments and all other direct moral guidance by God, as shown in the Bible. In such a scenario sin is eliminated since there can be no divine law or design to violate. Thus, Darwinism clearly undermines the foundations of biblical morality, yet our identity as Adventists lies heavily in the imperative to call people to obedience to God's commandments. How can we do so if our scientific paradigms eliminate the veracity of the Ten Commandments? It seems likely that Darwinism is quite toxic to this dimension of our mission as a church.

"The elimination of the Ten Commandments (since there is no more divine design) means one would eliminate the ability to sin, since there is no design to rebel against. Furthermore, judgment becomes impossible since there can be no moral design as a standard to which one can be held accountable. For Seventh-day Adventist theology, this is especially devastating due to the great emphasis on the 'investigative judgment.' Such a judgment is incompatible with Darwinism or deism, leaving man with no real accountability to God. Neither Deism nor Darwinism can sustain such a doctrine. Our mission of announcing the judgment and calling people to acknowledge their accountability to God is incompatible with the implications of Darwin's theory.

"This undermining of the doctrines of sin and judgment, in turn, removes the need for salvation from sin and its penalty, for there can be no sin or penalty without divine design and sovereignty. This would mean, therefore, that there would be no need for an incarnation and sacrificial death by Christ. Furthermore, the incarnation event was designed, planned, unnatural act incompatible with Darwinism or a deistic god who uses no design. Removing teleology [design] thus undermines several key pillars of Christian faith that are crucial to the salvific mission of the church.

"Additionally, if there is no divine design, how can such a theism have a meaningful eschatology? If suffering and death are tools of evolutionary progress, then death and suffering are natural. Death is no longer an enemy as the Scriptures declare (for example, 1 Cor. 15:26). If Darwin is right, then why should we hope for a world to come in which death and suffering will be no more (Rev 21-22)? Man's importance in the plan of salvation and divine future is replaced by an uncertain future of natural selection, personal insignificance, and death. There can be no special destiny since there is no divine design that calls for it.

"Today, the Christian church is faced with an apostasy as marked as that recorded by the prophet Ezekiel (8:3-17). Abominations are being committed in the name of Christian religion by bringing non-religious philosophies (e.g., Darwinian evolution) into the church and sanctifying them by acceptance. The leaders of such congregations are in rebellion against God and his word. Surely, the Lord will answer as he did anciently: 'Therefore I also will act in fury. My eye will not spare nor will I have pity; and though they cry in My ears with a loud voice, I will not hear them' (Ezek. 8:18)."

5. Four living creatures (seraphs) were present before the throne. What function are they shown performing?
Revelation 4:6 Before the throne *there was* a sea of glass, like crystal. And in the midst of the throne, and around the throne, *were* four living creatures full of eyes in front and in back.

Verses 8-10 *The* four living creatures, each having six wings, were full of eyes around and within. And they do not rest day or night, saying: "Holy, holy, holy, Lord God Almighty, who was and is and is to come!" Whenever the living creatures give glory and honor and thanks to Him who sits on the throne, who lives forever and ever, the twenty-four elders fall down . . . and worship . . . .

Isaiah 6:1-5 In the year that King Uzziah died, I saw the Lord sitting on a throne, high and lifted up, and the train of His *robe* filled the temple. Above it stood seraphim; each one had six wings: with two he covered his face, with two he covered his feet, and with two he flew. And one cried to another and said: "Holy, holy, holy *is* the LORD of hosts; the whole earth *is* full of His glory!" And the posts of the door were shaken by the voice of him who cried out, and the house was filled with smoke. So I said: "Woe *is* me, for I am undone! Because I *am* a man of unclean lips, and I dwell in the midst of a people of unclean lips; for my eyes have seen the King, the LORD of hosts."

Note: The identity of the creatures featured in Revelation is shown by reference to the texts in Isaiah. The four living creatures are identified here as seraphim (highest order of angels). These creatures ceaselessly honour the God they serve (cf. Ps. 121:4). Their eyes are symbolic of majestic brightness and intelligence and the wings of speed (Ezek. 1:4, 8, 9, 14; Dan. 9:21; Rev. 1:14). We are informed concerning Isaiah's vision that "Around the throne were seraphim, as guards about the great King, and they reflected the glory that surrounded them. As their songs of praise resounded in deep notes of adoration, the pillars of the gate trembled, as if shaken by an earthquake. With lips unpolluted by sin, these angels poured forth the praises of God" (AG 72).

6. What characteristic possessed by Christ do the seraphs highlight?
Revelation 4:8 last part And they do not rest day or night, saying: "Holy, holy, holy, Lord God Almighty, who was and is and is to come!"

Note: This chorus of affirmation by the seraphs assures us that God is eternal, linking the idea expressed in the title "I AM" (Exod. 3:14) to John's thought emphasized in Revelation that God is not dead: He "is" and "is to come." The second coming of the Lord is here kept foremost in the minds of the readers. This is a theme that permeates the Scriptures, especially the New Testament. However, the psalmist rejoiced that: "Our God shall come, and shall not keep silent; a fire shall devour before Him, and it shall be very tempestuous all around Him. He shall call to the heavens from above, and to the earth, that He may judge His people: 'Gather My saints together to Me, those who have made a covenant with Me by sacrifice.' Let the heavens declare His righteousness, for God Himself *is* Judge. Selah" (Ps. 50:3-6). Jesus Himself added to this witness (John 14:1-4): "Let not your heart be troubled; you believe in God, believe also in Me. In My Father's house are many mansions; if *it were* not *so,* I would have told you. I go to prepare a place for you. And if I go and prepare a place for you, I will come again and receive you to Myself; that where I am, *there* you may be also. And where I go you know, and the way you know."

7. The seraphs are described as having the likeness of living creatures. What are we meant to take from this symbolism?

Revelation 4:7, 8 first part The first living creature *was* like a lion, the second living creature like a calf, the third living creature had a face like a man, and the fourth living creature *was* like a flying eagle. *The* four living creatures, each having six wings, were full of eyes around and within.

Note: The choice of various animals symbolizes various features of Christ's character as follows. The lion denotes strength and fearlessness (Rev. 5:5); the dignified ox represents willingness, patience in toil and suffering (John 15:20; Acts 4:27, 30); man is noted on account of his intelligence, ability to sympathize and to communicate (Matt. 22:46; Mark 6:31; Luke 9:22); and the eagle represents swiftness, perceptiveness and the power to soar (Job 9:26; Isa. 40:31). These same ensigns were used (according to the "Talmudists"—Clarke 1825, 590) by the tribes located on the four sides of the earthly sanctuary (Num. 2:3, 10, 18, 25; Ezek. 1:10).

8. Who is shown sitting on the throne holding a scroll in chapter 5?

Revelation of 5:1 And I saw in the right *hand* of Him who sat on the throne a scroll written inside and on the back, sealed with seven seals.

Note: The person sitting on the throne holding the scroll is not identified, but probably refers to God the Father. When the angel asked who was able to unroll the scroll, nobody could be found worthy to do this (vss. 2, 3). At this revelation, John wept (vs. 4). However, he was not to be disappointed for long.

9. Who was found worthy to open the scroll and why?

Revelation 5:5, 6 But one of the elders said to me, "Do not weep. Behold, the Lion of the tribe of Judah, the Root of David, has prevailed to open the scroll and to lose its seven seals." And I looked, and behold, in the midst of the throne and of the four living creatures, and in the midst of the elders, stood a Lamb as though it had been slain, having seven horns and seven eyes, which are the seven Spirits of God sent out into all the earth.

Note: There is no question but that the "Lion of the tribe of Judah" is none other than Jesus Christ who was found worthy to open the scroll. This is evident from the following verses (and also verse 12), but is also evident from a perusal of the genealogy of Jesus recorded in the first chapter of Matthew (1:2).

The scroll is sealed with seven seals (vs. 1) meaning that it is thoroughly sealed and that only one individual could possibly open it. The single reason given that the Lamb is worthy to open the scroll is that He "has prevailed" against Satan. Even though He was slain in the encounter on earth, He rose. Satan was unable to bind Him in the shackles of death and hence we can rejoice that his reign will end in oblivion (Rev. 20:9-15).

The significance of the number seven resides in its reference to the perfection of God. The Lamb is shown having eyes and horns. This is meant to convey the thought that He possesses both perfect wisdom and strength (Deut. 33:17; Prov. 8:22-30; Lam. 2:3).

10. What information is contained in the scroll?

Revelation 5:8 first part, 9 last part Now when He [the Lamb] had taken the scroll, the four living creatures and the twenty-four elders . . . sang a new song, saying: "You are worthy to take the scroll, and to open its seals; for You were slain, and have redeemed us to God by Your blood . . . ."

Note: We can deduce from this account that the scroll has something to do with the process of completing the plan of redemption, for as soon as it is opened the surrounding observers highlight their joy at being redeemed. The scroll certainly contains details about the Great Controversy and climaxes with the second coming (refer to the next study). We are not told in these chapters about the events in heaven immediately preceding the second coming, but we will learn something about these in later chapters. Perhaps we can suggest that the scroll contains also a record of the principles used in deciding who will be saved and who will be lost and the names of those in each category. Indeed, we are informed that the sealed scroll does contain a record of those who were pivotal in arranging Christ's final suffering and death here on earth (COL 294).

11. When Christ takes the scroll, what reaction is shown by the beasts, elders and angels?

Revelation 5:8, 9 Now when He [the Lamb] had taken the scroll, the four living creatures and the twenty-four elders fell down before the Lamb, each having a harp, and golden bowls full of incense, which are the prayers of the saints. And they sang a new song, saying: "You are worthy to take the scroll, and to open its seals; for You were slain, and have redeemed us to God by Your blood out of every tribe and tongue and people and nation."

Verses 11, 12 Then I looked, and I heard the voice of many angels around the throne, the living creatures, and the elders; and the number of them was ten thousand times ten thousand, and thousands of thousands, saying with a loud voice: "Worthy is the Lamb who was slain to receive power and riches and wisdom, and strength and honor and glory and blessing!"

Note: The song of the elders and living creatures indicates their appreciation for the redemption offered by Christ. Both fallen and unfallen beings can sing this song, for had Christ failed to succeed in His encounters with Satan the future of the government of God would have been at risk. In fact, the entire creation is shown praising God for the deliverance offered (vs. 13). There will be no more suffering, death or parting (Rev. 21:4) and the humble creatures will no longer suffer want and pain (Romans 8:22).

12. A great deal of sanctuary language is used in chapters 4 and 5. Notice the summary (Table 9). What significance can be attributed to the use of this imagery?

Note: The main purposes of including the language of the sanctuary in the discourse is to establish the unity of the scriptural record, to clarify (for those inclined to be dismissive) that both the Old and New Testament records are relevant to Christian living, and to reaffirm the centrality of both mercy and justice in God's plan of salvation. Justice cannot function without law and so the immutability of God's law also is highlighted by the emphasis. Finally, the intimate involvement of Christ throughout recorded history is shown in the plan of salvation.

The wonderful news that this imagery conveys to us is that the sanctuary in heaven is real; it has real actors and a real purpose. This is the message that the apostle Paul conveys to us in the book of Hebrews (8:1, 2): "Now *this is* the main point of the things we are saying: We have such a High Priest, who is seated at the right hand of the throne of the Majesty in the heavens, a Minister of the sanctuary and of the true tabernacle which the Lord erected, and not man."

The activities in the heavenly sanctuary follow discrete phases. The first phase commenced soon after Christ's resurrection—at Pentecost (Acts 2:1-4, 32, 33). Christ carried on His mediatorial ministry and then in 1844 the second phase of His ministry began—His ministry in the pre-advent judgment. The Scriptures present Christ as the judge, for He alone has earned the right to represent sinful human beings. "[The Father] has given Him authority to execute judgment also, because He is the Son of Man" (John 5:27). This important point was made clear in the earthly sanctuary where the high priest represented Christ.

Symbol used or instruction given	Text in Revelation	Sanctuary reference
Glorious light, colour, sound (prelude to giving sanctuary instructions–Exod. 25:8)	Rev. 4:1, 3	Exod. 19:16; 20:18
Instruction to observe (prelude, as above)	Rev. 4:1	Exod. 19:24
White garment worn	Rev. 4:4	Lev. 16:3, 4
24 elders	Rev. 4:4	1 Chron. 24:1–19
Torches or lamps of fire/glory	Rev. 4:5	Exod. 29:43; Lev. 6:13; Num. 9:16
Seven lamps	Rev. 4:5	Exod. 37:17–23
Ensign imagery	Rev. 4:7	Exod. 28:15–21
Book written on both sides	Rev. 5:1	Exod. 32:15
Lamb slain	Rev. 5:6, 12	Exod. 29:38–42; cf. Exod. 12:3
Golden bowls/incense	Rev. 5:8	Exod. 30:8
Blood redeems	Rev. 5:9	Heb. 9:11–14
Kings and priests	Rev. 5:10	Exod. 19:6

Table 9. Sanctuary language used in Revelation chapters 4 and 5.

The following quote adds further emphasis: "Christ has been made our Judge. The Father is not the Judge. The angels are not. He who took humanity upon Himself, and in this world lived a perfect life, is to judge us. He only can be our Judge. . . . Christ took humanity that He might be our Judge" (9T 185).

Revelation chapters 4 and 5 present inauguration scenes of Christ in the heavenly sanctuary following His ascension. This event was recognized on earth by the pouring out of the Holy Spirit. The initial verses of chapter 8 (vss. 3-5) emphasize intercession and Revelation 11, verse 19, judgment.

13. What activity is all heaven shown to be engaged in as chapters 4 and 5 climax?
Revelation 5:14 Then the four living creatures said, "Amen!" And the twenty-four elders fell down and worshiped Him who lives forever and ever.

Note: The worship in heaven echoes to the worship that God wishes His followers to enter into on earth. This is the emphasis given by the first angel highlighted in Revelation 14 (vss. 6, 7). This is worship given in honour of both creation and redemption.

11.4 Opening the Seals

Introduction

The chapters in the book of Revelation dealing with the opening of the seven seals have been a point of special interest since early Christian history. The message of the seals is given in the context of Christ appearing before the Father in the heavenly sanctuary (Revelation, chapters 4 and 5). The account dealing with the opening of the seals is continuous until and including the sixth seal, and then there is an intermission where important information is given about God's final work of salvation on the earth. The seventh seal climaxes with the coming of Christ.

The seals commence with a glorious scene in heaven, which culminates in a victory announcement and shouts of praise to God. The purpose of this is to remind all readers that irrespective of world events and of the triumphs of evil, a final satisfactory outcome is assured. God will triumph with His saints.

The seven seals deal with "things which must take place after this" (Rev. 4:1). Indeed, as the seals are opened there is a progression reflecting increasing urgency. The instruction to come and see in the first four seals becomes a cry of "how long" under the fifth seal but ends with the instruction that the day of God's judgment "has come" under the sixth seal. Then silence in heaven is introduced under the seventh seal to indicate that a celestial rescue mission is in full swing.

The usual thinking is that the seven seals cover the same period of time as the letters to the seven churches. We will follow this view, but the reader should be warned that commentators differ on the time periods covered by each seal, particularly the first four. The information given under the seals differs from that spoken by the angels to the seven churches. It has been truly said: "Surely the Lord GOD does nothing, unless He reveals His secret to His servants the prophets" (Amos 3:7).

The Study

Read chapters 6, 7 and 8:1 then the Bible texts and notes below in answer to the questions posed.

1. What was Christ's first task after His enthronement in heaven?

Revelation 4:1 After these things I looked, and behold, a door *standing* open in heaven. And the first voice which I heard *was* like a trumpet speaking with me, saying, "Come up here, and I will show you things which must take place after this."

Revelation 5:5 But one of the elders said to me, "Do not weep. Behold, the Lion of the tribe of Judah, the Root of David, has prevailed to open the scroll and to lose its seven seals."

Note: Christ was enthroned in heaven and then the Holy Spirit was poured out. This enthronement occurred at Pentecost (Acts 2:1, 33). On that day the Spirit was poured out on the waiting, united disciples (Acts 2:1-4). In our parallel account in the book of Revelation, such a plentiful outpouring of the Spirit is indicated by reference to the seven Spirits of God (Rev. 4:5; 5:6).

Christ's enthronement represented His acceptance by the Father as the Mediator or Guide between heaven and earth. The apostle Paul emphatically declared: "For there is one God and one Mediator between God and men, the Man Christ Jesus" (1 Tim. 2:5). In the letter to the Hebrews Paul explains further, as follows: "For if the blood of bulls and goats and the ashes of a heifer, sprinkling the unclean, sanctifies for the purifying of the flesh, how much more shall the blood of Christ, who through the eternal Spirit offered Himself without spot to God, cleanse your conscience from dead works to serve the living

God? And for this reason He is the Mediator of the new covenant, by means of death, for the redemption of the transgressions under the first covenant, that those who are called may receive the promise of the eternal inheritance" (Heb. 9:13-15)

2. When the first seal was opened, what symbolic beast rode out?

Revelation 6:1, 2 Now I saw when the Lamb opened one of the seals; and I heard one of the four living creatures saying with a voice like thunder, "Come and see." And I looked, and behold, a white horse. He who sat on it had a bow; and a crown was given to him, and he went out conquering and to conquer.

Note: White is a symbol of purity (Ps. 51:7; Isa. 1:18). Indeed, up to this point in our study of the book of Revelation the colour white has been used to refer to Christ and His authentic followers (e.g., Rev. 1:14; 2:17; 3:4, 5; 4:4). The choice of a horse is to convey the idea of conquest (Jer. 8:6). Now in the time when the apostle wrote, conquering generals rode in triumph on white horses.

The rider on the horse when the first seal was opened is shown as a real person and as carrying a bow. He also was given a crown. Now the bow represents success in endeavour (Pss. 7:11, 12; 45:4, 5), as does the crown (1 Cor. 9:25; Jas. 1:12). It has been suggested that this picture is a fitting representation of Jesus Christ and the purity of the message that He gave and still gives to the world (cf. Rev. 19:11-16). The prophetic representation is also a fitting picture of the Christian church particularly in the first century of the present era when the message of the gospel went to the well known parts of the world (Col. 1:23).

The church made rapid advances in the period under review. This was not made without sacrifices or persecution. Doctrinal errors began to creep into the congregations, but the apostles and elders vigorously defended the truths delivered to them.

3. When the second seal was broken, what coloured horse emerged?

Revelation 6:3, 4 When He opened the second seal, I heard the second living creature saying, "Come and see." Another horse, fiery red, went out. And it was granted to the one who sat on it to take peace from the earth, and that *people* should kill one another; and there was given to him a great sword.

Note: The period of history covered by this rider is considered by some commentators to be from A.D. 100 into the fourth century (A.D. 313). The red colour of this horse reasonably can be taken to indicate that persecution and bloodshed would be experienced (cf. Rev. 17:6). Indeed, the remainder of the verse quoted above indicates that the sword would rule with much destruction of life. The rider is without identity, but took peace from the earth. Some have suggested that the emphasis being made here was that the pagan Roman emperors took up the sword of persecution and destruction against the Christian church.

Persecution of Christians actually commenced with the Jews as recorded in the book of Acts and was given impetus by Nero in A.D. 64. However, these examples represented localized persecution. The persecution arising from "imperial edict" commenced with the Emperor Decius and his successors in and after A.D. 250. The "great persecution" under Diocletian and his colleagues commenced in A.D. 303 (de Ste Croix 2006, 106, 107). The Emperor Constantine gave Christianity legitimacy by the Edict of Milan in 313, but persecution continued under Licinius until he was defeated by Constantine (A.D. 324). It was then that the "Christian religion had finally triumphed in the Roman world" (Odahl 2004, 153-160).

4. The breaking of the third seal revealed a black horse. What is the significance of the scales or balances?

Revelation 6:5 When He opened the third seal, I heard the third living creature say, "Come and see." So I looked, and behold, a black horse, and he who sat on it had a pair of scales in his hand."

Note: The emphasis being made under this seal is that the church had lost the purity of both its message and its mission. For example, its thinking became so confused that it took up the sword to further its own interests. This was against other Christians who believed or practiced somewhat differently to the official church and also against pagans. Beginning with Constantine the interests of the emperor and the church were similar and opened the way for the church to pursue its goals both politically and militarily. Controversies began to rage among Christian groups after the Diocletian persecutions and these tore at the Empire. Constantine sent troops against the Donatists (group who refused to accept priests and bishops who had at one time renounced their faith under persecution) and succeeding emperors wrestled with the Arians (group considered Christ as a created being). The historian Gibbon (2004, chapter 21) observed that "the enmity of Christians towards each other surpassed the fury of savage beasts against man" and further "the kingdom of heaven was converted by discord into the image of chaos, of a nocturnal tempest, and of hell itself." The pagans had begun to lose favour under Constantine. It was Theodosius I (A.D. 378-395 reigned) who especially was characterized by "religious intolerance" towards them. The laws he enacted allowed pagans to be killed and their temples to be destroyed, although it is uncertain what direct involvement he took in these activities. He was the "last emperor to rule the entire Christian empire" (Rohrbacher 2002, 278-288). All these activities brought the Christian church into disrepute.

The period of history over which these comments are especially relevant is taken here to be from A.D. 313 until A.D. 538. The starting date represents the time when the Edict of Milan (toleration given) was made by Constantine (A. D. 313). The latter date represents the point where the last of the Arian powers was neutralized in the city of Rome. The Emperor Constantine 'converted' to Christianity and favoured the church with lands, privileges and powers. Church and state were no longer separate—this is represented by the rider carrying the balances—the civil and religious powers acted as one. Pagan practices flooded into the church as the insincere joined. Such practices as the decoration of temples with ornaments, the use of holy water, holy days, processions, the use of images and praying towards the East are pagan in origin. These and other practices were "sanctified by their adoption into the Church" (Newman 1920, 373). Tradition began to flourish.

5. A voice was heard during the vision of the third horseman. What message was given?
Revelation 6:6 And I heard a voice in the midst of the four living creatures saying, "A quart of wheat for a denarius, and three quarts of barley for a denarius; and do not harm the oil and the wine."

Note: The third horse was indeed black, for the gospel's purity had been largely lost (cf. Matt. 4:16; John 1:5; 3:19). During the period of loss of purity and doctrinal controversies in the church, there was a famine for the word of God. The grain spoken about represents God's word (cf. Matt. 13:3-30; Luke 8:11). It was so scarce that the prophet tells us that a day's wages was needed to buy the bare necessities for survival (a quart represented the daily ration for a man and a denarius was a representative daily wage). However, despite this famine, the oil and wine was still assured. This is an assurance that the Holy Spirit was still active to convict and convert men and women and to keep alive the flame of truth (Isa. 55:1; Zech. 4:1-6).

6. The breaking of the fourth seal revealed a pale horse. Who was riding the horse?

Revelation 6:7, 8 When He opened the fourth seal, I heard the voice of the fourth living creature saying, "Come and see." So I looked, and behold, a pale horse. And the name of him who sat on it was Death, and Hades followed with him. And power was given to them over a fourth of the earth, to kill with sword, with hunger, with death, and by the beasts of the earth.

Note: The progression of horses revealed becomes even less inviting as we arrive at the pale animal. We now see a pale and sickly coloured horse with a rider called "Death" seated upon it. The rider, and his following companion "Hades" (the place of the dead), brought destruction, hunger and death on a portion of mankind.

For the purpose of this exposition, we are taking the time period involved from A.D. 538 until the beginning of the Protestant Reformation (Luther's theses that were posted in 1517 is a convenient date). The Crusades, the Inquisition and religious wars are highlights of this period. The period commenced under the rule of the Emperor Justinian the Great (A.D. 527-565). He understood that "public law contained the sacral law" hence he considered he had the right to deal with religious matters. His reign exerted "profound effects on the fate of the papacy and herewith on medieval—and eventually also modern—Europe" (Ullmann 2003, 43).

Charlemagne the Great (A. D. 768-814), king of the Franks, is significant to the history of Europe and to the fulfillment of this seal. He was the first king to be crowned by a pope. He continued the policies of the first king of the Franks, Clovis, who introduced Catholicism. They both regarded the church and the state as being "hardly distinguishable" (Koch 1997, 98). After Charlemagne's crowning, his "army was now an arm of the Roman Church" (Jones & Pennick 1995, 130). Through most of his life, he led religious crusades which were marked by ruthlessness and terror.

The Crusader movement is another fulfillment of the fourth seal. It is considered to have occurred between 1095 until 1291 when Christian armies attempted to restore their control over the holy land (occupied by Muslim forces). However, campaigns also were mounted against pagans, heretics and other enemies of the church. These included the Slavs, Jews, Orthodox Christians, Mongols, Cathars, Hussites, Waldenses and Old Prussians. The political enemies of the church were punished.

The Inquisition, established with the "Pope's blessing, [provided] the machinery for mass extermination" (Baigent & Leigh 1999, 21). It became active in 1234. Innumerable people were killed, imprisoned, exiled or consigned to other punishments. In Spain the Inquisition (commenced 1478) pursued "with unabated ferocity . . . its work for more than 200 years" (Baigent & Leigh 1999, 80). Other countries did not escape including the New World.

7. When the fifth seal was broken, no more horses emerged. Instead, what unusual scene was revealed and what request was made?

Revelation 6:9, 10 When He opened the fifth seal, I saw under the altar the souls of those who had been slain for the word of God and for the testimony which they held. And they cried with a loud voice, saying, "How long, O Lord, holy and true, until You judge and avenge our blood on those who dwell on the earth?"

Note: The history of bloodshed on behalf of so-called Christianity did not cease with the Reformation. The scene became overwhelming and the victims from the various periods are shown symbolically under the fifth seal as crying out to God pleading for deliverance because they continued to remain true to Him. Symbolically their blood (or soul—cf. Lev. 17:11) cried out for vengeance as righteous Abel's blood did

(Gen. 4:10). This seal is set in the time leading up to the judgment of investigation that commenced in heaven in 1844.

8. What gesture was made to those who had suffered oppression?
Revelation 6:11 Then a white robe was given to each of them; and it was said to them that they should rest a little while longer, until both *the number of* their fellow servants and their brethren, who would be killed as they *were,* was completed.

Note: This verse makes it quite clear that the judgment in heaven will reward those who have stood firmly for authentic truth. Justice will be done. However, the prophet reminds readers that the cup of human suffering has not yet been filled. "When the fifth seal was opened, John the Revelator in vision saw beneath the altar the company that were slain for the Word of God and the testimony of Jesus Christ. After this came the scenes described in the eighteenth of Revelation, when those who are faithful and true are called out from Babylon" [Rev. 18: 1-5 quoted] (MR 1423, 1993).

9. The announcement of the arrival of the time of the end commences with the opening of the sixth seal. How do the elements of nature announce the nearness of this event?
Revelation 6:12, 13 I looked when He opened the sixth seal, and behold, there was a great earthquake; and the sun became black as sackcloth of hair, and the moon became like blood. And the stars of heaven fell to the earth, as a fig tree drops its late figs when it is shaken by a mighty wind.

Note: God now calls on the elements of nature and heavenly bodies to answer to the events of history. Under the sixth seal an earthquake struck with great severity in the city of Lisbon, Portugal, on November 1, 1755. This devastating earthquake exerted a widespread influence over an area from the Caribbean to Scandinavia and induced people to ask questions about God. It was recognized as "a harbinger of the approaching advent" (Froom 1948, vol. II, 674-695). This was followed by the dark day of May 19, 1780 that was restricted to certain areas of North America, for which there is no satisfactory natural explanation. It too was regarded "as a token of the latter days" (Froom 1948, vol. IV, 290). The final sign in the heavens involved the Leonid shower of meteorites on November 12-13, 1833 over the area from the Gulf of Mexico to Halifax. Although the Leonid showers occur at 33 year intervals, the one observed in 1833 stands as one of the most spectacular and it had a sobering effect on observers. Many believed that God's judgments were falling on the earth. The science of meteorite astronomy importantly has its birthdate with the 1833 Leonid shower.

The significance of these signs must be judged in the context of the times and the reaction they generated. The question is not whether they were the greatest earthquake ever seen or the greatest display of the falling stars.

10. During the last phase of the sixth seal, what happens in the heavens?
Revelation 6:14 Then the sky receded as a scroll when it is rolled up, and every mountain and island was moved out of its place.

Note: The last part of the sixth seal has yet to be fulfilled. The universal signs spoken about will take place at the coming of the Lord (Rev. 16:17-20). One writer has expressed it thus: "The heavens are to be rolled together as a scroll. And then shall they see the Son of man coming in the clouds with power and great glory. The Son of man shall come in his glory, and all the holy angels with him; then shall he sit upon the throne of his glory" (RH Jan. 12, 1886).

11. How widespread is the expression of God's wrath and how do the wicked respond?
Revelation 6:15, 16 And the kings of the earth, the great men, the rich men, the commanders, the mighty men, every slave and every free man, hid themselves in the caves and in the rocks of the mountains, and said to the mountains and rocks, "Fall on us and hide us from the face of Him who sits on the throne and from the wrath of the Lamb!"

Note: All now recognize the sovereignty and superiority of God's government. None now question His existence and power.

12. God's wrath is not expressed upon all. Some people are spared. What do these people possess that permits them to escape?
Revelation 7:2, 3 Then I saw another angel ascending from the east, having the seal of the living God. And he cried with a loud voice to the four angels to whom it was granted to harm the earth and the sea, saying, "Do not harm the earth, the sea, or the trees till we have sealed the servants of our God on their foreheads."

Note: The discourse commences with a scene showing four angels standing at the four points of the compass (Rev. 7:1) making sure that God's people are sealed before the Spirit of God is removed from the earth and war and strife come, just before Christ's coming (cf. Jer. 25:31-34; 51:1, 2, 11).

Now in order to understand the sealing, we remember that a seal placed on documents was and still is a sign of ownership and authenticity. This figure of speaking is used to describe God's pleasure in saving His people and claiming them as His. For "Every soul in our world is the Lord's property, by creation and by redemption" (7BC 969). A graphic figurative description of this process is given by the prophet Ezekiel (Ezek. 9:4-6). Those who are sealed refuse to believe or partake in the "abominations" (vs. 4) committed on the earth. God finds many activities in this category; some of these are identified in the three angels' messages of Revelation 14, verses 6 to 12.

13. What characteristics might we infer are displayed by those sealed and protected from God's wrath?
Revelation 7:14 And I said to him, "Sir, you know." So he said to me, "These are the ones who come out of the great tribulation, and washed their robes and made them white in the blood of the Lamb."

Note: Those who are sealed have identified fully with Christ and His ways. They have depended wholly on His merits—hence the terms "washed their robes" and "in the blood of the Lamb." They acknowledge God as their Creator through the observance of His holy law. "This recognition of God is of the highest value to every human being. All who love and serve Him are very precious in His sight. He would have them stand where they are worthy representatives of the truth as it is in Jesus" (Letter 77, 1899).

The great time of trouble or tribulation spoken of in this verse is the same as that alluded to by Daniel (Dan. 12:1), which is unparalleled in both its extent and effects. In that time, "The restraint which has been upon the wicked is removed, and Satan has entire control of the finally impenitent" (GC 614). This means that Christ's work of intercessory atonement has ceased.

14. How many are sealed and what are we to make of the number given?
Revelation 7:4 And I heard the number of those who were sealed. One hundred *and* forty-four thousand of all the tribes of the children of Israel *were* sealed.

Note: The number is not to be taken literally but it symbolically represents the saved that have come through great trouble. We can be certain of this as two of the original 12 tribes of Israel (Ephraim and Dan) are not mentioned in the list (vss. 5-8).

15. When John looked again at the scene, how many victorious believers could he see?
Revelation 7:9 After these things I looked, and behold, a great multitude which no one could number, of all nations, tribes, peoples, and tongues, standing before the throne and before the Lamb, clothed with white robes, with palm branches in their hands.

Note: Joining the symbolic 144,000 is an innumerable multitude of redeemed from all ages and from all nations.

16. What universal shout comes from the saved and what answering prayer is uttered by the elders and living creatures?
Revelation 7:10, 12 [The prophet saw a great multitude standing before the throne, waving branches] and crying out with a loud voice, saying, "Salvation *belongs* to our God who sits on the throne, and to the Lamb!" All the angels stood around the throne and the elders and the four living creatures, and fell on their faces before the throne and worshiped God, saying: "Amen! Blessing and glory and wisdom, thanksgiving and honor and power and might, *be* to our God forever and ever. Amen."

Note: The universal shout of blessing and praise to God for His salvation ascends not only from the redeemed but from the angels as well. God's kingdom has been made secure forever. This is indeed a reason to praise Him.

17. Looking into the future, one of the elders told John something about the experiences of the redeemed in heaven. What details did he give?
They will serve and live with Christ (Rev. 7:15, 17).
They will not suffer discomfit or want (vss. 16, 17).

Note: This list is far from complete but assures those who long for a better land that we serve a personal God who is interested in us. The assurance is also given that the cause of suffering, Satan and his philosophies, will be eliminated forever along with his followers (Rev. 20:10, 15).

18. When the seventh seal was opened, what was heard?
Revelation 8:1 When He opened the seventh seal, there was silence in heaven for about half an hour.

Note: There is silence in heaven as the angels have accompanied Jesus when He comes as a mighty king to take His saints with Him (Matt. 25:31). All the heavenly angels come with Christ (accounting for the silence in heaven): "He is coming with His own glory, and with the glory of the Father. He is coming with all the holy angels with Him. While all the world is plunged in darkness, there will be light in every dwelling of the saints. They will catch the first light of His second appearing" (COL 420).The opening of the last seal assures us that God is prepared to give all heaven for our rescue. In reality He has done this already in the sacrifice of Jesus Christ.

11.5 Seven Trumpets Sound

Introduction

From the days of the apostles to the return of Christ, the prophetic record carries predictions that the church will be subjected to dramatic pressures. Jesus briefly lifted the curtain of history in Matthew 24 to His wondering disciples. They were unable to comprehend the magnitude of the events that He spoke about. It was to the apostle John through whom He chose to expand on these themes.

The trial of God's people through the ages has been highlighted from different perspectives in our studies thus far. When we studied the seven seals the emphasis was initially on the experiences of authentic believers in Christ under the persecution of the Christian church that had lost its direction. Then we looked at the signs in the natural world that heralded the Lord's soon return and His convincing victory over the forces of evil.

In this study, dealing with the seven trumpets, we will learn something about the experiences the authentic Christian church would go through after Christ's death and resurrection. The trumpets are arranged in chronological order and stand as warnings of judgment on mankind. They also give us significant information about two of the three monotheistic religions, Christianity and Islam, and their impact on authentic worshippers (Judaism, the remaining representative in this category, was mentioned in vision in Daniel chapter 9.9).

In Revelation chapter 8 we are assured in the opening verses that the high priest who is ministering in the heavenly sanctuary (Jesus Christ) is aware of the unfolding drama of human history and will not abandon His people. The seven angels under His direction sound in turn and the last one introduces the reader to the triumphant Christ.

The Study

Read chapters 8, 9, 11:14-19 then the Bible texts and notes below in answer to the questions posed.

1. The sounding of the trumpets and the breaking of the seals (that we have just studied), contain elements of similarity (refer to Table 10). What are these and how does this help us understand the meaning of the trumpets?

Number	Seals	Trumpets
	Horsemen	Warnings
1	White–Rev. 6: 2	Judgment on earth–Rev. 8:7
2	Red–vss. 3, 4	Judgment on sea–vss. 8, 9
3	Black–vs. 5	Destroying star falls on rivers and springs of water–vss. 10, 11
4	Pale–vss. 7, 8	Sun, moon, stars affected–vs. 12
	Judgment scene/second coming	Woes
5	Souls under altar/persecution–vs. 9	Darkness, torture by locusts–Rev. 9:1–3
6	Signs in heavens/Christ's return–vss. 12–17	Horsemen release slaughter–vss. 13–15; cf. 10; 11 as part of second woe
7	Silence in heaven–Rev. 8:1	Christ reigns–Rev. 11:15

Table 10. Similarities noted in the visions of the seals and trumpets.

Note: The trumpets, like the seals, have something to say about the history of the Christian church. The comparison in Table 10 makes it evident that the events dealt with stretch from John's time until Christ's coming. Both the seals and trumpets are divided in the same pattern with the focus changing in the latter part of the vision. Much symbolic language is used, but there are literal sections too.

2. In order to give us the correct perspective, Jesus gave John a view of activities in the temple in heaven. What activity was the special angel engaged in and does this correspond with the activities of the elders and living creatures?
Revelation 8:3, 4 Then another angel, having a golden censer, came and stood at the altar. He was given much incense that he should offer *it* with the prayers of all the saints upon the golden altar which was before the throne. And the smoke of the incense, with the prayers of the saints, ascended before God from the angel's hand.

Revelation 5:8 Now when He had taken the scroll, the four living creatures and the twenty-four elders fell down before the Lamb, each having a harp, and golden bowls full of incense, which are the prayers of the saints.

Note: The scene before us is again placed in the setting of Christ ministering or interceding in the heavenly sanctuary. The assurance is given through these texts that the prayers of those who trust in God are heard. The merits of Jesus' sacrifice ascend with the incense before the Father indicating that Jesus is pleased with those who have put their trust in His sacrifice. "Every sin acknowledged before God with a contrite heart, He will remove" (RH Sept. 29, 1896).

3. Finally what did the angel do with the censer containing the fire?
Revelation 8:5 Then the angel took the censer, filled it with fire from the altar, and threw *it* to the earth. And there were noises, thunderings, lightnings, and an earthquake.

Note: The loving God whom we serve is also the God of justice (Neh. 9:17). The angel revealed in this verse is telling us that ultimately God is in control of the affairs of nations and allows uncomfortable events to happen to permit the mystery of iniquity to run its course so as to convince all of its principles and to warn and appeal to people everywhere to turn to the true God (cf. Zeph. 3:1-7; Luke 24:47).

4. The sounding of the first trumpet resulted in destruction on the earth. What agents were used and what do they symbolize?
Revelation 8:7 The first angel sounded: And hail and fire followed, mingled with blood, and they were thrown to the earth. And a third of the trees were burned up, and all green grass was burned up.

Note: Jesus explained why He spoke in symbolic language and it is relevant for us to mention His reasons here. Symbolic language is used in order to clothe the uncomfortable truths of His word in language that only those who are earnest and honest in mind will enquire about and accept. While on earth, Jesus often spoke in parables (Luke 8:10). This devise protected the word of God from more vigorous attempts made to destroy it. Ultimately, the Bible contains the key to understanding the symbols used.

Trumpets were used anciently to announce events, including war. The fire, hail and blood simply convey the idea that destruction was associated with the activity of the powers represented (Isa. 28:1, 2; Ezek. 38:22, 23). This is the type of language that was used to describe the effects of the plagues in Egypt

(Exod. 7:17-21; 9:18-26). The trees represented people (Jer. 11:16, 17), as did the grass (Isa. 40:6, 7). This means that the trumpet informs us, through symbols, that many people would suffer (incomplete destruction is represented by reference to a third).

Many commentators understand that the trumpet represents the savage attacks carried out by the Visigoths (Germanic tribe and an Arian power) under the leadership of Alaric (A. D. 394-410). Their exploits extended over part of present day France and the Mediterranean lands. Rome was invaded in A.D. 410. The significance of this will become apparent as we go along. Suffice it to say at this juncture that the Western Roman Empire was being weakened through these activities and being prepared for the emergence of the papacy.

5. What spectacular event was associated with the sounding of the second trumpet?
Revelation 8:8 Then the second angel sounded: And *something* like a great mountain burning with fire was thrown into the sea, and a third of the sea became blood.

Note: The scene now shifts and trouble came via the sea as the trumpet revealed a smoking mountain being thrown into it. The reference to a mountain indicates a nation or government (Isa 2:2, 3; Jer. 51:24, 25). The angel used this language to convey information about the destructive activities of a nation. Some consider that the activities of another Arian power, the Vandals (originally of east Germanic origin) from their northern Africa stronghold, fit into this picture. Under their leader Genseric (c. A.D. 389-477) they overpowered the Roman fleet by sending fire ships among them. Rome was sacked and captives were taken. This event happened in A.D. 455. The Roman Empire was about to fall preparing the way for further distress in the area of religious warfare.

6. The third trumpet sounded and suddenly a burning star fell upon the waters (vs. 10). What effect did it have on them?
Revelation 8:10, 11 Then the third angel sounded: And a great star fell from heaven, burning like a torch, and it fell on a third of the rivers and on the springs of water. The name of the star is Wormwood. A third of the waters became wormwood, and many men died from the water, because it was made bitter.

Note: A star in Scriptures may represent a power or a dynamic leader (Num. 24:17; Dan. 8:10, 24). The star was called Wormwood or bitterness (Deut. 29:18) indicating the sorrow that this destructive force would bring. This picture fits the description of Attila the Hun (A.D. 434-453) who devastated parts of Europe (part of the Western Roman Empire) and Central Asia with great cruelty and savagery. The Huns were of Eurasian origin (beyond the Volga river).

7. The fourth trumpeter now revealed a strange sight in the heavens. What was seen there?
Revelation 8:12 Then the fourth angel sounded: And a third of the sun was struck, a third of the moon, and a third of the stars, so that a third of them were darkened. A third of the day did not shine, and likewise the night.

Note: Reference to the celestial bodies is taken in this context to be symbolic and hence refers to important persons (Gen. 37:9, 10; Dan. 8:10, 24). The trumpet messenger is informing us that important persons would cease to have influence in the Roman Empire that has been the focus of the prophetic utterances both in the book of Daniel and in this chapter. In the year A.D. 476 the Roman emperor located in the west was deposed by Odoacer, king of the Heruli (another Arian power). This is considered the time when the Western Roman Empire ceased to exist.

Why this is important to our study of prophecy can be judged when the following information is given. The Emperor Diocletian had commenced (A.D. 285) the practice of having a co-emperor appointed so as to administer the vast territory occupied by the empire. Constantine the Great shifted the seat of the empire to Constantinople (A.D. 330) in Asia and took sole charge. However, Emperor Theodosius I (reigned A.D. 379-395) gave the imperial office jointly to his sons and was the last emperor to reign over the entire empire. This meant that, less than a century later, when Romulus Augustus was deposed in Ravenna, northern Italy (A.D. 476), there was still an emperor in Constantinople. In fact, by this time the East treated the West with indifference; the West was in a weakened and decaying state.

Soon after the collapse of the Western Empire, the political situation in the city of Rome became such that the papacy had the opportunity to grow in strength. This was especially the situation when Emperor Justinian gave the Church in Rome an "exalted rank" by allowing it greater freedoms and authority (Ullmann 2003, 40-43). Finally, when the Arian powers were neutralized in the city the papacy was given additional freedom. This process starting in earnest in and after A.D. 538 when the Ostrogoths were expelled from the city of Rome by the troops of the Eastern Roman emperor. It gathered momentum after the Lombard invasion of Italy in A.D. 568. Of course, at the same time as all these events were occurring, a variation of religious belief was developing in Christianity. This force (Eastern Orthodox Church) would become more significant as time went past.

8. When the fifth trumpet (first woe) sounded a star fell from heaven that possessed a key. This enabled entry to a deep pit. What emerged from the pit when it was opened?

Revelation 9:1-3 Then the fifth angel sounded: and I saw a star fallen from heaven to the earth. And to him was given the key to the bottomless pit. And he opened the bottomless pit, and smoke arose out of the pit like the smoke of a great furnace. So the sun and the air were darkened because of the smoke of the pit. Then out of the smoke locusts came upon the earth. And to them was given power, as the scorpions of the earth have power.

Note: Reference to smoke and locusts both can indicate destructive activities (Deut. 28:38; Joel 1:4; Rev. 14:11). Many commentators consider that these texts refer to the land of Arabia and the spread of Islam. The symbolism of a star (Rev. 9:1) is similarly understood as the star spoken about under the third trumpet, that is, a power or a dynamic leader. The leader here spoken about is considered by many to be Muhammad the prophet and those that took up the banner of Islam. The bottomless pit or region of the abyss (vs. 1) can be taken to refer to the deserts of Arabia from whence the destructive forces emerged like locusts. Indeed, major territories plagued and damaged by the desert locust correspond significantly with the spread of Islam in the period of its great conquests after Muhammad's death (A.D. 632). The empire over this period extended from India to the Pyrenees. The most extensive acquisitions were in the western direction.

The turning point to the further progress of Islamic forces into Europe took place at the Battle of Tours (Poitiers) in 732 when the Muslim armies were soundly defeated. This was not the only significant battle, but it served to preserve Christianity in France and regions further afield. Soon after this decisive battle the Umayyad dynasty lost its power over most of its territories due to dissent and internal revolts. The dynasty is significant as it was the first dynasty of the Muslim caliphate. It exercised a dominating influence with some of the caliphs taking the title of "deputy of God" or more precisely "*Khalīfa* of God" (Berkey 2003, 79; Lewis 2004, xvii). This designation of the human instrument preceded that of the popes who eventually took the title "vicar of Christ" (Ullmann 2003, 182, 183).

The consequence of the 732 victory in France was that Europe was spared conquest by the Muslim forces and was preserved for the Protestant Reformation that allowed authentic faith to survive. It also ensured that the prophecy that we will speak about in chapter 11 could be fulfilled. It is hardly likely that the Scripture would be silent about such a significant force (monotheistic religious force) that exercised its strength in both the temporal and spiritual domains in the cradle of Christianity and that would contend with the pure faith delivered to the prophets and apostles.

9. What incredible features did the symbolic locusts possess?

Revelation 9:3-11—Read.

In summary we are told that the locusts possessed the sting of scorpions (vss. 3, 10), they appeared like horses (vs. 7), had human faces, crowns of gold and sported women's hair (vss. 7, 8). They also possessed lion's teeth (vs. 8) and breastplates (vs. 9).

Note: The description of the locusts being like horses but having human features is seen by some as very descriptive of the Muslim warriors on horseback with their turbans, long hair, robes and breastplates. Islam spread by conquest and the teeth and breastplates might be taken generally to represent the overpowering and seemingly impregnable nature of its forces. It is fitting to note that Muhammed regarded the locust as "the army of the most high God" and he forbade people to kill them (Philologos website).

10. Special command was given to the warriors not to destroy a group of people referred to as the grass of the earth and the trees (vs. 4). What special feature did these people possess that exempted them from the harshest punishment?

Revelation 9:4 They were commanded not to harm the grass of the earth, or any green thing, or any tree, but only those men who do not have the seal of God on their foreheads.

Note: Those who believed in the creator God, the God of Abraham, and valued the Old Testament Scriptures were spared. These included Jews and Christians. The historian Gibbon (2004, chapter 51) recorded that Abu-bekr, the successor to Muhammed, ordered the troops to: "let not your victory be stained with the blood of women and children. Destroy no palm-trees, nor burn any fields of corn. Cut down no fruit-trees, nor do any mischief to cattle . . . . [Those] retired in monasteries, and propose to themselves to serve God that way; let them alone, and neither kill them nor destroy their monasteries: and you will find another sort of people that belong to the synagogue of Satan, who have shaven crowns; be sure to cleave their skulls . . . ." It has been noted that the territory of peoples such as the Waldenses and Albigenses were spared the onslaught by the Muslim armies; these people groups were to shine amidst the dark times in the Christian church.

The special period of torment spoken of (vs. 5) is interesting, but interpretations differ. Using the skills we have acquired already by studying Daniel, five months represents 5×30 or 150 years. A number of dates are available to fit this time period but on account of the complex nature of Muslim wars and conquests, it is difficult to fix on an entirely convincing period. Some have even applied the prophecy to two separate time periods during the era of Muslim dominance, since the 150 year period is spoken of two times (cf. vss. 5, 10).

We have chosen to apply verse 5 of this prophecy to the initial period of Muslim domination as during this period the Muslim empire was established over a vast area (the star fallen from heaven was emerging—vs. 1). It was a power proclaiming monotheism and as such functioned to confuse the minds of people about the truths of God's word. To add to the confusion some of the caliphs took the title "deputy of God" (Berkey 2003, 79). During this period, the Christian nations were threatened with destruction, but ultimately were delivered. We contend that these events are sufficiently important to warrant mention in the prophetic record. Humanity certainly was tormented by the Muslim armies and some of the early caliphs acted unwisely by claiming to be God's deputy.

One application of the 150 year prophecy (A.D. 612 to 762), possibly fitting into the scheme presented here, is given by some evangelists as follows. In A.D. 612 Muhammed announced his mission concerning the one true God and made the call to abandon paganism, idolatry, materialism and greed. These ideas were pursued rather successfully through means of the sword after A.D. 622. This initiative was made principally in a westward direction under Muhammed's successors in the Umayyad caliphate located in Damascus. They occupied Palestine, Egypt, Syria, Persia, all northern Africa and Spain in a relatively short time. Ultimately, they were to lose power.

The succeeding caliph (Abbasids—commenced A.D. 750) established their new capital in Bagdad in 762. This was done in order to stabilize the dynasty because Damascus was too remote from the western provinces. These events meant that the Islamic Empire was divided with a rival caliphate being set up in Cordova, Spain, by the remnant of the Umayyad clan (A.D. 755). According to researchers Dumper and Stanley (2006, 56), the change of the capital to Bagdad "enabled him [al-Mansur] to control the major trade, agricultural production, and communication networks in the two-river valley [Tigris and Euphrates]." This meant that within decades Bagdad was the most important city in the region and this move heralded the Golden Age of Islamic culture, science and medicine. The Abbasids turned their focus to the east. The luxuries of the rulers and the emphasis on scholarship and science coincided with the end of a period of Islamic aggressive and expansionist warfare. Eventually, the Abbasids came to preside over an empire racked by schisms. However, their power continued until the 10th century.

11. Just before the sixth trumpet (second woe) was sounded, who did the prophet observe ruling over the locust kingdom?

Revelation 9:11 And they had as king over them the angel of the bottomless pit, whose name in Hebrew *is* Abaddon, but in Greek he has the name Apollyon.

Note: Locust hordes do not have a captain locust leading them. However, in symbolic language the king's name ruling over the locusts was called "Abaddon" or "Apollyon." The meaning of the word is the Destroyer and also damnation. The force controlled by the king arose out of the bottomless pit or *abussos*, which is the place where those who oppose God are figuratively seen to dwell (Rev. 20:1, 2, 7). This term aptly describes the activities of the Islamic forces that spread through the region by the power of the sword. We also notice that ultimately the name Destroyer refers to Satan who works through human agents (cf. Isa. 14:4, 12-17). Now others see this verse as an introduction to Othman (a name that means 'bone-breaker'—emerged in 1299). The victories of his armies were swift and extensive. His empire spanned three continents.

This king had power to "hurt" five months. We consider along with some others that the second mention of a five month period (vs. 10) is distinct from that identified in verse 5 as the activities of the "star" of the movement (who had the key to the bottomless pit—vs. 1) and the "king" over the locusts (vs. 11) appear to be different. We have taken the view that the "king" mentioned could only rule after the invention and the use of gunpowder weapons in warfare. We will take these points into consideration in the following section. In the scenario that we are painting, the information under the last portion of the fifth trumpet prepares the way to understand the sixth trumpet.

12. The sixth trumpet mentions another group of symbols. What similarities exist between the fifth and sixth trumpets and what can we conclude from this?
Revelation 9:13-19—Read and refer to Table 11.

Fifth trumpet	Sixth trumpet
Smoke from pit (vs. 2)	Smoke, fire and brimstone come from horses mouths (vs. 17)
Locusts like horses (vs. 7) with teeth like lions' teeth (vs. 8)	Heads of horses like lions' heads (vs. 17)
Breastplates of iron (vs. 9)	Riders have breastplates of fire and brimstone (vs. 17)
Tails like scorpions; carry sting in tail (vs. 10)	Tails like serpents; possess hurting ability (vs. 19)

Table 11. Similarities noted between the fifth and sixth trumpets of Revelation chapter 9.

Note: The similarity in the symbols is sufficient for us to suggest that basically the same forces are involved. Many think that the Seljuk and then the Ottoman Turks (forces that had converted to Islam and arose in the 10 and 14th centuries, respectively) are referred to under the sixth trumpet. The Seljuk Empire eventually fell to the Mongols and out of the chaos the Ottoman Empire made its "quiet entry into history" according to historian Shaw (1977, 11). In 1299 Osman I (Othman) began to establish his dominance in conjunction with other forces. These kingdoms were located at the cross roads of the Medieval world and regulated the east/west trade routes. They energetically pursued the claims of their religion and mass conversions occurred in a number of countries. The policy of tolerance was followed generally as long as those conquered accepted Muslim rule and paid the special tax to avoid military service. Sometimes child tribute also was required of Christians. These boys became part of the army and generally converted to Islam.

In 1299 Othman invaded Greek territories and added to the lands under his control. In the next century the Ottoman-controlled territories expanded to surround the Byzantine Empire with its capital in Constantinople. The Ottoman Empire continued its extension so that it came to occupy three continents. The significant event that we wish to focus on occurred in 1449 and involved the last Roman emperor to reign in Constantinople. In that year, Constantine XI sought the approval of the Turkish sultan before taking the throne. In this act he recognized his own weakness and the supremacy of the sultan. The 150 year prophecy mentioned in verse 10 is commonly believed to have been fulfilled during the period 1299 to 1449; it was not long before the conquest of Constantinople was accomplished in 1453. The Eastern Roman Empire then ceased to exist.

We might make the following points without trying to struggle through the minute details: The reference to 200 million horsemen is regarded as figurative (vs. 16). Some commentators see it as referring to the massed cavalry in the siege of Constantinople (1453) by the Ottoman Turks. The fire, smoke and brimstone coming from the mouths of the horses (vs. 17) might be considered to refer to the extensive use of gunpowder (based on sulphur and other ingredients) that produced much smoke. Now, it is informative to note that gunpowder (invented by Chinese) was not used by troops until towards the end of the thirteenth century. Canon made their first appearance in the Ottoman Empire and in North Africa. In the siege of Constantinople the use of canon was pivotal in breaching the outer walls of the city. Hand guns of various types followed.

The previous discourse has prepared the way to focus on the special period of prophetic time of an hour, a day, a month and a year spoken of in Revelation 9, verse 15. In prophetic time this equals 391 years according to the principles that we introduced in the book of Daniel. We have already mentioned that the last emperor of the Byzantine Empire, Constantine XI, ascended the throne under permission from the Turkish sultan. From this time (1449) until the Ottoman Empire was weakened in a political and military sense lasted 391 years (1449+391=1840). It is fitting to note that this time prophecy commenced with an expression of strength by the Turkish ruler and ended with an admission of his weakness, under strikingly parallel political environments.

What happened in 1840? The London Convention of 1840 was organized by foreign Christian powers and exercised its authority against Egypt's occupation of Syria (part of Ottoman Empire). In that year, Turkey needed to be protected by foreign powers against aggressors. Now, for the European powers "the dissolution of the Ottoman Empire was believed to be imminent" (Atli 2009). The sultan's independence had descended to such a low point that it was no longer true to say that he could effectively destroy men (Rev. 9:15). One early authority said of this event, "In the year 1840 another remarkable fulfillment of prophecy excited widespread interest [referring to Josiah Litch's outline] . . . . At the very time specified, Turkey, through her ambassadors, accepted the protection of the allied powers of Europe, and thus placed herself under the control of Christian nations. The event exactly fulfilled the prediction" (GC 334, 335).

This meant that the Ottoman Empire was being judged just as the Byzantine Empire had before it (the decline continued and finally the Empire gave way to the Turkish Republic in 1923). Some have observed also that from the fall of Constantinople in 1453 until 1844 was exactly 391 years, which marked the close of the 2300 year prophecy of Daniel 8. In 1844, all nations were being reviewed according to God's standard.

13. What lament did the sixth angel make concerning the effects of all these judgments on human behaviour?

Revelation 9:20, 21 But the rest of mankind, who were not killed by these plagues, did not repent of the works of their hands, that they should not worship demons, and idols of gold, silver, brass, stone, and wood, which can neither see nor hear nor walk. And they did not repent of their murders or their sorceries or their sexual immorality or their thefts.

Note: The Eastern Orthodox (Byzantine) Church rejected (A.D. 1054) some of the doctrines of the Catholic Church that did not have a scriptural basis such as papal infallibility, the Immaculate Conception and celibacy. However, it promoted its own human traditions such as the veneration of icons and the use of leavened bread in the communion service. The leaders failed to accept the Son's equal divinity with the Father and eventually joined the Catholic Church in sanctifying Sunday.

Other activities not repented of can perhaps be seen in exploits as follows. The Eastern Orthodox Church, through the emperor, was involved in efforts to find common ground with the Roman Church from 1274. At the Council of Ferrara-Florence (1438-1445), it agreed on some of the contentious positions advocated by Rome including purgatory and Roman primacy. It was "Political desperation and the fear of facing the Turks again, without western support, was the decisive factor that caused them to place their signatures of approval on the Decree of Union (July 6, 1439)." However, Constantinople fell before any significant changes took place.

Such an outcome (union) was assisted by the fact that "The life of Byzantium formed a unified whole, and there was no rigid line of separation between the religious and the secular, between Church and State: the two were seen as parts of a single organism." The Byzantine people identified their kingdom with the kingdom of God. However, "The tales of Byzantium duplicity, violence, and cruelty are too well known to call for repetition here. They are true—but they are only a part of the truth. For behind all the shortcomings of Byzantium can always be discerned the great vision by which the Byzantines were inspired: to establish here on earth a living image of God's government in heaven. The authority of the patriarch of Constantinople was motivated in a formal fashion by the fact that he was the bishop of the 'New Rome,' . . . ."–(*History of the Orthodox Church*).

The practice of making images and paintings of the saints and prophets was particularly detested by the Muslims. However, the judgments of God falling on Byzantine people did not change the thinking of the church leaders. There are lessons in this account for all to observe.

14. What dramatic announcement did the seventh angel make (third woe)?

Revelation 11:15 Then the seventh angel sounded: And there were loud voices in heaven, saying, "The kingdoms of this world have become *the kingdoms* of our Lord and of His Christ, and He shall reign forever and ever!"

Note: The information sandwiched between the sixth and the seventh trumpets will be considered in other lessons. This information is considered to be an extension of the sixth trumpet by some commentators (cf. 11:14). The message of the seventh angel is clear. Whatever kingdoms are established by mankind ultimately will be destroyed. Those who wish to triumph with the Lord will acknowledge Christ's sacrifice and the words of His witnesses (Luke 24:25-31; Rev. 22:11-14). Eternal life is assured to those who understand and practice the principles of God's kingdom.

It is important to note that the seventh trumpet was followed by the exhibition of the ark of the covenant in the heavenly sanctuary, which contains the law of God. "Sacrilegious minds and hearts have thought they were mighty enough to change the times and laws of Jehovah; but, safe in the archives of heaven, in the ark of God, are the original commandments, written upon the two tables of stone. No potentate of earth has power to draw forth those tables from their sacred hiding place beneath the mercy seat" (ST Feb. 28, 1878).

11.6 Eating a Book

Introduction

Near the end of the messages of the seven trumpets, two interesting topics seem to be inserted as an interlude before the seventh trumpet sounds. These topics, in actual fact, are an expansion of the sixth trumpet and together constitute the second woe (Rev. 11:4). Revelation chapter 10 deals with eating a little book and the sequel to that experience. As we study this prophecy, it will become evident that the sixth trumpet focused the attention of Bible students on events about to transpire in heaven as Jesus prepared to enter into the last phase of His ministry there.

The appearance of the mighty angel to deliver this message (Rev. 10:1) indicates that it has no ordinary significance. Indeed, after the destruction spoken about under the sixth trumpet, readers universally would be willing to welcome encouragement. This is given when we understand the identity of the angel and when the meaning of the announcement "there should be delay no longer" (vs. 6) is understood. In effect the angel was saying that no more delay would be made in finalizing the plan of redemption. Hence, the announcement was made that Christ was about to enter the final phase of His ministry in heaven and make His final appeal to earth's inhabitants.

However, before the announcement is made from heaven that Christ is coming, authentic believers were led through an unusual testing experience.

The Study

Read chapter 10 then the Bible texts and notes below in answer to the questions posed.

1. The mighty angel revealed in Revelation chapter 10 is similar to the one seen by the prophet Daniel. What comparisons may be made (refer to Table 12), and what does this tell us about the identity of the individual involved?

Daniel 10–12	Revelation 10
Appearance	
"Clothed in linen" and a golden girdle (10:5; 12:6)	"Clothed with a cloud" (vs. 1; cf. 1:7)
Face like "lightning" (10:6)	Face "like the sun" (vs. 1; cf. 1:16)
Eyes like "torches" of fire (10:6)	Rainbow on head (vs. 1)
Arms and feet like "burnished bronze" (10:6)	Feet like "pillars of fire" (vs. 1; cf. 1:15)
Voice like "voice of a multitude" (10:6)	Cried with "loud voice as when a lion roars" (vs. 3; cf. 1:15)
Positioned above the waters (12:7)	Standing on sea and land (vss. 2, 5)
Activities	
"Shut up the words," "seal the book until the time of the end" (12:4)	Open book in hand (vs. 2) Announced: "there should be delay no longer" (vs. 6)

Table 12. The characteristics of the mighty angel spoken about by the prophets Daniel and John.

Note: In the book of Daniel, chapters 10 and 12, the individual described is "Michael" and in Revelation he is called the "Son of Man" (1:13). This is none other than Jesus Christ. "The mighty angel who instructed John was no less a personage than Jesus Christ. Setting His right foot on the sea, and His left upon the dry land, shows the part which He is acting in the closing scenes of the great controversy with Satan. This position denotes His supreme power and authority over the whole earth" (7BC 971).

Just when we expect to hear the announcement that God's kingdom is to be established, John the apostle is instructed to prophecy again (Rev. 10:11). Important events are still to be identified before Christ returns. This message is to go to all peoples.

2. What object was the angel holding in his hand?
Revelation 10:2 first part He had a little book open in his hand.

Note: The identity of the book or little scroll that the angel held in his hand has been debated. We well remember that the complete understanding of the book of Daniel was sealed until the time of the end (Dan. 12:4, 9). "The books of Daniel and the Revelation are one. One is a prophecy, the other a revelation; one a book sealed, the other a book opened" (7BC 971).The message we are studying is inserted between the collapse of the Eastern Roman Empire and the decline of the Ottoman Empire and the end of time. Hence, there is every expectation that what we learn will be about the experiences of God's people during this time period. More precisely, the opening of the little book tells us about the final phases of Christ's atonement or God's plan of salvation. We well remember that the message of the trumpets was set in the context of the heavenly sanctuary (Rev. 8:2-5). What is more fitting than for it to conclude under the sixth trumpet in the same sanctuary?

3. What significant proclamation prefaced the angel's instruction regarding the little book? To what passage of Scripture does this direct the reader's mind?
Revelation 10:6, 7 And swore by Him who lives forever and ever, who created heaven and the things that are in it, the earth and the things that are in it, and the sea and the things that are in it, that there should be delay no longer, but in the days of the sounding of the seventh angel, when he is about to sound, the mystery of God would be finished, as He declared to His servants the prophets.

Exodus 20:9-11 Six days you shall labor and do all your work, but the seventh day *is* the Sabbath of the LORD your God. *In it* you shall do no work: you, nor your son, nor your daughter, nor your male servant, nor your female servant, nor your cattle, nor your stranger who *is* within your gates. For *in* six days the LORD made the heavens and the earth, the sea, and all that *is* in them, and rested the seventh day. Therefore the LORD blessed the Sabbath day and hallowed it.

Note: The angel invoked the authority of the creator God and drew attention to the principles of His kingdom and to the Sabbath provision in particular. The angel with the little book indicated that the last phase of God's plan of salvation would be delayed no longer. Verse 7 reminds the reader that the Great Controversy is coming to an end. The words "mystery of God" refer to the plan of redemption (Mark 4:11; Col. 2:2; 4:3; cf. 6T, 19).

Those among Christians who do not believe that God is the Creator or insist that He worked through the evolutionary process are in danger of misunderstanding the work that God wishes to do in the lives of all believers. God is warning all readers to develop clear lines of thinking. He is directing all readers to the contents of the law of the covenant in the ark of the Testimony in the Most Holy Place of the heavenly sanctuary.

4. What question asked by angel messengers in the book of Daniel is about to be answered?
Daniel 8:13 Then I heard a holy one speaking; and *another* holy one said to that certain *one* who was speaking, "How long *will* the vision *be* [about the 2300 year prophecy], *concerning* the daily *sacrifices* and the transgression of desolation, the giving of both the sanctuary and the host to be trampled underfoot?"

Daniel 12:6 And *one* said to the man clothed in linen, who *was* above the waters of the river, "How long shall the fulfillment of these wonders [spoken about in Daniel chapter 11] *be?*"

Note: An outstanding reason that we are able to make the suggestion that there is a relationship between Daniel's prophecies and John's relates to the experiences already mentioned under the sixth trumpet. We remember that in Revelation chapter 9, verse 15, the four angels were loosed for an hour, a day, a month and a year or 391 years. The end point of this prophecy has been applied by many commentators to the protection of the Ottoman Empire by European Christian powers under the London Convention (1840). By this act, the independence of the Ottoman Empire was brought into question. The convention forced Egypt to abandon its claim on Syria. It incidentally also substantiated the statement that Turkey was the "sick man of Europe" (Atli 2009). The historical reality is that this event focused attention on Bible prophecy (1499 to 1840=391 years) and naturally on the date 1844 that represented the year when the last great Bible prophecy reached its fulfillment. It was then that the last phase of Christ's ministry commenced in heaven.

5. What unusual instruction did the angel give to John concerning the open book that he held in his hand? What Old Testament prophet was given similar instruction and what did it signify?
Revelation 10:9 So I went to the angel and said to him, "Give me the little book." And he said to me, "Take and eat it; and it will make your stomach bitter, but it will be as sweet as honey in your mouth."

Ezekiel 3:1, 2 Moreover He said to me, "Son of man, eat what you find; eat this scroll, and go, speak to the house of Israel." So I opened my mouth, and He caused me to eat that scroll.

Note: The instruction to eat the manuscript was equivalent to saying that its contents were to be tasted and digested or understood (cf. Jer. 15:16). The first impressions were overwhelmingly attractive, but the later experience with this unusual item of food was distressing.

6. The angel predicted that Daniel's prophecies relating to end-time events would be understood and that much "sweet" joy would be experienced (Rev. 10:9). Which prophecy in particular was being referred to?
Daniel 7:26 'But the court shall be seated, and they shall take away his dominion, to consume and destroy *it* forever.'

Daniel 8:13, 14 Then I heard a holy one speaking; and *another* holy one said to that certain *one* who was speaking, "How long *will* the vision *be, concerning* the daily *sacrifices* and the transgression of desolation, the giving of both the sanctuary and the host to be trampled underfoot?" And he said to me, "For two thousand three hundred days; then the sanctuary shall be cleansed."

Note: After the fulfillment of the 1260 year prophecy in the capture and exile of the pope in 1798, many Bible scholars began to carefully reassess the significance of other time prophecies. They had initially understood that at the end of the 1260 years Christ would return. However, the one remaining time prophecy of Daniel 8 relating to the 2300 year prophecy had to be fitted into the puzzle. The general conclusion reached from an intense study of this time prophecy led scholars to suggest a fulfillment in the period 1843-1847. Eventually the date was settled on as October 1844. Again the event anticipated at this time was the second coming of Christ. This misunderstanding was commonly held, as the following quote indicates: "All felt that upon the events therein brought to view depended their brightest expectations and most cherished hopes. These prophetic days had been shown to terminate in the autumn of 1844. In common with the rest of the Christian world, Adventists then held that the earth, or some portion of it, was the sanctuary, and that the cleansing of the sanctuary was the purification of the earth by the fires of the last great day. This they understood would take place at the second coming of Christ. Hence the conclusion that Christ would return to the earth in 1844" (SR 375).

7. After the book of Daniel was understood (eaten), a bitter reaction occurred in the stomach (Rev. 10:9), yet the clear instruction was to prophecy again (vs. 10). What understanding (arising from investigating or measuring something) would make this possible?

Revelation 11:1, 2 Then I was given a reed like a measuring rod. And the angel stood, saying, "Rise and measure the temple of God, the altar, and those who worship there. But leave out the court which is outside the temple, and do not measure it, for it has been given to the Gentiles. And they will tread the holy city underfoot *for* forty-two months.

Note: The chapter divisions were not included in the original text. This means that the initial verses in chapter 11 help to finish the thought of chapter 10. The believers' fondest hopes were dashed on that October day in 1844 when they expected Christ to return. They experienced bitter disappointment just as the prophet John had indicated in verse 9. The disappointment was similar to but more intense than that experienced by the disciples who came to the empty tomb on Sunday morning after the crucifixion (EW 244, 245). After the intense disappointment of Christ failing to return, some of the believers began to reexamine the prophecy and discovered that rather than Christ coming to earth at the end of the 2300 year period He was, in fact, entering the last phase of His ministry in the heavenly sanctuary. They had "measured" and understood more clearly the truths about the sanctuary and Christ's work there.

We learn that "God designed to prove them . . . those who had looked with joyful expectation for their Saviour were sad and disheartened, while those who had not loved the appearing of Jesus, but embraced the message through fear, were pleased that He did not come at the time of expectation" (EW 235).

8. The earthly sanctuary was patterned after the heavenly one. What event happened once a year in the earthly sanctuary that gave the key to understanding the events occurring in heaven at the end of the 2300 year prophecy (1844)?

Hebrews 9:6, 7 Now when these things had been thus prepared, the priests always went into the first part of the tabernacle, performing *the services.* But into the second part the high priest *went* alone once a year, not without blood, which he offered for himself and *for* the people's sins *committed* in ignorance.

Note: In the earthly sanctuary two phases of ministry were highlighted, the daily and the yearly (Heb. 9:6, 7). The work performed in the sanctuary was a work of "forgiveness of sin and restoration to fellowship" (Hardinge 1991, 41). Every day, morning and evening sacrifices were made for the benefit of the people, indicating the ever readiness of God to minister to the needs of men and women. The sinner could avail himself or herself of this provision by faith irrespective of their place of residence. This sacrifice was made even on the Day of Atonement. Now on that day, the activities of the priest in the Most Holy Place involved "atonement and intercession" and the removal of sins from God's presence (White 1969, 27). It was and still is commonly held that "The Day of Atonement is the Day of Judgment" (Hershon in *Seventh-day Adventists Answer Questions on Doctrine* 1957, 363). The main emphasis on this day surrounded the "Lord's goat." It was only the blood of this goat that was shed (Lev. 16:15-20; cf. Heb 7:27). There was another goat (for Azazel or Satan), but this was led into the wilderness after the sins of the people for which the Lord's goat had died were laid upon it (Lev. 16:20-22). This goat was not sacrificed for sin.

One might say that the daily emphasis in the outer court and the Holy Place was on "release of the repentant sinner from the condemnation of the law" (White 1969, 38) and in the Most Holy Place the emphasis was to "govern and judge His people Israel" (Hardinge 1991, 534).

These ceremonies were a symbol of Christ's heavenly activities for He is now ministering in the sanctuary in heaven applying the benefits of His sacrifice to repentant sinners (Heb. 8:2; 9:14, 15). Taking the Day of Atonement on earth as an indicator, we understand that the heavenly sanctuary also needs to be cleansed (Heb. 9:23). This involves removal of the record of sin.

9. What evidence do the Scriptures provide to indicate that there is an investigation of the deeds of men (pre-advent judgment) before Christ returns?

Daniel 7:9, 10 "I watched till thrones were put in place, and the Ancient of Days was seated; His garment *was* white as snow, and the hair of His head *was* like pure wool. His throne *was* a fiery flame, its wheels a burning fire; a fiery stream issued and came forth from before Him. A thousand thousands ministered to Him; ten thousand times ten thousand stood before Him. The court was seated, and the books were opened.

Daniel 7:26 'But the court shall be seated, and they shall take away his dominion, to consume and destroy *it* forever.

Revelation 14:6, 7 Then I saw another angel flying in the midst of heaven, having the everlasting gospel to preach to those who dwell on the earth—to every nation, tribe, tongue, and people—saying with a loud voice, "Fear God and give glory to Him, for the hour of His judgment has come; and worship Him who made heaven and earth, the sea and springs of water."

Note: The judgment scene pictured by the prophet Daniel is one of the best indications that a judgment of investigation precedes the execution of punishment. Most people would expect such behavior from a just judge! Now, every person will be judged according to the heavenly records (Eccles. 12:14; Dan. 7:10; Rev. 20:12). This concept of judgment was upheld by Christ while on earth (Matt. 12:36; John 5:24).

10. In the pre-advent judgment what evidence is made available enabling just decisions to be made?

Ecclesiastes 12:14 For God will bring every work into judgment, including every secret thing, whether good or evil.

Daniel 7:10 A fiery stream issued and came forth from before Him. A thousand thousands ministered to Him; ten thousand times ten thousand stood before Him. The court was seated, and the books were opened.

Malachi 3:16, 17 Then those who feared the LORD spoke to one another, and the LORD listened and heard *them;* so a book of remembrance was written before Him for those who fear the LORD and who meditate on His name. "They shall be Mine," says the LORD of hosts, "On the day that I make them My jewels. And I will spare them as a man spares his own son who serves him."

Matthew 12:36 "But I say to you that for every idle word men may speak, they will give account of it in the day of judgment."

Revelation 20:12 And I saw the dead, small and great, standing before God, and books were opened. And another book was opened, which is *the Book* of Life. And the dead were judged according to their works, by the things which were written in the books.

Note: The decisions made by God are based on evidence kept in heaven as indicated in our texts quoted. To appeal to our earthly understanding, various books of record are spoken about in the Bible and these include books of life, remembrance, and perhaps others. Those who are saved have their names retained in the Book of Life (Exod. 32:33; Ps. 69:28). The judgment is for the benefit of the whole universe, so that all might be convinced of "His [God's] love and His justice." These have been "challenged by Satan and his hosts" *Questions on Doctrine* 1957, 421). He has presented God as unjust.

11. Who is the believer's advocate in the judgment?
1 John 2:1 My little children, these things I write to you, so that you may not sin. And if anyone sins, we have an Advocate with the Father, Jesus Christ the righteous.

Note: The good news is that Jesus is described as man's advocate. This does not infer that the Father, Holy Spirit and angels are against the saints, but it does say that the person who cared so much for mankind to die in our stead is now willing to represent sinners in the judgment. The completeness of God's interest in repentant sinners is expressed by the prophet Jeremiah who wrote: "For I [the Lord] will forgive their iniquity, and their sin I will remember no more" (Jer. 31:34). This thought is echoed by the writer Ellen White. "He [Jesus] took the burden of humanity that he might save men from the consequences of their sins. He is in one their Advocate and Judge. Having tasted the very dregs of human affliction and temptation, he is qualified to understand the frailties and sins of men, and to pronounce judgment upon them. Therefore, the Father has given this work into the hands of his Son, knowing that He who victoriously withstood the temptations of Satan, in behalf of man, will be all-wise, just, and gracious in his dealing with him" (2SP 168).

12. When the judgment process is nearing completion, what is the concluding act in the drama?
Leviticus 16:20-22 "And when he has made an end of atoning for the Holy *Place,* the tabernacle of meeting, and the altar, he shall bring the live goat. Aaron shall lay both his hands on the head of the live goat, confess over it all the iniquities of the children of Israel, and all their transgressions, concerning all their sins, putting them on the head of the goat, and shall send *it* away into the wilderness by the hand of a suitable man. The goat shall bear on itself all their iniquities to an uninhabited land; and he shall release the goat in the wilderness.

Revelation 20:10 The devil, who deceived them, was cast into the lake of fire and brimstone where the beast and the false prophet *are.* And they will be tormented day and night forever and ever.

Note: The final act in the earthly sanctuary was undertaken by the High Priest who took the second goat, for Azazel or Satan, and placed all the iniquities of the children of Israel to its account. This was done by laying his hands on its head. The goat was then led away by the hand of a fit person into the wilderness to die (Lev. 16:21, 22). This goat was not sacrificed by the shedding of blood. This goat represented Satan and on his head will be placed the responsibility for sin's presence and its promotion in the universe. Christ then returns to claim His saints. Satan is bound in solitude for a thousand years and then is joined by the raised wicked to receive the sentence of eternal death, which is the second death (Rev. 20:13-15). The wicked will be destroyed forever, but not by eternal punishment (Ps. 37:10, 11).

13. With this increased understanding, what burden of responsibility was placed on those who understood the message of the open book?
Revelation 10:11 And he said to me, "You must prophesy again about many peoples, nations, tongues, and kings."

Ezekiel 3:10, 11 Moreover He said to me: "Son of man, receive into your heart all My words that I speak to you, and hear with your ears. And go, get to the captives, to the children of your people, and speak to them and tell them, 'Thus says the Lord GOD,' whether they hear, or whether they refuse."

Note: It is incumbent on those who know important truths to tell those who might benefit from knowledge of God's word (Matt. 28:19, 20). The prophet in the above words was saying that the believers in the 1840s who misunderstood Bible prophecy must continue to study and witness again, for they had much still to learn about other prophecies. With the enlightened understanding about the event that happened in heaven in 1844, it then became evident to the believers that the three angels' messages of Revelation 14 had yet to be understood and then given to the world.

11.7 Two Witnesses Resurrected

Introduction

The vision of the two witnesses occurs seemingly as an interlude between the sounding of the sixth and seventh trumpets. In actual fact, Revelation chapter 11 is an extension of the sixth trumpet (together with chapter 10) and constitutes the second woe (Rev. 11:14). After the eating the little book, the apostle John was instructed to measure the temple of God in heaven and he also was led to understand the experiences of God's two witnesses on earth.

Through the act of measuring the temple in heaven, a greater understanding of Christ's ministry there would come to God's people. This would be encouraging. On the other hand, what the prophet was about to hear concerning the two witnesses was most distressing. These were clothed in sackcloth for 1260 years. Then they were killed, rose again and were glorified in the presence of God's enemies. No doubt John was appalled and intrigued by this prophecy.

The witnesses do not represent individuals, so what do they represent? We are about to discover the answer to this question. In the meantime, we are given the assurance that God's testimony on this earth will not cease. He is in charge.

The Study

Read chapter 11 then the Bible texts and notes below in answer to the questions posed.

1. The sixth trumpet ended with the date of 1840 emphasized. What particular topic was John requested to study in order to grasp the significance of the symbolism of the two witnesses?
Revelation 11:1, 2 first part Then I was given a reed like a measuring rod. And the angel stood, saying, "Rise and measure the temple of God, the altar, and those who worship there." But leave out the court which is outside the temple, and do not measure it, for it has been given to the Gentiles.

Note: The temple spoken about is the one in heaven. The prophet and readers are urged to understand both the furnishings of this temple and the services that occur there and to carefully consider God's nature and that He is inviting believers to be worshipers at the altar.

The Gentiles mentioned are those who have not identified with God. In the next and following questions we examine what some of these individuals have dedicated themselves to accomplishing in the world.

2. John observed the two witnesses prophesying for 1260 years. What were they dressed in and what meaning might we attribute to the imagery?
Revelation 11:2 last part, 3 And they [Gentiles] will tread the holy city underfoot *for* forty-two months. "And I will give *power* to my two witnesses, and they will prophesy one thousand two hundred and sixty days, clothed in sackcloth."

Note: The message of the Bible is cast in terms of a Great Controversy between Christ and Satan, the saints and the Gentiles, Jerusalem and Babylon or the "holy city" and "the great city." The last part of verse 2 above speaks about a 42 month period when those who refuse to accept God become active against Him. We immediately recognize that this time period is equivalent to 1260 days by reference to verse 3, for each prophetic month is considered to contain 30 days (42×30=1260). In practical terms, this period is taken as literal years and refers to the time between A.D. 538 and 1798. At the time of the first date, General Belisarius finally ousted the Ostrogoths from Rome on Emperor Justinian's initiative. This occurred in March, A.D. 538 and allowed Pope Virgilius, who was Justinian's recent appointee, in control of spiritual matters. In A.D. 533 Justinian recognized the pope as the head of all the churches. He said: "This See [bishop of Rome] is indeed the head of all churches, as the rules of the Fathers and the decrees of the Emperors assert, and the words of your most reverend piety testify. . . . We order all those who follow this law to assume the name of Catholic Christians, and considering others as demented and insane" (Scott 1932). The undertaking made in the year 533 could not be implemented fully until after 538 for antagonistic foreign powers were occupying the city of Rome. The papacy needed the ability to operate as an independent entity. The recognition that Justinian gave to the papacy at this and other times conferred on it enormous authority as the "Roman church *par excellence.*" In elevating the Church, he gave recognition of the fact that the city of Rome was the birthplace of the Empire. And Justinian was pacifying the church in preparation for his attempt to recapture the Western Empire (Ullmann 2003, 43). The privileges and authority conferred by emperors and councils was utilized effectively by the papacy until its power was broken for a period in 1798. After 1798, religious freedom was restored. In that year General Berthier, operating under instructions from Napoleon, took the pope captive. The pontiff died in exile the next year in the city of Valence, France.

During these long and difficult 1260 years, persecution raged with varying levels of intensity. God's word was hidden in a form not readily available to the people and it was corrupted by the traditions of men. "When the early church became corrupted by departing from the simplicity of the gospel, and accepting heathen rites and customs, she lost the Spirit and power of God; and in order to control the consciences of the people she sought the support of the secular power. The result was the papacy, a church that controlled the power of the State, and employed it to further her own ends, especially for the punishment of 'heresy'" (GC, 443). We already have dealt with some of these experiences when speaking of the Thyatira church (Rev. 2:18-29) and the pale horse of Revelation 6 (vss. 7, 8).

We remember that the time periods $3^{1/2}$ times, 42 months and 1260 days are speaking of the same period in history and are the linkage points to the little horn power. This makes our task easy, so we can search in both the books of Daniel and Revelation for identifying clues. Some characteristics of the power that undertook to cause the witnesses to dress in sackcloth are identified in Table 13. When we link this with the information that the power arose from the Roman Empire (Dan. 7:24) and uprooted three powers (Dan. 7:17, 23, 24), there is no doubt about its identity.

Little horn's activities	Reference
Speaks pompous words against God, responsible for blasphemy	**Dan. 7:20, 25; 8:25; Rev. 13:5, 6**
Persecutes saints, destroys, tramples on the saints	**Dan. 7:25, 8:24; 12:7; Rev. 11:2; 12:6, 13–16; 13:7**
Attempts to change times and law	**Dan. 7:25**
Has an issue with the commandments and testimony of Jesus	**Rev. 12:17**
Exalts in the human instrument	**Dan. 8:25**
Pursues sinister and deceitful schemes	**Dan. 8:23, 25**

Table 13. Significant activities of the little horn power.

The witnesses prophesied in sackcloth or mourning (2 Sam. 3:31). Such behaviour is an appropriate reference to those ruling in the dominant church hiding the word of God from the common people, promoting human traditions (Dan. 7:25), and insisting that the clergy alone could interpret God's love letter to mankind. In fact, the prophecy said they will "tread the holy city underfoot." The act of hiding the word of God was the foundation of the distressing experience that took place. "When the Word of God is set aside, its power to restrain the evil passions of the natural heart is rejected" (FLB 7).

3. What is the identity of the two witnesses?

Revelation 11:3, 4 "And I will give *power* to my two witnesses, and they will prophesy one thousand two hundred and sixty days, clothed in sackcloth." These are the two olive trees and the two lampstands standing before the God of the earth.

Zechariah 4:6 [In answer to the question what the two olive trees of verse 3 were] So he answered and said to me: "This *is* the word of the LORD to Zerubbabel: 'Not by might nor by power, but by My Spirit,' says the LORD of hosts.

Verse 14 So he said, "These *are* the two anointed ones, who stand beside the Lord of the whole earth."

Note: The scenes in Zechariah and Revelation speak of olive trees or lampstands and in the latter book they are called witnesses. The prophet Isaiah is very precise that the Scriptures are a clear witness of God (Isa. 8:20). He said, "To the law and to the testimony! If they do not speak according to this word, *it is* because *there is* no light in them." The word "testimony" may be translated "witness." The Scriptures witness to the foundations of God's throne (mercy and justice), which Satan has sought continually to destroy (cf. Ps. 85:10; 89:14; SR 427). Now "The two witnesses represent the Old and New Testament Scriptures. Both are important testimonies to the origin and perpetuity of the law of God. Both are witnesses also to the plan of salvation. The types, sacrifices, and prophecies of the Old Testament point forward to a Saviour to come. The Gospels and Epistles of the New Testament tell of a Saviour who has come in the exact manner foretold by type and prophecy" (4SP 188).

The Scriptures speak of the inerrancy of God's moral law and the certainty and simplicity of His salvation (1 Pet. 1:10-12; 1 John 5:9). These are the same truths as were taught in the Most Holy Place of the earthly sanctuary (the mercy seat overshadowed the tables of the law). The apostle Paul identified the nature of God's testimony powerfully, as follows: "And I, brethren, when I came to you, did not come with excellence of speech or of wisdom declaring to you the testimony of God. For I determined not to know anything among you except Jesus Christ and Him crucified" (1 Cor. 2:1, 2). Ultimately, God's word testifies to His character (Ps. 119:105, 130; John 5:39). His death was required on account of the fact that the just provisions of the Decalogue needed to be fulfilled (sin brings death), for God cannot change.

Jesus affirmed the reliability and significance of the Scriptures after His resurrection (Luke 24:25-27) and, in His last message through the prophet John, He is personally revealed as a God of constancy and care (Rev. 1:1). Later in the book we are told that God's smile is on those "who keep the commandments of God and have the testimony of Jesus Christ" (Rev. 12:17 last part). The central elements of the witness of Scripture are repeated in the three angels' messages of Revelation 14. Satan's accusations against God will finally be silenced just after the coronation of Christ. Notice: "His [Satan's] accusations against the mercy and justice of God are now silenced" (SR 427). This indentifies for us the two central emphasises of the Scriptures, which are God's witnesses.

4. What supernatural powers were attributed to the two witnesses? And to what episodes in the Old Testament is reference made?
Revelation 11:6 These have power to shut heaven, so that no rain falls in the days of their prophecy; and they have power over waters to turn them to blood, and to strike the earth with all plagues, as often as they desire.

1 Kings 17:1 And Elijah the Tishbite, of the inhabitants of Gilead, said to Ahab, "*As* the LORD God of Israel lives, before whom I stand, there shall not be dew nor rain these years, except at my word."

2 Kings 1:10 So Elijah answered and said to the captain of fifty, "If I *am* a man of God, then let fire come down from heaven and consume you and your fifty men." And fire came down from heaven and consumed him and his fifty.

Exodus 7:19-21 Then the LORD spoke to Moses, "Say to Aaron, 'Take your rod and stretch out your hand over the waters of Egypt, over their streams, over their rivers, over their ponds, and over all their pools of water, that they may become blood. And there shall be blood throughout all the land of Egypt, both in *buckets of* wood and *pitchers of* stone.'" And Moses and Aaron did so, just as the LORD commanded. So he lifted up the rod and struck the waters that *were* in the river, in the sight of Pharaoh and in the sight of his servants. And all the waters that *were* in the river were turned to blood. The fish that *were* in the river died, the river stank, and the Egyptians could not drink the water of the river. So there was blood throughout all the land of Egypt.

Note: The prophetic witnesses identified in Old Testament times brought judgment upon the earth (plagues) and controlled rainfall. If the entire accounts of these episodes are read, it will be observed that the Scriptures faithfully record how God worked through His servants first to warn men and women of the way of truth and then of His coming judgments.

Christ said of the Scriptures: "You search the Scriptures, for in them you think you have eternal life; and these are they which testify of Me" (John 5:39) and again He added: "And this gospel of the kingdom will be preached in all the world as a witness to all the nations, and then the end will come" (Matt. 24:14). This clearly indicates that Jesus witnessed to God's mercy (gospel) and coming judgment (justice—cf. Matt. 12:36; John 5:24). God's recorded dealings with the human race are found in the Bible. It contains powerful evidence that mercy and justice come from the same divine source. Thus the Bible can be said to function as two witnesses. These testify to the fact that God's mercy and justice kissed at the cross or was shown to be dependent on each other (Ps. 85:10; AG 74). Satan's contention has been that mercy is incompatible with justice. It was "Satan's purpose to divorce mercy from truth and justice. He sought to prove that the righteousness of God's law is an enemy of peace. But Christ shows [at the cross] that in God's plan they are indissolubly joined together; the one cannot exist without the other" (AG 74).

5. What fate did the witnesses suffer progressively and particularly near the end of the 1260 years? And who ultimately should be held responsible for this act?
Revelation 11:7 When they finish their testimony, the beast that ascends out of the bottomless pit will make war against them, overcome them, and kill them.

Note: Our previous texts have assured us that the Bible witnessed in sackcloth (vs. 3) and that there would come a time when the "beast" power would attack and destroy the effective witness of the Old and New Testament prophets (their writings are contained in the Bible). There is perhaps no more defined place in history than the French Revolution when the political powers of state were applied systematically to de-Christianize the nation or attempt to kill the witness of Christianity. It was a time when little justice and great loss of life and cruelty reigned, all in the name of "Liberty, Fraternity, Equality!" (Anon. 1991). Atheism reigned supreme and a goddess of Reason was crowned to indicate the rejection and abhorrence of divine revelation. Churches were desecrated and ransacked, books were burned and religion and its followers were insulted and mocked, even though there was in theory freedom of worship. In the city of Lyons the gospels were tied to a donkey's tail to indicate its total rejection. The calendar was changed so that no religious undertones remained. Priests were executed or sent to slavery. Ultimately, the power behind these non-Christian acts originated with Satan, the original dissenter against Christ.

6. The "dead bodies" of the words of God are said to have lain in the streets of spiritual Egypt and Sodom. What information does this imagery convey?

Revelation 11:8 And their dead bodies *will lie* in the street of the great city which spiritually is called Sodom and Egypt, where also our Lord was crucified.

Genesis 19:5 And they called to Lot [located in Sodom] and said to him, "Where are the men who came to you tonight? Bring them out to us that we may know them *carnally.*"

Ezekiel 16:49, 50 Look, this was the iniquity of your sister Sodom: She and her daughter had pride, fullness of food, and abundance of idleness; neither did she strengthen the hand of the poor and needy. And they were haughty and committed abomination before Me; therefore I took them away as I saw *fit.*

Exodus 5:2 And Pharaoh [in Egypt] said, "Who *is* the LORD, that I should obey His voice to let Israel go? I do not know the LORD, nor will I let Israel go."

Note: The reference in Revelation 11, verse 8, is to Sodom and Egypt. The activities characterizing Sodom are highlighted in our texts from Genesis and Ezekiel. Degenerate Sodom was known for its licentiousness, its total disregard for human dignity, and its rejection of sections of God's moral code. It was known above all for the immoral and unnatural acts of its citizens and the word 'sodomy' has come down in the English language in recognition of this. This vice was strengthened on account of the city's wealth and the abundance of the leisure time available.

It is recorded that during the French Revolution the cult of Reason was established as a religion. A beautiful actress (of doubtful morality) was enthroned as the goddess of Reason and was paraded as the ultimate exhibit of nature's perfection. Now "In domestic affairs the era of the Directory (1795-1799) was characterized by large-scale corruption. The revolution had demoralized public life, especially in Paris and the major cities. Profiteering in business, graft in politics and bureaucracy, extravagance in luxuries, and vulgarity in morals and manners, were the marks of the new regime" (*Citizendium*—French Revolution).

Egypt was known for its defiance of God. The pharaoh said to Moses the prophet that he had no respect for God or His word. Pharaoh was pompous and claimed god-like powers (Ezek. 29:3). Egypt stands for a nation that has no place for the God of Scripture and is atheistic at its core. This meant that no place would be found in such a city for the promulgation of the gospel of Christ. When we look at the historical records, this is precisely the picture that emerged in France during the French Revolution. The thought leaders of the de-Christianizing movement bent their energies to "overturn the religion of Christ, and eradicate from the human heart every religious sentiment." Their secret watch word was: "Crush Christ" (Buck 1831, 446, 447).

The whole thrust of the Revolution was to distance itself from any Christian remembrance and to put human reason and philosophy in its place; hence the goddess of Reason was worshipped and the calendar was changed. Others have continued in the footsteps of revolutionary France.

7. For how long would God's witnesses be without a voice and people rejoice over their death?
Revelation 11:9, 10 Then *those* from the peoples, tribes, tongues, and nations will see their dead bodies three-and-a-half days, and not allow their dead bodies to be put into graves. And those who dwell on the earth will rejoice over them, make merry, and send gifts to one another, because these two prophets tormented those who dwell on the earth.

Note: Denying burial to the dead witnesses conveys the idea that "an act of great indignity" had been perpetrated (Müller 2002, 38). The period of time when the Scriptures were figuratively lying dead in the streets of France can be located from around mid-November of 1793 for about three and a half years (using the principles that a day in prophecy is equal to a literal year). At that time, there was great rejoicing at the expulsion of religion and the elevation of reason; Bibles were burnt and churches were desecrated. The Festival of Reason held at Notre Dame Cathedral on November 10, 1793, has come to be regarded as a defining act in the de-Christianising movement. It was the climax of the de-Christianization acts of the revolution. The cathedral became the Temple of Reason. On November 23, 1793, all churches in Paris were consecrated to reason and closed and this movement was followed in the provinces. By its actions France, a Christian nation, deliberately renounced its trust in religion and hence commenced a modern atheistic movement.

8. When God's witnesses were given a voice again, what amazing turn around in prominence occurred?
Revelation 11:11, 12 Now after the three-and-a-half days the breath of life from God entered them, and they stood on their feet, and great fear fell on those who saw them. And they heard a loud voice from heaven saying to them, "Come up here." And they ascended to heaven in a cloud, and their enemies saw them.

Note: The abolition of religion in France lasted until June 17, 1797 when religious activity was again permitted officially. Following this act, freedom came to both the Protestant Christians and Jews. On that day the Council of Five Hundred received a report recommending that everyone be given the "liberty to follow the religion of their heart" (Thiers 1845, 724; Thiele 1959, 193). The Council gave its general consent. Further attempts to terrorise the clergy were largely ineffectual.

In the early part of the 1800s, a religious awakening, which had commenced earlier in various countries, blossomed and caught the people of France in its wake. Missionary societies flourished and Bibles were multiplied and were spread widely throughout many countries. Indeed, the witnesses had "ascended to heaven" in prominence (cf. Dan. 4:20–22; 4SP 193).

9. What significance can we attach to the reference to the great earthquake occurring after the witnesses were honoured?
Revelation 11:13 In the same hour there was a great earthquake, and a tenth of the city fell. In the earthquake seven thousand people were killed, and the rest were afraid and gave glory to the God of heaven.

Note: The interpretation of this verse has followed a number of lines. We are suggesting that the earthquake referred to was representative of the revolution of ideas and the significant changes that took place in both France and the territories annexed by it during the revolution and in the Napoleonic wars. The thousands slain in the upheaval might be taken to represent the fact that the church and state were separated and that the power and privileges of the nobility and Catholic Church were gone and were replaced by representative government by popular vote. In a figurative sense the power of the privileged group was "slain" or finished for the time being. Reference to the tenth part of the city and seven thousand slain can be interpreted to mean that a "minimum" of the city or country fell on the one hand and that a "remnant" of the church's powers remained and it would recover (Doukhan 2002, 98, 99). Glory was given to God when the witnesses were resurrected in that the rights of mankind now were formally recognized and the exercise of religion was permitted without the interference of priests or princes.

10 What attitude and activities on our behalf might increase the prominence of the two witnesses and what activities might in reality kill their influence?
Acts 17:11 These [believers] were more fair-minded than those in Thessalonica, in that they received the word with all readiness, and searched the Scriptures daily *to find out* whether these things were so.

2 Peter 1:19-21 And so we have the prophetic word confirmed which you do well to heed as a light that shines in a dark place, until the day dawns and the morning star rises in your hearts; knowing this first, that no prophecy of Scripture is of any private interpretation, for prophecy never came by the will of man, but holy men of God spoke *as they were* moved by the Holy Spirit.

Note: The text in Acts simply encourages us to trust the word of God, to take its literal, plain and simple sense. This is what the Bereans practiced and they were commended for their nobility. The historical-grammatical approach to the understanding of Scripture is the one spoken about by the apostle Peter who regarded it as authoritative, inspired and trustworthy. It has been given under the influence of the Holy Spirit for the edification of mankind, and hence it is consistent. "A familiar acquaintance with the Scriptures sharpens the discerning powers and fortifies the soul against the attacks of Satan. The Bible is the sword of the Spirit, which will never fail to vanquish the adversary. It is the only true guide in all matters of faith and practice. The reason why Satan has so great control over the minds and hearts of men is that they have not made the Word of God the man of their counsel, and all their ways have not been tried by the true test. The Bible will show us what course we must pursue to become heirs of glory" (1MCP 89).

Today we have many voices questioning the divinely inspired nature of the Bible. The supernatural events described there are doubted or rejected. Such a critical approach (historical-critical method) largely has swept away confidence in God's word, which is regarded as little more than an ordinary book by some religionists. The Scriptures predicted that a day would arrive when such an attitude would be expressed. "For the time will come when they will not endure sound doctrine, but according to their own desires, *because* they have itching ears, they will heap up for themselves teachers" (2 Timothy 4:3). Today, we assert, as in the Protestant Reformation, that the Bible and it alone is the basis of our faith. We are called upon by the Lord Himself to live by the word of God. Notice His instruction: "It is written, 'Man shall not live by bread alone, but by every word that proceeds from the mouth of God.'"(Matthew 4:4). Indeed, Satan through his agents seeks "to throw professed Christians and all the world into uncertainty about the Word of God" and "he leads them to doubt its divine origin" (EW 90).

11.8 The Woman and the Sun

Introduction

The imagery used at the commencement of Revelation chapter 12 reminds us of some of the tales coming from Greek mythology. However, the symbols used throughout the book are deliberate and full of meaning. Fortunately, the book of Revelation itself and other books of the Bible explain the meaning of the symbolic language used.

In this chapter we are introduced again to the Great Controversy theme and are directed particularly to the events surrounding Jesus' birth and the subsequent history of the endeavours of world powers to destroy the witness of the apostles and the believers to follow.

Although the chapter presents, at first sight, a view of the Church retreating before the onslaughts of evil forces inspired by Satan, it is comforting to observe that God is in charge of the affairs of men and that a faithful remnant is still present in the "time of the end." This group is shown elsewhere in the book of Revelation as triumphing along with those who have sacrificed for God's cause throughout history.

The chapter gives us an assurance that God will always have a faithful remnant to witness for the truths of the gospel and carry its light to the following generations. The remnant cherish and value God's gift of instruction in the Bible and respond to His gracious offer of salvation.

The Study

Read chapter 12 then the Bible texts and notes below in answer to the questions posed.

1. The women featured in chapters 12 and 17 are different. How is this difference expressed?
Revelation 12:1 Now a great sign appeared in heaven: a woman clothed with the sun, with the moon under her feet, and on her head a garland of twelve stars.

Revelation 17:1 "Come, I will show you the judgment of the great harlot who sits on many waters."

Verse 4 The woman [harlot] was arrayed in purple and scarlet, and adorned with gold and precious stones and pearls, having in her hand a golden cup full of abominations and the filthiness of her fornication.

Note: The difference observed in these verses is significant. One woman, clothed in the sun or bright and shining, is accepted by God (vs. 6) whereas the harlot dressed in gorgeous robes does not meet with God's approval, since she is responsible for the death of Jesus' followers (17:6).

2. Many symbols are used in chapter 12. What does the symbol of the woman clothed in the sun refer to?
Revelation 12:1 Now a great sign appeared in heaven: a woman clothed with the sun, with the moon under her feet, and on her head a garland of twelve stars.

Note: The symbol of the woman is frequently used in Scripture to refer to God's people. This is noted in both the Old and New Testaments (e.g., Isa. 54:5, 6; Jer. 3:20; 2 Cor. 11:2; Eph. 5:25-32). Following this lead, and considering our first question, the woman represents God's authentic followers who hold firm to the information delivered to them by the prophets and apostles. This conclusion is made firmer when we consider that the woman is clothed with the sun, which is symbolic of Christ and His purity (Mal.

4:1, 2). This woman wears a sign or symbol of victory on her head (cf. Rev. 2:10; 3:11), which refers to the victory she will experience through faith in Christ. Undoubtedly this text also refers to the fact that these authentic followers are firm believers in God the Creator who fashioned the sun, moon and stars on day four (Gen. 1:14-19). The moon may be taken also as a symbol to indicate that the followers of Christ reflect His glory. Their lives have been changed by their relationship with Jesus; they can be channels to others only of the gifts they have received from God. Ellen White affirmed this interpretation: "The people of God, symbolized by a holy woman and her children, were represented as greatly in the minority. In the last days only a remnant still existed. Of these John speaks as they 'which keep the commandments of God, and have the testimony of Jesus Christ'" (ST Nov. 1, 1899).

3. The woman (authentic church) finds itself in conflict with spiritual and political forces. Who is revealed as directing these political forces or powers?

Revelation 12:3 And another sign appeared in heaven: behold, a great fiery red dragon having seven heads and ten horns, and seven diadems on his heads.

Verse 13 Now when the dragon saw that he had been cast to the earth, he persecuted the woman who gave birth to the male *Child*.

Note: There is no question that the dragon or serpent is none other than the great apostate, Satan, who was cast out of heaven (vs. 9). This is the same individual responsible for tempting Eve in the Garden of Eden (Gen. 3:1-4). He is identified as the chief cherub or Lucifer elsewhere in Scripture (Isa. 14:12-15; Ezek. 28:14-16). First, he was the chief angel in the heavenly courts and after his rebellion he became known as Satan or the dragon.

Reference to political forces with interests in the spiritual domain is made through the description of the dragon given in verse 3. He is said to have "seven heads and ten horns, and seven diadems on his heads." The heads are taken to refer to political powers (cf. Rev. 17:9, 10). The reference to the heads bearing diadems or crowns is confirmation of this interpretation, as anciently royalty used the wearing of crowns to indicate their rulership. The horns are also symbolic of political powers (cf. Dan. 7:7, 8). It is obvious from the verses to follow that religious matters are of major concern to the dragon.

4. In what location in the universe did the Great Controversy between the dragon (Lucifer) and Christ begin?

Revelation 12:7, 8 And war broke out in heaven: Michael [Son of God] and his angels fought with the dragon; and the dragon and his angels fought, but they did not prevail, nor was a place found for them in heaven any longer.

Note: Rebellion broke out in heaven when the lead angel, Lucifer, became jealous of the attention given to the Son of God. He wished to possess the Son's throne (Isa. 14:12-15; Ezek. 28:12, 15). No excuse for the origin of evil is offered in the Bible.

Following the rebellion in heaven, the immediate leadership of heaven's loyal hosts was taken over by Michael or the Son of God. The prophet Daniel has introduced Him already to us as a "great prince" who is on the side of His people (Dan. 12:1). The name "Michael" means "Who is like God."

On account of Lucifer's unjustified rebellion he was removed from heaven. He was able to convince many of the holy angels and win them to his side through his mind games. "The influence of mind on mind, so strong a power for good when sanctified, is equally strong for evil in the hands of those opposed to God" (7BC 973). We are informed that "Satan was warring against the law of God." His rebellion was expressed by his resistance to the authority of Christ. He was prepared to "defend his place in heaven by force of might, strength against strength" (SR 17, 18).

5. Satan was expelled from heaven on account of his rebellion. What proportion of angels was expelled with him?
Revelation 12:4 first part His tail drew a third of the stars of heaven and threw them to the earth.

Note: When Lucifer or Satan was expelled from heaven, his sympathizers were cast out with him. Our text indicates that around a third of the angelic host had taken sides with Satan. These forces set about to derail the plan of salvation. Ever since the idea was made public that God had a plan to rescue mankind (Gen. 3:15), Satan had sought ways to frustrate its fulfillment. He was so successful early in his ventures that just eight people (a remnant) were saved at the time of the great flood (Gen. 7:7; 1 Pet. 3:20). In the days of King Ahasuerus and Queen Esther, there was a move to destroy the nation that God had chosen to represent Him. The plan failed utterly (Esth. 9:1-4). Again a remnant was saved. Other examples of remnant groups are provided in the Bible.

6. Where was the home base for Satan and his angels located after their expulsion from heaven? And when did they relocate?
Revelation 12:9 So the great dragon was cast out, that serpent of old, called the Devil and Satan, who deceives the whole world; he was cast to the earth, and his angels were cast out with him.

Ezekiel 28:13 You [Lucifer, refer to Isa. 14:12] were in Eden, the garden of God; every precious stone *was* your covering: the sardius, topaz, and diamond, beryl, onyx, and jasper, sapphire, turquoise, and emerald with gold. The workmanship of your timbrels and pipes was prepared for you on the day you were created.

Note: The earth was made the primary dwelling place of the evil forces. Ezekiel the prophet tells us that Satan was in the Garden of Eden, just as recorded in the book of Genesis (Gen. 3:1-4). By comparing the description given by Ezekiel with the record in Genesis, it is evident that Satan had lost his glorious appearance. Other evidence in Scripture informs us that he also enjoyed limited visiting privileges to other locations in the universe (Job 1:6, 7). We are not privileged to know a great deal about the heavenly realms, but we have been informed that at points in his experience Satan waited "just at the entrance [of heaven] to taunt the angels and seek contention with them" (SR 27).

7. The focus in chapter 12 is on the Child the woman was bearing. Who was the Child and what type of reception did He receive at His birth?
Revelation 12:2 Then being with child, she [the woman] cried out in labor and in pain to give birth.

Verse 4 last part And the dragon stood before the woman who was ready to give birth, to devour her Child as soon as it was born.

Note: Satan's attempts to derail God's plans to save the human race commenced in Eden. Following the murder of Abel, we find that Eve named the replacement child Seth that means "God has put," which links our minds to the putting of enmity between Satan and the woman spoken about in Genesis (Gen. 3:15). Christ arose from Seth's line in fulfillment of this prophecy (Doukhan 2002, 110). When the birth of Jesus was imminent, Satan made special efforts to upset the fulfillment of Christ's mission. When the wise men visited from the east and attempted to find the location of the King of the Jews, Herod was disturbed and sought to locate Him. When Herod's plan failed, Satan inspired him to kill all the male children of two years and under in an attempt to eliminate Jesus (Matt. 2:2-18). He was afraid of the King that the wise men from the east had come to worship. These plans also failed as Joseph fled to Egypt in response to a dream given by God and Jesus escaped (vss. 13-15).

We well remember that the wise men that came to honour the birth of Christ came from the east. Those who came were "rich and noble, the philosophers of the East." Now these wise men "had studied prophecy, and knew the time was at hand when Christ would come, and they were anxiously watching for some sign of this great event, that they might be among the first to welcome the infant heavenly King, and worship Him. . . . [To their amazement] a luminous star appeared, and lingered in the heavens. The unusual appearance of the large, bright star which they had never seen before, hanging as a sign in the heavens, attracted their attention, and the Spirit of God moved them out to seek this heavenly Visitor to a fallen world." Now, "this luminous star appeared, and lingered in the sky. It was neither a fixed star nor a planet, and the phenomenon excited the keenest interest" (TAA 161, 162). Indeed, this phenomenon appears to have been recorded in the astronomical records of China where in 5 B.C. a comet was clearly visible for over 70 days and its appearance was associated with unusual alignments of other heavenly bodies. Tradition has it that the wise men visiting Jesus were Magi who came from northern Persia and other areas under Zoroastrian influence. It is possible that the news of their visit to Bethlehem would have gone to China bearing in mind the mutual strong interest in astronomy.

8. Was Satan successful in his attempts to overcome Christ and destroy His plan of salvation?
Revelation 12:5 last part And her Child was caught up to God and His throne.

Verse 10 Then I heard a loud voice saying in heaven, "Now salvation, and strength, and the kingdom of our God, and the power of His Christ have come, for the accuser of our brethren, who accused them before our God day and night, has been cast down."

Note: Despite the attempts of Satan to destroy Christ, this prophecy informs us that his attempts would not succeed. Christ said "the ruler of this world is coming, and he has nothing in Me" or will find no sympathetic response from Me" (John 14:30). In practice this means that all the attempts to discourage, cause Jesus to become angry or seek an easy solution were unsuccessful. Then, too, all the attempts by those who killed Jesus to prevent His rising again were useless. In fact, the brightness of one angel was sufficient to cause the guards at His tomb to fall down as dead men. The stone was rolled back by one angel (Matt. 28:2) who broke the seal and released the resurrected Lord (vs. 6). Jesus rose by the divine power present in Himself at the call of the Father and with the quickening of the Spirit (John 10:18; Rom. 6:4; 8:11; Gal. 1:1; DA, 780, 785). He then ascended or was "caught up" to God in heaven (Mark 16:19; Acts 1:9-11).

Satan was first cast down when he was removed from heaven (Rev. 12:4, 8); the second and defining casting down of Satan occurred at the cross (John 12:31). It was then that "Satan . . . knew that his kingdom was lost" (SR 227). This represented the defining moment spoken of by our text. However, Satan was not about to give in. He is determined to take as many people with him to destruction as possible to limit Christ's success. Through Satan's devices he brought "A moral and intellectual paralysis . . . upon Christendom" for many years (SR 334) and continues to work along similar lines. He will finally be thrown into the lake of fire (Rev. 20:10). It has been suggested that the defining casting down of Satan at the cross was also the time when he was excluded from the councils in heavenly places (Job 1:6-12).

9. When will Jesus rule with a rod of iron?
Revelation 12:5 first part She bore a male Child who was to rule all nations with a rod of iron.

Note: Christ will rule with a rod of iron when He delivers the outcomes of His judgment on the nations of the world after His second coming (Rev. 11:15; 19:15).

10. Satan was furious with his failure to overcome Christ while He lived as a man on earth. What institution did he now seek to destroy?
Revelation 12:12, 13 "Therefore rejoice, O heavens, and you who dwell in them! Woe to the inhabitants of the earth and the sea! For the devil has come down to you, having great wrath, because he knows that he has a short time." Now when the dragon saw that he had been cast to the earth, he persecuted the woman who gave birth to the male *Child.*

Note: From the time when evil emerged, Satan's primary objective was to resist the authority of Christ and derail His plans. Satan's failure to upset either God's schedule or plan to provide a means to save mankind was now answered with fury against the followers of Christ. In our text the woman or church was persecuted in order to discourage and limit its success. In practice, the strategy of persecution has been partially successful. A more successful strategy now has been adopted. This involves introducing doubt about the word of God and the assimilation of 'humanistic' ideas into the church.

11. What means did God employ to protect the woman (authentic church) and for how long did this experience last?
Revelation 12:6 Then the woman fled into the wilderness, where she has a place prepared by God, that they should feed her there one thousand two hundred and sixty days.

Verse 14 But the woman was given two wings of a great eagle, that she might fly into the wilderness to her place, where she is nourished for a time and times and half a time, from the presence of the serpent.

Note: The term "wilderness" is often interpreted, as we might expect, as a desolate and deserted place. However, the Bible also uses the idea of a wilderness to express the concept that God's people would be found in unexpected places (Hos. 9:10). The time period of 1260 days or years specifically spoken of in our verse refers to the period between A.D. 538 and 1798, which has peculiar significance to events happening within the Roman Church. The date 538 is significant, as we have discovered already, in the overthrow of the Arian power of the Ostrogoths in the city of Rome, releasing the powers of the papacy to do their work until interrupted temporarily in 1798. It was in this latter year that the pope was taken captive by Napoleon's general during the French Revolution.

Reference to the woman fleeing (or to "fly") into the wilderness reminds the reader of the experience of the children of Israel as they escaped from Egypt. This is described as being accomplished on "eagles' wings" (Exod. 19:4; Deut. 32:11, 12), which is another way of saying that the persecuted people were God's chosen saints and He was helping them against the persecuting powers.

12. In a practical sense, what assistance did the earth offer sections of the authentic church?
Revelation 12:15, 16 So the serpent spewed water out of his mouth like a flood after the woman, that he might cause her to be carried away by the flood. But the earth helped the woman, and the earth opened its mouth and swallowed up the flood which the dragon had spewed out of his mouth.

Note: The 1260 year prophecy in this chapter is related specifically to the period of time between A.D. 538 and 1798. Satan has consistently used people to carry out his plans. Water in Bible prophecy refers to people (Rev. 17:15) and similar terminology refers to persecuting powers elsewhere (Pss. 69:1, 2; 124:2-5; Isa. 8:7, 8). Persecution of authentic Christians came from many quarters—Roman emperors, popes, military powers of princes and rulers (e.g., Inquisitors and individuals such as Justinian, Charlemagne and Timur). Christians were sent to the stake, to summary execution, to the arena, to slavery and exile. Then 'converts' were used to bring pagan practices and traditions into the church so that Christianity was corrupted. Others were used to question the authority of the Scriptures and to propose pleasing theories and interpretations (1 Tim. 6:20). Some have spoken of this as preparing a "river of deceit" (Stefanovic 2002, 392).

The persecutions were successful regionally. The history of the Albigenses (Cathars), the Huguenots and Waldenses is sufficient to allow all to understand the ferocity and barbarity of the war waged against God's word and the saints who chose to follow its teachings apart from the traditions of men. Suffice it to say that "The possession of an Old or New Testament was in itself seen as grounds for suspicion [against the Cathars] and was forbidden" (Barber 2000, 145). The crusades against these groups were seen as more important than contending with external enemies. There was urgency to accomplish the "extermination of the heretics." This was accomplished with cruelty and singleness of mind against the Cathars (Gardiner 2003, 50-57). Those unwilling to "submit to the supreme pontiff" were punished (Wilhelm 1910).

Selected Christian groups found refuge in geographically isolated locations and in places inaccessible politically (cf. Gen. 27:41-43; Exod. 2:11-15; 1 Kings 19:1-8; Matt. 2:13-15). Notable examples were the Waldenses in the Alps of northern Italy while the peoples of the Church of the East were located in regions not controlled by Rome. Of the first group it has been noted: "The mountain heights and rocky fastnesses have ever been the friendly refuge of God's people when oppressed and hunted by their enemies. For hundreds of years the Waldenses worshiped God amid the mountain solitudes, and there defied the armies of kings and emperors. On their rocky heights, in sight of their enemies, they sang the praise of Him who made the hills; and no opposing power could silence their hymns of lofty cheer (ST Feb. 2, 1882).

13. In the chapter under study, we are directed to several phases of church history other than the wilderness experience. What phases are mentioned?

Note 1: *Expectant period (vss. 1, 2, 4).* Our attention is first directed to the woman or church that looked with anticipation to the birth of the Saviour of the world. This phase stretched from the announcement in Eden of the coming Redeemer (Gen. 3:15) until the first advent. There was no lack of opportunities for Satan to deceive and seek to derail God's plans. We might refer to the rebellion that God sought to stem at the great flood (Gen. 9) and the apostasy of the children of Israel that led to the Babylonian captivity (Jer. 25:1-14) in order to illustrate this point.

Note 2: *Apostolic period (vs. 5).* The birth of Christ was followed by His anointing, ministry, death, resurrection and then ascension. These events are implied in our text. Subsequent to the ascension of Christ, the apostles lived by faith and looked for the second coming of Christ to set up His eternal kingdom and to rule with a rod of iron. All the apostles except one died a violent death inspired by Satan.

Note 3: *Wilderness period (vss. 6, 14).* The wilderness period is the one often emphasized. We are not belittling this period but wish to extend its meaning somewhat. The church after the time of Justinian was particularly anxious to preserve its dominance and it accomplished this by means of decree, persecution and elimination. The Emperor Justinian has the distinction of causing the *Corpus Juris Civilis* to be produced. This system of civil law influenced canon law and for the first time in A.D. 534 it was possible to "enforce orthodoxy with the Church's blessing—[a] condition without precedence in this form." This meant that those not connected with the church were considered non-citizens. Freedom of conscience consequently disappeared (Ando & Rüpke 2006, 124). It is said that "Pagan Greeks, Monophysite Christians, Jews and Samaritans were forced to convert to orthodox Christianity or suffer expulsion and even death" (Falk 1996, 353). The historian Gibbon records that "The insufficient term of three months was assigned for conversion or the exile of all heretics" (Gibbon 2004, chapter 13).

Various forms of persecution, repression and enforcement were attempted as the centuries rolled by with the strength of the now largely paganized church increasing. The Inquisition and brutal religious wars added to the tale of woe. Some Christian groups, such as the Waldenses, literally found refuge in desolate places in the mountains of southern France and northern Italy. Other groups such as the Cathars also had the advantages of access to mountain fortresses or relatively remote places, which offered them some protection.

Faithful groups existed in widely scattered locations. We will mention the Church of the East that stretched from Iran and India to China. It was isolated through distance and politics from the strangle hold of the Latin Church. This separation commenced in earnest from the time of Pope Victor I (A.D. 189-199), who excommunicated the Church of the East over the question of Easter observance. The separation gathered momentum following Justinian's decrees. The Church of the East maintained a strong missionary endeavour and evangelized much of the East. Their period of trials at the hand of the persecutor is not well recorded. However, persecution under Chinese rulers is recorded in A.D. 845. The Mongol Timur (A.D. 1336-1405) is noted in history for his cruel and ruthless behaviour and mass slaughter of Christians.

All these groups maintained their connection with the apostolic church. They attempted to hold fast to the teachings of the apostles rather than to traditions. They succeeded to varying degrees.

Note 4: *Remnant period (vs. 17).* God has preserved a remnant in all ages. However, the writer is informing us, by reference to the remnant in this verse, that Satan would be unsuccessful in extinguishing the light of truth through the period of the 1260 years. As a consequence, he would be especially angry at the groups focusing on Bible prophecy and its unalterable standards following the French Revolution.

14. What features characterize the believers, on whom God places His special care, in the last fragment of earth's history?

Revelation 12:17 And the dragon was enraged with the woman, and he went to make war with the rest of her offspring, who keep the commandments of God and have the testimony of Jesus Christ.

Note: The failure of all of Satan's schemes to disrupt God's plans will lead to desperate efforts using the well-tried approach of compromise (SR, 354). Naturally, the deceptions come in many guises. The focus of Satan's attention is specifically against those who reverence God's commandments and reject the traditions of mankind in favour of the words of Scripture. "Those who love and keep the commandments of God are most obnoxious to the synagogue of Satan, and the powers of evil will manifest their hatred toward them to the fullest extent possible" (7BC 974).

The second feature characterizing the remnant is that they "have the testimony of Jesus Christ." This means what it says. God has given "inspiration from above" (Doukhan 2002, 173). "The remnant lift up God's word and exhibits genuine manifestations of the gift of prophecy . . . that comes from Jesus and in which Jesus testifies about Himself" (Mueller 2000, 200). The only safety is in giving heed to the witness of Scripture and God's prophets (1 Pet. 1:19-21).

11.9 Beasts from Sea and Land

Introduction

The two beasts described in chapter 13 of Revelation are remarkably different in appearances, but as the discourse develops, they are shown to have a common goal in world affairs.

This is one of the most significant chapters that John the Revelator penned for it summarizes the end result of the fusion of politics with religion. Indeed, he commences the account by making a number of allusions to the writings of Daniel the prophet and to the influences coming into the church through contact with the pagan religions of the East. These developments led to the suppression or alteration of the truths of the Bible and to the heavy hand of persecution being felt by believers. This oppression was experienced for long ages by those who believed in the simple words of God.

Then the scene changes suddenly to reveal a seemingly gentle beast that joins forces with the great religio-political power of the Middle Ages to force men and women to worship or lend support to a philosophy directly opposed to God's word. This event is yet future. When this happens, a crisis point will have been reached in the history of the human race. All must make their stand for either God or for agents pretending to represent Him on earth. Severe civil penalties will be the reward of those who choose to follow God's words. The stakes are high and no one can excuse themselves from making a decision.

The Study

Read chapter 13 then the Bible texts and notes below in answer to the questions posed.

1. The prophet saw an unusual beast in his vision. What features did it display, and what meaning might be attributed to the symbols?
Revelation 13: 1 first part, 2 Then I stood on the sand of the sea. And I saw a beast rising up out of the sea, having seven heads and ten horns, and on his horns ten crowns . . . . Now the beast which I saw was like a leopard, his feet were like *the feet of* a bear, and his mouth like the mouth of a lion. The dragon gave him his power, his throne, and great authority.

Note: The vision of the beast arising from the sea is full of meaning. In the literature of the region a sea dragon represented the "enemies of the Creator" (Doukhan 2002, 114). However, the vision shows a beast with features already experienced when we studied the book of Daniel. There the leopard, bear and lion were spoken about (Dan. 7:2-6). The symbolism informs us that the power represented in this chapter displays essential characteristics derived from these previous civilizations. The ten horns remind us of the divisions seen in the fourth kingdom of Rome.

Indeed, the fact that Satan is intimately involved in the establishment, growth and prosperity of this leopard-beast power indicates that we are speaking of a political power with a keen interest in religious affairs.

2. What was written on the beast's heads? And how is the characteristic identified there shown in practice?
Revelation 13:1 last part And on his heads [was] a blasphemous name.

Revelation 13:6 Then he opened his mouth in blasphemy against God, to blaspheme His name, His tabernacle, and those who dwell in heaven.

Note: The thought expressed in our last paragraph is confirmed by the above segment of the text in verse 1. The leopard-like beast speaks against God and His ways specifically. In order to clarify the meaning of the word blasphemy, Merriam-Webster's Collegiate Dictionary, tenth edition (1996) offers the following helpful suggestions: "the act of insulting or showing contempt or lack of reverence for God" or "the act of claiming the attributes of deity" or "irreverence toward something considered sacred or inviolable." There are good examples in Scripture confirming these suggestions. Anciently Pharaoh said:" "Who *is* the LORD, that I should obey His voice to let Israel go? I do not know the LORD, nor will I let Israel go" (Exod. 5:2). Sennacerib blasphemed God by considering Him no better than the gods of the nations (2 Kings 18:35; 19:6). The Pharisees accused Jesus of claiming God's attributes when He said: "I and *My* Father are one" (John 10:30-33).These qualities were rightly His to claim, but they dismissed the claim and attempted to stone Him (vs. 31). Then we find that Nadab and Abihu acted blasphemously toward the sacred provisions of the sanctuary and its services by offering strange fire and were destroyed for their actions (Num. 3:4). With this as background, we can say confidently that presenting the doctrine of hell as a place of eternal suffering arranged by a loving God is a long standing example of blasphemy (GC 536). A modern version of blasphemy has been given by the outspoken evolutionist, Professor Dawkins, who recently said "The God of the Old Testament is a monster . . . He is a hyped-up Ayatollah Khomeini" (Miller 2009, 45).

We might expect that the power spoken about to participate in similar types of attitudes, statements or activities. Verse 6 tells us precisely that the power will speak unadvisedly about God's name, aspects of the plan of salvation (either connected with the earthly tabernacle or about features of Christ's ministry in the heavenly tabernacle), and make false representations about events happening in heaven or persons residing there. We will speak about these details when we have identified the power involved.

3. One of the heads of the leopard-like beast displayed remarkable features. Contrast these with the prophetic record found elsewhere (refer to Table 14). What new features are revealed about the little horn power highlighted in this new format?

Note: The leopard-like beast of Revelation 13, in all important respects, is seen to be a promoter of the policies and displays the attitudes previously attributed to the little horn power. This significant point will guide our discussion. The dramatic fall and subsequent restoration of this power, spoken about in chapter 13, verse 3, helps us to identify it precisely.

4. What additional defining clues are given about the leopard-like beast that allows us to identify it as the little horn power in its latter phases of development?
Revelation 13:3 And *I saw* one of his heads as if it had been mortally wounded, and his deadly wound was healed. And all the world marvelled and followed the beast.

Revelation 13:5 last part And he was given authority to continue for forty-two months.

Note: The period of papal dominance from A.D. 538 until 1798 has been written about already. One of the heads or powers reigned for 42 months or 1260 days (interpreted as literal years) and then it received a deadly wound. Now this wound was subsequently healed so that the entire world was transfixed by the recovery.

Leopard-like beast of Revelation 13	Other useful references to the power
Severely wounded, but wound is healed (vs. 3)	
Power given to beast by the dragon or Satan (vs. 4)	Does not operate by his own power (Dan. 8:24)
Speaks blasphemies against God, His tabernacle and those in heaven (vss. 5, 6)	Speaks pompous words (Dan. 7:8, 25). Attacks truth, opposes doctrine of salvation and Christ Himself (Dan. 8:12, 25)
Prominent for 42 months or 1260 years (vs. 5)	Prominent for $3^{1/2}$ times (Dan. 7:25; Rev. 12:6, 14–16)
Warred against the saints and overcame them (vs. 7)	Persecuted and destroyed saints (Dan. 7:21, 25; 8:24; 12:7)
Gained world-wide authority (vs. 7)	Changes conventions and destroys significant powers (Dan. 7:25; 8:24)
Receives world-wide worship with notable exceptions (vss. 3, 8)	

Table 14. Highlights of the leopard-like beast spoken about in the book of Revelation.

Let us review a few relevant details. Justinian's code of justice (A.D. 534) "rigidly suppressed all non-orthodox Christian faiths and practices in his empire" (Falk 1996, 353). Four years later (A.D. 538), the Arian powers were removed from the city of Rome by Justinian's General Belisarius leaving the pope to grow in power and prestige. Then the empire saw the reign of "a uniform yet various scene of persecution" (Gibbon 2004, chapter 13) that was responsible for the flight of the church into the wilderness to commence the 1260 years period spoken about in the prophecy. It was from Justinian's time that it could be truly said that "The Christian emperor had absorbed the ancient Roman emperor. . . . [His reign] had profound effects on the fate of the papacy and herewith on medieval—and eventually also modern—Europe" (Ullmann 2003, 43). Indeed, the papacy increased in power and wealth during this period.

The capture of the pope (Pope Pius VI—died in captivity) by Napoleon's general in 1798 was the deadly wound received by the papacy. Its subsequent recovery is a matter well-understood in history. The historian Thomson (1990, 104) remarked that Pope Pius VII in 1814 (after the abdication of Napoleon) "made a triumphal return to Rome" having gained much freedom and set about to reestablished various offices so that a period "like a second Counter-Reformation" occurred. The "recovery of Catholicism after its low ebb at the end of the eighteenth century was rapid and remarkable."

By the first Vatican Council held in 1870, the papacy was well on its way to recovery (even though it had lost the papal states in the same year during the establishment of the Italian kingdom). In that year the doctrine of papal infallibility was proclaimed. Today it is a world power. The pope was featured on *Time* magazine as the "Man of the Year" in 1962 and again in 1994 (Jan. 4 issue, 1963 and Dec. 26 issue, 1994, respectively), which illustrates this achievement.

5. Going back to a previous point, we indicated that some explanation would be provided concerning activities of the little horn power and of some other religious powers that could be considered blasphemous. We now offer a partial commentary on the following text.

Revelation 13:6 Then he opened his mouth in blasphemy against God, to blaspheme His name, His tabernacle, and those who dwell in heaven.

Note 1: *State in death.* It is blasphemy to assert that humans possess immortal souls when the Scripture clearly state that God alone possesses it (1 Tim. 1:17; 6:15, 16). This is a notion coming from Greek mythology and has captured most of the Christian church. This doctrine is one of Satan's most successful strategies that he has linked with its companion, eternal torment in hell. Hence, he is able to "hold up God before the people as a revengeful tyrant . . . instead of being loved and adored" (EW 218, 219). These two doctrines hold up God's character to ridicule.

Note 2: *Claims to the titles and authority of God.* It is recorded that from about the 1140s the pope designated himself the "vicar of Christ" and that he was regarded as the mediator between Christ and man "flesh from God's flesh, spirit from God's spirit" (Ullmann 2003, 182, 183). The papal bull of 1302, *Unam Sanctam*, proclaimed that the pope's authority was "not human but divine. . . . Therefore whoever resists this power ordained by God resists the ordinance of God." The Bible contains no authorization conferring such powers.

Note 3: *Mary mediatrix or coredemptrix.* The doctrine of Mary the mother of Christ being an advocate or mediatrix was already promoted from the time of Saint Irenaeus in the second century; this was confirmed in A.D. 373 by Saint Ephraem and his opinion was later supplemented by other church fathers. Vatican II declared that the doctrine had not been fully developed, but confirmed that it involves a participatory role for Mary. This is despite the full assurance of Scripture that states: "For *there is* one God and one Mediator between God and men, *the* Man Christ Jesus, who gave Himself a ransom for all, to be testified in due time" (1 Tim. 2:5, 6). The significance of this doctrine for the Christian churches is expressed as follows: "the full truth about Mary, far from being an obstacle to ecumenism, is in fact the very foundation of real Christian unity" (Vox Populi . . . Center 2009, 6). Well we might shudder at the thought expressed in some quarters of the church that the "virgin might be proclaimed a mediator and co-Savior figure, comparable to Jesus himself, even a fourth member of the Trinity" (Jenkins 2002, 118).

Note 4: *Tradition elevated.* In the Catholic Church there is a "formal equality between Scripture and tradition." However, practical priority is given to the Scripture (Rahner 1975, 168). Nevertheless, it is asserted that "God maintains the Christian (Catholic) church in truth such that Tradition cannot fundamentally err." And it is also observed that "from time to time [the Catholic Church has] elevated some portion of tradition to the status of dogma . . . even when the belief is not found clearly expressed anywhere in Scripture." This can be noted in the assertion that Mary conceived without the taint of original sin. By contrast the Reformation was based on the idea of *sola Scriptura* or Scripture alone or above all (Olson 2002, 64). This is the safe position and the one adopted by survivors of the scenes pictured in Revelation 13.

Note 5: *Sanctuary doctrine ignored in practice.* The sanctuary doctrine is specially understood and proclaimed by the Seventh-day Adventist church. This contrasts with most churches, whether Protestant or Catholic, which ignore its full message. This doctrine has to do with God's plan of salvation and the sinner's acceptance of it. It covers the ideas already commented upon above and establishes without controversy that the blood of Christ cleanses the sinner. This doctrine establishes that our works do not contribute to our salvation. However, it is taught in the Catholic tradition that the believer "should strive by works of mercy and charity, as well as by prayer and the various practices of penance, to put off completely the 'old man' and to put on the 'new man'" (*Catechism of the Catholic Church*, paragraph #1473). The related doctrine of indulgences even allows others to benefit: "The faithful can gain indulgences for themselves or apply them to the dead" (paragraph #1471). These doctrines clearly go beyond the clear evidence of the Scriptures as taught by the sanctuary doctrine.

6. One group of people refuses to worship the little horn power. What does the Scripture say about them?

Revelation 13:8 All who dwell on the earth will worship him, whose names have not been written in the Book of Life of the Lamb slain from the foundation of the world.

Revelation 7:14 last part "These are the ones who come out of the great tribulation, and washed their robes and made them white in the blood of the Lamb.

Note: These Scriptures are structured about the concept of a Great Controversy between good and evil. We have clearly seen this already in our study of Revelation chapter 12 (verse 7), namely: "And war broke out in heaven: Michael and his angels fought with the dragon; and the dragon and his angels fought." This conflict has been continued on earth. Those standing firmly for God are further identified in chapter 7 of Revelation. As a result of their stand they will suffer greatly. However, they choose to live by faith in Christ alone. This idea is shared with us through reference to the saints washing their robes in the "blood of the Lamb." In response to the information that their names are in the Book of Life, they do not go on to claim that they have contributed to this status. They have chosen to obey God and have been honoured by Christ.

7. In contrast to the leopard-like beast, a lamb-like beast is now revealed as we continue reading in chapter 13. The first beast arose from the sea, the second comes from the land. What significant detail can be derived from these symbols?

Revelation 13:1 first part (cf. 17:15) Then I stood on the sand of the sea. And I saw a beast rising up out of the sea.

Revelation 13:11 first part Then I saw another beast coming up out of the earth.

Note: The earth and sea are contrasted by these texts quoted above. The significance of the terms 'earth' and 'sea' is debated by commentators. We can be certain of one thing and that is the terms refer to the "universal and worldwide scope of Satan's end-time activities" (Stefanovic 2002, 414). Beyond that we might infer from Daniel 7, verse 3, that the sea refers to regions of the globe where population concentrations and political intrigue are well developed. In these regions of rich cultural diversity, the philosophies and practices of the people were destined to impact significantly on the perception of God's truth. We have commented already that the kingdoms of Babylon, Medo-Persia, Greece and finally Rome appeared from the sea (vs.1). This type of reasoning is confirmed in Revelation 17, verse 1, where similar language is used. The same beast is shown there sitting on "many waters," which represent peoples, nations and tongues—masses of people are indicated (Rev. 17:15).

We have discovered from our study of the previous chapter that the "earth helped the woman" (Rev. 12:16). We indicated there that, in practical terms, this meant that those who wished to obey God sometimes were able to locate themselves in rugged or desolate places or in locations where the political environment was conducive to worship. The lamb-like beast arose in a sparsely populated region of the world and initially displayed a temperament favouring the things of God—hence the use of the term 'lamb.'

8. The lamb-like beast possessed two horns. What interpretation might be given to this detail?
Revelation 13:11 Then I saw another beast coming up out of the earth, and he had two horns like a lamb and spoke like a dragon.

Note: In agreement with the comments in our last question, this prophecy is applied to the emergence of a powerful nation in the New World far away from the intrigue and turmoil in Europe and Asia. This we have taken to be the United States of America, which has now developed to be first among world powers. It is significant to notice that as the leopard-like beast was going "into captivity" (vs. 10) the lamb-like beast was arising. In 1798 the United States was a rising nation.

In common with our previous interpretations, the horns refer to the source of power. The United States was created by immigrants seeking to establish a safe dwelling environment on the "principles of civil and religious liberty" (Lawler & Schaefer 2005, 11). These were the founding principles of the nation established in 1776 through the union of states. No kingly power or "crowns" were involved; this nation operated by democratic principles from its commencement. However, the prophecy goes on to say that the spirit of the dragon or Satan would possess it over time and that it would become oppressive in its policies.

9. What powers does the lamb-like beast possess? What remarkable act does it "cause" the world to perform?
Revelation 13:12 And he exercises all the authority of the first beast in his presence, and causes the earth and those who dwell in it to worship the first beast, whose deadly wound was healed.

Revelation 13:14 And he deceives those who dwell on the earth by those signs which he was granted to do in the sight of the beast, telling those who dwell on the earth to make an image to the beast who was wounded by the sword and lived.

Note: The prophet now focuses on a time yet in the future when the civil powers will combine with other forces to cause people to give honour and even worship the papacy or its inventions. The liberty purchased by the American Revolution will disappear. This will be achieved, no doubt, through changes to the Constitution. Such changes have been proposed already (unsuccessfully). The prophecy predicts that ultimately they will be successful. The First Amendment to the Constitution states: "Congress shall make no law respecting the establishment of religion or prohibiting the free exercise thereof" (Duncan & Jones 2008, 42). The Supreme Court has and continues to struggle over the interpretation of this Amendment in the face of challenges to the separation of church and state. The Court has ruled already that Sunday laws may be enforced in the interests of "safeguarding the health and welfare of the American people" (Finley 2005, 10). Some justices on the Court favour abandoning the separation of church and state.

Already it has been observed that in time of crisis separation of church and state can be difficult to maintain. This was illustrated when President George Bush commenced his crusade against Muslim extremists after September, 2001. This crusade favoured the policies of the religious right. One commentator has remarked: "The events of 2001 not only changed the mentality of the American people, they also resulted in a fracture throughout the country . . . between those who believe that the struggle between Good and Evil is a last crusade to uphold the moral and religious values of Christianity, and those who maintain that God and religion have no place in domestic and foreign policy" (Victor 2005, 39). In practice, religious ideals were being implemented through foreign policy in the Bush era. The prophecy indicates even more directed policies in the future.

The signs that are performed in the name of the lamb-like beast (vss. 13, 14) are under the control of evil angels (cf. Job's experience recorded in Job 1:14-19). These agencies are effective in that they "deceived [men] by the miracles which . . . [they] have power to do, not which they pretend to do" (GC 553).

10. What meaning might be attributed to the phrase "he was granted power to give breath to the image of the beast"?

Revelation 13:15 He was granted *power* to give breath to the image of the beast, that the image of the beast should both speak and cause as many as would not worship the image of the beast to be killed.

Note: As incredible as it appears to us today, the Scriptures indicate that a time will come when obedience to religious demands will be associated with a death decree on all those who choose not to obey. This means that the spirit of the Dark Ages will be resurrected. One inspired writer has commented that "the Sabbath has become the special point of controversy throughout Christendom, and religious and secular authorities have combined to enforce the observance of Sunday . . . ." (GC 615). And further, "This prophecy will be fulfilled when the United States shall enforce Sunday observance" (GC 579). Some believe that "this century, like its predecessor, will be an American one" (Martinez 2010, 32). This could mean that the unprecedented dominance of the United States is destined to continue for some time.

11. The apostle John contrasts the mark of the beast and his number with the seal of God. Is there a third option?

Revelation 7:3 [An angel cried with a loud voice] saying, "Do not harm the earth, the sea, or the trees till we have sealed the servants of our God on their foreheads."

Revelation 13:16, 17 He causes all, both small and great, rich and poor, free and slave, to receive a mark on their right hand or on their foreheads and that no one may buy or sell except one who has the mark or the name of the beast, or the number of his name.

Note 1: No, there is not a third option! Jesus made it plain that "He who is not with Me is against Me, and he who does not gather with Me scatters abroad" (Matt. 12:30). No element of force is used when God places His seal in a person's forehead. In contrast, the mark of the beast is given under cover of threats. Study the details given in Table 15 relating to the contrast between the mark of the beast and the seal of God found in the book of Revelation.

Note 2: In order to understand the Bible message, some definitions are perhaps required. The word "SEAL" in Greek means to receive an "impression" or "inscription" that attests to the authenticity of the item (cf. Deut. 32:1-5). God's seal is thus a statement of fitness for heaven that by its very nature implies a process of investigation (hence, the idea of a pre-advent judgment is seen to be on a solid scriptural basis). This represents remarkable common sense, for any item of quality requires an investigation before a maker of quality goods will place his/her seal of approval on it. The word "MARK" in Greek means "impressed mark" or "engraving." Those with the mark of the beast have Satan's approval (endorsement) or display aspects of his character, for they have given allegiance to him (Horn 1960, 685, 974, 975;

Liddell & Scott 1961, 1742, 1976). It is clearly evident that no physical mark or distinction is being spoken about.

Mark of the Beast	Seal of God
Placed in right hand or on forehead (Rev. 13:16; cf. 14:9, 10)	**God's name placed on forehead (Rev. 14:1)**
Mark can be substituted for by the number of the beast (Rev. 13:17)	**No substitutes are permitted or issued (Rev. 7:2, 3)**
Mark holders worship beast and image (Rev. 13:15)	**Seal holders support and worship God the Creator and Judge (Rev. 14:6, 7; cf. 20:4)**
Marked individuals accept the blasphemous things the beast says (Rev. 13:5, 16)	**Sealed individuals accept and live by the words of God and by faith alone (Rev. 14:12)**

Table 15. Contrasting features of the seal of God and the mark of the beast.

The idea will be promoted widely just before Christ returns the second time that the "Temporal Millennium" has arrived (the doctrine declares that the world will be converted to Christianity and all peoples will live in peace for a thousand years). We understand that at this time the claim will be made that God has changed the Ten Commandments concerning the day of worship. This will pave the way for general agreement on Christian unity, especially as the claim is supported by signs, miracles and the appearance of angels (actually evil angels) among men. Those dedicated to upholding God's laws will be taunted and harassed for standing against the general community opinion. Their ability to buy or sell will be denied and they will be cast into great distress. God responds by supplying their needs through the ministration of heavenly angels (TA, 267, 268). It is firmly believed that "this prophecy [restricting buying and selling] will be fulfilled when the United States shall enforce Sunday observance" (GC 579). There should be extra care in presenting the truth about the true Sabbath as the seal of God and Sunday keeping as the mark of the beast. The fact that Sunday observance is widespread amongst Christians by itself is not to be considered as the mark of the beast. The decree to make Sunday keeping compulsory plays an important role in the prophetic timeline. "Sunday keeping is not yet the mark of the beast, and will not be until the decree goes forth causing men to worship this idol sabbath. The time will come when this day will be the test, but that time has not come yet" (MS 118, 1899).

12. What does Jesus Christ advise those to do who wish to triumph with Him?
Revelation 13:9 If anyone has an ear, let him hear.

Revelation 13:18 first part Here is wisdom. Let him who has understanding calculate the number of the beast.

Note: The emphasis here is that all should be willing to hear, to think and consider God's words and His message for these last days. We are told that the sealing of the Holy Spirit represents a "settling into the truth, both intellectually and spiritually, so they cannot be moved" (MS 173, 1902).

13. What are we to understand by the number 666?

Revelation 13:18 last part For it [the number of the beast] is the number of a man: His number *is* 666.

Note: Much debate has surrounded this number. It is unlikely to be connected with numerical values associated with the name *vicarius filii Dei* or "vicar of the Son of God." This name is connected with the fabrications contained in the Donation of Constantine (Valentine 2005, 317, 318). There is a surer basis to the interpretation of this number. The symbolism of numbers was at the root of ancient and medieval systems of mysticism and has its roots in astrology. We find, for example, that numerical values were given names of gods to indicate their place in the astrological system. A rich lore was associated with the numerical values of certain letters of the alphabet by ancient peoples. The number six is undoubtedly the number of the serpent, Lucifer. It is represented in many languages by the symbol of the snake. The greatest number in the mysteries was 666, the number found on sacred solar seals, for it represents the god of the heavens or cosmos—the Sun.

As part of the philosophy of numbers, we find the practice of assigning meaning to numbers. The numbers 1 to 36 were particularly significant as they represented the 36 rooms of the Zodiac. These numbers could be arranged in an astrological chart consisting of six columns and six rows (magic square). In any direction the numbers added to 111 and the summary number of the six rows or columns was 666. Now, the number "666 was a summary number of the Sun-god, because it was the sacred number as the Ruler of the Zodiac" (Sutton 1983, 67). We come across the magical squares again in the form of amulets (these could be worn to protect from trouble or bring health and happiness. It is fascinating to note that among the Arabians and Hebrews the "amuletum or cameo" of the sun (whose day was Sunday) consisted of six columns (added vertically, horizontally or diagonally they totalled 111); the grand total was 666 (Budge 1978, 12, 395, 396). Small wonder, then, that the mystic number 666 is referred to in the Scriptures as the symbol of apostate Christian religion (Rev. 13:18)—whose sign of authority is changing the day of worship to Sunday.

We briefly note some of the practices accepted by those in such communions. Slowly pagan practices from astrology infiltrated the Old and New Testament churches (e.g., Job 31:26-28; Jer. 32:34-36 in Old Testament; Acts 19:26; Rev. 2:13, 14 in New Testament). Some of the current manifestations of pagan practices are Christmas and Easter celebrations with their associated customs, Sunday sacredness, veneration of saints and Mary, festivals, processions and relic worship. The number of these practices is increasing! For example, Catholicism in the Americas has other iconic figures of significance (icons of Mary) such as the Virgin of Guadalupe in Mexico or La Virgen de la Caridad del Cobre, the queen and patron of Cuba; meanwhile in Korea, Confucian and shamanistic practices have been introduced in some Christian churches of other persuasions. Similar trends are seen in Africa.

Sunday is, without any question, the "Day of the Sun" (Sutton 1983, 266). This day was dedicated to the sun anciently and was adopted by the early church as a day of worship in place of the day ordained by God. There is no scriptural mandate for this change; its observance is an ordinance of man as indicated by the following quote: "Perhaps the boldest thing, the most revolutionary change the Church ever did, happened in the first century. The holy day, the Sabbath, was changed to Sunday. 'The day of the Lord' (dies Dominica) was chosen, not from any direction noted in the Scriptures, but from the (Catholic) Church's sense of its own power . . . . People who think that the Scriptures should be the sole authority, should logically become 7th Day Adventists, and keep Saturday holy" (Broderick 1995, 1).

14. What features are displayed by those who are sealed by God and what are the contrasting features of the group who are not sealed (refer to Table 16)?

Characteristics shown by marked individuals	Features found in those sealed by God
Standards accepted conform to societal norms or their own standards (Mal. 3:5)	Hold to pure doctrines (virgins), possess no guile and are without fault (Rev. 14:4, 5; cf. Matt. 5:5,8)
Do not have the spirit of repentance (Rev. 9:21)	Accept gospel fully and forsake sins (Rev. 14:6; 18:4)
Unrighteous and unholy (Rev. 22:11)	Accept justification by faith (Rev. 7:10, 14)
Genuine faith is alien to personal experience (Rev. 9:20)	Display patience and faith (Rev. 13:10; 14:12; cf. sanctification; Rev. 19:8)
Do not or do not wholly respect the Decalogue (Dan. 7:25; Rev. 9:21)	Respect the Decalogue (Rev. 12:17; 14:12)
Characterized by a liberal attitude towards the doctrines delivered by the prophets and apostles (Dan. 8:12; Rev. 2:14)	Respect testimony of Jesus and his word (Rev. 12:17; cf. 19:10; 22:18). They are faithful (Rev. 17:14)
Unbelieving and worship demons and idols (Rev. 9:20; 21:8)	Honour miracle working Creator (Rev. 14:7)
Do not practice justice (Rev. 22:11)	Accept and understand that mercy is balanced with justice (Rev. 14:6, 7)
Practice abominations (Rev. 21:8; 22:11, 15)	Protest the abominations practiced in the name of religion (Ezek. 9:4)
Obsessed with material wealth and prestige among the nations (Dan. 8:24)	Honour and respect God's book of nature (Rev. 11:18)
Characterized by intolerance and forcing the consciences of others (Dan. 8:24, 25)	Follow peace with all people (Heb. 12:14; cf. Matt. 5:9)

Table 16. Contrasting features shown by marked and sealed individuals.

Note: It should be explained that not all the features noted against those bearing the mark of the beast are possessed by all people. By contrast all the sealed of God show the features highlighted. It is also important to note that God is fair in dealing with His children who have not yet had the chance to hear the good news. "There are many who have never had the light. They are deceived by their teachers, and they have not received the mark of the beast. The Lord is working with them; He has not left them to their own ways. Until they shall be convicted of the truth and trample upon the evidence given to enlighten them, the Lord will not withdraw His grace from them" (Letter 7, 1895).

11.10 Angels Proclaim Hope

Introduction

The scene immediately presented in Revelation chapter 14, as an interlude, is one of triumph in heaven after the disturbing scenes outlined in chapter 13. There you will remember that the great religious and political powers of the world had combined to deny freedom of religion. Satan was shown as using both types of forces to accomplish his purposes and to deny God a resounding victory in the great clash of ideologies taking place in the world. Now God is assuring His people that the death decrees enacted by men really have no power over the destiny of those who have given themselves in dedication and service to God. There will be a remnant that is prepared to remain loyal to God. However, the scene of triumph now changes quickly. We find ourselves back on earth by verse 6. In order to achieve the glorious rest in heaven, the remnant group has serious work to undertake on earth.

Before the close of human probation, God undertakes earnestly to reach as many people as possible with the penetrating truths for this time. He causes three great messages to be proclaimed around the world with urgency—these messages are shown as being carried by flying angels. Angels certainly assist in giving this message, but the idea is clearly presented that it is the duty of true-hearted believers to share the information they have received. The reader should carefully note that these messages were first proclaimed in the nineteenth century and still are being given to the world. Today, we see prophecy being fulfilled before our eyes.

The Study

Read chapter 14 then the Bible texts and notes below in answer to the questions posed.

1. The scene in chapter 14 opens with the triumph of the sealed saints (144,000) before God's throne (vss. 1-3). Why is all heaven engaged in excited celebration?
Revelation 14:4 last part, 5 These are the ones who follow the Lamb wherever He goes. These were redeemed from *among* men, *being* first fruits to God and to the Lamb. And in their mouth was found no deceit, for they are without fault before the throne of God.

Note: The heavenly hosts join with the redeemed in proclaiming the end of sin, sinners and its originator (Satan). The triumph of Christ is complete. Death and the grave have no place in the world made new. Those who are found worthy have maintained their fidelity to God in the face of gross departures from the teachings of the Bible and amidst threats to their lives.

2. What special acts are the redeemed able to participate in?
Revelation 14:3, 4 first part They sang as it were a new song before the throne, before the four living creatures, and the elders; and no one could learn that song except the hundred *and* forty-four thousand who were redeemed from the earth. These are the ones who were not defiled with women, for they are virgins.

Revelation 7:14, 15 And I said to him [in answer to the question, "Who are these arrayed in white robes"–vs. 13], "Sir, you know." So he said to me, "These are the ones who come out of the great tribulation, and washed their robes and made them white in the blood of the Lamb. Therefore they are before the throne of God, and serve Him day and night in His temple. And He who sits on the throne will dwell among them.

Note: The song that the saints sing is a song of both experience and victory. This is the song that those who have passed through the tribulations described in chapter 13 are able to sing. They have gone through very troublesome times and have maintained their faith and trust in God. Actually, the parable of the ten virgins told by Christ is relevant here. It informs us that the saved people have enjoyed a living experience with Christ (Matt. 25:1-13). They have remained true to God through the trials and discouragements they have experienced on earth (cf. 2 Cor. 11:2, 3).

There have been several theories proposed regarding the composition of the 144,000. Ellen White offered the following counsel. "Christ says that there will be those in the church who will present fables and suppositions, when God has given grand, elevating, ennobling truths, which should ever be kept in the treasure house of the mind. When men pick up this theory and that theory, when they are curious to know something it is not necessary for them to know, God is not leading them. It is not His plan that His people shall present something which they have to suppose, which is not taught in the Word. It is not His will that they shall get into controversy over questions which will not help them spiritually, such as, Who is to compose the hundred and forty-four thousand. This those who are the elect of God will in a short time know without question" (7BC 978).

3. Those who have been sealed and saved have responded to the rousing end-time calls given by three special angels. How does the Bible summarize the sealed saints' commitment?
Revelation 14:12 Here is the patience of the saints; here *are* those who keep the commandments of God and the faith of Jesus.

Note: One thing is clear from chapter 14. The Decalogue delivered by God to mankind is still intact. He has not changed either His will or ways for He is unchangeable (Num. 23:19; Jas. 1:17). We can be very glad that God has this quality to His character, for otherwise the sacrifice offered by Christ would have been of doubtful value and our salvation would not be secure. Serving a fickle God is not an attractive option; the Bible presents a picture of a stable, trustworthy God. This is why the redeemed are able to display steadfast faith in Jesus Christ. In fact, we find that they show true sanctification by "a conscientious regard for all the commandments of God, by a careful improvement of every talent, by a circumspect conversation, by revealing in every act the meekness of Jesus" (ST June 12, 1901).

4. The first angel declares that he has the everlasting gospel. What is understood by this?
Revelation 14:6 Then I saw another angel flying in the midst of heaven, having the everlasting gospel to preach to those who dwell on the earth—to every nation, tribe, tongue, and people.

Note: The everlasting gospel was first given to Adam and Eve. Its purpose was to restore the image of God in mankind that so recently had been lost through disobedience to His commands. This gospel is understood "not [to be] limited to the good news of His pardon and forgiveness. It presents the ellipse of truth that reveals the integrity of God's grace as including His forgiveness and His power to transform" (Douglass 2001, 150; cf. SC 62, 63). Through God's offer of mercy, He "imparts all the powers, all the grace, all the penitence, all the inclination, all the pardon of sins, in presenting His righteousness for man to grasp by living faith—which is also a gift of God" (FW 24). This means that man's works can account for nothing. The believers' responsibilities are to respond to God's offer of mercy and to cooperate with Him by using their powers as agents to do His will. They are to become channels of the benefits received and to give them to others. In fact, the mind of the believer is given in "willing consecration and service to God." This is the fruit of faith. Such faith understands that the salvation of mankind purchased by Christ does "not change or annul or lessen in the slightest degree the law of Ten Commandments." Such faith also "works by love and purifies the soul" (FW 25-27, 30, 49).

5. The first angel's message gives three commands, what are these and what is their relevance?
Revelation 14:7 Saying with a loud voice, "Fear God and give glory to Him, for the hour of His judgment has come; and worship Him who made heaven and earth, the sea and springs of water."

Compare Psalm 96:8, 9 Give to the LORD the glory *due* His name; bring an offering, and come into His courts. Oh, worship the LORD in the beauty of holiness! Tremble before Him, all the earth.

Note 1: *Fear.* To fear God is to awe and respect Him and render obedience to Him through faith (1 Sam. 12:14; 2 Chron. 6:31; Jer. 44:10). This is a truth very clearly outlined in the Old Testament (Deut. 10:12, 13) and was illustrated in the life and experience of Abraham (Gen. 22:12) and Job (Job 1:1). It is informative to note that the prophet Moses carefully recorded the relationship that always existed between the state of respect for God and obedience. Notice this in Deuteronomy 5:29 (cf. Deut. 6:2; 8:6) "Oh, that they had such a heart in them that they would fear Me and always keep all My commandments, that it might be well with them and with their children forever!" This same thought is echoed by King Solomon (Eccles. 12:13) and others (e.g., Ps. 128:1; Acts 10:35).

Note 2: *Glory.* Giving glory to God is to experience and gratefully acknowledge His salvation. The psalmist tells us gratefully that "In God *is* my salvation and my glory; the rock of my strength, a*nd* my refuge, *is* in God" (Ps. 62:7) and adds "Behold, You desire truth in the inward parts, and in the hidden *part* You will make me to know wisdom. Purge me with hyssop, and I shall be clean; wash me, and I shall be whiter than snow" (Ps. 51:16, 17). So here again the hearer is urged to accept the offer of God's gracious salvation by faith and develop a daily, living association with Jesus (cf. Matt. 5:16). There is no question that honest hearers will offer willing obedience to God (Eccles. 12:13). It has been well said "To give glory to God is to reveal His character in our own, and thus make Him known" (7BC 979).

Now giving glory to God has yet another dimension that we must mention. This is highlighted in 1 Corinthians 10, verse 31 as follows: "Therefore, whether you eat or drink, or whatever you do, do all to the glory of God." Healthful living is part of God's last day plan to bring glory to Him. He is directing our attention to the diet given in Eden. Indeed, we are reminded that "The world at large are given to gluttony and the indulgence of base passions. The light of health reform is opened before the people of God at this day, that they may see the necessity of holding their appetites and passions under control of the higher powers of the mind. This is also necessary, that they may have mental strength and clearness, to discern the sacred chain of truth, and turn from the bewitching errors and pleasing fables, that are flooding the world. Their work is to present before the people the pure doctrine of the Bible. Hence health reform finds its place in the preparatory work for the second appearing of Christ" (2SP 44). We can hardly ignore this advice, for Dietetic Associations that do not pretend to hear God's voice, are fully supportive of a vegetarian dietary choice.

Note 3: *Worship.* The basis of all true worship is identified in our text. This involves an acknowledgment that God is the Creator. We worship a miracle-working God. No credibility is given to the idea that God simply started the life processes and then stepped back to observe what would happen through evolutionary mechanisms. We declare this truth about His creatorship most sincerely by praising God for His mercy and goodness on the memorial day of creation, the seventh-day Sabbath (DA 283; GC 437).

True worship can be offered only by those who allow the renewing power of the Holy Spirit to change the life and produce a spirit of "willing obedience" to God's revelations (9T 156). There is no question that the end-time events will involve both issues of worship of God as Creator and acknowledgement of the day He set aside specifically for worship—the seventh-day Sabbath.

6. What additional understandings are given during the sounding of the first angel's message?
Revelation 14:7 middle section "The hour of His judgment has come."

Note: The text is properly understood to mean that an announcement has been made that the judgment has commenced and that this process is part of the gospel message. This act of judgment is understood as the pre-advent investigation phase, not the execution phase of the judgment. In the first angel's message there is a clear understanding given that the pre-advent phase of judgment cannot be divorced from the idea of God's mercy (salvation). It is emphasized in verse 6 that mercy always accompanies such judgment.

The plan of salvation outlined in the Old Testament sanctuary system highlighted the fact that God's plan to save mankind would end in the elimination of sin and the source of evil (Satan represented by Azazel). Indeed, the executive judgment was illustrated anciently in the final scenes of the Day of Atonement ceremonies. Since the final ministry on this Day took place in the Most Holy Place, we conclude that, as in the earthly sanctuary so in the heavenly, the basis on which judgment is made resides in the principles of the Decalogue housed there (Rom. 3:20; 1 John 3:4). The results of God's investigation in the heavenly sanctuary will be declared and administered commencing at the second coming.

The scriptural concept of judgment means that any ideas of the immortality of the soul must be abandoned. God's execution of judgment occurs at the end of probationary time and not at death (2 Cor. 5:10; Heb. 9:27). The outcome of all cases is announced and/or the rewards are given at Christ's second coming and at the end of the millennium (1 Thess. 4:13-18; 2 Pet. 2:9; Rev. 20:11-15).

7. The second angel announces that Babylon has fallen. To what attitude in worship does the term Babylon apply?
Revelation 14:8 first part And another angel followed, saying, "Babylon is fallen, is fallen, that great city, because she has made all nations drink of the wine of the wrath of her fornication."

James 4:4 Adulterers and adulteresses! Do you not know that friendship with the world is enmity with God? Whoever therefore wants to be a friend of the world makes himself an enemy of God.

Jeremiah 11:10 "They have turned back to the iniquities of their forefathers who refused to hear My words, and they have gone after other gods to serve them; the house of Israel and the house of Judah have broken My covenant which I made with their fathers."

Note 1: *General comments.* The twice mentioned fall of Babylon is understood to indicate the certainty of the event. The uncleanness exhibited by Babylon is seen in her acceptance of worldly practices and philosophies. It really "is a spirit of self-sufficiency that dates back at least to the story of the Tower of Babel . . . ." (Haffner 2009, 14). Babylon also stands for the systems of worship inspired by Satan that are fundamentally opposed to God. Nimrod, the founder of the city of Babel, led the peoples of his day in rebellion and defiance of God (Gen. 10:8-10; 11:3-6; cf. Isa. 21:9). Nimrod's worldly greatness was memorialized after his death in that he became a deity and was worshipped in the Babylonian mysteries.

He was associated with the sun god and with the generation of a system of counterfeit worship based on salvation by performing ceremonies and practices devised by man.

The term Babylon means confusion. Today such confusion is seen also among Christian groups with "widely conflicting creeds and theories," all ostensibly derived from the Bible, but marred on account of people seeking the favour of secular powers (GC 383). The prophet Isaiah associated Lucifer (Satan) with Babylon (Isa. 14:4, 12-14). This city was the place where astrology and the magical arts and the worship of heavenly bodies were highly developed. Rebellion against God was perfected there. Indeed, the city is "symbolic of all apostate religious organizations and their leadership from antiquity down to the close of time" (7BC 830). In the end-time period, Babylon is called "great" and this conveys the idea that a massive association of religious systems will form to oppose God and His people (cf. Rev. 16:19). For a brief period, the Christian churches will agree on how to present their distorted witness.

Note 2: *Wine.* The wine may be understood in reference to Daniel 5, verses 3 and 4. These texts refer to the behaviour of King Belshazzar on the night of his overthrow by the Medes and Persians. The multitude of revelers used fermented wine (symbol of sin) in the holy vessels of the temple of God. Hence, they mixed the sacred and profane by filling the sacred cups with the products of corruption or fermentation (Exod. 34:25; 1 Cor. 5:8). On account of this, God called down on Belshazzar vengeance and judgment. Any attempt to change the pure truths of the Scripture by introducing practices from profane sources is similarly regarded. Ignoring God's purposes, His provisions and His words in favour of man's ways are the sins of Babylon.

Note 3: *Fornication.* The verse in Jeremiah is typical of many others found in the Old Testament that speak of the people breaking their agreement with God by following other systems of worship. The specific shortcoming mentioned there was Israel's habit of taking on pagan practices (cf. Isa 21:9; Jer. 7:18; 19:5; Ezek. 16:26-32; Jas. 4:4). These practices were accompanied by other unbiblical ideas such as a conscious state in death (Isa. 8:19, 20).

The dwellers of Babylon may appear to sing a pleasant song, but they fail to do the deeds suggested by their song (Ezek. 33:31, 32). This may be shown in many ways in unacceptable interpersonal and community relationships and the abuse of power. All this evil is done under the cloak of religion (Ezek. 22:1-16). By this means, the name of God is brought low. Today, similar practices are seen in the worship of those who say they follow God but have added an extensive number of practices from paganism (e.g., Easter and Christmas rituals, use of holy water, relic and image worship, penance, honouring the day of the sun—Sunday). This trend is escalating among the so-called global Southern churches (churches found in South America and Africa). It has been noted by one observer. "Many Southern churches are syncretistic, they represent a thinly disguised paganism, and all in all they make for 'a very superstitious kind of Christianity,' even 'post-Christianity'" (G. C. Oosthiuzen quoted in Jenkins 2002, 121).

8. God consistently has called true hearted people to abandon the deceptions of false religious philosophies. What Bible examples may be cited in support of this claim?

Genesis 12:1 The LORD had said to Abram, "Leave your country, your people and your father's household and go to the land I will show you."

Joshua 24:2 And Joshua said to all the people, "Thus says the LORD God of Israel: 'Your fathers, *including* Terah, the father of Abraham and the father of Nahor, dwelt on the other side of the River in old times; and they served other gods.'"

Verse 14 "Now therefore, fear the LORD, serve Him in sincerity and in truth, and put away the gods which your fathers served on the other side of the River and in Egypt. Serve the LORD!"

Note: Abram was asked by God to leave Ur of the Chaldeans for he sought to separate Abram from the influences both of his family and the culture and practices of the surrounding peoples (cf. PP 125). God's removal of the children of Israel from Egypt was for a similar purpose.

9. When, in terms of apostasy, might it be truly said that Babylon has fallen?
Revelation 13:15 He was granted *power* to give breath to the image of the beast, that the image of the beast should both speak and cause as many as would not worship the image of the beast to be killed.

Note: We have discussed the above text already. The day has not yet arrived where the political powers of the world combine with powerful religious elements to impose worship practices. However, these end-time events are hastening to reality. God's pre-advent judgment activities commenced in 1844 and this prophecy began to be fulfilled as a fuller understanding about God's last messages to the world found in Revelation chapter 14 were rejected by the churches. It will be complete when the churches of Christendom show "indifference to the testing truths of our time" and antagonism towards those who accept God's instructions undiluted by human traditions (GC 389). Today, many Christian religious organizations in the Third World continue to be or have become politically active, so there is a "distinctly Christian politics" in this region (Jenkins 2002, 142).

10. The third angel was particularly emphatic in giving the first part of his message. Why was the call so urgent?
Revelation 14:9, 10 first part Then a third angel followed them, saying with a loud voice, "If anyone worships the beast and his image, and receives *his* mark on his forehead or on his hand, he himself shall also drink of the wine of the wrath of God, which is poured out full strength into the cup of His indignation."

Note: The cry of the third angel was and continues to be urgent for Jesus is "making His final intercession for all those who have ignorantly broken the law of God" (EW 254). Man's probation is fast coming to an end and a merciful God is eager to save just one more individual. When the probation of mankind has ended, God's wrath will be poured out undiluted with mercy. This has been explained by one author as follows: Because God's *agape* "means a completely reckless giving, it also demands unlimited devotion . . . it becomes an annihilating judgment on the selfish life which will not let itself be re-created into a life of love and refuses the offered fellowship" (Nygren 1982, 104).

11. In summary what is the nature of the worship that is approved by God and the rejection of which calls down His wrath on mankind?
Revelation 14:12 Here is the patience of the saints: here are they that keep the commandments of God, and the faith of Jesus.

Note: This verse in reality summarizes the interest of the last day saints in "the law and the gospel" (1SM 385). The first focus of the third angel was and is without question on God's law. Already in our study of Revelation 11, verses 1 and 19, we noticed the instruction to "measure" or investigate the temple of God. Such activity leads to an understanding of Christ's ministry in the heavenly sanctuary. Two things are made clear from such an investigation. First, the reader is brought face to face with the various phases of Christ's ministry of salvation and understands that the final phase of atonement is almost complete. Secondly, it reveals that the standard in the judgment is none other than the despised law of God (EW 255; Letter 110, 1896). It is clearly seen by readers today that the ark of the Testimony, testament or covenant (Exod. 30:6; Rev. 11:19) actually contains the "tablets of the Testimony," that is none other than the Decalogue (Exod. 31:18). In succinct terms, "God's testimony [is found] in the ten commandments" (4SGa 8). Deliberate rejection of this testimony brings God's judgment on mankind.

The other significant conviction held by those who study Christ's ministry in heaven is that the law of God can be kept only through the enabling power of Christ. After all, the mercy seat in the Most Holy Place in the earthly sanctuary overshadowed the law to indicate that its requirements could be met only through the blood of Christ (cf. 1 John 5:8-12). The apostles Paul and James comprehensively outline the relationship among faith, law and works (Rom. 3:20-26; Jas. 2:8-26), which complements the words of the prophets of old (e.g., Deut. 10:12, 13; Eccles. 12:13; Isa. 8:20). The consistent acknowledgment of the prophets is both to the necessity and adequacy of Christ's ministry and sacrifice (Rev. 19:10). Everything is dependent upon Christ and His merits. One writer has said of this text that it deals with "Christ's righteousness and His love for the world" (RC 82). That is exceedingly good news.

The people who respond to the three angels' messages "are not called to resistance and protest but to endurance and perseverance" (Stefanovic 2002, 454). They are overjoyed and energized by the simplicity of the gospel story and are determined to depend on God by faith, trusting in Him to strengthen them to keep His commandments. In their minds and lives the law and the gospel are held in balance and works of faith follow.

12. What startling discovery is made when the ark of the covenant is opened? What sudden realization and response comes from those who discover that God's law has not been changed by God's authority?

Revelation 11:19 Then the temple of God was opened in heaven, and the ark of His covenant was seen in His temple. And there were lightnings, noises, thunderings, an earthquake, and great hail.

Exodus 20:9, 10 Six days you shall labor and do all your work, but the seventh day *is* the Sabbath of the LORD your God. *In it* you shall do no work: you, nor your son, nor your daughter, nor your male servant, nor your female servant, nor your cattle, nor your stranger who *is* within your gates.

Daniel 7:25 He shall speak *pompous* words against the Most High, shall persecute the saints of the Most High, and shall intend to change times and law. Then *the saints* shall be given into his hand for a time and times and half a time.

Note: Those following Christ's ministry suddenly realize that "The commandment [fourth] reads as when spoken by the voice of God in solemn and awful grandeur upon the mount [Sinai] . . . it is the same as when written with His own finger on the tables of stone" (EW 255). The Sabbath institution was kept in Eden before the Fall. God Himself rested and so did "all the heavenly host" (EW 217). We can hardly doubt the continuing significance of this day.

The papacy has changed many things regarding the Christian faith. The boldest act claimed on its behalf is as follows: "Perhaps the boldest thing, the most revolutionary change the Church ever did, happened in the first century. The holy day, the Sabbath, was changed from Saturday to Sunday. 'The day of the Lord' (dies Dominica) was chosen, not from any direction noted in Scriptures, but from the (Catholic) Church's sense of its own power" (Broderick 1995, 1).

Following such a realization, those who are true servants of God confess their error, pray for forgiveness and work to tell others of the issues at hand. They have a thirst to understand all of God's ways and His instruction for them (EW 256).

13. In what manner does God cause the message of the third angel to become more prominent?
Revelation 18:1 After these things I saw another angel coming down from heaven, having great authority, and the earth was illuminated with his glory.

Verse 4 And I heard another voice from heaven saying, "Come out of her, my people, lest you share in her sins, and lest you receive of her plagues."

Note: The angel spoken of here unites with the third angel to bring God's last warning message to the peoples of the world. The instruction is simple: Come out of the spiritual adultery in which you dwell and join with those God is preparing to save (EW 277, 279). It is fascinating to notice that the "health principles must be united with this message" (CD 75; 3T 62). In practical terms, this means that the angels' messages can be enhanced today in the eyes of the people, for the scientific world is supportive in general of the vegetarian life style that gives clarity of thought and vigour of life (cf. 3T 62).

There is a parallel between the warnings given to God's people to come out of Babylon and Jesus' earthly ministry that we might notice. "When Jesus began His public ministry, He cleansed the temple from its sacrilegious profanation. Among the last acts of His ministry was the second cleansing of the temple. So in the last work for the warning of the world, two distinct calls are made to the churches. The second angel's message is, 'Babylon is fallen, is fallen, that great city, because she made all nations drink of the wine of the wrath of her fornication.' And in the loud cry of the third angel's message a voice is heard from heaven saying, 'Come out of her, my people, that ye be not partakers of her sins, and that ye receive not of her plagues. For her sins have reached unto heaven, and God hath remembered her iniquities'" (RH Dec. 6, 1892).

14. What special manifestation of God's blessing will be seen among the believers as a result of the mighty angel's activities?
Joel 2:23 Be glad then, you children of Zion, and rejoice in the LORD your God; for He has given you the former rain faithfully, and He will cause the rain to come down for you—the former rain, and the latter rain in the first *month.*

Verses 28, 29 "And it shall come to pass afterward that I will pour out My Spirit on all flesh; your sons and your daughters shall prophesy, your old men shall dream dreams, your young men shall see visions. And also on *My* menservants and on *My* maidservants I will pour out My Spirit in those days."

Note: Before the coming of the Lord, the last outpouring of the Holy Spirit will take place in abundance and visions, dreams and prophecies will be part of the experience. In fact, all the gifts of the Spirit will be evident in order to give impact to the last warning messages to the world (AA 55; GC, 611; cf. Acts 2:4, 16-21; Eph. 4:8, 11-16). The gift of prophecy was seen in the life and works of Ellen White in a marked manner. This manifestation was timed to accompany the proclamation of the three angels' messages, with their last great call of mercy. Other Spirit-activated events occurred in many parts of the world where manifestations and dreams were experienced. For example, the well known child preachers in Sweden in the early 1840s represent an extraordinary manifestation of the Spirit's activities. It is said that "some appeared to be in vision or a trancelike state while preaching" (Maxwell 1985, 356). The appearance of angels in the clouds in parts of Papua New Guinea also falls into the category of manifestations. There they heralded important events about to happen in heaven (Omahi Jackway, personal communications). These experiences are not dead in the church and continue to be seen in various parts of the world, as has been attested to by current witnesses. We will yet see the fuller expression of the Spirit's power before Christ comes.

15. The Scriptures promise that an Elijah type message again will be given before Christ returns (Mal. 4:5, 6). Do the three angel's messages form part of the fulfillment of this prediction? Study the accompanying Table 17.

Feature	Elijah 1 Kings 18	John the Baptist Gospels	Remnant people Revelation
Repentance	vs. 39	Matt. 3:2	3:19; 14:6
Invitation	vs. 30	Matt. 3:7	3:15; 14:6; 18:4
Reformation			
1. Abandon human traditions and accept the certainty of God's word	vss. 18, 36	Matt. 3:3, 7	14:8, 12
2. Identify fully with God	vs. 21	Luke 1:16–19; 3:4–6	14:9; 22:17
3. Truths and acceptable practices restored	vs. 36	Matt. 3:7	11:1; 14:12
4. Human works will not save; faith in Jesus saves	vss. 26–29	Matt. 3:8	3:18; 7:13, 14; 14:12
5. Focus worship on the miracle working God	vss. 31, 32	Matt. 3:11	3:20; 14:7
6. Pray for the Holy Spirit's manifestation	vss. 36, 38; cf. Acts 2:2–4	Luke 3:16, 22	3:18 (eyesalve); 7:3, 4; 14:1; cf. Eph. 4:30
Judgment	vs. 40	Matt. 3:10, 12	3:16; 14:7, 10

Table 17. Features of Elijah type messages spoken about in Scripture.

Note: There is no question that John the Baptist represented the call of Elijah at the time of Jesus' first coming to prepare people's minds for His ministry (Luke 3:2-6). Similarly, the prophet Malachi informs us that a call to repentance and reform will be an outstanding feature of the last day events to enable preparation for the second coming of Christ. We are told that "Elijah was a type of the saints who will be living on the earth at the time of the second advent of Christ . . . ." (PK 227). This means that an Elijah-type call is being made to honest minded people everywhere today.

The emphasis in all three instances is to call people, whether in the churches or outside, to accept God's great offer of mercy and accept His standard of conduct. Following this call lost truths were restored, such as the sanctuary and Sabbath truths (1 Kings 18:36; Rev. 11:1; 14:12). Others may follow. In our day "Those who are to prepare the way for the second coming of Christ are represented by faithful Elijah . . . ." (FLB 290).

16. By giving the angel's special warning messages to all people, what event is God seeking to shelter them from?

Revelation 14:10, 11 [The third angel said that if the beast or his image was worshipped then] "He himself shall also drink of the wine of the wrath of God, which is poured out full strength into the cup of His indignation. He shall be tormented with fire and brimstone in the presence of the holy angels and in the presence of the Lamb. And the smoke of their torment ascends forever and ever; and they have no rest day or night, who worship the beast and his image, and whoever receives the mark of his name."

Note: God is seeking to save just one more person. However, His judgments are about to fall on the world unmixed with mercy. Human probation is about to end. Then God will perform His "unusual act" (Isa. 28:21, 22). The idea behind the severe language used in the above texts is not to suggest that there is a living, eternal torment, but that evil will come to an absolute end. Judgment is final, sin and suffering has ceased. Just as fire burns until nothing is left, so the imagery used in the text above conveys the idea of an eternal nothingness for sin and sinners. They both cease to exist. These ideas are conveyed fully when similar passages are studied concerning God's judgments (e.g., Mal. 4:3; cf. Isa. 13:19-22; Jude 1:7).

11.11 Bowls of Wrath

Introduction

The account given in Revelation chapters 15 and 16 represents divine judgments on the wicked. This means that God has closed the avenues to His mercy. The three angel's messages of chapter 14 have ceased to be proclaimed. God's justice on the wicked and unrepentant is about to be revealed before the second coming of Christ in glory.

It is informative to note that judgment events are associated with the temple in heaven where Christ is ministering. When the "tabernacle of the testimony" (Exod. 38:21, KJV) or witness, which contains the tables of witness or Decalogue is opened, the seven angels carrying the plagues emerge to do their dreadful work.

The plagues are not meant to bring men and women to repentance. The Holy Spirit has been poured out in the later rain, as at Pentecost. None is left in doubt as to the issues. Hence the plagues reveal the sentiments that control the minds of the people. They remain resolutely rebellious to the end. In fact, the first five plagues clearly reveal this state of mind as the people continue to blaspheme God.

The sixth plague introduces a scene where all the forces of evil combine to molest and attempt to overcome those who have given their allegiance to God. The last great confrontation between the forces of good and evil takes place figuratively in a great battle at a place called Armageddon. There the people of God are called to endure the ultimate test of faith just before the coming of Christ.

The pouring out of the seventh plague represents the turning point in the battle. God brings the test of faith to a decisive and sudden end as the forces of nature respond to His voice.

The Study

Read chapters 15 and 16 then the Bible texts and notes below in answer to the questions posed.

1. A great voice from heaven was heard by John instructing the seven angels to pour out God's wrath on mankind (16:1). What event immediately preceded this announcement?

Revelation 15:8 The temple was filled with smoke from the glory of God and from His power, and no one was able to enter the temple till the seven plagues of the seven angels were completed.

Note: The temple or sanctuary in heaven was seen in vision as being filled with the glory of God and hence we conclude that it is unavailable to service any future needs of unrepentant humanity. Probation or the day of opportunity has closed (cf. Exod. 40:34, 35). The day of God's wrath has come unmixed with mercy. The third angel's message has been delivered fully and the image to the beast has been made. Its mark has been applied to unrepentant or uncaring mankind. The scene presented in chapter 13 through to 15 is reminiscent of the events preceding the great flood.

2. As a further indication that the day of God's mercy has closed, who does John see standing victorious on the sea of glass just as the plagues are about to be poured out?

Revelation 15:2 And I saw *something* like a sea of glass mingled with fire, and those who have the victory over the beast, over his image and over his mark *and* over the number of his name, standing on the sea of glass, having harps of God.

Note: At the beginning of the chapters on the plagues, the righteous are seen as being secure. The destinies of all have been decided before the plagues are poured out. However, we must not think that those who are to be saved are not affected in the slightest by the epidemics and upheavals in nature. They suffer want and privation and suffer at the hands of their enemies, but the plagues are not poured out on them. They have to cope with the general chaos that is being generated on a world-wide basis.

3. What is the nature of the song that the redeemed sing?
Revelation 15:3, 4 They sing the song of Moses, the servant of God, and the song of the Lamb, saying: "Great and marvellous *are* Your works, Lord God Almighty! Just and true *are* Your ways, O King of the saints! Who shall not fear You, O Lord, and glorify Your name? For *You* alone *are* holy. For all nations shall come and worship before You, for Your judgments have been manifested."
Note: The song that the redeemed sing is about their experience and deliverance. It is a song of redemption where "The church history upon the earth and the church redeemed in heaven all centre around the cross of Calvary. This is the theme, this is the song,—Christ all and in all,—in anthems of praise resounding through heaven from thousands and ten thousand times ten thousand and an innumerable company of the redeemed host. All unite in the song of Moses and of the Lamb. It is a new song, for it was never before sung in heaven" (TM 433).

The Song of Moses recorded in Exodus, chapter 15, is a song of great deliverance and of a new beginning (a type of re-creation). It contains many notes of gratitude (vs. 1; cf. Ps. 66:5-12; TM 433) for the salvation experienced (vss. 2, 13, 16). It is also a song of exultation over the forces of evil (vss. 3-8). Such a victory was gained initially against seemingly hopeless odds, for death was determined on God's people (vs. 9). The song implies faith in the ultimate destruction of God's foes, for God is over all (vss. 6, 7). It is also a song of vindication (vss. 15, 16). God gloriously fulfilled the covenant promises including the giving of a new dwelling place (vss. 16-19). Through all of history, God has not compromised His principles in seeking deliverance of His people from spiritual Egypt. God's people eventually will receive the greatest reward of all time—"life that measures with the life of God" (MS 92, 1908).

4. In the judgments God delivers through pouring out the plagues, what standard does He use to determine who is worthy and who is unworthy of heaven?
Revelation 15:5 After these things I looked, and behold, the temple of the tabernacle of the testimony in heaven was opened.

Note: The "tabernacle of witness" (Num. 17:7, 10) refers to the temple that houses the "tablets of Testimony" or the Decalogue (Exod. 31:18) found in the "ark of the Testimony" in the Most Holy Place (Exod. 30:6).

5. Why are the plagues poured out when there is no further hope of salvation?
Revelation 16:1 Then I heard a loud voice from the temple saying to the seven angels, "Go and pour out the bowls of the wrath of God on the earth."

Genesis 6:3 first part And the LORD said, "My Spirit shall not strive with man forever."

Verse 5 Then the LORD saw that the wickedness of man *was* great in the earth, and *that* every intent of the thoughts of his heart *was* only evil continually.

Verse 12 So God looked upon the earth, and indeed it was corrupt; for all flesh had corrupted their way on the earth.

Note: Like the experience at the Noachian flood, mankind will not be moved to repentance by the plagues (Rev. 16:9, 11, 21). The spirit that activates them becomes fully evident (cf. Rev. 13:15-17) and God's justice is fully revealed (GC 670). Mercy without the corresponding display of justice is poured out on those who have rejected so great opportunities to be saved and then enter into outright rebellion against God. The saints are vindicated and in the destruction of the false leaders they are led "to acknowledge that God has loved them because they held fast the truth and kept God's commandments . . . ."(EW 124).

6. The first plague is targeted to a particular group of people. Which group qualified to receive it?
Revelation 16:2 So the first went and poured out his bowl upon the earth, and a foul and loathsome sore came upon the men who had the mark of the beast and those who worshiped his image.

Note: The first plague is located principally in Christendom where the movement to set up the image to the beast and the application of his mark is particularly strong. Those who are eager to shed the blood of the righteous are its targets too (cf. GC 628). It is impossible to know the nature of the illness spoken about but several possibilities might be suggested to illustrate that microorganisms already exist capable of causing distressing sores that are difficult to cure. Such organisms are antibiotic resistant staphylococci, flesh eating streptococci and the buruli ulcer (caused by *Mycobacterium ulcerans*). Even though existing organisms might be used, the nature of the epidemic on the wicked and the protection of the righteous from its effects undoubtedly involve miraculous elements.

7. The second and third plagues are similar. What distressing events are predicted under these?
Revelation 16:3, 4 Then the second angel poured out his bowl on the sea, and it became blood as of a dead *man;* and every living creature in the sea died. Then the third angel poured out his bowl on the rivers and springs of water, and they became blood.

Note: The sea and rivers of water become blood. The exact meaning of this is a matter of conjecture, but what is important to us is that the oxygen requiring organisms living in these waters die. Furthermore, the fresh water supplies become non-potable. A contrasting plague was poured out on Egypt by Moses when he turned the Nile into a brownish red, unusable body of water, which led to the death of the fish and similar organisms (Exod. 7:17, 18). Now, the people of Egypt worshipped Hapi, god of the Nile. He was the god of fertility and bounties, including fish and birds. He was called "father of all the gods, prince of the waters, who feedeth Egypt, from whose rising come plenty, and riches, and life to all" (Wiedemann 2001, 147). Obviously this plague showed the powerlessness of such a god to provide food. The people had to access alternative sources of water to satisfy their needs (Exod. 7:24).

We are probably correct to surmise that a similar judgment will occur under the second plague. The turning of the sea to blood is a judgment on the obsession to gain wealth through buying and selling by means of international trade. Such trade commonly has associated with it a philosophy of greed, a wanton usage of earth's resources and a scant regard for degradation of the environment. On the other hand, judgment on the rivers may be a statement about the destructive attitude of the wicked towards those who choose to follow God (cf. Rev. 16:6) or due to their failure to acknowledge God as Creator and Redeemer (vs. 5).

8. During the fourth plague, intensely hot weather will be experienced. What effect will this have on the attitude of those who are adversely affected?

Revelation 16:8, 9 Then the fourth angel poured out his bowl on the sun, and power was given to him to scorch men with fire. And men were scorched with great heat, and they blasphemed the name of God who has power over these plagues; and they did not repent and give Him glory.

Note: No amount of speculation will allow us to predict with any accuracy either the cause or total effects of this plague. At the outset, we remember that the bowls of wrath are poured out by God's angels. Hence, we are not discounting the miraculous. At the same time, God is able to work through nature. Humanity has shown scant regard for the world, its resources, or its preservation. This judgment falls on those who do not have regard for God's second book of information—nature. It is a fulfillment of the statement that God "should destroy those who destroy the earth" (Rev. 11:18). The destruction of the ozone layer by man's activities may be proposed as one possibility for a dramatic increase in the temperature of the world and hence of scorching heat being felt.

9. The fifth plague is experienced at the headquarters of the beast power. What is the nature of this judgment?

Revelation 16:10, 11 Then the fifth angel poured out his bowl on the throne of the beast, and his kingdom became full of darkness; and they gnawed their tongues because of the pain. They blasphemed the God of heaven because of their pains and their sores, and did not repent of their deeds.

Note: The "seat" or "throne" of the beast represents its nerve centre. This is viewed by some commentators as a prediction of literal darkness descending on the beast's headquarters or equally it may be seen as a prediction that a painful disease will affect the eyesight of the leaders of this enterprise (cf. EW 289). The pain experienced during this plague seems inexplicable if literal darkness alone is postulated. Possible causes of debilitating eye diseases are bacterial, protozoan and virus infections, all of which can be very painful. Of course we are not discounting organisms/causes of other types being involved.

We notice in passing that the group of people highlighted here evidently is still suffering from the sores contracted during the first plague (cf. vs. 2). The attitude of those suffering from the plagues continues to be unhelpful and defiant in that they blaspheme God.

10. When the sixth plague is poured out, the waters of the river Euphrates are dried up. What does this symbolism mean and what does this event allow the kings of the east to do?

Revelation 16:12 Then the sixth angel poured out his bowl on the great river Euphrates, and its water was dried up, so that the way of the kings from the east might be prepared.

Note: We can begin to understand this text after reviewing a little history. The armies of Cyrus had approached the ancient city of Babylon and entered by way of the river Euphrates. The seemingly impregnable city had been taken by stealth (cf. Isa. 45:1), for Cyrus had drained the river into a nearby lake thereby lowering the water level and allowing his troops to enter via the stream bed that flowed through the city. When they came to the gates inside the city leading down to the river, they were open just as prophecy had foreseen (Isa. 45:1).

In spiritual Babylon, when the waters or support of the people (cf. Rev. 17:15) comes to an end, then the great religio-political kingdoms assembled at the end of time will be brought to the point of instability. This instability will come into play just before the coming of Christ. It is interesting to notice that the Bible often pictures God's deliverances as coming from the east. Cyrus, a servant doing

God's bidding, represented a power coming from the eastern regions (Isa. 45:1). God's glory came from the east to fill the temple in Ezekiel's day (Ezek. 43:2) and God's sealing angel comes from the east (Rev. 7:2). It is no small wonder that the sign of deliverance of God's people appears in the east (GC 640, 641).

11. Before Christ comes, the forces of evil make one last great effort to convince the nations of the world about the righteousness of their cause. What forces combine in order to rally the people into cooperation?
Revelation 16:13, 14 And I saw three unclean spirits like frogs *coming* out of the mouth of the dragon, out of the mouth of the beast, and out of the mouth of the false prophet. For they are spirits of demons, performing signs, *which* go out to the kings of the earth and of the whole world, to gather them to the battle of that great day of God Almighty.

Note: The beast, false prophet and dragon are identified as the forces involved in the deception of the people. The beast of Revelation 13 and 16 is none other than the papacy. It is supported by political powers in the pursuit of its religious goals (Rev. 17:3, 5). It has many accomplices in the religious world too. In fact, the organization is said to be the "Mother of harlots" or to be joined by others in disregard of God's word (vs. 5). These others are referred to as the false prophet and are represented by the adoring Protestant churches that follow the papacy's example of rejecting the plain words of Scripture. We have learnt already that the lamb-like beast of Revelation 13 (vss. 11-17) represents the United States of America. The Protestant churches of America will be foremost in leading down a pathway of compromise and will become sponsors of the papacy (GC, 588). The dragon or Satan is behind all these powers but has always enjoyed unparalleled expression of his antagonism to God and to His requirements through the pagan religious movements of the world. These are filled with evidences of the operation of evil agencies such as spiritism (reincarnation is a belief held by some spiritists). However, spiritism and spiritualism is not limited to them. Through all these agencies, the peoples of the world are prepared for the last great showdown with God.

12. Where does the gathering together take place for the last great conflict between good and evil?
Revelation 16:16 And they gathered them together to the place called in Hebrew, Armageddon.

Note: The term Armageddon (Rev. 16:16) means hill of Megiddo. The name brings to mind two remarkable events outlined in Scripture. Megiddo was the place where ancient Israel, under the leadership of Barak and Deborah (the prophetess), gained a remarkable victory under God's direction against vastly superior forces (Judg. 4, 5). God instructed His people to gather on Mount Tabor (the hill or mountain across the valley from Megiddo) in order to draw Sisera's army towards them. This battle strategy gained them the victory, as they demonstrated their faith in and obedience to God's words (Judg. 4:6, 7, 14, 15).

Mount Carmel was also in the vicinity of ancient Megiddo. Now a most remarkable contest took place on this mountain, in which worship was the central issue. The thrilling account of the prophet Elijah's lone challenge to the wicked Ahab, his priests and his subjects is recorded in Scripture for our benefit. Elijah urged the people to choose whom they would worship. The great issues he raised concerned the honour of God and the form of worship they chose. God was vindicated in a most remarkable manner on the mountain by Elijah's faithfulness (1 Kings 18).

In the final crisis to engulf the world, God's faithful people will again be at the apparent mercy of the wicked and with no hope of deliverance (Rev. 13). "The faith of individual members of the church will be tested as though there were not another person in the world" (MS 1a, 1890). The good news is that God will deliver His people, as they stand upon the principles enunciated in His word. In essence they take their stand on the hill of "faith and obedience," as did ancient Israel on Mount Tabor and Elijah on Mount Carmel (G. Pfandl, personal communications). The battle at Armageddon thus takes place, in the end-time setting, wherever God's faithful are surrounded by the servants of Satan intent upon their destruction. This contest at Armageddon is a world-encompassing event. The forces of Satan will be utterly destroyed, as they continue to defy their Creator.

13. Assembly for the battle of Armageddon takes place at the end of the sixth plague. How is this battle described?
Revelation 16:12-21— Read.

Note: In reality we are left to conjecture somewhat about the type of battle this is. Some commentators assert that it is literal. However, verse 13 informs us that various religio-political powers combine with the unseen forces of Satan to convince the kings of the earth to support their repression of those who have sought to serve God. This chapter must be read with the closing verses of chapter 13. When we do this, it is more prudent to suggest that the battle is of an intensely spiritual nature where the principles of God are under attack from satanic forces. This is not to deny that force of arms may be used against the righteous. However, there is no convincing evidence that two literal armies will face each other.

14. What assaults of the forces of nature accompany the coming of Christ associated with the final phases of the battle of Armageddon?
Revelation 16:18 And there were noises and thunderings and lightnings; and there was a great earthquake, such a mighty and great earthquake as had not occurred since men were on the earth.

Verse 21 first part And great hail from heaven fell upon men, *each hailstone* about the weight of a talent.

Note: The language used here suggests that a literal earthquake is predicted under the last plague. Joined with this are the sickening effects of giant hailstones (~30 kilograms), which accomplish their own devastation (this is many times larger than anything experienced on earth to date). Amidst the general destruction, the cooperative arrangements (religio-political) between the nations also disintegrate or are shaken apart.

15. What is the end result of the battle of Armageddon?
Revelation 16:20 Then every island fled away, and the mountains were not found.

Verse 21 And great hail from heaven fell upon men, *each hailstone* about the weight of a talent. Men blasphemed God because of the plague of the hail, since that plague was exceedingly great.

Note: The unity previously seen in the city or Babylon the great is now destroyed so that cooperation between the papacy, wayward Protestantism and neo-pagan religions comes to an end. This tendency also is encountered among the political support groups. We may observe that this thought is conveyed in the expression "the cities of the nations fell" (Rev. 16:19). Not only does political support for the papacy and her associates vaporise, but the anger of the nations is now focused on these powers and their leaders (Rev.

17:16, 17; cf. GC 655, 656). General destruction of the earth and its people takes place. The words of inspiration add, "Then I was shown that the seven last plagues will be poured out, after Jesus leaves the Sanctuary. Said the angel—It is the wrath of God and the Lamb that causes the destruction or death of the wicked" (RH Nov. 1, 1850).

16. What special experience do the people of God go through about the time the plagues are poured out?

Daniel 12:1 "At that time Michael shall stand up, the great prince who stands *watch* over the sons of your people; and there shall be a time of trouble, such as never was since there was a nation, *even* to that time. And at that time your people shall be delivered, everyone who is found written in the book."

Note: At the close of probation, the angels holding back the elements of war and strife (Rev. 7:1) are removed and "The whole world will be involved in ruin more terrible than that which came upon Jerusalem of old" (GC 614). Then, for the righteous, begins the "time of Jacob's trouble" (Jer. 30:5-7; GC 616). Just as Jacob's faith was severely tested on the night before he met Esau who was determined to destroy him (Gen. 32:24-30), so the people of God will be tempted to despair of their acceptance with God and their safety (GC 618, 619). However, their faith does not fail and they overcome as did Jacob.

The time of trouble is associated with the passing of the death decree that we have mentioned already in Revelation 13 (vs. 15). When the world seems to be conspiring against the saints, God will deliver the faithful following the announcement "It is done!" (Rev. 16:17). The forces of nature respond in violence and revenge (vss. 18-21).

11.12 Babylon Finally Falls

Introduction

We have dealt with the pouring out of the seven plagues in Revelation chapters 15 and 16. It is during the battle of Armageddon that Babylon the great falls and Christ prepares to come (16:16-19). As we turn to chapter 17, the first verse informs us that one of the seven angels is prepared to reveal details about the soon coming judgments on the "great whore." Looking a little closer at this chapter, we observe that verses 3 to 6 are concerned with the symbolic vision John saw. Then the following texts give the explanation of the vision (vss. 8-18). This explanation is complex and a number of views have been expressed about their meaning. We do not intend to review these opinions in any detail but rather we will paint a broad picture. This appears to be reasonable as the fulfillment of the prophecy is in the future and its meaning will become readily apparent then. The details are not essential for our salvation.

Moving onto the next chapter, we discover that chapter 18 is not written in proper sequence of events. You will remember that we already have dealt with verses 1 to 6 that relate to events just before the close of probation. The mighty angel featured in verse 1 adds his voice to that of the third angel of Revelation 14 in order to warn earth's inhabitants of coming events. At the end of verse 6, we find that God's offer of mercy has come to an end and that He is about to give appropriate rewards to the wicked. We have included verses 7 to 24 of the chapter in this lesson as they inform us about the activities of Babylon the great, her fall and the reaction of the political powers that have profited by her activities.

The record found in chapter 19, verses 1 to 7 represents a hymn of thanks and rejoicing over the fall of Babylon the great. These verses appear to relate to events that transpire immediately following the finishing of the seventh angel's work.

The Study

Read chapters 17 to 19 then the Bible texts and notes below in answer to the questions posed.

1. Chapter 17 commences with a declaration that God will judge "the great whore" (vs. 1). What is the meaning of this term?

Revelation 17:1 Then one of the seven angels who had the seven bowls came and talked with me, saying to me, "Come, I will show you the judgment of the great harlot who sits on many waters."

Note: The woman of chapter 17 contrasts sharply with the woman of chapter 12. Whereas a pure woman was spoken about in chapter 12, here an impure woman or harlot is introduced. A harlot or whore is a prostitute, hence the verse is speaking about judgment on the apostate systems that have changed the purity of God's word into something different and convinced others of the truthfulness of their philosophy. The Scriptures speak in these terms frequently in the Old Testament (e.g., Jer. 3:8; Ezek. 23:30, 36-39). The many waters represent the peoples of earth (Rev. 17:15) that Babylon influences and on which it depends for its powers.

2. Who did the impure woman or whore consort with?

Revelation 17:2, 3 "With whom [i.e., the whore] the kings of the earth committed fornication, and the inhabitants of the earth were made drunk with the wine of her fornication." So he carried me away in the Spirit into the wilderness. And I saw a woman sitting on a scarlet beast *which was* full of names of blasphemy, having seven heads and ten horns.

Note: The "kings of the earth" are political powers. The text is saying to us that the leaders of popular Christianity, and perhaps other sympathetic religious groups, will cooperate with the leaders of the nations in order to allow the fulfillment of the purposes of the false church. Through the combined activities of the religio-political consortium the inhabitants of the earth are "made drunk" or are deceived as a result of the policies and worldview promulgated in the name of Christianity (Jer. 51:7; 2 Thess. 2:8-10; GC 624).

Verse 3 confirms this interpretation for the apostate church (woman) sits on a scarlet coloured or evil beast (cf. Isa. 1:18). This beast represents political powers (cf. Dan. 7:3-7, 17; 8:3, 5, 20, 21). The combined powers of church and state act against God's cause and, in fact, become blasphemous in their claims. This is a fitting description of the activities of apostate religion under the guise of Christianity.

3. By what descriptive name is the impure woman or unfaithful church called?
Revelation 17:5 And on her forehead a name *was* written: MYSTERY, BABYLON THE GREAT, THE MOTHER OF HARLOTS AND OF THE ABOMINATIONS OF THE EARTH.

Note: The term Babylon the great represents the unfaithful religious groups whose leaders misrepresent God's word and will at the end of time. The components of this consortium of popular religious systems that has elevated tradition and laid aside the plain words of Scripture undoubtedly include Roman Catholicism, apostate Protestantism and religious enterprises based on or using spiritism (or "communicating with the dead"–Tibbs 2007, 287) and spiritualism (an important idea held is that "the soul of man is a spiritual substance"–Pace 1912; Rev. 16:13). In partial illustration of unhelpful activities within Protestantism, and as examples among a number possible, we are reminded of the efforts of Evangelicals in the United States to find common ground with the Catholic Church (1994) and the rush by traditional Anglican churches applying to join the Catholic Church (2010; first union accomplished Jan. 15, 2011). The move by the Evangelicals cost them clarity of expression about the topic of righteousness by faith, which is the heart of the Reformation.

4. What is the origin of the name Babylon? And what did the act of building this first city represent?
Genesis 10:9, 10 He [Nimrod] was a mighty hunter before the LORD; therefore it is said, "Like Nimrod the mighty hunter before the LORD." And the beginning of his kingdom was Babel, Erech, Accad, and Calneh, in the land of Shinar.

Genesis 11:5-9 But the LORD came down to see the city and the tower which the sons of men had built. And the LORD said, "Indeed the people *are* one and they all have one language, and this is what they begin to do; now nothing that they propose to do will be withheld from them. Come, let Us go down and there confuse their language, that they may not understand one another's speech." So the LORD scattered them abroad from there over the face of all the earth, and they ceased building the city. Therefore its name is called Babel, because there the LORD confused the language of all the earth; and from there the LORD scattered them abroad over the face of all the earth.

Note: The name "Babylon" means confusion, as this is the place where the language of the people was confused after they rebelled against God. The original plan laid out in the Garden of Eden called for country living. After the disaster of the great flood, God repeated His covenant with mankind. However, some did not respect His will and set about congregating together and entered into huge building projects. This was in actuality an expression of distrust, defiance of God, and an expression of independence and glory seeking (PP 118, 119).

5. What is the nature of the crimes committed by Babylon (refer to Table 18)?
Revelation 17:3-6 So he carried me away in the Spirit into the wilderness. And I saw a woman sitting on a scarlet beast *which was* full of names of blasphemy, having seven heads and ten horns. The woman was arrayed in purple and scarlet, and adorned with gold and precious stones and pearls, having in her hand a golden cup full of abominations and the filthiness of her fornication. And on her forehead a name *was* written: MYSTERY, BABYLON THE GREAT, THE MOTHER OF HARLOTS AND OF THE ABOMINATIONS OF THE EARTH. I saw the woman, drunk with the blood of the saints and with the blood of the martyrs of Jesus. And when I saw her, I marveled with great amazement.

Characteristic	Babylon the great Revelation	Ancient Babylon Old Testament references
Involved in impure and corrupt practices	17:1–5; 18:2	Jer. 50:14; Ezek. 23: 17
Behaviour marked by luxury and pride	18:16, 17	Isa. 13:19; 47:1, 8
Ambitions to rule the world	17:14, 18; 18:7	Isa. 47:7, 8; cf. Dan. 3
Antagonistic towards the righteous	17:6; 18:24	Isa. 47:6; Jer. 51:49
Cooperates with worldly powers to accomplish her purposes	17:9, 10, 12; 18:23	Isa. 47:13, 15
Ensnares people of earth by controlling their minds	17:2, 8; 18:3	Jer. 51:7, 13; Dan. 5:19, 23
In league with Satanic agents	16:13, 14; 18:2	Isa. 14:4, 12
Fate and reaction		
God will judge	16:17, 19; 17:1; 18:8	Jer. 25:12, 28–30; Dan 5:26, 27
Judgment will annihilate	18:21–23	Isa. 14:9, 11, 15; Jer. 51:42, 63, 64
Worldly powers turn against Babylon but are sorrowful about her fate	17:16; 18:9–11, 15–18	Isa. 13:4; 47:13–15; Jer. 50:13; 51:27–30
Accomplices will be judged by God, too	16:19	Jer. 25:31, 33; 51:49
Heaven rejoices at the destruction of evil	18:20	Jer. 51:48

Table 18. Comparison of Babylon the great with ancient Babylon. Sample references are provided (refer 7BC, 866-869).

Note: Parallels between Babylon the great and ancient Babylon are evident from Table 18. We are actually dealing with some of the characteristics of those who have set themselves against God in the Great Controversy. The attitudes of those operating in both ancient and modern times are similar. However, many deceived people are in Babylon and these God seeks to win to His kingdom (Jer. 51:6, 45; Rev. 18:4).

6. What does the woman have in her hand and with what is it filled?

Revelation 17:4 The woman was arrayed in purple and scarlet, and adorned with gold and precious stones and pearls, having in her hand a golden cup full of abominations and the filthiness of her fornication.

Jeremiah 51:7 Babylon *was* a golden cup in the LORD's hand, that made all the earth drunk. The nations drank her wine; therefore the nations are deranged.

Note: The text in Revelation has clear parallels with Jeremiah's description of Babylon of old. This parallel informs us of the similarities between the ancient mysteries and their modern counterparts. The Chaldean mysteries were characterized by their connection with the worship of a woman bearing a cup (Semiramis or later Venus). These ceremonies were idolatrous in their emphasis and licentious in their practices.

Initiates into the Chaldean mysteries took a fermented beverage that intoxicated the drinkers and prepared them to participate in the secret rites. The symbolism represented here was faithfully accepted and reproduced by Pope Leo XII who in 1825 struck a medal with his own image on one side and on the other side the Church of Rome. The Church was symbolized as a "'Woman,' holding in her left hand a cross, and in her right hand a CUP, with the legend around her, 'Sedet super universum,' 'The whole world is her seat'" (Hislop 1976, 6).

The history of the church shows the gradual but systematic acquisition of rites and ceremonies from paganism, especially Mithraism, into it. Mithraism represents the form of religion that evolved in Babylon when the Persians came to prominence in the Middle East region. The practices of this religion eventually passed over in altered form to Rome and some came into the Catholic Church in the time of Constantine the Great when great numbers of pagans joined the church. Since that time other practices have been added that are regarded as "absolute truth." These include a special place for Tradition, the intercession ministry of the Virgin Mary, the practice and meaning of Eucharist, and the position of the Pope as God's representative (Gulley 2000, 208, 209).

7. What major issues do the Scriptures identify as being particularly repugnant to God? How does this contrast with Babylon the great's sins? Refer to texts shown in Table 19.

Note: Babylon the great has the wrong attitude towards God and His revealed will. Pride has taken control of the emotions of those devoted to the worldview accepted by Babylon, as it did with Lucifer, Nimrod and a long line of men and women throughout history.

8. On account of the crimes committed, what sentence or judgment is declared against Babylon the great?

Revelation 17:7, 8 But the angel said to me, "Why did you marvel? I will tell you the mystery of the woman and of the beast that carries her, which has the seven heads and the ten horns. The beast that you saw was, and is not, and will ascend out of the bottomless pit and go to perdition. And those who dwell on the earth will marvel, whose names are not written in the Book of Life from the foundation of the world, when they see the beast that was, and is not, and yet is."

Note: The angel offered to interpret the mystery of the beast (vss. 8-17) and the woman (vs. 18). The significant aspect that we wish to note here is that the judgment that God will execute will end in utter destruction, which is another way to convey the idea that these powers will "go to perdition."

Issues identified as repugnant to God	Unacceptable practices found in Babylon the great	God's ideal identified in Scripture
Attempting to change God's law or arguing that it has been altered after the Cross	Dan. 7:25; cf. Ezek. 23:36–38; Rev. 14:12	Exod. 20:2–17; Deut. 10:12, 13; Rev. 12:17
Obscuring Christ's sanctuary ministry—the atonement	Dan. 8:11–13; cf. Ezek. 23:36–38; Rev. 14:12	Heb. 5:5–11; 8:1–6; 9:11–28
Exalting oneself to virtual equality with God	Dan. 8:11; cf. Rev. 17:14	Acts 4:12; 1 Tim. 2:5; cf. 2 Thess. 2:3, 4
Traditions of mankind developed or adopted as being equal or superior to God's word	Rev. 13:14–16	Mark 7:7, 9, 13; Deut. 4:15–24
Adopting pagan practices and incorporating divergent philosophical thoughts into the religious worldview or into ceremonies	Rev. 17:2; cf. Ezek. 23:30	Exod. 20:3–5, 7–11; 2 Cor. 4:5, 6
Doctrine of salvation through works promoted (to gain merit) or the adoption of sacraments to gain access to salvation	Rev. 18:2, 11–13	Hab. 2:4; Rom. 3:28–31; Gal. 3:11; Jas. 2:14–20
Excuses all types of iniquity under the cloaks, e.g., modernism/post-modernism	Rev. 18:2, 3	Ezek. 22:1–16
Focuses on spectacular displays of ceremony and wealth to feed prideful ambitions	Rev. 18:7, 16	Prov. 8:13; Mic. 6:8; Mark 8:36, 37; Luke 12:16–21
Source of inspiration/strength		
Consorts with the unscrupulous and deceptive	Rev. 18:9, 17, 23	Prov. 1:8–19; 15:27; 16:11: Ezek. 22:13
Controlled by Satanic agencies	Rev. 16:13, 14; 18:2, 23	Isa. 8:19, 20; 2 Thess. 2:9, 10
Aspirations/strategy		
Plans to dominate in world affairs and gain the supremacy	Rev. 17:15, 18; 18:7	Mark 10:42–45; Jas. 4:4; 1 John 2:15–17; cf. Dan. 4:29–37
Antagonistic towards God's saints, persecutes them and forces the consciences of men	Rev. 17:6; 18:24; 19:2	Rom. 13:10; Rev. 21:7, 8.
Controls men's minds (or "sits on many waters")	Rev. 17:1, 8, 15; cf. 18:13	Matt. 10:28; cf. 2 Cor. 4:6; Phil. 4:6, 7; 2 Thess. 2:9–12

Table 19. Practices, associations and aspirations found unacceptable to God and the status of Babylon the great in relation to these.

9. What details are given about the political powers (beast powers) supporting the apostate church?

Revelation 17:8-12 partial text [Regarding] "The beast . . . . Here *is* the mind which has wisdom: The seven heads are seven mountains on which the woman sits. There are also seven kings. Five have fallen, one is, *and* the other has not yet come . . . ."The ten horns which you saw are ten kings who have received no kingdom as yet, but they receive authority for one hour as kings with the beast."

Note: The identity of the beast introduced here has been suggested by some as the same as in Revelation 13. This is made on the basis that both beasts are given to blasphemy (Rev. 17:3; cf. 13:6), both are associated with the power of Satan (the "dragon" or individual making "war with the Lamb"–Rev. 13:4; 17:14; cf. 12:7) and both depend on political powers or kings for their dominance (Rev. 17:2; cf. 13:11, 12). Equally, both are enemies of God and His people. There are also differences between the beasts of chapters 13 and 17 that we will not discuss in this lesson. The important point is that both beasts are enemies of God.

The exact identity of the political powers has been debated. Suffice it to say that it is not our intention to struggle through these complex verses for this is beyond the purposes of this course. However, one notable commentator has added the following helpful thoughts: "In the warfare to be waged in the last days there will be united, in opposition to God's people, all the corrupt powers that have apostatized from allegiance to the law of Jehovah. In this warfare the Sabbath of the fourth commandment will be the great point at issue; for in the Sabbath commandment the great Lawgiver identifies Himself as the Creator of the heavens and the earth." And further, "'These have one mind.' There will be a universal bond of union, one great harmony, a confederacy of Satan's forces. 'And shall give their power and strength unto the beast.' Thus is manifested the same arbitrary, oppressive power against religious liberty, freedom to worship God according to the dictates of conscience, as was manifested by the papacy, when in the past it persecuted those who dared to refuse to conform with the religious rites and ceremonies of Romanism" (Mar 187).

10. A day will come when Babylon the great loses her power. How will the great city perish and what reaction is seen from worldly powers?

Revelation 18:8-10 "Therefore her plagues will come in one day—death and mourning and famine. And she will be utterly burned with fire, for strong *is* the Lord God who judges her. The kings of the earth who committed fornication and lived luxuriously with her will weep and lament for her, when they see the smoke of her burning, standing at a distance for fear of her torment, saying, 'Alas, alas, that great city Babylon, that mighty city! For in one hour your judgment has come.'"

Note: The nations of the world who have cooperated to oppose God's will and that have rejected the salvation He offers have benefited through their partnership with Babylon the great. Now they mourn its fall, but they do so with admiration for her past greatness.

11. How does heaven announce the finality of Babylon's fall?

Revelation 18:21 Then a mighty angel took up a stone like a great millstone and threw *it* into the sea, saying, "Thus with violence the great city Babylon shall be thrown down, and shall not be found anymore."

Note: It takes a mighty angel to bring Babylon the great to nothing. Its fate is sealed as it is thrown violently into the deepest sea. The language expresses the finality of its fall. It will not arise a second time to be wondered at by the nations.

12. What reaction comes from heaven after the fall of Babylon?

Revelation 18:20 "Rejoice over her, O heaven, and *you* holy apostles and prophets, for God has avenged you on her!"

Revelation 19:1-3 After these things I heard a loud voice of a great multitude in heaven, saying, "Alleluia! Salvation and glory and honor and power *belong* to the Lord our God! For true and righteous *are* His judgments, because He has judged the great harlot who corrupted the earth with her fornication; and He has avenged on her the blood of His servants *shed* by her." Again they said, "Alleluia! Her smoke rises up forever and ever!"

Note: The fall of Babylon the great represents the end to the reign of evil. The Great Controversy has entered its final phase and Satan is about to be punished for his rebellion. The saints rejoice in the surety of their salvation.

13. What event follows quickly on the fall of Babylon?
Revelation 19:1-6—Read.
Revelation 19:7 Let us be glad and rejoice and give Him glory, for the marriage of the Lamb has come, and His wife has made herself ready."

Note: The song of rejoicing over the defeat of the forces of evil is heartfelt. The song is sung after the judgment of the great whore, which takes place under the seventh plague (Rev. 16:19; 17:1). This event occurs close to the second coming of Christ (TM 432).

11.13 Defeat of the Forces of Evil

Introduction

In our study of Revelation chapters 19 and 20, we follow the story of redemption to the point where the originator of sin, Satan, is destroyed. Fittingly, our study commences with a song of praise sung by the redeemed in heaven with the heavenly hosts. They sing because Christ is about to triumph conclusively over the forces of evil. This is a song of joy at the redemption offered by God and that is soon to be experienced in heaven.

Then the scene changes to reveal the actual coming of Christ with the armies of heaven to destroy rebellious mankind with the brightness of His coming and as a result of the turmoil of nature (Ps. 50:3, 4; Isa. 30:27-30; Rev. 6:14-17; 16:17-21). Those who witness this grand and awesome event include those who participated in Christ's crucifixion (Matt. 26:64; Rev. 1:7), as well as those "who have died in the faith of the third angel's message" (GC 637,643-645, 657).

The scene then changes in chapter 20 to reveal a desolate earth. The saints have been transported to heaven and the wicked are dead. Satan alone with his angels wander through a desolate earth and reflect on their rebellious acts (Isa. 14:12-17; GC, 666). Meanwhile, in heaven the saints are occupied by the serious business of reviewing the evidence God has used in deciding who was counted worthy to inherit eternal life (1 Cor. 6:2, 3; Rev. 20:4). Christ returns to the earth a third time and comes with the saints. The New Jerusalem descends to the location of the Mount of Olives that has been leveled and specially cleansed for the purpose (Zech. 14:4, 5, 9; EW 52; GC 622, 623). It is then that Satan marshals the recently raised wicked and attempts to overthrow the city of God. They are halted in their ambitious attempt by the "final coronation of the Son of God" (Rev. 20:11; GC 666). They stand condemned by their deeds and their rejection of Christ. The consuming fires of cleansing take them away to oblivion and a time of eternal peace is about to be ushered in.

The Study

Read chapters 19 and 20 then the Bible texts and notes below in answer to the questions posed.

1. Chapter 19 opens with a song of praise. The universe is overwhelmed with gratitude at the death of Babylon the great (vss. 1-7). What important announcement is made at this praise session?
Revelation 19:7-9 "Let us be glad and rejoice and give Him glory, for the marriage of the Lamb has come, and His wife has made herself ready." And to her it was granted to be arrayed in fine linen, clean and bright, for the fine linen is the righteous acts of the saints. Then he said to me, "Write: 'Blessed *are* those who are called to the marriage supper of the Lamb!'" And he said to me, "These are the true sayings of God."

Note: The marriage of the Lamb or Christ is announced at the end of the praise session. We understand by this that Christ is about to receive His kingdom of glory. In this scene, the bride is the New Jerusalem and the guests at the marriage ceremony are the saints (Rev. 21:9, 10). The parable that Jesus gave His disciples about the marriage supper is about to be fulfilled. In this parable, only those wearing a wedding garment (representing the righteousness of Christ) are allowed to participate in the marriage celebrations (Matt 22:1-14).

2. What was John's reaction and what vital information is given concerning the attitude shown to God and His word by those who are redeemed?

Revelation 19:10 And I fell at his [the angel's] feet to worship him. But he said to me, "See *that you do* not *do that!* I am your fellow servant, and of your brethren who have the testimony of Jesus. Worship God! For the testimony of Jesus is the spirit of prophecy."

Note: At the end of the vision showing the redeemed and the heavenly beings praising God, John fell down to worship the angel. This he forbade but delivered the meaningful admonishing to worship God and Him alone. The meaning of the phrase "who have the testimony of Jesus" has caused some debate. One writer has pointed out the parallelism found in the above verse and Revelation 22, verses 8 and 9. The meaning of the phrase in this latter text is "who keep the words of this book" (Doukhan 2002, 173). The words of the book of Revelation are God's words, they are inspired. The whole book is a testimony about Jesus. Every reader is challenged to keep these words because they talk about mercy and judgment; gospel and law. They give the reader hope through faith in the Lord Jesus Christ. All true prophets make similar affirmative testimonies about Jesus.

3. We have been introduced previously to a rider on a white horse. Who is now shown coming to this earth in glory?
Revelation 19:11-16 Now I saw heaven opened, and behold, a white horse. And He who sat on him *was* called Faithful and True, and in righteousness He judges and makes war. His eyes *were* like a flame of fire, and on His head *were* many crowns. He had a name written that no one knew except Himself. He *was* clothed with a robe dipped in blood, and His name is called The Word of God. And the armies in heaven, clothed in fine linen, white and clean, followed Him on white horses. Now out of His mouth goes a sharp sword, that with it He should strike the nations. And He Himself will rule them with a rod of iron. He Himself treads the winepress of the fierceness and wrath of Almighty God. And He has on *His* robe and on His thigh a name written: KING OF KINGS AND LORD OF LORDS.

Note: We now step back a little in time to observe the fate of the wicked that takes place before the scenes shown in the verses previously studied. We encountered the white horse when we looked at the seals (Rev. 6:2). You will remember that the rider on that horse represented the person leading in the great period of expansion of the gospel following Christ's resurrection and ascension. The same person is revealed here coming with many crowns to execute judgment—hence the sharp sword imagery is used. The identity of the rider is "The Word of God" or "King of kings and Lord of lords," who is none other than Christ (John 1:1, 14; Rev. 17:14). His garments are red with the blood of those who have been slain (cf. Isa. 63:1-6).

4. What dramatic events does Christ, the rider on the white horse, engage in? How does this engagement between the forces of good and evil end?
Revelation 19:19-21 And I saw the beast, the kings of the earth, and their armies, gathered together to make war against Him who sat on the horse and against His army. Then the beast was captured, and with him the false prophet who worked signs in his presence, by which he deceived those who received the mark of the beast and those who worshiped his image. These two were cast alive into the lake of fire burning with brimstone. And the rest were killed with the sword which proceeded from the mouth of Him who sat on the horse. And all the birds were filled with their flesh.

Note: The battle of Armageddon that is described in the verses above is preceded by an announcement from heaven delivered by an angel inviting the carrion eating birds to gather for the feast of the dead that is about to be prepared for them (vss. 17, 18). Christ enters the battle and captures the beast and false prophet. These are destroyed by fire and the political powers (the kings of the earth and their armies) are killed by the word of Christ. None of the wicked remains alive. The devil or Satan has been captured by circumstances and is yet to meet his end (cf. Mar 307).

5. What ultimate purpose of God is fulfilled by Christ giving Himself for humanity?
1 John 3:8 He who sins is of the devil, for the devil has sinned from the beginning. For this purpose the Son of God was manifested, that He might destroy the works of the devil.

Note: The purpose of the great plan of salvation is to overcome evil with good and to secure the universe against evil arising the second time. Only a universe operating according to the principles of selfless love can continue forever. It also stands to reason that all those inhabiting the heaven and earth made new have both whole-heartedly accepted and experienced these principles.

6. After the defeat of the forces of evil, what sentence is pronounced on Satan?
Revelation 20:1-3 Then I saw an angel coming down from heaven, having the key to the bottomless pit and a great chain in his hand. He laid hold of the dragon, that serpent of old, who is *the* Devil and Satan, and bound him for a thousand years; and cast him into the bottomless pit, and shut him up, and set a seal on him, so that he should deceive the nations no more till the thousand years are finished. But after these things he must be released for a little while.

Note: The seven last plagues are poured out after Christ's ministry in the heavenly sanctuary is finished. The upheavals of nature associated with the plagues and during the coming of Christ have left the earth in a desolate and unrecognizable state (Rev. 16:18, 20; Jer. 25:33; GC, 644, 657). The earth has been reduced to a similar state it had "in the beginning" before God's creative hand moulded it into Edenic beauty (GC 658, 659; cf. Gen. 1:2; Jer. 4:23-26). Hence, it is termed the "bottomless pit."

All human beings present at the beginning of the battle of Armageddon now are either in heaven (righteous) or dead (wicked) upon the earth. There are no human beings to tempt. Hence Satan (the dragon), with his angels, is left in solitary circumstances with nothing to do.

7. What service enacted during Old Testament times foreshadowed this event?
Leviticus 16:20-22 "And when he has made an end of atoning for the Holy *Place,* the tabernacle of meeting, and the altar, he shall bring the live goat. Aaron shall lay both his hands on the head of the live goat, confess over it all the iniquities of the children of Israel, and all their transgressions, concerning all their sins, putting them on the head of the goat, and shall send *it* away into the wilderness by the hand of a suitable man. The goat shall bear on itself all their iniquities to an uninhabited land; and he shall release the goat in the wilderness.

Note: The scene described under Question 6 was presented in a slightly different form in the sanctuary services of the Old Testament. At the conclusion of the Day of Atonement (or Judgment) ceremonies, the Azazel goat (representing Satan) was taken into the wilderness bearing the ultimate responsibility for the sins of those who had placed their faith in Jesus Christ. These sins were placed symbolically on the head of the one who tempted them to sin—Satan (GC 658).

8. What is the experience of the righteous at the commencement of the 1000 years (millennium) during which Satan is chained?
Revelation 20:4 And I saw thrones, and they sat on them, and judgment was committed to them. Then *I saw* the souls of those who had been beheaded for their witness to Jesus and for the word of God, who

had not worshiped the beast or his image, and had not received *his* mark on their foreheads or on their hands. And they lived and reigned with Christ for a thousand years.

Note: During the period of Satan's imprisonment on this desolate earth, those who have stood firmly for God's principles are shown reigning with Christ in heaven. These saints have been either translated without seeing death or have been resurrected and taken to heaven. When the prophet speaks of seeing "souls" of people, he is not thinking in terms familiar to many in the Christian church. He is not talking of souls as the immortal, conscious and spiritual part of mankind as some groups view it. The text is speaking of the "whole person" with all the faculties operating (Doukhan 2002, 181). The true meaning of the word translated "soul" (from Hebrew *nephesh* or its Greek equivalent *psuché*) is found in the following examples (Gen. 34:3; Pss. 103:1; 107:9; 143:6; Isa. 55:2).

9. What name is given to the resurrection of the righteous dead before the 1000 years of Satan's sentence begins?

Revelation 20: 6 Blessed and holy *is* he who has part in the first resurrection. Over such the second death has no power, but they shall be priests of God and of Christ, and shall reign with Him a thousand years.

Note: Those who have died in Christ are resurrected in the first resurrection. This is in perfect agreement with the pattern of thought that Daniel the prophet encouraged his readers to consider (Dan. 12:2). The righteous dead are resurrected at Christ's second coming. This makes the meaning of the first part of verse 5 a little clearer. This sentence relates to the wicked dead as indicated in the New International Version of the Bible. In this version, the first sentence appears as follows: "(The rest of the dead did not come to life until the thousand years were ended.) This is the first resurrection." This devise of placing a sentence in brackets tells us that it is awkwardly placed. It makes better sense if placed immediately after verse 3.

10. What great event happens simultaneously with the first resurrection? And what happens to the righteous who have survived the horrific events surrounding Christ's coming?

1 Thessalonians 4:15-17 For this we say to you by the word of the Lord, that we who are alive *and* remain until the coming of the Lord will by no means precede those who are asleep. For the Lord Himself will descend from heaven with a shout, with the voice of an archangel, and with the trumpet of God. And the dead in Christ will rise first. Then we who are alive *and* remain shall be caught up together with them in the clouds to meet the Lord in the air. And thus we shall always be with the Lord.

Note: The resurrected ones are present to welcome Christ at His coming. However, the apostle Paul makes it abundantly clear in his first letter to the Corinthians that not all the saints will be in the grave when Jesus comes. The living saints will be transformed and will join with the resurrected saints at His coming at the "last trumpet" (1 Cor. 15:51-55). No secret departure of the saints is spoken about in these and other texts. The concept of people departing secretly is foreign to the Bible. It presents the coming of Christ as a well orchestrated, global event full of light, glory and sound (Matt. 24:27; Luke 9:26; 1 Thess. 4:16). Nor does the Bible present the idea that the souls of human beings escape at death to be with God (e.g., Eccles. 9:5; Job 14:13, 21).

11. Where are the risen saints taken?

1 Thessalonians 4:17 Then we who are alive *and* remain shall be caught up together with them in the clouds to meet the Lord in the air. And thus we shall always be with the Lord.

Note: When the saints leave the earth at the coming of the Lord, they go to heaven (cf. Acts 1:9-11). There is no Golden Age during which they reign on earth before they are translated. There are a number of theories in the Christian world about the future fulfillment of God's promises to ancient Israel. Some consider that Christ will rule the world from Jerusalem at His second coming. In other words, God's dealings with the Jewish nation have been interrupted, but will be reestablished and there will be national salvation. This and similar ideas are fanciful, based on an imperfect understanding of the Old Testament prophecies regarding Israel.

12. Some Christians believe that the Old Testament prophecies made to Israel will be fulfilled and that a Golden Age (millennium) will yet occur on this earth in relation to the prophecy of Revelation 20. On what misunderstanding is this interpretation based?

Exodus 19:5 Now therefore, if you will indeed obey My voice and keep My covenant, then you shall be a special treasure to Me above all people; for all the earth *is* Mine.

Note: The highly significant word in this text is "if". The promises to Israel throughout the Old Testament were conditional on obedience (e.g., Deut. 8:19; 28:13; Jer. 18:6-10; Zech. 6:15). Israel failed to obey and the kingdom promises were lost when they rejected Jesus (Matt. 21:42, 43). These promises will never be fulfilled through Israel (PK 374, 375). The Christian church became the inheritor of the promises of Israel (Rom. 11:2-5; Gal. 3:26-29). In spiritual Israel, there is no distinction made between Jews, Greeks or others (Gal. 3:28).

As pointed out in our study in Revelation 13, the last great movements before Christ returns in glory will be associated with a proclamation by religious leaders that a Golden Age or Temporal Millennium on earth is about to begin. This is considered to be a period when the whole world is converted to Christianity. God's authentic followers will be placed under intense pressure, for it is claimed by religious authorities that the Commandments have been changed and that Sunday is the sacred day of worship rather than Saturday. "They [religious authorities] declared that they had the truth, that miracles were among them, that angels from heaven talked with them, and walked with them, that great power, and signs and wonders were performed among them, and this was the Temporal Millennium, which they had been expecting so long. The whole world was converted and in harmony with the Sunday law, and this little feeble people stood out in defiance of the laws of the land, and the laws of God, and claimed to be the only ones right on the earth" (Mar 209).

13. What tasks are the righteous engaged in during the 1000 years?

Revelation 20:4 And I saw thrones, and they sat on them, and judgment was committed to them. Then *I saw* the souls of those who had been beheaded for their witness to Jesus and for the word of God, who had not worshiped the beast or his image, and had not received *his* mark on their foreheads or on their hands. And they lived and reigned with Christ for a thousand years.

Verse 12 last part And the dead were judged according to their works, by the things which were written in the books.

Note: The saints participate in a review of the evidence during the 1000 years and decide the appropriate punishments to be allocated to those who have not accepted God's invitation of mercy and who have opposed His will and God's people (cf. 1 Cor. 6:2, 3; Luke 12:47, 48; EW 52, 53, 290, 291). At the end of the process the saints do not disagree with the decisions reached by Christ. They regard Him as a righteous judge. The knowledge they have gained through this process aids in the fulfillment of the prophecy made by Nahum (1:9) that evil will not arise a second time in the universe. Indeed, in an overwhelming sense "The sacrifice of Christ for a fallen world draws not only men, but angels unto Him [in] bonds of indissoluble union," so that there is no danger that sin will arise again (TA 296).

14. Before the execution of judgment, what evidence is considered?
Revelation 20:12 first part And I saw the dead, small and great, standing before God, and books were opened. And another book was opened, which is *the Book* of Life.

Note: This verse and the succeeding one clearly teach that the judgment is universal. No one is excused and position does not have a bearing on the outcome. The dead are not literally standing before God. The language used is figurative. Their names come up in the record books and in that sense they stand before God. The Scriptures tell us that all are ultimately responsible for the deeds they have done during their life. All will be held personally responsible for their own choices (2 Cor. 5:10). The final phase of Jesus executive judgment takes place only after the saints have looked at the evidence.

It is worth noticing that God also is interesting in keeping the records of our good deeds, which are the fruits of our salvation. "All heaven is interested in our salvation. The angels of God are walking up and down the streets of these cities, and marking the deeds of men. They record in the books of God's remembrance the words of faith, the acts of love, the humility of spirit; and in that day when every man's work shall be tried of what sort it is, the work of the humble follower of Christ will stand the test, and will receive the commendation of Heaven" (RH Sept. 6, 1890).

15. What principles are used to decide whose names are retained in the Book of Life?
Revelation 20:13 The sea gave up the dead who were in it, and Death and Hades delivered up the dead who were in them. And they were judged, each one according to his works.

James 2:14 What *does it* profit, my brethren, if someone says he has faith but does not have works? Can faith save him?

Verses 20-22 But do you want to know, O foolish man, that faith without works is dead? Was not Abraham our father justified by works when he offered Isaac his son on the altar? Do you see that faith was working together with his works, and by works faith was made perfect?

Note: Attitudes and acts determine the destiny of mankind. In the Christian context, this means that the saints accept the promptings of God's Spirit and freely acknowledge that their evil tendencies cannot be overcome in human strength. All must come to the foot of the cross asking for help in faith. This continual experience will lead to a change in thinking and will be reflected in the acts committed. Such individuals are born again and are obedient to God's words (John 14:21; 15:14; YI June 15, 1893).

The most exciting command that Jesus gave to His disciples was that "you love one another; as I have loved you, that you also love one another" (John 13:34). Now the reality is that this command contains all others, because God is love (1 John 4:8). Our responsibilities and potential to do good are enormous. "All of us, as beings blessed of God with reasoning powers, with intellect and judgment, should acknowledge our accountability to God. The life He has given us is a sacred responsibility, and no moment of it is to be trifled with; for we shall have to meet it again in the record of the judgment. In the books of heaven our lives are as accurately traced as in the picture on the plate of the photographer. Not only are we held accountable for what we have done, but for what we have left undone. We are held to account for our undeveloped characters, our unimproved opportunities" (RH Sept. 22, 1891).

16. What happens to Satan and the wicked dead at the end of the 1000 years? What does Satan then immediately do?
Revelation 20:7, 8 Now when the thousand years have expired, Satan will be released from his prison and will go out to deceive the nations which are in the four corners of the earth, Gog and Magog, to gather them together to battle, whose number *is* as the sand of the sea.

Note: The Scriptures clearly tell us that just as there will be a resurrection of the righteous there will be a resurrection of the wicked (John 5:28, 29; Acts 24:15). The prophetic discourse given to us in Revelation informs the reader that the resurrection of damnation or condemnation occurs at the end of the 1000 years (cf. vs. 5 first part). This provides us a clue to the meaning of the releasing of Satan. Now he has people to interact with and tempt (cf. vs. 3); he immediately plans a new battle with his war cabinet. The new battle is similar to that waged at Armageddon, but this time the forces are called Gog and Magog. These names refer to the "nations of the wicked" gathered (4BC 704; cf. Ezek. 38:1, 2).

There is an interesting contrast between the first resurrection (the righteous) and second (the wicked). "At the first resurrection all come forth in immortal bloom, but at the second, the marks of the curse are visible upon all. All come up as they went down into their graves. Those who lived before the Flood, come forth with their giant-like stature, more than twice as tall as men now living upon the earth, and well proportioned. The generations after the Flood were less in stature" (3SG 84, 85).

17. When Satan observes the multitudes of the wicked, what audacious plan does he devise?
Revelation 20:9 first part They went up on the breadth of the earth and surrounded the camp of the saints and the beloved city.

Note: The 1000 years that Satan will spend in solitude with his angels will have no effect on his attitude towards God. In fact, if anything his determination and resolve to overthrow God's government has become intensely focused. In his last attempt to accomplish his mission, he assembles all the wicked around the New Jerusalem that has recently descended from heaven to this earth (GC 662-665).

18. What answering response comes from God to Satan's intended assault on the saints of God?
Revelation 20:9 last part, 10 And fire came down from God out of heaven and devoured them. The devil, who deceived them, was cast into the lake of fire and brimstone where the beast and the false prophet *are*. And they will be tormented day and night forever and ever.

Note: This is the end of sin and sinners. Those who challenge God are destroyed by consuming fire and raging elements (cf. Ezek. 38:22, 23: 39:6—speaking of Gog and Magog). They are destroyed forever (GC 672, 673).

19. What important acknowledgment ceremony precedes the destruction of the wicked?
Revelation 20:11-13 Then I saw a great white throne and Him who sat on it, from whose face the earth and the heaven fled away. And there was found no place for them. And I saw the dead, small and great, standing before God, and the books were opened. . . . And they were judged, each one according to their works.

Note: These verses give the scene after the resurrection of the wicked and as they surround the New Jerusalem intent on its capture. At that time, "The final coronation of the Son of God takes place" (GC 666). His throne is high above the massed inhabitants of both in the New Jerusalem and outside its walls. Christ opens the books of record and in panoramic view the life history of all rushes through their memories. To this is added the scenes of Christ's life, suffering and sacrifice. All the lost are constrained to acknowledge God's principles, His justice and His supremacy. They all fall down and worship Him. At this time, the wicked turn on Satan in a universal expression of rage (Ezek. 28:6-8; 16-19; GC 672). The fires of God mercifully end the scene (Mal. 4:1; 2 Pet. 3:10).

20. The fires of destruction that consume the wicked usher in a special type of death. What is it called?
Revelation 20:14 Then Death and Hades were cast into the lake of fire. This is the second death.

Note: The death that the wicked die is eternal. There is no possibility of another resurrection. This is the second or final death. It is interesting to note that death also comes to an end. Death is an unknown word in the dictionary of the new heavens and earth.

21. When the Bible speaks of tormenting the Devil "forever and ever" (20:10), what are we to understand this to mean?
Psalm 37:10 For yet a little while and the wicked *shall be* no *more;* indeed, you will look carefully for his place, but it *shall be* no *more.*

Verse 20 But the wicked shall perish; and the enemies of the LORD, like the splendor of the meadows, shall vanish. Into smoke they shall vanish away.

Malachi 4:3 You shall trample the wicked, for they shall be ashes under the soles of your feet on the day that I do *this,*" says the LORD of hosts.

Ezekiel 28:18 "You defiled your sanctuaries by the multitude of your iniquities, by the iniquity of your trading; therefore I brought fire from your midst; it devoured you, and I turned you to ashes upon the earth in the sight of all who saw you."

Note: The term used in Greek that is translated "forever and ever" means literally "unto ages of ages" (7BC 882). When we take the other verses of Scripture noted above into consideration, the practical meaning is that this death will mean annihilation forever (cf. Mal. 4:1). It does not remotely imply eternal suffering. The concept of Purgatory and Hell circulating in many Christian circles represent ideas coming from paganism. A merciful God has no pleasure in inflicting pain for eternity. Such an act is against His nature; the idea is blasphemous.

22. During this process of annihilation of the wicked, what happens to the present earth?
2 Peter 3:10-13 But the day of the Lord will come as a thief in the night, in which the heavens will pass away with a great noise, and the elements will melt with fervent heat; both the earth and the works that are in it will be burned up. Therefore, since all these things will be dissolved, what manner *of persons* ought you to be in holy conduct and godliness, looking for and hastening the coming of the day of God, because of which the heavens will be dissolved, being on fire, and the elements will melt with fervent heat? Nevertheless we, according to His promise, look for new heavens and a new earth in which righteousness dwells.

Note: The wicked and their works are consumed in cleansing fires that will remove all traces of sin and disease. God will create a new earth according to His plan at the beginning. The new earth will be even more beautiful than the Eden of old. During this cleansing process, the New Jerusalem is protected (3SG 87, 88; and refer to the introduction to this lesson).

11.14 Harmony Re-established

Introduction

The Great Controversy between good and evil has come to an end and this rebellious planet is cleansed by fire to obliterate all traces of mankind's sinful ways and to remove all life forms remaining. God will create a new heaven and earth to replace that which has been despoiled. And God's will populate "heaven with the human family" (TA 49, 287).

God will locate a splendid city on the remade earth. This will contain reminders of the Garden of Eden and of Christ's sacrifice. Real people will dwell in the city. In fact, the righteous will inhabit the city and rejoice in its splendor. Besides their dwellings in this glorious place they will have country dwellings and will grow plants for pleasure and food. There will be no reminders of death or destruction in the earth made new and all will partake of a healthy diet (non-meat) as designed by God in the beginning.

Christ will be the constant companion of the redeemed, fulfilling His desire to dwell with His people. Besides this delightful undertaking, there will be many surprises in store for those who are saved. The account in chapters 21 and 22 of Revelation represents the anti-typical fulfillment of the Festival of Ingathering in the sanctuary system spoken about in the Old Testament.

The Study

Read chapters 21 and 22 then the Bible texts and notes below in answer to the questions posed.

1. What did John see in vision after the earth has been purified by fire?
Revelation 21:1 Now I saw a new heaven and a new earth, for the first heaven and the first earth had passed away. Also there was no more sea.

Note: The replacement of the earth and atmospheric heavens is necessary on account of the contamination wrought by sin (Rom. 8:19-22). No half measures are sufficient here. We discovered in our last lesson that the earth was cleansed by intense heat. One surprise in the new earth is the absence of an extensive sea. This may be more an expression of an "end of forces hostile to God and humanity" than about how large the bodies of water will be in the new earth (Stefanovic 2002, 575). One other commentator has remarked: "Thank God, in the earth made new there will be no fierce torrents, no engulfing ocean, no restless, murmuring waves" (7BC 988). The emphasis here is on separation of friends and unpleasant memories associated with cruelties received by saints at the hands of their persecutors.

2. What spectacular event did John now see happening on the newly created earth?
Revelation 21:2 Then I, John, saw the holy city, New Jerusalem, coming down out of heaven from God, prepared as a bride adorned for her husband.

Verse 10 And he carried me away in the Spirit to a great and high mountain, and showed me the great city, the holy Jerusalem, descending out of heaven from God,

Note: This is a space event greater than envisaged by most serious engineers. An enormous city is here seen coming from heaven and being located on earth (cf. John 14:1-3). As we will discover, the architectural features are both unusual and superb, like a bride. This is no wonder as the architect is God (Heb. 11:10; 12:22). The city will be filled with His glory.

3. What significant actions will God undertake in the new earth and New Jerusalem?
Revelation 21: 3, 4 And I heard a loud voice from heaven saying, "Behold, the tabernacle of God *is* with men, and He will dwell with them, and they shall be His people. God Himself will be with them *and be* their God. And God will wipe away every tear from their eyes; there shall be no more death, nor sorrow, nor crying. There shall be no more pain, for the former things have passed away."

Note: The presence of God means that pain, suffering and death are no longer possible, especially since sin, sinners and Satan are no more. The former things have no place in this new world, for they are contrary to the principles of love.

4. What assurance did John personally receive that all he had seen and heard was genuine?
Revelation 21:5, 6 first part Then He who sat on the throne said, "Behold, I make all things new." And He said to me, "Write, for these words are true and faithful." And He said to me, "It is done! I am the Alpha and the Omega, the Beginning and the End."

Note: The credentials of the dignified person sitting on the throne are clarified in this text. He is the same as identified at the beginning and end of the book of Revelation (1:8; 22:13). The person who declares, "It is done!" is none other than Christ.

5. What ceremony in the Old Testament sanctuary system foreshadowed the activities described by John in the verses we have just read?
Leviticus 23:34 "Speak to the children of Israel, saying: 'The fifteenth day of this seventh month *shall be* the Feast of Tabernacles *for* seven days to the LORD.'"

Note: The Feast of Ingathering or Tabernacles was held at the end of the religious year (Exod. 34:22) and just after the Day of Atonement ceremonies. It was a commemoration of God's blessings of salvation and expressed thanks for His continual leading (Deut. 16:13-17). In fact, "It marked a point of transition between the pleasant memories of God's past goodness, and the joyous hopes for the future" (PP 540, 541). As such it pointed to the final act of ingathering by God when He sends His angels to gather the elect to enjoy their inheritance. Indeed, the prophet Zechariah indicated that the ingathering ceremony will be kept in the world made new (Zech. 14:16). These reminders assure us of the unity of the Scriptures and of the significance of the Old Testament types and ceremonies to our understanding of God's purposes.

6. What note of assurance is given today to those who respond to God's love?
Revelation 21:7 "He who overcomes shall inherit all things, and I will be his God and he shall be My son."

Note: This is the oft repeated assurance given in our study of Revelation chapters 2 and 3. The assurance given in this verse is contrasted in the next verse. Those who do not value God's principles, seek His guidance and overcome through His strength are not found among those who are rewarded with a mansion in heaven (vs. 8). The saved will have a close relationship with God. They will be counted as His children. There can be no greater assurance than this.

7. The New Jerusalem is of immense proportions. What area does this city occupy?

Revelation 21:16, 17 The city is laid out as a square; its length is as great as its breadth. And he measured the city with the reed: twelve thousand furlongs. Its length, breadth, and height are equal. Then he measured its wall: one hundred *and* forty-four cubits, *according* to the measure of a man, that is, of an angel.

Note: In the description of the city, we have chosen to commence with the area it occupies. The city described here pales all others into insignificance if we accept the description as speaking of a literal city. This city is about 2200 kilometres in circumference in the view of many. The thickness of the walls is given as around 64 metres and we are informed that the wall itself is very high (vs. 12).

8. The city possesses high walls and twelve gates. What significance might be attached to the number of gates and foundations?

Revelation 21:12 Also she had a great and high wall with twelve gates, and twelve angels at the gates, and names written on them, which are *the names* of the twelve tribes of the children of Israel.

Verse 14 Now the wall of the city had twelve foundations, and on them were the names of the twelve apostles of the Lamb.

Note: The twelve gates are named after the tribes of Old Testament Israel. We carefully note in verse 14 that there are also twelve foundations and these contain the names of the twelve apostles. It has been suggested that through the use of this symbolism the important point is conveyed that "Old and New Testament Israel" is represented in the city (Stefanovic 2002, 256). This is a city for all peoples, whatever their ethnic background (cf. Luke 13:29).

The walls, gates and streets radiate brilliance and opulence (Rev. 21:18-21). The foundations are of different coloured stones. The spendour of the city is beyond human comprehension. The Scriptures inform us that humans have not seen nor are our imaginations capable of comprehending the splendours reserved for the redeemed (1 Cor. 2:9; GC 675).

9. What types of buildings cannot be found in the city?

Revelation 21:22 But I saw no temple in it, for the Lord God Almighty and the Lamb are its temple.

Note: A temple was not necessary in the Garden of Eden and neither is it in the Eden restored. God is there and is worshipped in person by the saints. When sin became part of the human experience, it was no longer possible to communicate directly with God (Isa. 59:2). In the earth made new sin and sinners will be no more and each of the redeemed will continue to be the temple of the Holy Spirit (1 Cor. 3:16, 17). Each will have a perfect right to associate freely with Christ as sons and daughters of God.

10. How is the city lighted?

Revelation 21:23-25 The city had no need of the sun or of the moon to shine in it, for the glory of God illuminated it. The Lamb *is* its light. And the nations of those who are saved shall walk in its light, and the kings of the earth bring their glory and honor into it. Its gates shall not be shut at all by day (there shall be no night there).

Revelation 22:5 There shall be no night there: They need no lamp nor light of the sun, for the Lord God gives them light. And they shall reign forever and ever.

Note: The glory of the Lord filled the earthly temple. When Moses glimpsed the back parts of the Lord on Sinai, he was enveloped in glorious light (Exod. 33:20-23). Christ was called the "light of the world" when He was on earth (John 8:12). This can be understood variously, but in the context of the new earth, the glory of God's righteous character fills the city and its reflective surfaces make it unnecessary to have further light (cf. Isa. 60:19, 20). In today's world, we welcome the night time as it offers us rest. In the world made new, weariness will not be an issue and the pursuit of the most strenuous mental exertions will not exhaust the saints (GC 676, 677).

11. What splendid items are described as being present in the New Jerusalem?
Revelation 22:1-3 And he showed me a pure river of water of life, clear as crystal, proceeding from the throne of God and of the Lamb. In the middle of its street, and on either side of the river, *was* the tree of life, which bore twelve fruits, each *tree* yielding its fruit every month. The leaves of the tree *were* for the healing of the nations. And there shall be no more curse, but the throne of God and of the Lamb shall be in it, and His servants shall serve Him.

Note: The river of life contains pure water and those who drink of it are not subject to diseases or dangerous contaminants. The tree of life spans the river and yields abundant fruit. This is none other than the original tree from the Garden of Eden. All are given free and ready access to the tree. It contains components essential to eternal existence (1T 288).

There is a parallel between this tree's potential to bear 12 different fruits and our life and work on earth. "Let all bear in mind that the tree of life bears twelve manner of fruits. This represents the spiritual work of our earthly missions. The Word of God is to us the tree of life. Every portion of the Scripture has its use. In every part of the Word is some lesson to be learned" (Letter 3, 1898).

12. What indication is given that the new heavens and earth will be inhabited by real people?
John 14:2, 3 "In My Father's house are many mansions; if *it were* not *so,* I would have told you. I go to prepare a place for you [speaking to the disciples]. And if I go and prepare a place for you, I will come again and receive you to Myself; that where I am, *there* you may be also."

Philippians 3:20, 21 For our citizenship is in heaven, from which we also eagerly wait for the Savior, the Lord Jesus Christ, who will transform our lowly body that it may be conformed to His glorious body, according to the working by which He is able even to subdue all things to Himself.

Note: These are Scriptures that indicate to us clearly that complete human beings will inhabit heaven. The text in Philippians indicates that the bodies of the redeemed will be like Christ's body after the resurrection. The apostle Luke tells us plainly that Christ looked and acted like usual people and He also ate with them (Luke 24:36-43).

13. What type of activities will the redeemed be engaged in?
Isaiah 65:17 "For behold, I create new heavens and a new earth; and the former shall not be remembered or come to mind."

Verses 21, 22 "They shall build houses and inhabit *them; t*hey shall plant vineyards and eat their fruit. They shall not build and another inhabit; they shall not plant and another eat; for as the days of a tree, *so shall be* the days of My people, and My elect shall long enjoy the work of their hands."

Note: In the world described by Isaiah there was productive activity. Whereas the prophet was speaking of the blessings God would have given to Israel after the Babylonian captivity if it had have been faithful, there are some principles that can be derived from his statements that may be applied to heaven. Death, pain, suffering will be forever excluded from heaven (cf. Rev. 21:4). The time in heaven will not be spent in idleness and revelry. The word of inspiration informs us that there will be a new order of things that will bring great enjoyment. New skills will be acquired and old mysteries explored (Isa. 51:3; Ed 202, 304, 307, 308). In actual fact, "The privileges of those who overcome by the blood of the Lamb and the word of their testimony are beyond comprehension" (RH March 9, 1886).

14. What type of unusual animal behaviour might the redeemed expect to observe?
Isaiah 11:6 "The wolf also shall dwell with the lamb, the leopard shall lie down with the young goat, the calf and the young lion and the fatling together; and a little child shall lead them."

Isaiah 65:25 "The wolf and the lamb shall feed together, the lion shall eat straw like the ox, and dust *shall be* the serpent's food. They shall not hurt nor destroy in all My holy mountain," says the LORD.

Note: Again in the heavenly places, the rule of tooth and claw does not take place. There will be a different order of things, in which destruction and pain do not have a place. Meat eating for both man and animals will be at an end. All creation will rejoice at the redemption of mankind.

15. Who will be the constant companion of the redeemed?
Revelation 14:4 These are the ones who were not defiled with women, for they are virgins. These are the ones who follow the Lamb wherever He goes. These were redeemed from *among* men, *being* first fruits to God and to the Lamb.

Note: The Creator's intention was to associate in the Garden of Eden with the new order of creatures He had made (Gen. 2:19; 3:8). This plan was interrupted by the arrival of sin. His plans were put on hold. Nevertheless, as the Israelites departed from Israel and travelled through Sinai, God reminded them of His desire to dwell with them. This He did through giving them His visible presence in the earthly sanctuary (Exod. 25:8; 29:43). Following the same theme, Christ came and lived with mankind in fulfillment of His promise to provide a plan to save sinners (Matt. 1:23; 12:6). In the heaven made new, when harmony is restored, Christ will dwell with His people forever, thus fulfilling His original purpose. It can be seen from these examples that the intermediary between earth and heaven has been Christ throughout human history. This is illustrated rather well in the vision given to Jacob the fugitive. The ladder between heaven and earth that he saw in a dream represented Christ (Gen. 28:12). Since the entrance of sin, Christ has been the connecting link between heaven and earth (John 1:51; PP 184).

16. In order to have Jesus as our constant companion in heaven, what invitation must we accept now?
Revelation 22:16, 17 "I, Jesus, have sent My angel to testify to you these things in the churches. I am the Root and the Offspring of David, the Bright and Morning Star." And the Spirit and the bride say, "Come!" And let him who hears say, "Come!" And let him who thirsts come. Whoever desires, let him take the water of life freely.

Note: Some of the texts previously studied have assured us that every promise made about the completeness of the redemption offered will be fulfilled in Christ (Rev. 21:3-6; 22:3-5). The urgent invitation is to accept

His invitation of mercy now, today. Such an acceptance must be made by each individual separately, as carefully outlined by the prophet Ezekiel (18:4, 20). If we accept Christ, confess our sins and day by day maintain our relationship, our previous sinful life will not condemn us (Ezek. 18:21, 22). The invitation is to "whoever desires." This means that none is excluded and that none are predestined to destruction.

Acceptance with God means understanding and accepting His will (Rev. 22:14). A special warning is given by Christ Himself that none should seek to alter or obscure the important messages of the book of Revelation (vss. 18-20). He does not wish there to be any possibility of confusion or failure to accept God's invitation.

17. What great truth does the prophet John declare concerning the basis for the continuing harmony in God's universe?

Revelation 22:14 Blessed *are* those who do His commandments, that they may have the right to the tree of life, and may enter through the gates into the city.

Note: Satan's basic strategy from the beginning of the Great Controversy has been to attack the principles of God's government through minimizing or denying the significance of the law of love. Here at the end of the scriptural record it is affirmed that "no heart that is stirred with enmity against the law of God is in harmony with Christ" (FW 95). Now that "One great pulse of harmony and gladness beats through the vast creation" (GC 678), it follows that all have the utmost respect for God's will. There are no dissenting voices in the universe. All honour God's will as expressed in the Decalogue.

Basic References

The references used in the construction of the studies are detailed below. We chose to note sources only where quotations were taken directly from articles. This was done in an effort to simplify the text and make it easier to read.

Abbasid Dynasty. *Encyclopaedia Britannica*. Online: http://www.britannica.com (11/08/2009).

Alföldi, A. 1948. *The Conversion of Constantine and Pagan Rome*. Oxford: Clarendon Press.

Anderson, M. J. 1995. Catholics vs. Evangelicals. Online: http://www.catholiceducation.org/articles/apologetics/ap0025.html (01/01/2011).

Anderson, R. A. 1978. *Unfolding the Revelation*, revised. Mountain View, California: Pacific Press Publishing Association.

Ando, C. & Rüpke, J. Eds. 2006. *Religion and Law in Classical and Christian Rome*. Stuttgart: Franz Steiner Verlag.

Anon. Revelation. Online: http://www.hajinformation.com/main/b2103.htm (11/06/2009).

Anon. Some notes on the visibility of the 5 B.C. Chinese star. Online: http://www.astrosurf.com/comets/cometas/Star/Visibility_Star.htm (May 4, 2010).

Anon. 1835. *The Epistles of Ignatius and Polycarp with an Account of Their Martyrdom*. Lexington, KY: J. Clarke & Co., Printers.

Anon. 1991. Jean-Baptiste-Henri Dominique Lacordaire. *Religion & Liberty*, vol. 1(2). Online: http://www.acton.org/pub/religion-liberty/volume-1-number-2/jean-baptiste-henri-dominique-lacordaire (12/09/2010).

Anon. 2007. The Mongol Empire. All History Empires Forum. Online: www.allempires.com/article.php?=The_Mogol_Empire (18/06/2009).

Atli, A. 2009. The Sick Man of Europe. Online: http://www.turkeyswar.com/prelude/sickmanofeurope.htm (23/12/2010).

Aulard, A. 1927. *Christianity and the French Revolution*. London: Ernest Benn Limited.

Bacchiocchi, S. 1977. *From Sabbath to Sunday.* Rome: Pontifical Gregorian University Press.

Baigent, M. & Leigh, R. 1999. *The Inquisition*. London: Viking.

Barber, M. 2000. *The Cathars: Dualist Heretics in Languedoc in the High Middle Ages*. Singapore: Pearson Education Asia Pte Ltd.

Barbero, A. 2004. *Charlemagne*. Berkeley: University of California Press.

Baron, S. W. 1952. *A Social and Religious History of the Jews*, vol. II. New York: Columbia University Press.

Bauer, S. 2009. Darwin and the gospel commission: How does our view of origins impact the evangelistic mission of the church? *Journal of the Adventist Theological Society*, vol. 19 (1/2), 209-229.

Bautista, R. 2009. What is Spiritism? The Spiritist philosophy and how it differs from Spiritualism. Online: http://www.suite101.com/content/what-is-spiritism-a128876 (08/02/2011).

Berkey, J. P. 2003. *The Formation of Islam: Religion and Society in the Near East, 600-1800*. Cambridge: Cambridge University Press.

Boettner, L. 1974. *Roman Catholicism*, eleventh printing. Philadelphia, Pennsylvania: The Presbyterian and Reformed Publishing Company.

Bouyer, L. 1990. *The Christian Mystery: From Pagan Myth to Christian Mysticism*. Edinburgh: T. & T. Clark.

Bright, J. 1960. *A History of Israel*. London: SCM Press Ltd.

Broderick, L. 1995. Pastor's page. *Saint Catherine Catholic Church Sentinel*, vol. 50(22), p. 1. Online: http://biblelight.net/st-cath.htm (11/01/2011).

Buchanan, B. J. 2006. *Gunpowder, Explosives and the State: A Technological History*. Burlington, Vermont: Ashgate.

Buck, C. 1831. *A Theological Dictionary*, new edition. Philadelphia: Joseph J. Woodward.

Budge, E. A. W. 1978. *Amulets and Superstitions*. New York: Dover Publications, Inc.

Burckhardt, J. 1949. *The Age of Constantine the Great*, translated by M. Hadas. London: Routledge & Kegan Paul Limited.

Burn, A. R. 1984. *Persia and the Greeks: the Defence of the West, c. 546-478 B.C.*, second edition. Stanford, California: Stanford University Press.

Burrill, R. 1993. *The New World Order*. Washington, D.C.: Review and Herald Publishing Association.

Carroll, M. P. 1986. *The Cult of the Virgin Mary*. Princeton, New Jersey: Princeton University Press.

Catechism of the Catholic Church. Online: http://ccc.scborromeo.org.master.com/texis/master/search/?sufs=0&q=church+possesses+power+to+forgive+the+sins&xsubmit=Search&s=SS (15/01/2011).

Catholic Encyclopedia, 1909-1912. Articles: Diocletian; Donatists; French Revolution; Heresy, Spiritism. Online: http://www.newadvent.org/cathen/ (18/09/2009).

Citizendium. Article: French Revolution. Online: http://webcache.googleusercontent.com/search?q=cache:UUjRvMYOqmIJ:en.citizendium.org/wiki/French_Revolution+licentiousness+french+revolution&cd=11&hl=en&ct=clnk (11/09/2010).

Cist, S. T. O. 2011. Vatican Information Service on the Establishment of the Ordinariate and the First Ordinary. *The Anglo-Catholic*, Jan. 15. Online: http://www.theanglocatholic.com/2011/01/vatican-information-service-on-the-establishment-of-the-ordinariate/ (16/01/2011).

Clarke, A. 1825. *The Holy Bible containing the Old and New Testaments: the Text with a Commentary and Critical Notes*, First American Royal Octavo Edition, vol. 1. New York: N. Bangs and J. Emory.

Colson, F. H. 1927. *The Week*. Cambridge: The University Press.

Cowan, H. 1910. *Landmarks of Church History*. London: A. & C. Black.

Crow, W. B. 1972. *A History of Magic, Witchcraft and Occultism*. London: Abacus.

Cumont, F. 1956a. *The Mysteries of Mithra*, translated by T. J. McCormack. New York: Dover Publications, Inc.

Cumont, F. 1956b. *Oriental Religions in Roman Paganism*, authorized translation. New York: Dover Publications, Inc. de Ste. Croix, G. M., Whitby, M. & Streeter, J. Eds. 2006. *Christian Persecution, Martydom, and Orthodoxy*. Oxford: Oxford University Press.

Diamond, J. 2005. *Guns, Germs, and Steel*. New York: W. W. Norton & Company.

Douglass, H. E. 2001. What is the "Everlasting Gospel"? *Journal of the Adventist Theological Society*, vol. 12(2), 145-151.

Doukhan, J. B. 1989. *Daniel: The Vision of the End*, revised edition. Berrien Springs, Michigan: Andrews University Press.

Doukhan, J. B. 2000. *Secrets of Daniel*. Hagerstown, Maryland: Review and Herald Publishing Association.

Doukhan, J. B. 2002. *Secrets of Revelation.* Hagerstown, Maryland: Review and Herald Publishing Association.

Dumper, M. & Stanley, B. E. Eds. 2006. *Cities of the Middle East and North Africa.* Santa Barbara, California: ABC-CLIO.

Duncan, A. W. & Jones, S. L. Eds. 2008. *Church-state Issues in America Today: Religion and Government*, vol. 1. Westport, Connecticut: Praeger Publishers.

Durant, W. 1944. *The Story of Civilization: Part III. Caesar and Christ.* New York: Simon & Schuster.

Falk, A. 1996. *A Psycholanalytic History of the Jews.* Cranbury, New Jersey: Associated University Presses, Inc.

Ferguson, J. 1970. *The Religions of the Roman Empire.* London: Thames and Hudson.

Ferraris, L. 1858. *Prompta Bibliotheca Canonica Juridica Moralis Theologica, Ascetica, Polemica, Rubristica, Historica,* vol. V, article II: Papa, column 1823. Petit-Montrouge (Paris): J. P. Migne, Online: http://www.hol.com/~mikesch/1823r.gif and translation given at http://www.topix.com/forum/topstories/TV910R5AL0932P9RK/p7122 (07/09/2010).

Finley, M. A. 2005. Is the United States the final superpower? *Adventists Affirm*, vol. 19(3), 6-12.

Froom, L. E. 1948. *The Prophetic Faith of Our Fathers*, vols II & IV. Washington, D.C.: Review and Herald Publishing Association.

Frye, R. N. 1975. Mithra in Iranian history, pp. 62-67. In: *Mithraic Studies*, vol. 1, ed. J. R. Hinnells. Manchester: Manchester University Press.

Gardiner, J. 2003. *Faiths of the World*, vol. 1. Whitefish, Montana: Kessinger Publishing.

Gibbon, E. 2004. *The Decline and Fall of the Roman Empire*, ed. J. B. Bury. Rockville, Maryland: Wildside Press LLC.

Goetz, P. W. Ed. 1988a. *The New Encyclopaedia Britannica: Micropaedia* (15th ed.). Article: Week, vol. 12. Chicago: Encyclopaedia Britannica, Inc.

Goetz, P. W. Ed. 1988b. *The New Encyclopaedia Britannica: Macropaedia* (15th ed.). Article: Pythagoreanism, vol. 25. Chicago: Encyclopaedia Britannica, Inc.

Goldstein, C. 1994. *The Remnant.* Boise, Idaho: Pacific Press Publishing Association.

Guénon, R. 2004. *The Spiritist Fallacy.* New York: Sophia Perennis.

Gulley, N. R. 2000. Will Christ return in the year 2000. *Journal of the Adventist Theological Society*, vol. 10(1/2), 191-213.

Haffner, K. 2009. Mission of hope in the midst of hopelessness. *Record*, vol. 14(34), 13-15.

Hardinge, L. 1991. *With Jesus in His Sanctuary.* Harrisburg, Pennsylvania: American Cassette Ministries.

Hastings, J. Ed. 1918. *Dictionary of the Apostolic Church.* Edinburgh: T. & T. Clark.

Hastings, J. Ed. 1967a. *Encyclopaedia of Religion and Ethics.* Article: Gnosticism, vol. VI. Edinburgh: T. & T. Clark.

Hastings, J. Ed. 1967c. *Encyclopaedia of Religion and Ethics.* Article: Sunday, vol. XII. Edinburgh: T. & T. Clark.

Hawkes, J. 1962. *Man and the Sun.* London: The Cresset Press.

Hawting, G. R. 2000. *The First Dynasty of Islam: the Umayyad Caliphate AD 661-750*, edition 2. New York: Routledge.

Herbermann, C. G. Ed. 1913. *The Catholic Encyclopedia.* Article: Mithraism, vol. 10. New York: The Encyclopedia Press.

Hershon, P. I. 1882. *Treasures of the Talmud*, p. 97. Quoted in *Seventh-day Adventists Answer Questions on Doctrine* (refer to basic reference).

Hinnells, J. R. Ed. 1975. *Mithraic Studies.* Manchester: Manchester University Press.

Hislop, A. 1976. *The Two Babylons*. London: S. W. Partridge & Co.

History of the Orthodox Church. Articles: Byzantine Christianity about AD 1000; Relations between Church and state. Online: http://www.kosovo.net/history.html (10/09/2010).

Holbrook, F. B. Ed. 1986. *Symposium on Daniel*. Daniel and Revelation Committee Series, vol. 2. *Introduction and Exegetical Studies*. Hagerstown, Maryland: Review and Herald Publishing Association.

Horn, S. H. 1960. *Seventh-day Adventist Bible Dictionary*. Washington, DC: Review and Herald Publishing Association.

Hughes, D. 2000. Stars at Christmas. *New Scientist*, vol. 165(2218), 82.

Humphreys, C. 1958. *Buddhism*. Harmondsworth, Middlesex: Penguin Books.

Humphreys, C. 1995. The star of Bethlehem. *Science & Christian Belief*, vol. 5 (Oct. 1995), 83-101. Online: http://adsabs.harvard.edu/full/1991QJRAS.32.389H (4/5/2010).

Jacob, S. Proctor, C., Riddle, J. E. & M'Conechy, J. 1854. *History of the Ottoman Empire*, 2nd revised edition. London: Richard Griffin and Company.

James, E. O. 1960. *The Ancient Gods*. London: Weidenfeld and Nicolson.

Jemison, T. H. 1959. *Christian Beliefs*. Mountain View, California: Pacific Press Publishing Association.

Jenkins, P. 2002. *The Next Christendom: The Coming of Global Christianity*. Oxford: Oxford University Press.

Jones, H. 1989. *The Epicurean Tradition*. London: Routledge.

Jones, P. & Pennick, N. 1995. *A History of Pagan Europe*. New York: Routledge.

Kane, J. P. 1975. The Mithraic cult meal in its Greek and Roman environment, pp. 313-351. In: *Mithraic Studies*, vol. II, ed. J. R. Hinnells. Manchester: Manchester University Press.

Kee, A. 1982. *Constantine versus Christ*. London: SCM Press Ltd.

Kennedy, E. 1989. *A Cultural History of the French Revolution*. New Haven: Yale University Press.

Koch, C. 1997. *A Popular History of the Catholic Church*. Winona, Maine: Saint Mary's Press.

Kidd, B. J. 1922. *A History of the Church to AD 461*, vol.1. Oxford: The Clarendon Press.

Knight, G. R. Ed. 2003. *Questions on Doctrine*, annotated edition. Berrien Springs, Michigan: Andrews University Press.

Koranteng-Pipim, S. 1996. *Receiving the Word*. Berrien Springs, Michigan: Berean Books.

Lawler, P. A. & Schaefer, R. M. 2005. *American Political Rhetoric: A Reader*, edition 5. Lanham, Maryland: Rowman & Littlefield.

Lewis, B. 2004. *The Crisis of Islam*. London: Phoenix.

Liddell, H. G. & Scott, R. 1961. *A Greek-English Lexicon*, revised edition by H. S. Jones & R. McKenzie. Oxford: Clarendon Press.

Lindsay, J. 1971. *Origins of Astrology*. London: Frederick Muller.

Livingstone, T. 2010. Anglican breakaways in rush to the Vatican. *The Australian*, March 27. Online: http://www.theaustralian.com.au/news/nation/anglican-breakaways-in-rush-to-the-vatican/story-e6frg6nf-1225846180092 (15/01/2011).

London Convention. 2009. *Mideast & North African Encyclopedia*. Online: http://www.answers.com/topic/london-convention-1 (11/06/2009).

MacMullen, R. 1984. *Christianizing the Roman Empire (A.D. 100-400)*. New Haven: Yale University Press.

Madden, T. F. 2005. *The New Concise History of the Crusades*. Lanham, Maryland: Rowman & Littlefield.

Marr, T. 2006. *The Cultural Roots of American Islamicism*. Cambridge: Cambridge University Press.

Martinez, A. 2010. The next American century. *Time*, vol. 175(11), 30-32.

Martyr, Justin. Fragments from the lost work of Justin on the resurrection. Online: http://www.earlychristianwritings.com/text/justinmartyr-resurrection.html (26/03/2010).

Maxwell, C. M. 1981. *God Cares*, vol. 1. *The Message of Daniel for You and Your Family*. Mountain View, California: Pacific Press Publishing Association.

Maxwell, C. M. 1985. *God Cares*, vol. 2. *The Message of Revelation for You and Your Family*. Mountain View, California: Pacific Press Publishing Association.

McManners, J. 1969. *The French Revolution and the Church*. London: S. P. C. K.

Metzger, B. M. 1987. *The Canon of the New Testament*. Oxford: Clarendon Press.

Miller, L. 2009. Darwin's Rottweiler. *Newsweek*, Sept. 26. Online: http://www.newsweek.com/id/216206?tid=relatedcl (12/01/2011).

Miller, N. P. 2005. The king of the North, the king of the South, and the sanctuary. *Adventists Affirm*, vol. 19(3), 80-86.

Moskala, J. 2007. The Sabbath in the first creation account. *Perspective Digest*, vol. 12(2), 45-53.

Mueller, E. 2000. The end time remnant in Revelation. *Journal of the Adventist Theological Society*, vol. 11(1/2), 188-204.

Müller, E. 2002. The two witnesses of Revelation 11. *Journal of the Adventist Theological Society*, vol. 13(2), 30-45.

Nabarz, P. 2005. *The Mysteries of Mithras: the Pagan Belief that Shaped the Christian World*. Rochester, Vermont: Inner Traditions-Bear & Company.

New Encyclopaedia Britannica: Macropaedia (15th ed.). 1974. Article: Time, vol.18. Chicago: Encyclopaedia Britannica, Inc.

Neufeld, D. F. & Neuffer, J. Eds. 1962. *The Seventh-day Adventist Bible Commentary*, vol. 9. *Source Book*. Washington, D.C.: Review and Herald Publishing Association.

Newman, J. H. 1920. *Essay on the Development of Christian Doctrine*. London: Longmans Green & Company.

Nichol, F. D., Cottrell, R. F., Neufeld, D. F. & Neuffer, J. Eds. 1953. *The Seventh-day Adventist Bible Commentary*, vol. 1, 290. Washington, D. C.: Review and Herald Publishing Association.

Nichol, F. D., Cottrell, R. F., Neufeld, D. F. & Neuffer, J. Eds. 1953-1957.*The Seventh-day Adventist Bible Commentary*, vols 1-7. Washington, D. C.: Review and Herald Publishing Association.

Nosotro, R. 2008. The Ottoman and Seljuk empires. Online: http://www.hyperhistory.net/apwh/essays/comp/cw17seljukottoman.htm (06/05/2009).

Nygren, A. 1982. *Agape and Eros*, translated by P. S. Watson. Chicago: Chicago University Press,

Odahl, C. M. 2004. *Constantine and the Christian Empire*. New York: Routledge.

Odom, R. L. 1977. *Sabbath and Sunday in Early Christianity*. Washington, D.C.: Review and Herald Publishing Association.

Olson, R. E. 2002. *The Mosaic of Christian Belief: Twenty Centuries of Unity and Diversity*. Downers Grove, Illinois: InterVarsity Press.

Pace, E. 1912. Spiritism. In: *The Catholic Encyclopedia*. New York: Robert Appleton Company. Online at *New Advent*: http://www.newadvent.org/cathen/14221a.htm (09/02/2011).

Palanque, J. R., Bardy, G., de Labriolle, P, de Plinval, G. & Brehier, L. 1949. *The Church in the Christian Roman Empire*, vol. 1. *The Church and the Arian Crisis*, translated by E. C. Messenger. London: Burns Oates & Washbourne Ltd.

Pettibone, D. 2007. Martin Luther's views on the antichrist. *Journal of the Adventist Theological Society*, vol. 18(1), 81-100.

Pfandl, G. Principal contributor. 2004. *Daniel*. Senior Sabbath School Lessons, Fourth Quarter 2004. Online: http://www.absg.adventist.org/Archives.htm (17/04/2009).

Philologist website. Topic: locusts. Online: http://philologos.org/bpr/files/l004.htm (20/12/2010).

Rahner, K. Ed. 1975. *Encyclopedia of Theology: the Concise Sacramentum Mundi.* New York: Continuum International Publishing Group Inc.

Raphael, C. 1990. *The Festivals: A History of Jewish Celebration.* London: Weidenfeld and Nicolson.

Reid, G. W. 1998. Faith under pressure: the Sabbath as case study. *Journal of the Adventist Theological Society*, 9(1-2), 141-149.

Riley-Smith, J. 2005. *The Crusades: A History*, edition 2. New York: Continuum International Publishing Group.

Roberts, A. & Donaldson, J. Eds. 1973. *The Anti-Nicene Fathers.* Grand Rapids, Michigan: Wm B. Eerdmans Publishing Company.

Rohl, D. M. 1995. *A Test of Time*, vol. 1. *The Bible-from Myth to History.* London: Century Ltd.

Rohl, D. M. 1998. *Test of Time*, vol. 2. *Legend: The Genesis of Civilization.* London: Arrow Books Limited.

Rohrbacher, D. 2002. *The Historians of Late Antiquity.* New York: Routledge.

Rollin, C. 1836. *The Ancient History of the Egyptians, Carthaginians, Assyrians, Babylonians, Medes and Persians, Grecians and Macedonians; Including a History of the Arts and Sciences*, vol. 1. New York: George Dearborn, Publisher.

Rudolph, K. 1983. *Gnosis: the Nature and History of an Ancient Religion.* Edinburgh: T. & T. Clark Limited.

Sandbach, F. H. 1975. *The Stoics.* New York: W. W. Norton & Company, Inc.

Saunders, D. A. Ed. 1952. *The Portable Gibbon: The Decline and Fall of the Roman Empire.* Hammondsworth, England: Penguin Books Ltd.

Schaff, P. & Wace, H. Eds. 1982. *A Select History of Nicene and Post-Nicene Fathers of the Christian Church* (Second series), vol. I. *Eusebius: Church History, Life of Constantine the Great and Oration in Praise of Constantine.* Grand Rapids, Michigan: Wm B. Eerdmans Publishing Company.

Scott, J. 1832. *Luther and the Lutheran Reformation.* London: R. B. Seeley and W. Burnside.

Scott, S.P. 1932. *Corpus Juris Civilis* (The Civil Law, the Code of Justinian). Cincinnati: Central Trust Company, Cincinnati, vol. 12, 9-12. Online: http://biblelight.net/jus-code.htm (18/09/2009).

Seventh-day Adventists Answer Questions on Doctrine. 1957. Washington, D.C.: Review and Herald Publishing Association.

Seznec, J. 1961. *The Survival of the Pagan Gods*, translated by B. F. Sessions. New York: Harper & Brothers.

Shaw, S. J. 1977. *History of the Ottoman Empire and Modern Turkey*, vol. 1. *Empire of Gazis: The Rise and Decline of the Ottoman Empire 1280-1808.* Cambridge: Cambridge University Press.

Shea, W. H. 2001.Supplementary evidence in support of 457 B.C. as the starting date for the 2300 day-years of Daniel 8:14. *Journal of the Adventist Theological Society*, 12(1), 89-96.

Shea, W. H. 2002. Azazel in the pseudepigrapha. *Journal of the Adventist Theological Society*, 13(1), 1-9.

Shea, W. H. 2005. *Daniel: A Reader's Guide.* Nampa, Idaho: Pacific Press Publishing Association.

Shipton, W. A. & Jackson, G. D. 1999. *The Pattern of Salvation.* Warburton, Victoria: Signs Publishing Company.

Smalley, W. A. 1991. *Translation as Mission.* Macon, Georgia: Mercer University Press.

Smith, R. F. 1975. *Prelude to Science; an Exploration of Magic and Divination.* New York: Charles Scribner's Sons.

Smith, W. 1884. *Smith's Bible Dictionary.* Online: http://dictionary.babylon.com

Soboul, A. 1974. *The French Revolution 1787-1799.* London: NLB.

Stanton, M. & Hyma, A. 2000. *Streams of Civilization: Earliest Times to the Discovery of the New World*, vol. 1. Arlington Heights, Illinois: Christian Liberty Press.

Stefanovic, R. 2002. *Revelation of Jesus Christ: Commentary on the Book of Revelation.* Berrien Springs, Michigan: Andrews University Press.

Sutton, W. J. 1983. *The New Age Movement; and the Illuminati 666.* United States of America: The Institute of Religious Knowledge.

Thiele, E. R. 1959. *Outline Studies in Revelation.* Michigan, Berrien Springs: Andrews University.

Thieme, P. 1975. The concept of Mitra in Aryan belief, pp. 21-39. In: *Mithraic Studies*, vol. I, ed. J. R. Hinnells. Manchester: Manchester University Press.

Thiers, M. A. 1845. *The History of the French Revolution.* London: Whittaker and Co.

Thomson, D. 1990. *Europe Since Napoleon.* London: Penguin Books.

Tibbs, C. 2007. *Religious Experience of the Pneuma. Communication with the Spirit World in 1 Corinthians 12 and 14.* Tübingen, Germany: Mohr Siebeck.

Tolhurst, A. 1983. "Cut off" or "Determined"? *Australasian Record and Advent World Survey*, vol. 88(41), 6, 7, 14.

Ullmann, W. 2003. *A Short History of the Papacy in the Middle Ages*, second edition. London: Routledge.

Unam Sanctam. Online: http://www.papalencyclicals.net/Bon08/B8unam.htm (12/01/2011).

Valentine, G. M. 2005. *W. W. Prescott: Forgotten Giant of Adventism's Second Generation.* Hagerstown, Maryland: Review and Herald Publishing Association.

Vance, M. 1991. *The Trail of the Serpent.* Pune, India: Oriental Watchman Publishing House.

Victor, B. 2005. *The Last Crusade.* London: Constable & Robinson Ltd.

Vox Populi Mariae Mediatrici Petition Center. 2009. A New Marian Dogma? Coredemptrix, Mediatrix of All Graces, Advocate. Online: http://www.catholicculture.org/culture/library/ view.cfm?id=360&CFID=5112617&CFTOKEN=48444376 (11/09/2009).

Warner, M. 1976. *Alone of All Her Sex.* London: Weidenfeld and Nicolson.

Waterhouse, S. D. 1982. The planetary week in the Roman West, pp. 308-322. In: *The Sabbath in Scripture and History*, ed. K. A. Strand. Washington, D. C.: Review and Herald Publishing Association.

Weigall, A. 1928. *The Paganism in Our Christianity.* New York: G. P. Putnam's Sons.

Whiston, W. circa 1936. *The Life and Works of Flavius Josephus. Antiquities of the Jews*, bk XVII, chap. III. Philadelphia: John C. Winston Company.

White, E. G. 1969. *Christ in His Sanctuary.* Mountain View, California: Pacific Press Publishing Association.

Wiedemann, A. 2001. *Religion of the Ancient Egyptians.* Boston: Adamant Media Corporation.

Wilhelm, J. 1910. *The Catholic Encyclopedia.* Article: Heresy. New York: Robert Appleton Company. Online at *New Advent*: http://www.newadvent.org/cathen/07256b.htm (10/02/2011).

Wilkinson, B. G. 1944. *Truth Triumphant: the Church in the Wilderness.* Mountain View, California: Pacific Press Publishing Association.

Wills, G. 2003. *Why I Am a Catholic.* New York: Mariner Books.

Witt, R. E. 1975. Some thoughts on Isis in relation to Mithras, pp. 479-493. In: *Mithraic Studies*, vol. II, ed. J. R. Hinnells. Manchester: Manchester University Press.

Zerubavel, E. 1985. *The Seven Day Circle.* New York: The Free Press.

Zustiak, G. B. The animal actions of Nebuchadnezzar-boanthropy? Online:
http://davidfish.info/ot%20history%20spring%202006/Boanthropy.pdf (13/04/2009).